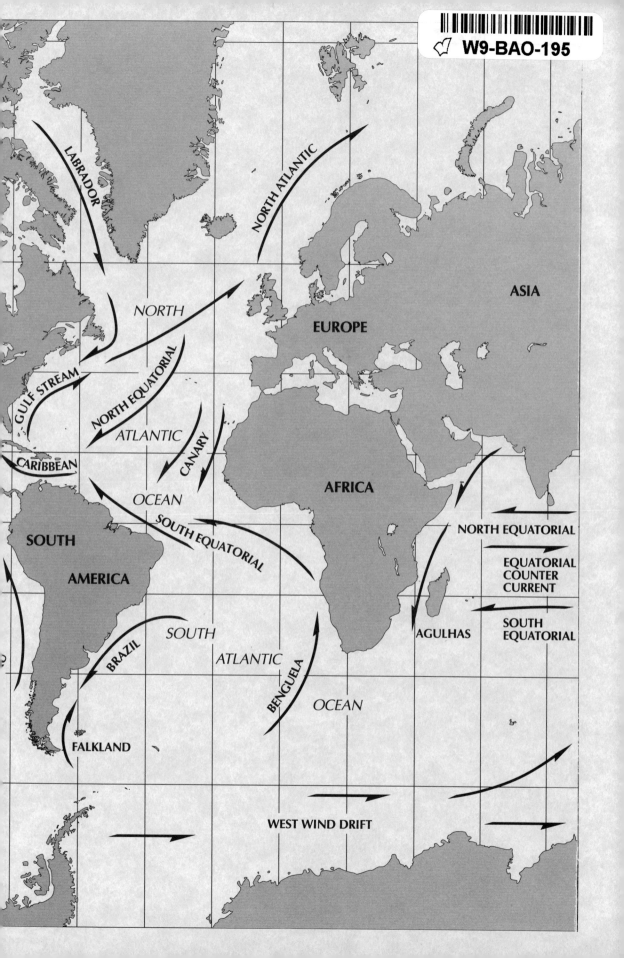

LABRADOR

NORTH ATLANTIC

ASIA

NORTH

EUROPE

GULF STREAM

NORTH EQUATORIAL

ATLANTIC

CANARY

AFRICA

CARIBBEAN

OCEAN

NORTH EQUATORIAL

SOUTH EQUATORIAL

EQUATORIAL
COUNTER
CURRENT

SOUTH

AMERICA

SOUTH
EQUATORIAL

SOUTH

BRAZIL

ATLANTIC

BENGUELA

AGULHAS

OCEAN

FALKLAND

WEST WIND DRIFT

LEGEND and LORE
of the Americas before 1492

An Encyclopedia of Visitors,
Explorers, and Immigrants

LEGEND and LORE
of the Americas before 1492

An Encyclopedia of Visitors, Explorers, and Immigrants

Ronald H. Fritze

ABC-CLIO

Santa Barbara, California
Denver, Colorado
Oxford, England

Library of Congress Cataloging-in-Publication Data

Fritze, Ronald H., 1951–
    Legend and lore of the Americas before 1492 : an encyclopedia of
visitors, explorers, and immigrants / Ronald H. Fritze.
        p. cm.
    Includes bibliographical references and index.
    1. Indians—Origin. 2. Indians—Legends. 3. Indians—History—Sources.
    4. America—Discovery and exploration. I. Title.
    E61.A72 1993   970.01—dc20   93-13367

ISBN 0-87436-664-X

99 98 97 96 95 94 93   10 9 8 7 6 5 4 3 2 1

ABC-CLIO, Inc.
130 Cremona Drive, P.O. Box 1911
Santa Barbara, California 93116-1911

This book is printed on acid-free paper ⊖.
Manufactured in the United States of America

For Karen

But seeing on the one side we know for certain that many years ago there were men inhabiting these parts [the Americas], so likewise we cannot deny but the scriptures teach us clearly that all men are come from the first man, without doubt we shall be forced to believe that men have come here from Europe, Asia, or Africa, yet must we discover by what means they travelled. . . . Wherefore these two things should be considered wonderful and worthy of admiration, yes, to be numbered among the secrets of God. The one is, how man could make so huge a journey by sea and land; the other is, that there being such multitudes of people they have yet been unknown for so many ages.

José de Acosta
The Natural and Moral History of the Indies, *1590*

Some would derive the Americans from the Jews; others, from the ten Tribes of Israel, carry'd into captivity. The ground of which Opinion is, That the Jews and Israelites were scatter'd amongst all Nations; therefore they conclude, that America was also Peopled by them.

John Ogilby
America: Being the Latest, and Most Accurate Description
of the New World, *1671*

Inform me, Whence the Tawny People came?
Who was their Father, Japhet, Shem, or Cham?
And how they straddled to th' Antipodes,
To look another World beyond the Seas?
And when, and why, and where they last broke ground,
What Risks they ran, where they first Anchoring found?

Nicholas Noyes
"Prefatory Poem," in Cotton Mather's
Magnalia Christi Americana, *1702*

And it came to pass that after we [Nephi and his family] had sailed for the space of many days we did arrive at the promised land; and we went forth upon the land, and did pitch our tents; and we did call it the promised land.

1 Nephi 18:23
The Book of Mormon, *1830*

Of course America had often been discovered before [Columbus] but it had always been hushed up.

Attributed to Oscar Wilde

"The only question in my mind," said Giordino, "is whether the fleet turned north or south."

"Neither." Pitt moved the light arrow through the Gibraltar Straits and across the Atlantic. "Venator led his fleet west to the Americas."

His statement was greeted with stunned disbelief.

"There is no archaeological evidence supporting pre-Columbian contact in the Americas," Lily stated firmly.

"The *Serapis* is a pretty good indicator they could have made such a voyage," said Sandecker.

"It's a heated controversy," admitted Pitt. "But there are too many similarities in Mayan art and culture that cannot be ignored. Ancient America may not have been as isolated from European and Asian influences as we once thought."

"Frankly, I buy it," said Yaeger, his enthusiasm restored. "I'll bet my Willie Nelson record collection the Phoenicians, the Egyptians, Greeks, Romans and Vikings all landed on North and South American soil before Columbus."

Clive Cussler
Treasure, *1988*

Contents

Preface

The observation of the quincentennial of Columbus's voyage has come and gone, but not without acrimony. During a recent trip to Denver just a few days before the 500th anniversary celebration of Columbus Day, I was walking down the corridors of Stapleton Airport in the company of six large Native Americans. Since they were dressed like cowboys, I simply assumed that they were in town for some rodeo. I later learned they were there to stop the Columbus Day parade that the Italian-Americans were planning. They did stop it, by the way.

Such controversy over Columbus Day is nothing new. In 1892, the Scandinavian-Americans bitterly resented the attention paid to Columbus on the 400th anniversary of his voyage and the relative neglect accorded to Leif Ericsson and the Norse voyages to America. That resentment helped to produce the hoax of the Kensington Rune Stone. Twenty years ago, few people would have had a problem with answering "Columbus" to the question—Who discovered America? Nowadays, for many people the proper answer to that question is those Stone Age hunters who crossed the Bering land bridge to become the first Americans.

Interestingly enough, the contention that Columbus was the first person to visit the Americas after the Native Americans has always been controversial. The orthodox position gives Columbus the credit for permanently revealing the Americas to Europe. As the historian William McNeill of the University of Chicago recently pointed out, thanks to Columbus, the earth became one world rather than many separate worlds.

However, in the opinion of many people and in the popular culture, that orthodoxy has never been fully accepted. A recent poll by CNN revealed that 70 percent of Americans believed that other people reached America before Columbus, 20 percent thought Columbus was first, and 10 percent did not know. The 70 percent group may represent subtle thinkers who rightly credit Native Americans with being first, as well as other informed individuals who know that the Norse most certainly reached the Americas 500 years before Columbus. If that is the case, the people in the 70 percent category are more correct than the 20 percent giving priority to Columbus. Many of those who believe that other people reached the Americas before Columbus, however, are not thinking of either the first people across the Bering land bridge or the Norse, but of Phoenicians, Atlanteans, Romans, or some other group. Professional archaeologists and anthropologists work hard to debunk such beliefs, but these fallacies are seemingly immortal. The work of professional scholars was put to naught when in January 1992 the venerable *Weekly Reader* put out a classroom map/poster of pre-Columbian explorers to the Americas that included the Welsh, Phoenicians, and Chinese.

Theories of pre-Columbian contacts find a ready audience with the general reading public, as indicated by the steady stream of books and articles over the years. John L. Sorenson and Martin H. Raish's excellent *Pre-Columbian Contact with the Americas across the Oceans: An Annotated Bibliography* (1990) lists 5,613 items on the topic, and it is not exhaustive. The concept also frequently appears in fictional settings. Clive Cussler's novel *Treasure* (1988) is based on the premise that ancient Romans hid part of the great library of Alexandria on the Texas side of the Rio Grande.

There are many more examples. *Hercules against the Sons of the Sun* is one of those Greco-Roman costume movies perennially popular in Italy that supplies the fodder for viewing events like Hercathons on the TNT channel. In this film Hercules is the sole survivor of a Greek ship wrecked on the shores of ancient South America. After an initial encounter with nasty Incas, he is rescued by some nice Incas. The goal of Huascar, their leader, is to oust his evil brother Atahualpa from the capital of Tiahuanaco. Hercules joins his rescuers and uses his might to make things right as usual. Needless to say, the movie is an anachronistic mess. Besides the fact that Hercules is a mythological figure, well over 2,000 years separated him from the time of the Incas. Huascar and Atahualpa are the names of two real Incan princes locked in a civil war just before Francisco Pizarro arrived in Peru in 1532. Tiahuanaco was not an Incan city, but rather the center of an earlier Andean civilization that flourished from about 100 to 1100. While that is earlier than the Incas, it is still much later than any hypothetical age of Hercules. Ironically, Hercules has never been the object of any theory about pre-Columbian visitors—unless his Isles of the Hespérides were actually the Americas.

People have a strong desire to believe that other people came to America between the time of the Stone Age migrations across the Bering land bridge and the arrival of Columbus. All kinds of theories have been proposed, and this encyclopedia is intended to serve as an introductory guide to them. Anyone reading through this work will quickly realize that the question of the origin of Native Americans and the question of the existence of pre-Columbian visitors to the Americas are often the same question for many people.

The geographical scope of this book is worldwide. Supposed pre-Columbian explorers from Africa, Asia, and Europe are all listed. While I have included Atlanteans and Lemurians, I have drawn the line at extraterrestrials. Chronologically some entries extend back to the never-never land that Theosophists believe existed millions of years ago. From there it proceeds to the time when the Siberians crossed Beringia about 15,000 years ago and into the historical eras of antiquity and the middle ages. It concludes, on the eve of Columbus's voyage of 1492, with the shadowy exploits of the merchants of Bristol and Jean Cousins of Dieppe, who supposedly preceded Columbus by merely a year or two.

My intended readers are the general public, high school students, and college students, although some specialists will hopefully find the work useful. My original goal was to make this encyclopedia exhaustive. I have since learned that researching theories about pre-Columbian visitors to the Americas is like peeling a very large onion layer by layer. I only hope that this encyclopedia is comprehensive and at least touches on all the major topics.

The encyclopedia consists of 216 alphabetically arranged entries that range from fifty to several thousand words in length. Each entry provides brief introductions to significant persons, authors, places, concepts, and groups associated with the topic of pre-Columbian visitors to the Americas. Most entries include bibliographical citations for those seeking more information, but brief entries refer the reader to longer, related entries and their bibliographies. Cross-references within entries are indicated by **boldface type,** and *see also* references are used when a relevant cross-reference is not directly mentioned. A complete bibliography appears at the back of the volume.

Throughout this work I have attempted to use the term *Native American* for the aboriginal peoples of the Americas whenever possible rather than the traditional term *Indian*. It was not always possible. Legends of Welsh Indians and White Indians abounded along the frontiers of the Americas. To call them Welsh Native Americans or White Native Americans is both unaesthetic and incomprehensible. *Paleo-Indians* is the term used by anthropologists and archaeologists to refer to the hunter-gatherers that inhabited the Americas from 14,000 years ago up until 9,000 years ago. In other words, they were the first Americans. Throughout I have tried to use the *Americas* rather than the *New World*, although this was not always possible in certain contexts. That leaves the problem of what to call the rest of the world. For that purpose I continued to use *Old World*. I tried using *eastern hemisphere*, but it seemed too clumsy. My desire is to inform and entertain, not to offend.

Acknowledgments

It is always a pleasure to finish writing a book, and this one is no exception despite the very fascinating subject matter. I have many people to thank for their help and inspiration. The idea for this book developed while I was teaching a class on Columbus and the European expansion of the fifteenth and sixteenth centuries. I would like to thank the members of the fall 1990 class for helping to inspire me. Thanks to Andy Anderson, the chair of the history department, along with Janice Trammell and Mike Read of the Lamar University off-campus education department, for the opportunity to teach that class.

My true academic specialty is early modern England, but I have always had a fascination with pre-Columbian America and the era of the conquest. That interest stems from the fact that William H. Prescott's classic books *The Conquest of Mexico* and *The Conquest of Peru* were the first serious histories I ever read. Years later, while working on my master's degree, I took a course in the Indian civilizations of Central and South America from Robert West of Louisiana State University. He turned out to be one of the finest professors I ever had. During that same period, I also had the opportunity to attend a lecture by Robert Wauchope of Tulane University, whose *Lost Tribes and Sunken Continents* served as both an inspiration and a guidepost for my own work.

Lamar University has a fine record of supporting scholarship at many levels. The reference and interlibrary loan staff of the Gray Library of Lamar University were patient, helpful, and prompt. Samuel Johnson's oft-repeated quote that an author must "turn over half a library to make one book" is true. In my case, the wonders of interlibrary loans allowed me to turn over books from dozens of libraries. Lamar University was generous with direct support for this project. My colleagues in the history department and the College of Arts and Sciences kindly allowed me a reduced teaching load for two semesters. The Faculty Senate awarded me a much-needed development leave for the summer of 1991. I received a very welcome research enhancement grant from the Research Council of Lamar University. The grant included provision for a research assistant, and I was most fortunate to have Ms. Shannon McIntire capably and conscientiously filling that position. Lamar University has good reason to be proud of its support for faculty research. My hope is that such support will be sustained and expanded in the future. As for me, I would like to thank them all once again.

After learning that I was writing this book, Professor Pat Harrigan of the Department of Communication at Lamar University steered me to Clive Cussler's *Treasure* and even loaned me his personal copy of the book. He was right on target. Besides being an enjoyable action novel, it had much to say about pre-Columbian visitors to the Americas. I would also like to thank Joyce Owens of the President's Office at Lamar University for being my guide through the intricacies of *The Book of Mormon*. The materials she loaned me were most helpful. Another individual to whom I owe gratitude is my colleague in the history department, Professor

Acknowledgments

Paul Isaac, who introduced me to the mysterious Melungeons of Tennessee. Without his help I might have missed them.

The people at ABC-CLIO have been a joy to work with on this project, but that is standard operating procedure for them. Heather Cameron contracted this book and has been a major source of encouragement and support all along the way. I am sorry I missed our deadline by several months. Tracey Butler, Sallie Greenwood, and Amy Catala have been very helpful with the development, picture research, and editing. Their efforts have made the book significantly better.

My cat Flacius provided his usual literary assistance by lying around my desk and checking out what I was doing.

My wife Karen Campbell has been a great source of support for the book and has graciously suffered the presence of this project in our lives. She hiked up Fort Mountain in Georgia with me during a drizzle just to look at a supposed medieval Welsh fort. We crossed Mobile Bay together on an open ferry in a driving rain with no umbrella just to see where Prince Madoc was supposed to have landed. Down at Chichén Itzá we climbed the pyramid of Kukulcan on a humid 85-degree day and vainly searched Mayan bas-reliefs for pictures of bearded men. In Texas we spent over two hours standing in line on the Galveston waterfront during an on-again, off-again rain waiting to see reproductions of the ships of Columbus. Of course, stops at secondhand bookstores in search of the odd book on pre-Columbian visitors have also been a common occurrence in our life together. So far, it has never rained on us in one of those bookstores. I won't say she hasn't complained at times, but then I don't always suffer in silence when we do something that she enjoys and I dislike. She is a good sport, a good friend, and the love of my life.

LEGEND *and* **LORE**
of the Americas before 1492

An Encyclopedia of Visitors,
Explorers, and Immigrants

The great North African historian Ibn Khaldun (1332–1406) does not even credit Abubakari with having reigned as a mansa of Mali. Other sources and oral traditions place him as a mansa during or before the years 1307–1311. According to these oral traditions, Abubakari thought there were lands on the other side of the western Atlantic, so in 1307 he sent out an expedition of about 400 ships. Only one returned, reporting that an enormous and powerful current carried off the others to the west before land had been sighted. Undaunted, Abubakari gathered an even bigger fleet (according to some reports numbering over 2,000 ships), and prepared to sail west with himself in personal command. In 1311 (or 1307), he appointed his brother Kankan Mūsā (i.e., Mansa Mūsā) as regent, and then departed. He was never heard from or seen again.

The story of Abubakari II is based on oral traditions passed on by the West African griots, who specialize in learning and narrating the oral history of their people. Research has shown that the griots' historical narrative is often remarkably accurate, although not invariably so. Many questions arise concerning the historicity of Abubakari's voyage. First, was Abubakari ever a mansa of Mali? That is by no means certain. Second, why was the size of his fleet so suspiciously large? Even if they were dugout canoes or reed boats with crews of only four to ten, 2,000 ships are still a very large expedition with which to sail off into the unknown. It just does not ring true. Third, Ivan Van Sertima and other supporters claim that many such voyages were made. But the legends of Abubakari belie that contention. To Abubakari and his people, the western Atlantic Ocean was a great mystery, with no memory of previous African voyages to guide them. That simply does not seem credible if so many earlier voyages took place. The story of Abubakari probably has less basis in historical events than the

Abubakari II, Western Voyages of (ca. 1307–1311)

Also known as Abu Bakr, this king or emperor of Mali, or of the Mandingo, supposedly sailed a huge fleet from West Africa in the Atlantic Ocean and was never seen again. Advocates of pre-Columbian **African voyages** to the Americas claim that he reached the other side safely.

Abubakari II was the grandson of Sundiata (fl. the first half of the thirteenth century), the founder of the dynasty of the mansas (or rulers) of Mali, and was the brother of Mansa Mūsā (d. 1332?), the most famous ruler of medieval Mali. A paucity of reliable documentation makes impossible the compilation of an accurate listing of the mansas of Mali and the years of their reigns.

fictional travels of Sir John Mandeville in the Middle Ages.

Bibliography: Davidson, Basil, "Africans before Columbus?" *West Africa* 27 (1969): 641; Fingerhut, Eugene R., *Who First Discovered America? A Critique of Pre-Columbian Voyages*, 1984; Niane, D. T., ed., *Africa from the Twelfth to the Sixteenth Century*, 1981; Van Sertima, Ivan, *They Came before Columbus*, 1976.

Acosta, Father José (or Joseph) de (1539 or 1540–1600)

In his *The Natural and Moral History of the Indies* (1590), this Spanish priest and historian first advanced the theory that the ancestors of the Native Americans first arrived in the Americas by traveling across a land bridge from Asia (see also **Bering Land Bridge/Strait Theory**).

Acosta was born at Medina del Campo about 1540 and received an excellent humanistic education from the Jesuits, becoming a novice in the Society of Jesus while still a boy. After a distinguished career as a student of theology and philosophy at the University of Alcalá, he entered the priesthood at age 26. In 1570 the Jesuits sent him to the Americas, and Acosta spent the next 16 years doing missionary work. He resided for brief periods of time in the Antilles and Panama before pushing on to his assignment in Peru. Once there Acosta evangelized the Andean natives and assisted viceroy Francisco de Toledo in ruling the country.

Acosta spent most of his 14 years in Peru at the Jesuit seminary of Juli at Lake Titicaca. He developed a great interest in the ways of the New World, and by 1583 he had learned enough of the native languages of Quechua and Aymara to produce a trilingual catechism. He also collected notes on the natural history, customs, and history of Peru. Acosta resided in Mexico from 1586–1587, gathering information on that country with the help of his fellow Jesuit Juan de Tovar. In 1586 he completed the manuscript of his Latin work *De natura novi orbis* (On the nature of the New World) based on his researches in Peru and Mexico, and it was published in 1588. Returning to Spain in 1587, Acosta translated his *De natura* into Spanish and made it part of his *Historia natural y moral de las Indias* (Natural and moral history of the Indies), completed in 1588 and published in 1590.

This latter book earned him the high regard of later historians, geographers, and anthropologists. It is a massive work based on comprehensive observations and research, rigorous objectivity, and logical organization. Like many of his contemporaries, Acosta was curious about the origins of Native Americans. As an orthodox Christian he believed in monogenesis, the single-creation theory of human origin. He therefore needed to determine how the ancestors of Native Americans got from the Old World to the New. Acosta accepted the possibility that ancient peoples made sea voyages to the New World, and mentioned stories by the Carthaginians and others. Ultimately he rejected such voyages as a significant means for populating the New World with humans, animals, and plants after the destruction of the universal flood of Noah. He also disbelieved the theories that Atlanteans and Hebrews were their ancestors. Instead, Acosta postulated the existence of an undiscovered land bridge or strait in the northwestern part of North America connecting it to Asia. Furthermore, he speculated that their ancestors had been primitive hunters who gradually spread through the Americas, ultimately developing independent civilizations.

Acosta's theory anticipated the triumph of the modern Bering Strait theory by some 300 years. During those intervening centuries, despite their excellent basis in scholarly research, Acosta's ideas faced stiff competition from other now-discredited theories.

Authors from many nations, particularly the eclectic **Gregorio García,** continue to offer a variety of theories involving transoceanic voyages to the New World to account for the origins of Native Americans.

Bibliography: Acosta, José de, *The Natural and Moral History of the Indies,* 2 vols., [1880], 1970; Arocena, Luis A., "Father Joseph de Acosta (1540–1600)," in *Latin American Writers,* edited by Carlos A. Solé, 3 vols., 1989; Huddleston, Lee Eldridge, *Origins of the American Indians: European Concepts, 1492–1729,* 1967.

Adair, James
(ca. 1709–1783)

This American historian and frontier trader authored the classic *History of the American Indians* (1775), which attempted to prove that Native Americans were descendants of ancient **Hebrews.**

James Adair was probably born in the county of Antrim, Ireland, and attended school to at least the secondary level. Moving to South Carolina around 1735, he participated in trading in the western part of the colony with the Catawba and Cherokee tribes. In 1744 he moved to the area of present-day Mississippi, where he lived and traded with the Chickasaw tribe. He played a role in the rebellion of the Choctaw tribe against the French in 1746 and led a group of Chickasaws who were fighting alongside the colonists from the South Carolina colony during the Cherokee War of 1759–1761.

Meanwhile Adair began writing his *History of the American Indians.* As he would later inform his readers, he accomplished that task while a Chickasaw woman provided him with intimate companionship. By 1768 the work was nearly complete and he began seeking support for both its publication and his views on Indian affairs. Traveling to New York, Adair visited Sir William Johnson, the royal superintendent for In-

dian affairs, who introduced him in late 1768 to Sir Thomas Gage, the commander of British forces in North America. To Adair's great disappointment, little came of this trip and its meetings. During 1769 he took out advertisements soliciting subscribers for his history. Various problems delayed publication for several years until Adair traveled to London and personally saw the book to press in 1775. His history received favorable reviews in British periodicals, and American readers also considered it an authoritative account. In 1782 it was translated into German.

The *History of the American Indians* is a curious work. Almost half its length is devoted to the argument that Native Americans descended from Hebrews. From the time of its publication to the present, scholars have respected its largely accurate and insightful descriptions of Cherokee, Creek, and Chickasaw customs. It has been convincingly argued that Adair's belief in Hebrew origins rather enhanced his pioneering anthropological work by providing him with both a fairly valid framework for cultural comparison and a greater respect for his subjects.

Adair based his arguments on the assumption of a single creation (or monogenesis), the idea that all humanity had a common origin in Adam. He rejected theories that Native Americans descended from **Chinese, Tartars,** or **Scythians** because their customs were dissimilar and, never having been maritime nations, they had no way of getting to the Americas. Although he did not state it explicitly, Adair apparently believed that the Native Americans' ancestors arrived by sea in the area around the Gulf of Mexico and Central America, then spread north and south. Later in the book, however, he argued that it was more probable that the Hebrews made their way across Asia to America to escape captivity by the Assyrians than that storms had driven them to America. Adair was aware that Asia and America were separated only by the narrow and easily navigable Bering Strait. In fact, he used that knowledge to bolster his own argument. The main thrust of his theory was based on comparisons of the two groups' customs and beliefs, which he presented as 23 detailed arguments forming the first half of his history.

Adair was not unique in espousing the idea of Hebrew origins. Such a theory had been around virtually from 1492 and Columbus's first contacts with Native Americans, and continued to flourish well into the nineteenth century. Unlike many advocates, Adair was a highly intelligent and accurate observer and able to produce a well-written account. Those qualities allow Adair's book to remain an important source for the history of the southeastern tribes of the United States despite an organization based on a now-discredited theory.

Bibliography: Hudson, Charles, "James Adair as Anthropologist," *Ethnohistory* 24 (Fall 1977): 311–328; Washburn, Wilcomb E., "James Adair's 'Noble Savages,'" in *The Colonial Legacy*, edited by Lawrence H. Leder, vol. 3, 1973.

Adam of Bremen's Chronicle (ca. 1075)

This clerical history of the archdiocese of Hamburg-Bremen contains the only explicit reference to the existence of **Vinland** in a non-Viking source from the Middle Ages.

Adam of Bremen (ca. 1040–after 1085) came from Bamberg, where he received a thorough classical education. About 1066 Archbishop Adalbert made him a canon of the cathedral of Bremen; by 1060 he was master of the cathedral school. Between late 1072 and 1075 or 1076, Adam composed in Latin the first version of his history *Gesta Hammaburgensis Ecclesiae Pontificum* (Deeds of the archbishops of the church of Hamburg). He continued to revise it be-

tween 1076 and 1081, and possibly as late as 1085. Adam's history consists of four books. The first two provide a history of the archdiocese of Hamburg up to 1043, the beginning of Adalbert's tenure as archbishop. The third book describes Adalbert's reign in Hamburg until his death in 1072. In the fourth book Adam supplied a geographical and ethnographical description of the northern islands of the Atlantic Ocean and the North and Baltic seas, commenting on the possibilities for missionary work there.

His geographical section qualifies Adam as the earliest German geographer and one of the first medieval European geographers. When he compiled his description of the northern seas, Adam used traditional classical sources that included fantastic stories of monstrous races and strange places. However, he also correctly believed that the world was a sphere. Not confining his researches to written records, he relied heavily on knowledge provided by contemporary travelers such as the merchants of Hamburg and Bremen. Information about Viking settlements in Iceland, Greenland, and Vinland came from his visit to the court of Svend Estudsen, king of Denmark. Adam's brief description of Vinland reports that wild grains and grapes grew there in abundance, the grapes producing an excellent wine. Adam did not think of Vinland as part of a vast, unexplored continent, but rather an Atlantic island like Iceland. Hearing that a recent expedition led by Harold Hadrada of Norway found nothing but ice and darkness and barely made its way home, he believed that no habitable lands existed beyond Vinland.

Although Adam's comments on Vinland are brief, they serve to confirm the stories told in the **Vinland Sagas**, which some regard as mere fiction. His chronicle provides the only definite evidence of non-Viking knowledge of Vinland. Some scholars suggest that the *Historia ecclesiastica* of Orderic Vitalis, written before 1143, refers to Vinland and not Finland when it lists the lands ruled by the kings of Norway. Even if both sources indicate the existence of some knowledge of the Vinland discoveries in northern Europe during the eleventh century, they also show how fleeting that knowledge was. Moreover, it is highly doubtful that this information influenced the geographical ideas of Columbus, since it appeared in little-used manuscripts located in northern Europe.

Bibliography: Adam of Bremen, *History of the Archbishops of Hamburg-Bremen*, translated by Francis J. Tschan, 1959; Phillips, J. R. S., *The Medieval Expansion of Europe*, 1988.

Aethicus of Istria's *Cosmography*

Also known as Pseudo-Aethicus, his seventh-century or late eighth-century account of a fictional journey around the world indicates that trans-Atlantic voyages were considered theoretically possible by early medieval Europeans.

The text of *Cosmography* professes to have been written in Greek by Aethicus from Istria, located at the mouth of the Danube River. It further falsely claims that St. Jerome translated it into Latin. It appears that an associate of encyclopedist Isidore of Seville wrote the *Cosmography* sometime during the seventh century in Merovingian Gaul. Another attribution identified the true author as the Irish missionary Ferghil or Virgil, bishop of Salzburg during the late eighth century.

In the *Cosmography*, Aethicus, a Christian neophyte, tells the story of his journey around the world. His account is full of the standard fantasies and legends that medieval people believed and enjoyed: dog-headed men, sirens, griffins, and the savage descendants of Gog and Magog. Despite the credulity of his geography, or perhaps because of it, Aethicus was widely read and cited over

the centuries by many people including such respected intellectuals as **Roger Bacon** and Sir Walter Raleigh. Furthermore, works like Aethicus's *Cosmography* provide strong evidence that early medieval Europeans considered westward trans-Atlantic voyages to Asia a theoretical possibility.

Bibliography: Beazley, C. Raymond, *The Dawn of Modern Geography*, 3 vols., [1897–1906] 1949; Phillips, J. R. S., *The Medieval Expansion of Europe*, 1988.

African Voyages to Pre-Columbian America

With the increase of black African studies in the twentieth century, the idea that sub-Saharan Africans visited the Americas in pre-Columbian times has grown in popularity among writers. (See also **Arabic Voyages to the Americas** and **Egyptians in Ancient America**.)

According to most writers, the two main periods for African visits to the Americas before 1492 occurred during the Olmec era in Mexico from ca. 1500–300 B.C. and during the fourteenth and fifteenth centuries. African visitors to the Olmecs were supposedly the inspiration for the great stone heads known by the archaeological nickname "babyfaces." White diffusionist writers such as James Bailey in *The God-Kings and the Titans* (1973) and Constance Irwin in *Fair Gods and Stone Faces* (1963) assume that black Africans came to the Americas as slaves or mercenaries of the **Phoenicians**. However, anthropologist Ivan Van Sertima, himself a black, contends that the blacks were Nubians who had conquered Egypt and ruled it as the twenty-fifth dynasty from 750–650 B.C. Coming to Mexico as the leaders of expeditions manned also by Egyptians and Phoenicians, the Nubians made themselves part of the Olmec ruling elite (see also **Nubian-Egyptians in Ancient America**). During the fourteenth and fifteenth centuries,

The supposed Negroid features on giant sculptured heads found at San Lorenzo and La Venta in Mexico have led some scholars to theorize about contacts between the Olmecs and Africa.

the **Mandingo** and **Songhay** peoples of West Africa visited the Americas for trade and colonization. Harvard professor of Slavic languages **Leo Wiener** pioneered this theory in the early 1920s; it was revived by Ivan Van Sertima in 1976.

Evidence for these African visits comes from several sources. One is the transfer to America of plants native to Africa or vice versa. Tobacco and **maize** (or corn) are cited as evidence, but they have also been discredited as genuine pre-Columbian transfers. **Cotton** is also cited, and its evolution appears to prove that contact took place. But that contact probably took the form of drifting seeds in the distant past rather than transport by humans. Certainly the chronology of domestic cotton growing in the Old World and the Americas does not support the African theory. Supposed Negro skeletal remains of pre-Columbian provenance are not widely accepted as genuine or convincing evidence. Skeletally, the races are not that distinct; these bones may actually be those of Native Americans.

The purported representations of Negroid people in pre-Columbian statues and pictures may simply be depictions of Native Americans with Negroid features or some artistic convention not yet understood. Some diffusionist scholars prefer to see true black Africans in these representations. Alexander von Wuthenau, a German expatriate living in Mexico, is the great advocate of using artistic portraiture to prove contacts between the Americas and the Old World. In his *Unexpected Faces in Ancient America: The Historical Testimony of the Pre-Columbian Artist* (1975), he sees the presence of all sorts of Old World peoples, including black Africans. Most scholars are skeptical of this sort of evidence, since much remains to be learned about the artistic conventions of the ancient Americans. Some Native Americans had Negroid features but had never been in contact with Africans. Various types of

physiognomies are distributed in all races, weakening the impact of von Wuthenau's evidence. Certain oral traditions and legends have been cited to prove the occurrence of Mandingo voyages to the Americas. Unfortunately, **Abubakari II,** the king of Mali who supposedly sponsored these voyages, is such a shadowy figure that there is some doubt as to whether he actually reigned.

Still, efforts to prove African contacts with pre-Columbian America continue. In 1981, Canadian writer Michael Bradley seconded Van Sertima's 1976 book *They Came before Columbus* by publishing his own *The Black Discovery of America: Amazing Evidence of Daring Voyages by Ancient West African Mariners.* Its conclusions are very similar to those of Van Sertima, almost redundantly so. Van Sertima has completed a new book tentatively titled *African Voyages before Columbus* that is scheduled to appear in 1993.

Bibliography: Feder, Kenneth L., *Frauds, Myths, and Mysteries: Science and Pseudoscience in Archaeology,* 1990; Van Sertima, Ivan, ed., *African Presence in Early America,* [1986], 2nd ed., 1992; Williams, Stephen, *Fantastic Archaeology: The Wild Side of North American Prehistory,* 1991.

Albania Superior

Or simply Albania, it is another name applied to the Arctic regions, **Greenland,** and the area of Norse explorations in eastern North America. Derived from *albus* (Latin for white), it is simply a Latinate version of the Norse **Hvítramannaland** or **White Man's Land.** See also **Irish Monks in America** and **Great Ireland.**

Alexander the Great, Lost Fleet of (ca. 323 B.C.)

Harold S. Gladwin's (1883–1983) theory attributes the higher civilizations of the ancient Americas to the arrival of a fleet of Greeks,

Campbell Grant's drawing of Gladwin's image of Alexander the Great's fleet landing in Peru. Grant's illustration mimics John Vanderlyn's famous Landing of Columbus *in the United States Capitol Building.*

Phoenicians, and **Egyptians** originally gathered together by Alexander the Great.

History records in various sources that Alexander the Great gathered possibly 800 vessels for exploration and colonization at the time of his death in 323 B.C. His admiral, Nearchus, abandoned the fleet to join Antigonus, one of Alexander's successors, in Asia Minor. Because of the silence of surviving records, the fate of the fleet remains a mystery. According to Gladwin's book *Men out of Asia* (1947), the fleet did not disintegrate but rather sailed east. Starting from the Persian Gulf, the fleet was a multinational enterprise of Greeks, Egyptians, Phoenicians, and Persians. Along its eastward course, the fleet stopped at various places in India, Burma, Thailand, Malaysia, and Indonesia. Some ships and crews stayed behind at various stopping points. Replaced in turn by Indians, Malaysians, and other peoples, the fleet became ever more heterogeneous.

Passing beyond New Guinea, the fleet mixed with the existing Negroid population of Melanesia. It sailed to then-uninhabited Polynesia and populated the islands with some of its own company, thus becoming the ancestors of Polynesians. The remainder of the great fleet sailed on to reach the coasts of Peru and Panama. The company spread out and encountered various groups of natives, to whom they brought the foundations of higher civilization. The fleet's leaders became the inspirations for the various **white god legends.** In Gladwin's opinion, the chronology of higher civilization in the Americas is too short for the indigenous peoples to have developed it in complete isolation. Only **diffusion** from the eastern hemisphere could explain its supposed rapid appearance.

Gladwin supplies numerous examples of cultural traits found in the Americas that he believes had their origin in diffusion from the crew of Alexander the Great's fleet rather than through parallel diffusion. One such cultural artifact was the peaked helmet worn in Peru, the Pacific Northwest, and Polynesia. According to Gladwin, the helmet designs could be traced back to the ancient

Greeks. Various weaving and metallurgical techniques were also attributed to Old World sources. Gladwin also cites the existence of the Hindu game of **pachisi** in pre-Columbian Mexico, which he credited to Alexander's fleet.

Like most diffusionists, Gladwin believed that humans were not very inventive. Specifically, he thought poorly of the intellectual talents of Native Americans. He felt that the best aspects of their civilizations originated from sources in the Old World. Gladwin believes that, left to themselves, the Native Americans often let the civilizing gifts of Alexander the Great's fleet degenerate. Most professional archaeologists and anthropologists would disagree strongly with these assumptions. No evidence supports the existence of any visit by Alexander the Great's fleet to the Americas. Other diffusionists also generally reject Gladwin's theory. In fact, Harvard archaeologist Stephen Williams persuasively suggests that *Men out of Asia* was actually an elaborate joke by Gladwin on his erstwhile friend Alfred V. Kidder, the professional archaeologist. Kidder was the model for the caricature of Gladwin's straw man, Professor Phuddy Duddy (Ph.D.), the archetypal stodgy, professional archaeologist, in the series of cartoons by Campbell Grant illustrating *Men out of Asia*.

Bibliography: Gladwin, Harold S., *Men out of Asia*, 1947; Williams, Stephen, *Fantastic Archaeology: The Wild Side of North American Prehistory*, 1991.

Anian, Strait of

This hypothetical strait divided the unexplored northwest part of North America from Asia. The early-modern European name Anian remained in use from the sixteenth century until 1728, when **Vitus Bering** discovered the real strait subsequently named in his honor.

The name Anian derived from a land of Ania mentioned by Marco Polo as being located in the extreme northeastern part of Asia. Jacopo Gastaldi published a pamphlet in 1562 containing the first mention of the Strait of Anian. He cited a lost map of contemporary Venetian geographer Mateo Pagano as his source for this information. A few years later Bolognino Zaltieri drew the earliest surviving map to show the Strait of Anian, which remained a common feature on maps of the world until Vitus Bering's explorations in 1728.

The geographical concept of a Strait of Anian was significant to sixteenth- and seventeenth-century people for two reasons. First, unless such a strait existed and thus divided Asia from North America, then neither a northwest nor northeast passage would provide a much desired sea route to China or Japan. Second, a land bridge between Asia and North America, or at least a narrow strait such as the supposed Strait of Anian, provided a possible land route from Asia for the ancestors of Native Americans. This theory was first put forward by **José de Acosta** and is the ancestor of the modern **Bering Land Bridge Theory**.

Bibliography: Ramsay, Raymond H., *No Longer on the Map: Discovering Places That Never Were*, 1972.

Anthrosophy

This schismatic group of European Theosophists was founded in 1913 under the leadership of Rudolph Steiner (1861–1925). They initially broke away from the main body of **Theosophy** in 1907 as a protest against Annie Besant's deification of the Indian savant Krishnamurti, but retained the basic theosophical doctrines including those dealing with **Lemuria** and **Atlantis**.

Theosophy attracted many followers in Europe, but many of the converts objected to the growing domination of Eastern religious and philosophical ideas. The German Rudolph Steiner and his followers wanted a greater emphasis placed on spiritual powers and clairvoyance. Their secession from the parent organization in 1907 was just one manifestation of their objections to Theosophy's overly enthusiastic adoption of ideas from Hinduism and Buddhism. The break became permanent in 1913 when Steiner founded the independent Anthrosophical Society.

In most ways, Theosophy and Anthrosophy remained quite similar. Steiner continued to believe in the existence of root races, Atlantis, and Lemuria, but he added some new insights into the mental processes of the ancient Lemurians and Atlanteans. In 1923 he wrote and published *Atlantis and Lemuria,* which explained how Lemurians lacked memory or reason but had a highly developed faculty of will power. On the other hand, Atlanteans possessed excellent memories but little ability to reason. They survived by mastery of the "life force," which gave them control over and harmony with nature. But as the fourth root race of the Atlanteans approached its final days, that power faded. The fifth root race of modern humans developed the ability to reason as a compensation. Apart from these additions, like the Theosophists, Steiner credited the Atlanteans with colonizing and civilizing both the eastern and western hemispheres in the distant past. Steiner's ideas also had a big influence on the teachings of Max Heindel of the **Rosicrucian** Fellowship.

Bibliography: de Camp, L. Sprague, *Lost Continents,* [1954], 1970; McDermott, Robert A., "Anthrosophy," in *Encyclopedia of Religion,* edited by Mircea Eliade, 10 vols., 1987.

Antillia

This legendary island of the western Atlantic was widely believed by fifteenth-century Europeans to be a real place. It was sometimes thought to be the island of the legendary **Seven Cities.**

The name Antillia probably derives from a combination of the Latin words meaning opposite island. **Martin Behaim's** globe of 1492 contained an annotation next to Antillia stating that a Spanish ship sighted it in 1414. The earliest datable appearance of Antillia on a map occurs in the nautical **map of Zuane Pizzigano** of Venice from 1424. Antillia is shown as a rectangular island with a north-south orientation located directly west of Portugal and approximately the same size as that country. Zuane Pizzigano's map also located the legendary Seven Cities on Antillia, a detail often omitted on later maps.

Antillia appeared frequently on maps during the rest of the fifteenth century, often as the largest of a group of islands. Other important mapmakers such as Fra Mauro ignored its existence. Nevertheless, it was widely assumed that Antillia existed and had been visited by the Portuguese. Around 1481 Paolo Toscanelli dal Pozzo recommended it to Columbus as a potential stopover and resting place during any trans-Atlantic voyage to Asia. Columbus took that advice and included the stop in his itinerary. After the European discovery of the New World, the West Indies were assumed to be related to Antillia and came to be called the Antillies by the Dutch and French. Meanwhile, the failure to find the Seven Cities caused some people to shift Antillia's location to the mainland of South America.

Today some scholars speculate that the appearance of the legendary Antillia on fifteenth-century maps vaguely reflects a visit by European seamen to Cuba. This intriguing suggestion is based on the assumption that the unknown voyagers sailed by a route that took them to Cuba and Jamaica but caused them to miss Haiti and Puerto Rico. Whether or not it was based on some

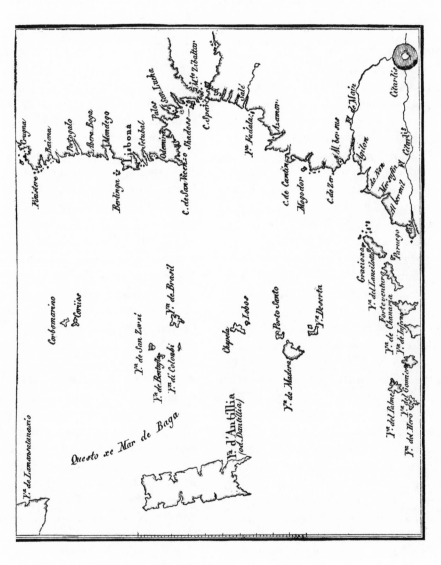

Antillia as it appeared on Andrea Biancho's map of 1436.

forgotten voyage, belief in the existence of Antillia provided a significant encouragement to those contemplating a trans-Atlantic voyage during the fifteenth century.

Bibliography: Babcock, William H., *Legendary Islands of the Atlantic: A Study in Medieval Geography*, 1922; Nebenzahl, Kenneth, *Rand McNally Atlas of Columbus and the Great Discoveries*, 1990.

Antipodes

In classical and medieval Europe this geographical concept postulated the existence of unknown and possibly inhabited regions in other quarters of the spherical earth, encouraging the possibility of travel.

Belief in the sphericity of the earth became common among educated Greeks by the fifth century B.C. due to the teachings of the Pythagorean philosophers. Beginning with Parmenides (fl. 450 B.C.), they also divided the earth into five climatic zones. At the north and south ends of the globe were two uninhabitable frigid regions. Along the equator lay a torrid or fiery zone that was uninhabitable because of heat. In the regions between the Arctic and torrid zones lay the temperate zones, capable of sustaining human life. This zonal theory of climate persisted, with modifications, as an organizing principle of geography through the Middle Ages and Renaissance into the modern era.

The ancient Greeks called the known inhabited world the *oikoumene*. Because they believed the earth was a sphere, they also recognized that the oikoumene constituted only a portion of the globe. Another common belief of the Greeks and others was that the known world was surrounded by ocean. Combined with the concept of a spherical earth, that belief led some Greek thinkers to suggest the existence of two great dividing oceans: one girdled the earth running north and south, while the other divided the earth east and west. The effect was to split the earth into four quarters. During the second century B.C., Crates (or Krates) of Mallus formalized this theory. Besides the known oikoumene, he identified three other regions. Directly south of the oikoumene lay the *antoikoi,* or "opposite men," which would have been where southern Africa is located. In that land, the seasons were reversed. Located directly on the opposite side of the northern hemisphere from the oikoumene was the *antipodes,* or "opposite feet men." It corresponded to the quarter of the globe occupied by North America, and its night and day were the reverse of the oikoumene. Finally, south of the antipodes lay the *antichthones,* or "those of the opposite land." South America is located where the antichthones were thought to be. In that land both day and night and the seasons were the reverse of the oikoumene. Crates's theory created the possibility that three other inhabitable regions existed on the earth. It is important to remember that the classical and medieval usage of the names for these quarters was often imprecise. *Antoikoi* and *antichthones* were not commonly used, while the term *antipodes* frequently referred to all three "opposite" quarters, not just the northern one.

For the ancient Greeks, Crates's theory of the "opposite" quarters suggested two important questions: Were they inhabited and could they be reached from the oikoumene? Initially it was thought that the torrid zone could not be crossed because of its deadly heat. By the time of the great geographer Claudius Ptolemy (fl. A.D. 127–148), sufficient evidence accumulated to show that the tropics were inhabited and so could be crossed safely.

The decline of the Roman empire after the time of Ptolemy also led to a decline in the store of human knowledge, including geography. Older, discredited ideas crept back into acceptance and challenged belief in the existence of the antipodal regions. The Christian apologist Lactantius (ca. 250–325) was a determined believer in the flat-earth theory. He based his arguments against the existence of the antipodes on the contention that if the earth were a sphere, everything would fall off the bottom half. At the same time, the idea that the torrid zone was uninhabitable and uncrossable regained general acceptance in medieval Europe. Nevertheless, Crates's theory of the four quarters also survived because of support from two fourth-century scholars: Ambrosius Theodosius Macrobius and Martianus Capella. Both men's writings were quite popular among the scholars of the early Middle Ages.

The loss of so much geographical knowledge from the classical era, during the Roman Empire, left Crates's theory vulnerable to challenges and modifications during the Middle Ages. **Aristotle** (384–322 B.C.), a Greek philosopher whose writings were considered authoritative by the scholars of medieval Europe, never accepted the existence of the northern antipodes. Instead, he concluded that only a relatively narrow Atlantic Ocean lay between the west coast of Europe and the east coast of Asia. As a result, most medieval geographical thinking, including that of Christopher Columbus, did not speculate about the existence of northern antipodes. Because Aristotle lived before it was proven that the torrid zone was inhabited, he wrote that the torrid zone was too hot to be crossed, a belief that persisted into the sixteenth century despite much evidence to the contrary.

Aristotle's belief caused conceptual problems for many Christian writers. It meant that the southern antipodes were completely cut off from contact with the oikoumene, the known world. Although some speculated that the temperate zone of the antipodes was inhabited, this belief was theologically unacceptable to the early fathers of the Christian church, particularly St. Augustine of Hippo (354–430). St. Augustine asked two questions. If there was only one creation, where did any antipodeans come from? If the antipodes were inaccessible, how could the gospel of Christ be preached throughout the world as the Bible said it was? The possibility of **multiple creations** (polygenesis) or multiple incarnations of Christ were considered heretical by the church. Therefore any belief in the existence of antipodeans was unbiblical and, in the opinion of many churchmen, contained the seeds of potential heresy. During the eighth century, Bishop Virgil of Salzburg received condemnation from Pope Zachary for just that belief. Still, the church never officially declared the belief to be a heresy. St. Augustine and others who followed him, such as Cosmos in the sixth century and the Venerable Bede (ca. 673–735), accepted the existence of the antipodes as a logical consequence of the sphericity of the earth. But they denied belief in the existence of antipodeans because of its theological unacceptability.

Despite the danger potential for the church hierarchy, various scholars speculated about the antipodes and even antipodeans during the Middle Ages. Lambert of St. Omer wrote his *Liber floridus* about 1130, which vaguely described the earth as a sphere divided into five climatic zones and split by the great equatorial ocean. He included antipodes, but believed they were uninhabited and inaccessible because of the deadly heat of the torrid zone. It was a theologically correct view of the world, but not one with which everyone agreed. In the next century, both Albertus Magnus (1206–1280) and **Roger Bacon** in his *Opus maius* of around 1266 argued that the antipodes were inhabited, but their ideas failed to achieve general acceptance. Even at the beginning of the fifteenth century, Cardinal Pierre d'Ailly, in his influential *Imago mundi*

15

of 1410 and his *Compendium cosmographiae* of ca. 1414, adhered to the belief that high temperatures of the torrid zone prevented humans from living there or traveling through.

Belief in the antipodes frequently became confused with another prevalent idea: the existence of a great southern continent (see also **Terra Australis**). Most importantly, however, belief in the antipodes provided considerable encouragement for speculation about the existence and accessibility of unknown lands up to and during the great Age of Discovery in the fifteenth and sixteenth centuries.

Bibliography: Ramsay, Raymond H., *No Longer on the Map: Discovering Places That Never Were*, 1972; Wright, John Kirtland, *The Geographical Lore of the Time of the Crusades*, [1925], 1965.

Arabic Voyages to the Americas

Although no definite historical evidence exists to bolster their claims, a number of writers maintain that Arabic sailors reached the Americas during the Middle Ages and possibly established sustained contact.

Arabic seamanship in the Indian Ocean had long followed the traditions and high standards of the legendary Sinbad the Sailor. On the Atlantic, however, Arabic sailors usually hugged the coast from fear of the dangerous **Green Sea of Darkness.** Modern scholars Ivan Van Sertima and M. D. W. Jeffreys dispute this picture of unadventurous seamanship and claim that Arabic sailors maintained a steady trade with the mysterious land of **Mu-lan-p'i** up to the twelfth and thirteenth centuries. They also assert that Arabic sailors introduced American **maize** to Africa during the pre-Columbian era. These claims, based on medieval Chinese writings, are not corroborated by the works of the great Arabic geographers al Massoudy (Abū-l-Hasan 'Alī ibn al-Husayn ibn 'Alī

al-Mas'ūdī; d. 956) or Edrisi (Abū 'Abd Allāh Muhammad al-Idrīsī; 1099–1180). Both men knew of the Canary Islands, and Edrisi appears to have known about Madeira, but neither indicated knowledge of any mysterious western lands.

Although both al Massoudy and Edrisi expressed the typical fears of the Atlantic (their Green Sea of Darkness), they told tales of people who successfully dared its terrible waters. Al Massoudy related how Khoshkhash, a young man from Cordova, sailed into the Atlantic. For a long time no one heard of him and it was assumed he was lost at sea. Then, unexpectedly, he returned with a very rich cargo. Khoshkhash's story circulated through Muslim Spain and may have inspired the central figures in Edrisi's story of high-seas travel on the Atlantic, the *Maghrurín,* which has been variously translated as the "Wanderers" or the "Deceived men."

The Wanderers of Lisbon were eight brothers or first cousins (Edrisi is unclear on that point). They departed from Lisbon on an east wind in a ship fitted for ocean travel and provisioned with water and food for many months. After sailing 11 days they reached a region where the water was thick and smelled of decay, a description corresponding to the Sargasso Sea. Faced by these strange, dangerous waters with their many concealed reefs, the Wanderers turned south. Twelve days of sailing brought them to an uninhabited island full of sheep, which is identified as Madeira. They continued south for 12 more days and found an island inhabited by people living in houses and practicing farming. The natives immediately captured the Wanderers and took them to a coastal city. Their captors were tall and tan-colored with straight black hair, a description that led some people to identify the islanders as a group of Native Americans or Indians. A far better alternative is that the unknown islanders were the aboriginal inhabitants of the

Canary Islands—the Guanches. This identification fits the physical and geographical descriptions far better than any place in the Americas. A Canarian identification is further reinforced by the fact that the island's ruler had an Arabic-speaking interpreter, which would not have occurred if the Wanderers had reached the Americas. When the interpreter asked the Wanderers what they wanted, they replied that they sought to learn about the ocean and its full extent. The ruler informed them he had sent a ship west manned by slaves. It had returned after a month without finding anything but a region of darkness. Later the islanders decided to release the Wanderers and returned them to the African coast. The Wanderers made their way home to Lisbon, where a street was named in their honor. Edrisi does not date the voyage of the *Maghrurín,* but it had to have taken place before 1147, the year Lisbon fell to Christian armies.

Evidence for Arabic contact with the pre-Columbian Americas is sparse and unconvincing. It is implausible that Edrisi would not have known about any strange western lands that might have been contacted by Arabic ships. It is even more inconceivable that he would not have known about any sustained trade with the Americas or the mysterious land of Mu-lan-p'i. Arabic sailors simply never crossed the Atlantic in the Middle Ages.

Bibliography: Beazley, C. Raymond, *The Dawn of Modern Geography,* 3 vols., [1887–1906], 1949; Haven, Samuel, *Archaeology of the United States,* [1856], 1973; Kimble, George H. T., *Geography in the Middle Ages,* [1938], 1968; Van Sertima, Ivan, *They Came before Columbus,* 1976.

Aristotle
(384–322 B.C.)

A famous Greek philosopher, his writings were considered by medieval Europeans from 1100 to 1500 to be authoritative works on most branches of human knowledge. These supposedly included the story of a Carthaginian discovery of America in 590 B.C.

Scholars during the age of explorations in the sixteenth century frequently quoted Aristotle's writings when they formulated their ideas or defended their opinions. Columbus quoted Aristotle's opinion that it would take only a few days to sail across the Atlantic from Europe to Asia. Aristotle's ideas on slavery were used by some Spaniards to justify enslaving Native Americans. A less well known contribution involved the belief, common among many sixteenth-century writers, attributing Aristotle as the source of a story that Carthaginian merchants discovered a large and pleasant island in the Atlantic about 590 B.C. The merchants wanted to colonize the new land, but the Senate of Carthage grew fearful of the project. In the opinion of the Senate, an enemy might later conquer such a rich colony and use it to threaten Carthage. They forbade anyone to visit the island and ordered its discoverers put to death to preserve the secret. Spanish historian **Gonzalo Fernández de Oviedo y Valdés** (1478–1557) identified it as the Americas and cited this story as an example of a pre-Columbian visit to the New World. Ferdinand Columbus, a contemporary of Oviedo and the son of the famous discoverer, rejected the story as nonsense, but to no avail.

Oviedo's account, based on Aristotle, became the foundation of a persistent belief that the Carthaginians visited the Americas. But in fact, the story lacked Aristotle's authority. The real source was the *Admirandis in natura auditis* by Theophilus de Ferrariis, who claimed to have taken it from *De mirabilibus auscultationibus,* a work long thought to be Aristotle's but written between A.D. 100 and 500. Because this spurious document was written some 400 to 800 years after the events it describes, it is a very unreliable source of information about the activities of Carthaginian sailors. Since Aristotle was not the author of the work, he no longer has any direct role in these debates.

Bibliography: Hammond, N. G. L., and H. H. Scullard, eds., *The Oxford Classical Dictionary*, 2nd ed., 1970; Huddleston, Lee Eldridge, *Origins of the American Indians: European Concepts, 1492–1729*, 1967.

Atlantis

The most famous of all the legendary **lost continents,** it was first mentioned by the Greek philosopher **Plato** (ca. 429–347 B.C.) who located it in the Atlantic Ocean where it sank with great loss of life and total destruction about 12,000 years ago. Many people consider Atlantis to be the original home of humanity and the source of civilization. The higher civilizations of the ancient Americas, particularly the Maya, have been credited to the Atlanteans.

The first written reference to Atlantis occurred in Plato's dialogue *Timaeus,* followed by more information in his unfinished dialogue *Critias*; both were written toward the end of his life. According to the narrative in *Timaeus*, the famous Athenian lawgiver **Solon** learned of the existence of Atlantis while visiting with some Egyptian priests about 600 B.C. The account was supposedly passed on orally by members of his family until it was written down by Plato toward the end of his life. The story told how Athens was the leading city of the eastern Mediterranean world about 9500 B.C. Suddenly and without warning, the armies of Atlantis, a great island beyond the Strait of Gibraltar, invaded the Mediterranean region. The brave Athenians managed to drive the invaders back, but a series of earthquakes

and floods devastated the area. Athens suffered immense damage, but Atlantis sank beneath the ocean.

Plato returned to the subject in his next dialogue, *Critias,* and gave more details of that mysterious land. Poseidon, god of the sea, first settled Atlantis by mating with the mortal Kleito. The couple produced five sets of male twins who became the ancestors of the Atlantean population. Thanks to their divine ancestry, the Atlanteans grew quite powerful. They built a huge circular city with a large citadel at its center and surrounded by three rings of canals. Beyond the city lay a large irrigated plain. The Atlanteans also organized a large navy of 1, 200 ships and a gigantic army of 10,000 chariots. Their society was a rich and prosperous one in which agriculture and trade flourished while gold and silver abounded. But such riches did not corrupt the Atlanteans. For many years they remained virtuous, sober, and self-controlled. Unfortunately, as the Atlanteans married mortal women over the years, their divine aspects became diluted and gradually they grew more greedy and selfish. When Zeus, king of the gods, saw this, he called the gods together to discuss punishing the Atlanteans to reform their behavior. Just what the gods decided to do is not known because here the dialogue stopped. This ending, however, marked the beginning of a debate over the historicity of the Atlantis story that continues to this day.

Initially, Greek and Roman writers did not discuss Atlantis very much. Strabo's *Geography*, which appeared 300 years after Plato, contained the next surviving reference to Atlantis. It includes a quote from **Aristotle** that states, "its inventor [Plato] caused it [Atlantis] to disappear," which indicates that Aristotle thought Atlantis was a purely fictional place. Other writers such as Poseidonius (ca. 135–51 B.C.) and Lysios Proklos disagreed with Aristotle, but modern scholarship supports him. Archaeological evidence

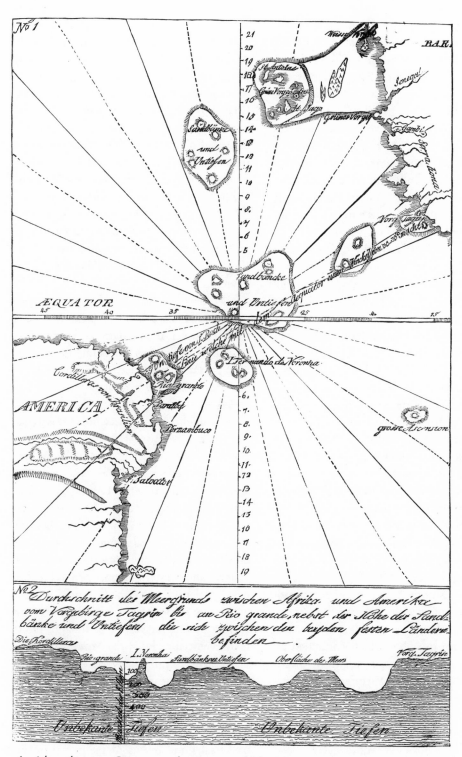

An eighteenth-century German map showing traces of Atlantis.

clearly shows that the great Athens that fought the Atlanteans to a standstill never existed; there are no ruins or artifacts on the site of Athens from that era. No legitimate archaeological evidence from Atlantis has ever been found. Scholars of classical literature also point out that internal evidence from Plato's dialogues gives further credence to the position that Atlantis was a fictional creation like those described in Sir Thomas More's *Utopia* and Samuel Butler's *Erewhon*. In *Timaeus*, it is mentioned that the Atlantean story was told as part of a storytelling festival in Athens—a good clue to its origins. Later in *Critias*, the description of Atlantis conforms so closely to Socrates's earlier description of what an ideal state should be like that even characters in the dialogue commented on it. This strikes most scholars as a case of Plato joking with his readers over the fictionality of his story. Although some writers claimed Plato's Atlantis story was a true history, it was really not that widely discussed. During the Middle Ages it almost disappeared from the writings of scholars.

Columbus's revelation of the existence of the Americas quickly reopened discussions about Atlantis that continue unabated. Prompting the renewed interest in Atlantis was the problem of the origin of the Native Americans or Red Indians—where had they come from? The first person to suggest an Atlantean origin was Spaniard **Francisco López de Gómara** in 1552. Within a few years, Augustin de Zárate, another Spanish historian, published his very popular *Historia del descumbrimiento y conquista de la provincia del Perú* in 1555, which contained an elaboration of Gómara's Atlantean origin theory. In 1572 **Pedro Sarmiento de Gamboa** wrote his *Historia de los Incas*, which traced descendants of Noah to Atlantis and from there to the Americas. By 1674, Englishman John Josselyn even suggested that Atlantis and the Americas were one and the same.

Initially Gómara's Atlantis theory was quite popular, although not without its skeptics. The great scholar **Father José de Acosta,** in his *Natural and Moral History of the Indies* of 1590, rejected the historicity of Atlantis, writing "I believe that all which he [Plato] has written of this Island [Atlantis] . . . cannot be held for true but among children and old folks." Other writers reached the same conclusion, and by 1600 the Atlantis theory lost most of its support. But not all; over the years the Atlantis theory periodically revives. Mexican writer Benito Jerónimo Feijoo y Montenogro used it in 1729 to attack the theories of **multiple creations** put forward by free-thinker Isaac de La Peyrère.

Modern theories claiming Atlantean origins for Native Americans can be traced to two people. **Abbé Charles Étienne Brasseur de Bourbourg's** inaccurate translation of the Mayan book *Codex troano* in 1864 seemed to indicate a clear connection between Atlantis and the Americas. But the most influential Atlantis scholar was Ignatius Donnelly (1831–1901), a multiterm Populist congressman from Minnesota. Donnelly was a reader with wide interests and inexhaustible energy. Out of his reading and research emerged the 1882 classic *Atlantis: The Antediluvian World.* He argued for the existence of a real Atlantis as the source of all succeeding civilizations in both the eastern and western hemispheres. He believed Atlantis established a great empire with colonies in Egypt, Mesoamerica, the Iberian peninsula, Peru, and Ireland. Donnelly even claimed that the **Mound Builders** of the Mississippi Valley were the descendants of Atlantean colonists. Just as Plato had written over 2,000 years earlier, earthquake and flood overwhelmed Donnelly's Atlantis. According to Donnelly, the various universal flood myths of peoples from all over the globe are a memory of its tragic sinking. This, along with other supposedly shared cultural traits, proved that Atlantis existed.

Advances in science render Donnelly's theory obsolete, untenable, and even ridiculous. But given the state of scientific knowledge in 1882, *Atlantis: The Antediluvian World* was initially considered a work of serious scholarship rather than a piece of crackpot literature. In his day, Donnelly's theories were quite believable even though he had a strong tendency to be overly credulous in his use of sources and evidence. He also worked inductively from the assumption that Atlantis existed and gleaned his evidence in such a way as to prove it. Still, compared with the many books about Atlantis claiming spiritual communications as their main sources of information, Donnelly's scholarship remains far and away the finest. His book remains the best of those advocating that a real Atlantis once existed out in the Atlantic Ocean.

Modern scholars can now counter many of Donnelly's arguments for the existence of Atlantis. Close studies of the various universal flood myths show that they do not refer to the same great flood or the sinking of Atlantis. His geological arguments are also shown to be erroneous. Explorations of the Atlantic Ocean's floor reveal no trace of Atlantis's existence. Donnelly's arguments for the diffusion of various cultural traits from the common source of Atlantis also prove faulty. There is no relationship between Egyptian obelisks and Mayan stelae, Egyptian and Mesoamerican pyramids, or the metallurgies practiced in the Old World and the Americas. Donnelly's book simply fails to prove that Atlantis existed.

Donnelly was only the beginning of modern Atlantis scholarship. **Rosicrucians, Theosophists,** and **Anthrosophists** incorporated Atlantis and other lost continents into their religious beliefs. During the 1920s, mythologist Lewis Spence contributed a series of Donnellylike attempts to prove the existence of Atlantis in a scholarly manner. His efforts began with *The Problem of Atlantis* (1924), which was followed by *Atlantis in America* (1925) and *The History of Atlantis* (1926). More books followed, including one on the lost continent of **Lemuria** in 1933. Other writers followed suit; popular writer and lost-continent-literature expert L. Sprague de Camp estimated that by 1954 some 2,000 books had been written about Atlantis. Hundreds more have been written since that date.

Scholars agree that the Atlantis of Plato and Donnelly never existed. Atlantean colonists or refugees did not create the Mayan civilization, or any other, in the Americas or the Old World. Many serious scholars suggest, however, that some ancient catastrophe may have been the inspiration for the Atlantis legend. Many cite the gigantic volcanic explosion that destroyed the Greek island of Thera about 1500 B.C. as a possible candidate. More recently a new book, *The Flood from Heaven: Deciphering the Atlantis Legend* (1992) by Eberhard Zangger, argues that Atlantis was ancient Troy. Whether or not that theory proves to be true, it is safe to say that while the Atlanteans did not beat Columbus to the Americas, more new books about Atlantis will follow Zangger's.

Bibliography: de Camp, L. Sprague, *Lost Continents*, [1954], 1970; Donnelly, Ignatius, *Atlantis: The Antediluvian World*, [1882], 1976; Feder, Kenneth L., *Frauds, Myths, and Mysteries: Science and Pseudoscience in Archaeology*, 1990; Pellegrino, Charles, *Unearthing Atlantis: An Archaeological Odyssey*, 1991.

Avalon

This mythical western island in Celtic mythology is associated with the legendary King Arthur.

Pre-Christian Celtic mythology contains a highly developed image of the Atlantic

Ocean dotted with otherworldly islands, some pleasant and others disagreeable. Arthur's Avalon combines this belief with that of classical Greco-Roman civilization about the existence of the **Fortunate Isles.** Geoffrey of Monmouth's (d. 1155) *History of the Kings of Britain* and *Vita Merlini*, written between 1129 and 1151, are the oldest written sources that mention Avalon; he refers to Avalon as *Ynys Avallach,* which in Welsh means the "isle of apples." Avalon is the place where the magic sword Excalibur (Caliburnus) was forged and where, after the Battle of Camlann, the pilot **Barinthus** took the mortally wounded Arthur. There the sorceress Morgan le Fay, a kindly figure in early versions of the Arthurian romance, ruled a benevolent community of nine women. The women healed Arthur's injuries, but he remained in Avalon a long time to recover his full health.

Although Avalon was obviously a nonexistent place of legend, some scholars contend that the persistent early medieval discussions of it and other mythical Celtic otherworlds supposedly located in the western Atlantic indicate a vague knowledge of the Americas.

Bibliography: Ashe, Geoffrey, *Avalonian Quest,* 1982; Ashe, Geoffrey, *Mythology of the British Isles,* 1990.

B

earth and its general circumference, as well as the concept of latitudes and longitudes for mapping. He believed in the existence of the **antipodes,** and that they were inhabited. Although he knew about recent European contacts with China, he exhibited no knowledge of **Iceland's** existence or the **Vinland** voyages of the Norse. Basing his opinions on **Aristotle,** Pliny, and the Book of Esdras in the Old Testament Apocrypha, he argued that Asia extended farther eastward than Ptolemy had believed. This concept meant that the Atlantic Ocean was much smaller and created a greater possibility for a successful western oceanic voyage to Asia. Although Bacon did not directly advocate such a venture, Pierre d'Ailly quoted and incorporated Bacon's geographical ideas into his *Imago mundi* (1410). This treatise exercised great influence on fifteenth-century geographical thought, particularly that of Christopher Columbus. Roger Bacon exemplified the highest level of geographical knowledge achieved by thirteenth-century Europe.

Bibliography: Hackett, Jeremiah M. G., "Roger Bacon" in *Dictionary of the Middle Ages,* edited by Joseph R. Strayer, 12 vols., 1982–1989; Phillips, J. R. S., *The Medieval Expansion of Europe,* 1988.

Bacon, Roger
(ca. 1213–1291)

This English Franciscan scholar wrote *Opus maius* (1266–1267), which disagreed with the views of the second-century geographer Ptolemy and made trans-Atlantic voyages to Asia seem more possible.

Although born in England, Bacon taught at the University of Paris, where he advocated a greater emphasis on secular subjects. Modern scholars consider Bacon a good example of the beginnings of a scientific worldview in European society. *Opus maius* summarized the state of human knowledge and served as a statement of Bacon's ideas on educational reform. Part four discussed mathematics, under which Bacon subsumed the subject of geography. Bacon showed awareness of the sphericity of the

Barcía Carballido y Zúñiga,
Andrés González de
(d. 1743)

In 1729 this Spanish historian published a revised and expanded second edition of **Father Gregorio García's** *Origen de los indios del nuevo mundo, e Indias occidentales* (Origins of the Indians of the New World and the West Indies) (1607), a massive but uncritical compendium of theories on the origins of Native Americans and pre-Columbian visitors to the Americas.

Its publication demonstrates the continuing popularity during the eighteenth century of theories claiming that trans-Atlantic voyagers were the ancestors of Native Americans. These theories continued to attract adherents even though the more plausible Asian Land Bridge Theory of **José de Acosta** was well known among scholars. Although Barcía's scholarship was sophisticated, he based his methodology on superficial comparisons of cultural traits among different societies, and failed to benefit from the pioneering ethnographic work of Acosta and other seventeenth-century practitioners of Acostan methodology. Nevertheless, Barcía and García's massive study provided adherents of fringe theories with vast and varied amounts of material to support their arguments.

Bibliography: Huddleston, Lee Eldridge, *Origins of the American Indians: European Concepts, 1492–1729*, 1967.

Barinthus

This Irish monk visited his kinsman **St. Brendan** and informed him of the existence of the Land of Promise of the Saints across the ocean to the west.

Barinthus appears at the beginning of the medieval tale *Navigatio Sancti Brendani* and serves as the mechanism to set St. Brendan on his own voyage to the west. Unlike St. Brendan he is almost certainly not a historical person. It is interesting to note that the *Navigatio* does not portray either St. Brendan or Barinthus as the discoverer of the Land of Promise of the Saints. Barinthus learns of it from his (spiritual?) son Mernoc, a monk residing on the idyllic Isle of Delights. Together they visit the Land of Promise of the Saints and determine that it is a vast land mass and not simply an island.

The story of Barinthus and Mernoc illustrates the proclivity of early medieval Irish monks to sail the seas seeking remote sites for their monasteries. It may also indicate their widespread belief in, or knowledge of

and visits to, a western land that may be the North American continent. See also **Irish Monks in America.**

Bibliography: "Navigatio Sancti Brendani," in *The Age of Bede*, edited by D. H. Farmer, 1965.

Basques

Many theories claim that the Basques reached the Americas before Christopher Columbus, ranging from the Basques being survivors of **Atlantis** and therefore ancestors of the Native Americans to Basque fishermen reaching Newfoundland well before 1492.

The Basques are a people of mystery and for good reason. They are a pre-Indo-European people who speak a language called Euskara, which is linguistically related to no other language, and call themselves the Euskadi. Their lands border the Bay of Biscay and are centered on the Pyrenees; their territory is located in what are now Spain and France. Over the centuries they struggled to maintain their independence and preserve their ethnic identity. The novel character of their language prompts considerable speculation about their origins. One theory states that an ancient language used during the ice age is the source of many widely scattered languages such as Ainu, Aboriginal Australian, Bushman, Basque, and the Tupi of South America. Obviously, considerable migration and diffusion must have taken place in the prehistoric past to produce these alleged connections. If this theory turns out to be true, the generally accepted theories about prehistoric migration patterns would have to be scrapped.

A more common but even less respectable theory of Basque origins claims that they were survivors of the destruction of Atlantis. Annie Besant, a successor to Madame Helena P. Blavatsky's leadership of **Theosophy**, specifically identifies the Basques as descendants of Atlantean refugees. So does Lewis Spence, another well-known and prolific early twentieth-century writer on Atlantis and other lost continents. A Basque-Atlantis connection also helped explain the so-called linguistic similarities between the Basque language and various Native American languages such as the Nahua of the Aztecs. These comparisons are superficial, however, and linguistically insignificant. An even more telling argument against this theory is the overwhelming scientific evidence and scholarly consensus that Atlantis never existed in the Atlantic Ocean as described by **Plato.**

More recently **Barry Fell,** a popularizer of extreme **diffusionist** theories, includes the Basques among the many peoples he claims traveled to North America during the Bronze Age. The Basques formed part of the so-called Celt-Iberian people who regularly visited the Americas between 1500 and 250 B.C. Fell's methods and proof are widely criticized by professional archaeologists, anthropologists, and historians; his ideas about the Basques definitely fall under the classification of cult archaeology.

The most important and longest lived theory is that Basque fishermen and whalers discovered the Newfoundland region of America 100 years or more before Columbus's famous voyage of 1492. Medieval Basques were renowned as sailors; they needed to be because their coastline bordered the treacherous Bay of Biscay. Adventurous and forever on the lookout for new fishing and whaling grounds, the Basques eventually made their way to Newfoundland and the Grand Banks during the Middle Ages. Some suggest that the Beothuk Indian tribe were the descendants of Basque whalers. The dying **Unknown Pilot** who supposedly showed Columbus the way to America was a Basque in some accounts of that tale.

Historical research shows this theory to be as false as all the others. No evidence has been found that French or Spanish Basques reached Newfoundland before perhaps 1526 or definitely 1528. French geographer and historian of the New World André Thévet (1502–1590) did not mention any Basque discovery of the Americas when he wrote his *La cosmographie universelle* in 1575.

In 1609 when Marc Lescarbot published *Histoire nouvelle France,* he mentioned seeing a map, now lost, by geographer Guillaume Postel (1510–1581) that mentioned Gauls visiting the Americas some 1,600 years earlier. Therefore he claimed it was the French, not the Spanish, who discovered America. Lescarbot also mentioned that the name Bacalos for Newfoundland derived from *bacaillos,* the Basque word for codfish. Modern scholars think it most likely that Lescarbot unconsciously misquoted Postel to reach his unique claim for French priority. In 1629 another French historian, Pierre de Bergeron, published a history of French discoveries titled *Traicte de navigations* in which, elaborating on Lescarbot, he credited Basques, Bretons, and Normans with pre-Columbian visits to Newfoundland some centuries before 1492.

Finally in 1647 Étienne Cleirac, in his well-respected book on maritime law *Us et coustumes de la mer,* shortened the time to only one century. He also identified the Unknown Pilot as a Basque visitor to Newfoundland. It is, however, interesting that no local Basque traditions support these literary legends. From Cleirac's time onward, this fully developed story appeared regularly in the works of French writers, even as part of an article in that great achievement of the Enlightenment, Denis Diderot's *Encyclopedie* of 1751. Although the entry's contributor adopted a somewhat skeptical tone, the legend of Basque discovery thrived with such prominent recognition. In 1829, although the great historian of exploration Martin Fernandez de Navarette expressed doubts about the legend, he failed to disprove it and so gave it new life. Finally, by 1900 the combined archival researches of Spanish historian Cesaro Fernandez Duro and French historian Henri Harrise proved that the legend had no documentary basis preceding the unwarranted speculations of Lescarbot and Cleirac.

It is easy to understand how stories of Basque, Breton, Norman, **Bristolian,** or Portuguese pre-Columbian visits to Newfoundland got started. Once John Cabot's voyage to Newfoundland in 1497 revealed the rich fishing of the Grand Banks, many European fishermen flocked there. Bretons and Normans arrived in 1504, well before French explorer Jacques Cartier's voyage in 1534. Basques quickly became so prominent in the fishing and whaling industry around Newfoundland that it was easy to assume they had always been there. So 100 years later Lescarbot made his erroneous speculation, which through repetition became fact for many people until the beginning of the twentieth century, and even now remains so for a stubborn few.

Bibliography: de Camp, L. Sprague, *Lost Continents*, [1954], 1970; Fell, Barry, *America B.C.,* [1976], rev. ed. 1989; Sanderson, Ivan T., *Follow the Whale,* 1956; Scisco, Louis Dow, "Precolumbian Discovery by Basques," *Proceedings and Transactions of the Royal Society of Canada* (3rd Series) 18 (1924): 51–61.

Behaim, Martin
(ca. 1436–1507)

Also spelled Behem, the Portuguese referred to him as Martinho of Bohemia. This geographer of Nuremberg has been variously credited with discovering the Cape of Good Hope before Bartolomeu Dias, the Americas before Christopher Columbus, and the Strait of Magellan before Ferdinand Magellan, all on slight and dubious evidence.

Martin Behaim was born into a family whose ancestors came from Pilsen in Bohe-

mia (now the Czech Republic). Standard reference works claim he was born about 1436, but also that he first arrived in Portugal at age 25. Since his date of arrival was as early as 1482 but more likely 1484, the year of his birth would actually be either 1457 or 1459. Once the young Behaim arrived, Portugal became his lifelong home. Some scholars suggest that he accompanied Portuguese explorer Diogo Cão on his second voyage down the African coast from Portugal to Walvis Bay in 1485. The evidence for this is both suspect and ambiguous. What is certain is that Behaim made a good impression

Martin Behaim.

on the Portuguese. King João II of Portugal knighted him as a member of the Order of Christ in 1485 and appointed him to the Royal Council of Mathematicians. Some maintain that the awards were recognition for his explorations with Cão, but there is no evidence for that contention. Sometime between 1486 and 1488 Behaim married Joana, a daughter of Jobst Van Hurter (or Joz d'Utra), a Fleming and the first donatory (i.e., gift of the king) captain of the islands of Faial and Pico in the Azores. Interestingly, Jobst Van Hurter's son and heir Joz d'Utra married Isabel, the daughter of **João Vaz Côrte-Real,** another supposed pre-Columbian discoverer of the Americas in 1472 or 1474. The claims for Côrte-Real's discoveries become considerably more dubious when it is pointed out that Behaim, who was in an excellent position to know, did not mention any such voyage in his copious notes about Portuguese explorations on his world globe of 1492.

It has also been suggested that Behaim sailed from the Azores with another Fleming, **Ferdinand Van Olmen,** on his western voyage of 1487. Van Olmen's royal charter mentions an unnamed "German knight who is going with them." Again, however, Behaim failed to mention Van Olmen's voyage in the notes on his globe. Given his tendency to be more than comprehensive with these notes (he included voyages that never took place), it seems highly unlikely that Behaim sailed with Van Olmen or that Van Olmen even sailed at all, let alone that together they discovered America before Columbus.

Behaim returned to Nuremberg in 1491 for an extended visit. During 1492 he constructed his famous globe of the world, the first ever produced. In 1493 he returned to Portugal, spending most of the remainder of his life in obscurity on Faial but dying in Lisbon in 1507. In Nuremberg that same year, Hartman Schedel published his *Liber chronicarum,* commonly known as the *Nuremburg Chronicle.* The Latin version, but not the German, contains a passage stating that Behaim sailed south along the African coast with Diogo Cão (Cam) in 1483 but turned west and discovered a new world. On that basis, some claim that Behaim discovered America before Columbus. Unfortunately, the passage presents certain problems. First, a check of the handwriting of the original

manuscript indicates that the passage was added later by someone other than Schedel. Second, Diogo Cão made his African voyages in 1482 and 1485, not 1483. Finally, Behaim's own globe reveals no knowledge of the existence of the Americas. For that matter, his globe's errors of African geography indicate that the maker had not even sailed down the west coast of Africa, let alone all the way to the Cape of Good Hope, as some claim.

Behaim is also credited with the discovery of the Strait of Magellan well before Magellan, based on Behaim's globe correctly showing a cape at the southern end of South America. That claim, however, is based on an erroneous identification of a later sixteenth-century globe. None of the claims for Martin Behaim making great discoveries is based on substantial evidence. It is far more likely that construction of the first globe will remain his one true claim to fame.

Bibliography: Diffie, Bailey W., and George D. Winius, *Foundations of the Portuguese Empire, 1415–1580,* 1977; Ravenstein, Ernest G., *Martin Behaim—His Life and His Globe,* 1908.

Bering, Vitus
(1681–1741)

The 1728 voyage of this Danish explorer in the service of Tsar Peter the Great of Russia proved the existence of a strait between Asia and North America.

During the early sixteenth century, after they realized that the Americas were not simply part of Asia, Europeans slowly became aware of the true extent of the continents of North and South America. Some people had long suggested that North America was connected to Asia. Others theorized that the two continents were separated by a narrow body of water, which they named the **Strait of Anian.** Although no European had visited or sailed through this strait, it began

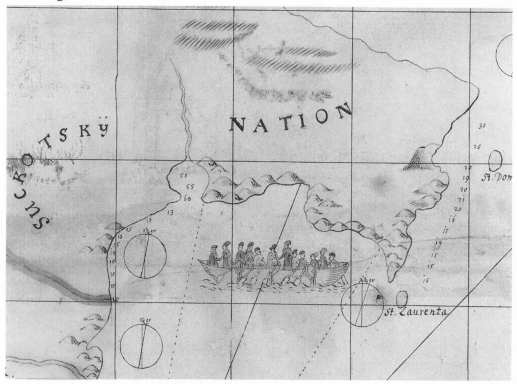

From a contemporary map of Vitus Bering's discoveries.

appearing on many late–sixteenth-century and early–seventeenth-century maps of the world. Some particularly cogent thinkers, such as **Father José de Acosta,** correctly theorized that this narrow strait was the original route by which the ancestors of Native Americans first came from Asia.

Meanwhile the Russian empire steadily expanded into Siberia from the mid-sixteenth century onward. By 1640 Cossack explorers reached the Sea of Okhotsk on Siberia's Pacific coast. More expeditions followed, including the controversial journey of Semyon Ivanovich Dezhnyov (1605–1672). Dezhnyov was a Cossack leader who took a small fleet of boats down the Kolyma River into the Arctic Sea in 1648. They sailed eastward along the northern coast of Siberia and passed through the Bering Strait some 80 years before Vitus Bering. Passing down the coast perhaps as far as the Kamchatka Peninsula, they turned inland once again. Because Dezhnyov was not a good

report writer, his achievement received little recognition until twentieth-century Russian historians tried to revive the Cossack's reputation as an explorer for nationalistic reasons.

Tsar Peter the Great of Russia (1682–1725) was anxious to strengthen his control over the vast lands of Siberia and expand his influence into other lands bordering the Pacific Ocean. In particular, he was anxious to know if the Strait of Anian really existed. Some suggest that vague stories of the western land of **Fusang** and other Chinese explorations across the Pacific Ocean also inspired Peter's enthusiasm for exploration. In 1724 the dying tsar chose Danish sailor Vitus Bering to lead the first of several expeditions to the Pacific Ocean. Leaving Moscow in early 1725, Bering's mission was to reach Kamchatka and sail north through the strait. Apparently Peter the Great gave little credence to Dezhnyov's discoveries because Bering's instructions were to sail all the way to the Kolyma River in order to confirm fully the existence of the strait.

Delayed by the vast distances across Siberia, Bering finally sailed north from Kamchatka in July 1728. During August he sailed through the strait that has since become known as the Bering Strait. But he refused to sail for the Kolyma River; he feared being trapped so far north in winter. On 17 August Bering discovered the Diomede Islands, but fog prevented him from seeing the American mainland. Unlike Dezhnyov, Bering knew he had found the long-sought strait. Back in Moscow he faced official displeasure for not sailing to the Kolyma River. That crisis passed, and in 1732 the Russian government named the efficient Bering commander of the Great Northern Expedition, which lasted from 1733–1742. In 1741 Bering sailed from Kamchatka to Alaska all the way to the Gulf of Alaska. Scurvy killed Bering on the return trip, and he was buried on Bering Island in the Commander group of islands.

Although Bering was probably preceded by Dezhnyov in sailing through the Bering Strait, he still deserves credit for bringing its existence firmly into Europe's growing store of geographical knowledge. His discovery also bolstered the theory that Native Americans were descendants of early Asian tribes who had crossed the narrow strait or some land bridge left uncovered during the last ice age. See also **Bering Land Bridge/Strait Theory** and **Beringia**.

Bibliography: Fisher, Raymond H., *Bering's Voyages: Whither and Why*, 1977.

Bering Land Bridge/Strait Theory

Advocates claim that the first Americans arrived from Asia by crossing a land bridge between Siberia and Alaska that had been uncovered by the lowering of the world's sea levels during the last ice age. Modern anthropologists and archaeologists overwhelmingly agree it is the best explanation for the original peopling of the Americas.

When Europeans realized the Americas were not a part of Asia, they needed to determine where the Native Americans fitted into the family of humanity. These aboriginal peoples had been largely isolated from the Old World from time beyond memory. Where did they come from and how did they get to the Americas? Numerous theories soon abounded. During the sixteenth and seventeenth centuries, some suggested the possibility of **multiple creations,** or polygenesis, which meant that God created more people than just Adam and Eve. Because the Roman Catholic and Protestant churches viewed such a suggestion as rank heresy, few people accepted this explanation. It still needed to be explained how the Americas had become populated in the era from Noah's flood to 1492, a relatively short interval of only a few thousand years that scarcely seemed sufficient. Meanwhile, various theories about peopling by **Hebrews, Carthaginians, Atlanteans, Romans,** and many other groups were in common circulation. These groups supposedly reached the Americas by sea, which posed a different but equally thorny problem.

The Americas were full of unique plants and animals not found in the Old World. If all life had been destroyed by Noah's flood, where did these strange species come from? Accepting that they came from the Old World, someone still needed to bring them in a ship. If that happened, then why did these early settlers bring dangerous wild animals like rattlesnakes and jaguars but not useful domestic animals such as horses, cows, and pigs?

Faced by such paradoxes, early historian and ethnographer **Father José de Acosta** suggested in 1590 that Native Americans came from Tartary or Siberia in Asia. These early settlers reached America by crossing a narrow strait or sea that Acosta assumed separated Asia from North America. No one knew if such a strait really existed, but the trends of the Asian and North American coastlines indicated that the two continents should come close together or even touch somewhere in the Arctic regions. During the seventeenth century, this theory continued to attract both supporters and detractors. Among the English writers, natural historian Thomas Morton attacked it in his *New English Canaan* of 1637, while renegade priest Thomas Gage in 1648 and sailor John Josselyn in the 1670s defended the narrow strait theory. This hypothetical passage even had a name—the **Strait of Anian**—and it frequently appeared on sixteenth- and seventeenth-century maps of the world. **Vitus Bering** finally proved its existence in 1728, and it was named the Bering Strait in his honor. Fifty years later, Captain James Cook's voyage further confirmed its existence.

By the end of the eighteenth century, support for the Bering Strait Theory increased. In 1787, during the writing of *Notes on the State of Virginia*, Thomas Jefferson considered the Bering Strait a very plausible route for the ancestors of Native Americans to have followed. In 1794 the German priest, traveler, and scholar Ignaz Pfefferkorn expressed the virtual certainty that Native Americans had first arrived by crossing the Bering Strait. Jefferson and Pfefferkorn were not alone in their conclusions. Several decades later Samuel Haven (1806–1881), librarian of the American Antiquarian Society and a premier early archaeologist, wrote his classic *Archaeology of the United States* (1856), which was a survey of the state of the young nation's archaeological knowledge. He was firmly in favor of Asia as the original home of Native Americans. By 1856 the embryonic profession of archaeology largely accepted the Bering Strait Theory.

Haven's magisterial scholarship did not end wild speculations about the **Mound Builders** and other transoceanic origin theo-

ries for all or some Native Americans. Such theories continued to appear for the rest of the nineteenth century and sometimes received serious scholarly consideration. Even into the twentieth century, variations of the same theories arose, but scholars and the general public became more skeptical. By 1900 the orthodox position of American archaeologists and anthropologists, led by the careful but dogmatic scholars William Henry Holmes (1846–1933) and Ales Hrdlicka (1869–1943), was that people had come across the Bering Strait less than 4,000 years ago, or about 2000 B.C.

Continued archaeological research led to refinements of the Bering Strait Theory and converted it to the Bering Land Bridge Theory. This new research also conclusively pushed back the arrival date to a time far earlier than Holmes or Hrdlicka would have accepted. Almost identical plants and animals of eastern Siberia and Alaska caused geologist Angelo Heilprin to propose in 1887 that Asia and North America had once been connected by a land bridge. Initially it was thought that movements of the earth's crust or shifts of the continents caused the two landmasses to separate. In 1934 another geologist, R. A. Daly, put forward the idea that the world's sea levels had risen and fallen significantly as the earth went through ice ages and periods of warming. The lowering of the Pacific Ocean by as much as 300 feet created the land bridge that scientists call **Beringia,** located in the shallowest waters of the Bering and Chukchi seas. During a period approximately 15,000 to 25,000 years ago, this land bridge connected Asia and North America with a wide expanse of tundra and forest, allowing humans to cross from Asia to North America for the first time. Until then, the Bering Strait would have blocked people of the Upper-Paleolithic culture because they lacked the maritime technology and skills to cross treacherous Arctic waters.

Early hunters moved into Beringia from Siberia, probably following their favorite prey—the great woolly mammoth—which also moved into Beringia at that time. The earliest known archaeological site for these Siberian hunters cannot be reliably dated to more than 15,000 years ago, although a caribou bone tool found at Old Crow, Alaska, is claimed to be 27,000 years old. Most archaeologists are skeptical of that particular evidence. Further movement by these Arctic hunters was halted by vast ice sheets that separated Beringia from the rest of the Americas. About 14,000 years ago, a warming trend caused the great glaciers to start melting, and ocean levels began to rise. By 10,000 years ago the Bering land bridge was submerged again. However, openings to the south had appeared in the great ice sheets, resulting in an ice-free corridor between the Cordilleran Ice Sheet covering the Canadian Rockies and the Laurentides Ice Sheet centered on Hudson's Bay. Another ice-free area along the Pacific Northwest coastline also began to appear. Not until less than 14,500 years ago would climatic and terrain conditions moderate sufficiently for the inhabitants of Beringia and Alaska to move south. By 12,000 years ago humans had arrived in the area of the present-day states of Washington, Oregon, and Idaho. Finally, about 11,500 years ago the Clovis culture of big-game hunters appeared and quickly spread across North America. It was tentatively suggested that these hunters moved so rapidly through the Americas that they reached southern Argentina about 10,500 years ago. If so, by that date Paleo-Indians had spread throughout the entire western hemisphere to begin development of the multitudinous local adaptations that would produce the myriad cultures and tribes living in the Americas well before 1492.

Some archaeologists suggest far earlier dates for the arrival of the first Americans. Louis Leakey, the investigator of remains of the earliest humans found in Africa's Olduvai Gorge, claimed in 1968 that materials dug up at Calico Hills, California, are the remains of human occupation dating back 100,000 to 200,000 years. Leakey's claim, based on flimsy evidence, gained virtually no support. Other more reasonable claims include the site of Meadowcroft, Pennsylvania; artifacts found there supposedly date back 20,000 years. Archaeologist Richard MacNeish, on the basis of several finds, dates the first humans in Mexico to between 20,000 and 30,000 years ago. Artifacts from the Taima-Taima site in Peru are dated as early as 20,000 years ago, while the Brazilian site of Pedra Furada yielded supposedly human artifacts dating back 32,000 years. These datings do not fit with the standard theory that early hunters moved south from Alaska no earlier than 14,500 years ago, creating the Clovis culture by 11,500 years ago. These supposedly earlier archaeological sites with their anomalous dates for artifacts suffer from the confusing problem of jumbled strata in the layers of occupation. Even more serious, some of the artifacts may have been produced by nature rather than human hands. The debates over dating the arrival of the first Americans are by no means finished.

After the first migrations of Arctic hunters moved into the Americas between 10,500 and 14,500 years ago, two more groups from Asia followed. The second migration consisted of the Athabascan or Na-Dene people and occurred about 12,000 to 14,000 years ago. This group occupied most of Alaska and the Yukon, where they remain, except for groups that later migrated to the Southwest region of the present United States, forming the Navajo and Apache tribes. Finally, a third migration occurred about 12,000 years ago or less and brought the ancestors of the Aleuts and **Eskimos** to the North American Arctic. The Aleuts remained in southern coastal Alaska and its islands, while the Eskimos eventually expanded from Alaska to **Greenland.** The archaeological evidence for these two later migrations is quite good. Furthermore, linguistic and biological evidence also confirms the distinctiveness of the Athabascan and Aleut-Eskimo peoples from the Paleo-Indians of the first migration. Studies of the blood types and teeth of all three groups confirm their common northeast Asian origin; however, close investigation of the variations in their blood proteins (called Gm allotypes) demonstrates that the Paleo-Indians, Athabascans, and Aleut-Eskimos crossed the Bering Strait or land bridge as three separate peoples.

Bibliography: Fagan, Brian M., *Ancient North America: The Archaeology of a Continent,* 1991; Fagan, Brian M., *The Great Journey: The Peopling of Ancient America,* 1987; Willey, Gordon R., and Jeremy A. Sabloff, *A History of American Archaeology,* 2d edition, 1980.

Beringia

Also called the Bering land bridge, this area appeared out of the Bering and Chukchi seas when the glaciation of the Wisconsin/Würm Ice Age lowered the world's sea levels and uncovered a land connection between Siberia and Alaska, allowing early man to enter the Americas about 15,000 years ago.

The Wisconsin/Würm Ice Age began about 125,000 years ago and ended about 14,000 years ago. Within that ice age there were several fluctuations of warm and cold weather, with the last cold phase starting about 30,000 years ago and lasting about 16,000 years. During that very cold phase the water levels of the world's oceans dropped some 300 feet below those of modern times as vast amounts of water were locked in massive glaciers. The great weight of these ice sheets caused various parts of the earth's crust to shift. New land emerged where the sea had been, while dry land became buried under miles of ice.

The Bering and Chukchi seas bordering the Bering Strait are fairly shallow because of their location over a large continental shelf. When sea levels dropped, a substantial land bridge between Siberia and Alaska emerged. Interestingly enough, this new land, which scientists call Beringia, was mostly free of glaciation. Environmentally it was an extension of the Siberian landscape since it was dry, desolate tundra and forest. Despite the harsh climate, Beringia supported a wide variety of plant life, which in turn attracted the giant herbivores, or megafauna, of the ice age. Predators were quick to follow these large grazing animals, particularly the woolly mammoth, which was the Upper-Paleolithic hunter's prey of choice. Just when these first humans entered Beringia is not known, but they probably arrived sometime between 15,000 and 25,000 years ago in the course of following herds of mammoths. Archaeologists are unable to discover much about these first Americans because the sea's return in warmer climates covers the most promising areas for their early campsites.

Before 25,000 years ago, the Bering land bridge would have been submerged and a water crossing impossible. Early Siberian hunters did not have the knowledge to make boats capable of navigating the narrow but highly dangerous seas that separated Siberia from Alaska. Once in Beringia, glaciers prevented the Stone Age hunters and their prey from moving farther into Alaska until about 14,500 years ago. So, the first Americans arrived by land, not by sea. The path to their new homeland lay across the challenging terrain of Beringia.

Bibliography: Fagan, Brian M., *The Great Journey: The Peopling of Ancient America,* 1987; Hopkins, D. M., ed., *The Bering Land*

Bridge, 1967; Hopkins, D. M., et al., eds., *The Paleoecology of Beringia*, 1982.

Biancho, Map of Andrea (1448)

Also spelled Bianco, since 1895 various scholars have cited this map as evidence that the Portuguese discovered Brazil in South America sometime before 1448.

Andrea Biancho was a Venetian navigator and cartographer. He produced a very conventional world map in 1436 that showed little advance over Petrus Vesconte's chart dated about 1320. Some scholars suggest that this 1436 map may have served as the model for the **Vinland map.** Later, in 1448 while living in London, Biancho produced a more up-to-date world map that included recent Portuguese discoveries in West Africa and the Azores. That map is now in the Ambrosian Library of Milan.

In 1895 English geographer H. Yule Oldham suggested a new interpretation of a peculiar feature on Biancho's 1448 map. An island is located about 100 miles southwest of Cape Verde, but a notation in the Venetian dialect of Italian reads "ixiola otinticha xe longa a ponente 1500 mia," which can be variously translated as "authentic island extends to the west 1,500 miles" or "authentic island distant to the westward 1,500 miles." According to Oldham, the "authentic island" could be both Brazil and the golden island of the **Seven Cities,** which sixteenth-century historian Antonio Galvão claimed the Portuguese had discovered in 1447. Oldham's hypothesis of a pre-Columbian discovery of Brazil supported by Biancho's 1448 map attracted supporters, including the historian of geography J. Batalha-Reis in 1897 and later the Portuguese scholar Jaime Cortesão. It was a controversial assertion in 1895, and most scholars still find it unacceptable.

Samuel Eliot Morison, the distinguished American historian of exploration, suggests that the "authentic island" represented some vague awareness of the Arquipélago dos Bijagós just off the west African coast. The Portuguese did not officially discover these islands until Alvise Cadamosto reached them in 1455–1456 (unless one accepts historian F. C. Wieder's 1938 suggestion that Biancho went on a secret voyage to the Bijagós before 1448). It is far more plausible that African informants provided vague reports that came to Biancho's attention while composing his map in 1448. It seems most improbable that a Portuguese ship sailed to distant Brazil before 1448 when Portuguese seamen had only reached Cape Verde on Africa's west coast in 1444 and the Gambia River, a hundred miles farther south, perhaps as early as 1446. Certainly the supposed voyage to Brazil had no discernible impact on Portugal's geographical knowledge and explorations. Bailey W. Diffie, a specialist in the history of early Portuguese explorations, concludes that the Biancho map does not depict Brazil and that the "authentic island" cannot be matched with any known location.

Bibliography: Batalha-Reis, J., "The Supposed Discovery of South America before 1448, and the Critical Methods of Historians of Geographical Discovery," *Geographical Journal* 9 (February 1897): 185–210; Diffie, Bailey W., and George Winius, *Foundations of the Portuguese Empire, 1415–1580*, 1977.

Blessed Isles

Irish Christian monks of the sixth, seventh, and eighth centuries believed in the existence of paradisiacal islands in the western Atlantic, which they called the Blessed Isles. The *Navigatio Sancti Brendani* refers to these islands as the **Land of Promise of the Saints.**

Some writers suggest that **Irish monks** seeking the Blessed Isles may have reached North America during the early Middle Ages. See also **Avalon; Brendan the Navigator, Voyage of St.;** and **Irish Monks in America.**

The Book of Mormon

This controversial sacred book is accepted as holy writ only by the religious groups collectively known as Mormons, who claim that it is a supplement to the Bible. Its title page calls it both "Another Testament of Jesus Christ" and "a record of God's dealings with the ancient inhabitants of the Americas," that is, the **Nephites, Lamanites, Mulekites,** and **Jaredites.** Great controversies exist between Mormons and non-Mormons, as well as among Mormons themselves, regarding its authenticity and historicity.

Origin

Mormons believe that *The Book of Mormon* is a translation of sacred writings made on metal plates left behind by the Nephite prophets Nephi, Mormon, and Moroni. As the Nephite nation faced destruction, Mormon condensed their existing records. Moroni, his son, finished the work and in 421 buried the metal plates at Hill Cumorah in upstate New York. Moroni returned on 21 September 1823 as a "glorified, resurrected being" and showed the young **Joseph Smith, Jr.,** where the golden books were hidden. After giving Smith the urim and thummin (supernatural tools needed to read the plates), the task of translation began. Once this was completed, Moroni took back the plates and Smith published the translation as *The Book of Mormon* in 1830. The Mormon movement grew and, along with *The Book of Mormon,* attracted considerable controversy and opposition.

Mormons stoutly defend *The Book of Mormon*'s authenticity. From the beginning non-Mormons were skeptical and attacked the book. One persistent theory that appeared shortly after its publication maintained that *The Book of Mormon* was simply a plagiarized version of an unpublished romantic novel written by Solomon Spaulding (d. 1816). The novel was set in pre-Columbian America and focused on the adventures of a civilized white nation surrounded by hostile dark-skinned barbarians. Modern scholarship no longer takes the Spaulding theory seriously since it was basically the creation of implacable anti-Mormon elements. Advanced textual analysis does not support the plagiarism charge against Joseph Smith, Jr. Some scholars, particularly those of the early twentieth century, preferred a psychomedical explanation, which postulated that epilepsy and hereditary mental illness caused Smith to imagine he was having visions. This theory foundered on a lack of evidence that Smith had epilepsy or any other psychological problems.

Traditional Mormon apologists argue that the uniqueness of *The Book of Mormon*'s subject matter proves its authenticity. But modern scholarship, by both Mormon and non-Mormon scholars, shows that *The Book of Mormon* clearly reflects the intellectual, cultural, and social concerns of the United States in the 1820s. Early–nineteenth-century Americans were keenly interested in the question of Native American origins. They were also well aware of the former existence of higher pre-Columbian civilizations in Mexico and Peru. Intriguingly, many parts of the eastern United States were generously sprinkled with mounds built by ancient Native Americans.

Speculations about the origins of both the mounds and the builders were common. One particularly popular theory sought to identify the Native Americans as descendants of the **Ten Lost Tribes of Israel** or some other **Hebrew** or Jewish migration. **James Adair,** the early ethnographer of the Chickasaw and Creek tribes, and Elias Boudinot (1740–1821), the author of *A Star in the West; or A Humble Attempt To Discover* *the Long Lost Ten Tribes of Israel* (1816), helped popularize the Ten Lost Tribes theory among Americans. Many Americans concluded that Native Americans, or Red Americans, were incapable of having built the many impressive mound complexes located in eastern North America. Someone else must have done it, and that someone was a highly civilized white race tragically annihilated by an invasion of dark-skinned barbarians, the ancestors of Red Americans. This **Mound Builder** myth remained popular and respectable through most of the nineteenth century.

In 1826 Ethan Smith (1762–1849) (no relation to Joseph Smith, Jr.) published his *View of the Hebrews; or The Tribes of Israel in America,* which combined the Ten Lost Tribes theory with the Mound Builder myth. Ethan Smith's book proved quite popular and may have influenced Joseph Smith's thinking, because the similarities between *View of the Hebrews* and *The Book of Mormon* are quite striking. Certainly Ethan Smith lived in the same geographical vicinity as Joseph Smith. Ethan was a preacher at Poultney, Vermont, and Joseph lived in nearby Palmyra, New York.

The Book of Mormon also reflects other concerns of the common people of a rural Protestant United States in the 1820s. It emphasized the country's role as a promised land of liberty, a belief widely held by Americans during the early nineteenth century. Democratic practices and values frequently came in for special praise in its pages. The anti-Masonic and anti-Catholic sentiments prevalent in that era are reflected in *The Book of Mormon*'s condemnation of the secret society of the Gadianton robbers (i.e., the Masons) and "the great and abominable church" (i.e., Roman Catholicism). Scholars also point out *The Book of Mormon*'s adherence to the values of moderate Christian revivalism. These intellectual and cultural connections firmly place *The Book of Mormon* in the historical setting of Joseph Smith's upstate New York of the 1820s.

Structure and Historical Contents

The Book of Mormon consists of 15 books, although one of the briefer books is titled the Words of Mormon. Altogether they basically describe the history of the Americas from about 600 B.C. to A.D. 421. They tell how Jewish prophet Lehi and his sons fled into the Arabian desert to escape the evil of King Zedekiah's reign over the doomed Kingdom of Judah and its impending destruction by King Nebuchadnezzar of Babylon. After several years in the desert, God directed Lehi and his sons to build a ship. They sailed out of the Red Sea and across the Indian and Pacific oceans to a promised land in the east. Arriving on the west coast of that promised land, they formed a settlement, but trouble broke out soon after Lehi's death. A long-standing animosity between Lehi's son Nephi, who was God's chosen prophet, and his older brothers Laman and Lemuel caused a division among the settlers. Nephi and his supporters took up a settled, agricultural life and became the nation of the Nephites, while Laman, Lemuel, and their followers became nomadic hunters and began the nation known as the Lamanites. Because the Lamanites disobeyed God's will, he punished them with dark skins, while the obedient Nephites remained "white and delightsome." Divine disapproval notwithstanding, the Lamanites multiplied faster than the Nephites, and warfare raged between the two nations. The Lamanites exterminated the last of the Nephites in the great battle at Hill Cumorah in 385.

Some 800 years elapsed, however, before the last stand and destruction of the Nephites. During those centuries, the Nephites went through numerous cycles of prosperity that led to corruption, corruption that led to disaster, and disaster that led to repentance, followed by reform and a return of prosperity. Along the way the Nephites founded the city of Nephi, but later abandoned it to the encroaching Lamanites. The Nephites took refuge at the city of Zarahemla about 130 B.C. Around the same time, the Nephites discovered the remains of the extinct race of Jaredites. The Jaredites migrated to America after the confusion of languages at the Tower of Babel hundreds of years earlier. They populated and civilized their new land, but sin led them into evil and they destroyed themselves in a series of suicidal civil wars. The most significant event described in *The Book of Mormon* is Jesus Christ's visit to the Americas in A.D. 34, after his death and resurrection. He established his church, and for 200 years peace and prosperity endured among both Nephites and Lamanites. After that the people again fell into sin, resulting in the total destruction of the Nephites and the degeneration of the Lamanites into savagery.

Geographical and Chronological Setting

The geographical statements in *The Book of Mormon* provide no clear clues for determining their correspondence with actual places in the Americas. Lehi and his people landed on the west coast of their new land at a place they called First Inheritance. As time went by they discovered that their new home consisted of a Land Southward and a Land Northward, divided by a Narrow Neck of Land. The lands of Nephi and Zarahemla were located in the Land Southward. On the east coast of the Land Southward and just below the Narrow Neck of Land was the location of the lovely Land Bountiful. Just north of it lay the fearsome Land of Desolation, "a land which was covered with bones of men, and of beasts, and was also covered with ruins of buildings of every kind" (Mosiah 8:8). This was the final battleground of the Jaredites and would later be the site of the last stand of the Nephites.

Traditionally Mormons believe that the Land Southward is South America, the Land Northward is North America, and the Narrow Neck of Land is the Isthmus of Panama. Hill Cumorah is located in upstate New York, right where the Angel Moroni led Joseph Smith to the golden books. In the late nineteenth century, many Mormon scholars tried to reduce the geographical scope of *The Book of Mormon* to southern Mexico and Guatemala. Various archaeological sites were identified with places in *The Book of Mormon,* but no consensus emerged. Reconstructions of *The Book of Mormon* geography, especially the traditional one, are plagued by serious internal contradictions and incongruities when matched with actual geographical settings.

Chronologically the events associated with the Nephites and Lamanites in *The Book of Mormon* took place during the times referred to by professional archaeologists as the late preclassic (600 B.C.–A.D. 300) and the very early classic (A.D. 300–400) periods of Mesoamerican history. This era includes the great Monte Albán (600 B.C.–A.D. 900) and Teotihuacán (A.D. 100–700) cultures of Mexico. In the Peruvian region the same time period corresponds to the Chavin and Nazca cultures. The earlier Jaredites (ca. 3000–600 B.C.) are frequently identified with the Olmec culture (1500–300 B.C.) of Mexico. Little agreement over these identifications exists between Mormon and non-Mormon archaeologists.

Criticisms and Contradictions

The Book of Mormon was subjected to intense scrutiny and criticism from its first appearance. Critics note the archaic English used in the translation and suggest that such usage is an indication of someone attempting to imitate the style of the King James or Authorized Bible widely owned by and available to early–nineteenth-century Americans. Mormon defenders argue that the antique style is how God instructed Joseph Smith to translate the golden plates. Other critics point out that the Nephites act more like nineteenth-century American Protestants than the Old Testament Hebrews they supposedly were. This circumstance is also cited as evidence of *The Book of Mormon*'s purely nineteenth-century origins.

Some serious historical anachronisms occur in the pages of *The Book of Mormon*. It mentions steel weapons, horses, and cows among the Nephites, and all those things among the Jaredites plus elephants, pigs, and mysterious animals called cureloms and cumons, which were said to be particularly "useful unto man" (*Ether* 9:19). Neither steel nor any of the animals were present in the Americas before the Spanish conquest of the sixteenth century. Mormon scholars try to explain these problems by suggesting that more advanced metallurgical skills existed in the Americas but were lost by the degenerate Lamanites. They also claim that the elephants of the Jaredites were mastodons or mammoths that supposedly became extinct much later than non-Mormon archaeologists thought. Cureloms and cumons are variously identified as tapirs, sloths, or mammoths. *The Book of Mormon*'s horses and cows are supposedly deer or bison, while the pigs are peccaries. According to the explanations of Mormon scholars, the Nephites simply attached the names of familiar Old World animals to the strange animals of the Americas that resembled them. Such explanations, while satisfactory to Mormons, tend to leave non-Mormons somewhat skeptical.

The Book of Mormon is a fascinating document whether or not one considers it to be divinely inspired. Traditional Mormons claim that it tells the story of the origins of all Native Americans, but more liberal Mormons limit its coverage to the southern Mexico and Guatemala regions of Mesoamerica. Liberal Mormons do not claim that *The Book of Mormon* provides an explanation of how all Native Americans reached the Americas. They readily accept that other peoples arrived via the **Bering Land Bridge/Strait.** But whether *The Book of Mormon* applies to the history of all the Americas or just a part of Mesoamerica, it is one of the most detailed accounts of supposed pre-Columbian visitors to the Americas.

Bibliography: Madsen, Brigham D., ed., *Studies of the Book of Mormon*, 1985; O'Dea, Thomas F., *The Mormons*, [1957], rev. ed. 1964; Vogel, Dan, *Indian Origins and the Book of Mormon*, 1986; Williams, Stephen, *Fantastic Archaeology: The Wild Side of North American Prehistory*, 1991.

Brasseur de Bourbourg, Abbé Charles Étienne (1814–1873/1874)

This pioneer archaeologist of Central America whose voluminous writings appeared largely during the third quarter of the nineteenth century lost the respect of most of his fellow archaeologists during his later years by his advocacy of theories that included **Atlantis** as the source for the various Native American civilizations.

Born at Bourbourg in northern France, Brasseur showed an early interest in history and archaeology as well as a talent for languages. However, circumstances did not allow him to pursue the study of archaeology; instead, during his early twenties he made a living as a Paris journalist and writer of romance novels and religious works. Five years later he studied for the priesthood, completing his training at Rome where he received excellent instruction in linguistics and archaeology. At the age of 31 Brasseur was ordained, and his first assignment was to teach church history at the seminary in Quebec. He visited Boston and read William H. Prescott's *Conquest of Mexico,* which finalized his decision to pursue the study of American archaeology.

Returning to Rome in late 1846, Brasseur began his study of American antiquities in the Vatican Library. In 1848 he traveled to Mexico, immersing himself in manuscript sources for pre-Columbian Mexican history. He published *Lettres pour servir d'introduction à l'histoire primitive*, his first book about ancient America, in 1851 shortly before he returned to Europe. It was well received and brought him to the attention of prominent Americanists E. G. Squier and J. M. Aubin. During 1854–1856 he returned to Mexico

Charles Étienne Brasseur de Bourbourg.

for a second period of intense research. Back in Paris in January 1857, he completed work on the first volume of his magnum opus, *Histoire des nations civilisées du Mexique et de l'Amérique central.* Between 1857 and 1859 it appeared in four volumes totaling 2,600 pages, earning him recognition as one of the foremost Americanists. In the years that followed, Brasseur produced scholarly translations and editions of important manuscripts, adding further to his reputation.

Around 1857 Brasseur's hitherto fine scholarship deteriorated into mysticism. He became convinced that much of the ancient history he had recovered from the forgotten documents was actually myth serving as allegory for various natural disasters. Although earlier in his career Brasseur rejected the existence of Atlantis, he later became a passionate believer. He claimed that Atlantis had been destroyed 6,000 or 7,000 years earlier but that survivors reached Central America and Egypt, where they kept their civilization alive. These ideas appeared in his book *Quatre lettres sur le Mexique . . .* in 1868, beginning the ruin of his academic reputation. Brasseur also periodically maintained that both ancient Scandinavians and **Egyptians** had sustained contacts with the early civilizations of Central America. Despite his late lapse of judgment, Brasseur remains an important early contributor to the advancement of the pre-Columbian history of Central America.

Bibliography: Brunhouse, Robert L., *In Search of the Maya: The First Archaeologists*, 1973; Wauchope, Robert, *Lost Tribes and Sunken Continents*, 1962.

Brazil, Island of

Also known as Bersil, Brasil, Brazir, Breasil, Hy-Brasil, O'Brassil, or O'Brazil, about 1300–1550 Europeans commonly thought that this mythical island in the western Atlantic Ocean really existed.

The name Brazil, which is only indirectly connected to the modern South American country, has two possible derivations. Brazil was an Irish personal name derived from the words "breas" and "ail," connoting praise or admiration. A second source was the valuable product red dye-wood, which was sometimes thought to be that mythical island's main export.

The Island of Brazil was first shown on the 1325 map of Angellinus Dalorto of

Genoa as a round island in the Atlantic Ocean to the west of southern Ireland. This same form and position appeared on most maps from the late Middle Ages and the Renaissance. Reports described the island as a very pleasant place and well worth visiting. In some cases, Brazil seems to have been confused with the island of Terceira in the Azores. Another variation occurred on the Catalan map of 1375, which depicted it as a ring of land surrounding a circular lake dotted with small islands. Some authorities feel that this ring island may represent a medieval visitor's impression of the Gulf of St. Lawrence on the east coast of Canada. On the Catalan map of 1480, the Island of Brazil appeared in the position of Labrador or Newfoundland, again possibly indicating some pre-Columbian knowledge of North America's existence. In 1498 Pedro de Ayala, the Spanish ambassador to England, reported to Ferdinand and Isabella of Spain that fishermen of Bristol explored the western Atlantic looking for Brazil prior to Columbus's voyage of 1492. Geographer William H. Babcock suggests that the Island of Brazil was simply a little-used alternate name for **Great Ireland** (North America) given by seafaring monks of early Christian Ireland.

Bibliography: Babcock, William H., *Legendary Islands of the Atlantic: A Study in Medieval Geography*, 1922; Ramsay, Raymond H., *No Longer on the Map: Discovering Places That Never Were*, 1972.

Brendan the Navigator, Voyage of St.

During the last seven years of his life, this prominent **Irish monk** (ca. 486–575) supposedly sailed throughout the North Atlantic, visiting the Americas along the way.

Little is known for certain about the life of St. Brendan. He was born near Tralee in western Ireland about 486 during the twi-

light of the Roman Empire when Ireland was an isolated haven of devout Christianity and scholarship. Very much a part of this religious culture, Brendan became a monk and a priest. He later founded the monastery of Clonfert around 559, as well as several other monastic houses. In those days, Irish monks commonly sailed the seas in their **curachs** seeking remote spots where they

St. Brendan and his crew encounter a siren.

could set up monasteries and conduct devotions. St. Brendan figured prominently in such sailing activities. In addition to his legendary voyage around the Atlantic, he was widely reputed to be a great traveler throughout Christendom, visiting Scotland, Wales, and Brittany.

The story of St. Brendan's legendary seven-year Atlantic voyage comes from the *Navigatio Sancti Brendani*. This medieval manuscript book was probably written by an Irish monk living in the Low Countries or the Rhineland in 870 or shortly thereafter. It must have been very popular because 116 manuscript copies survive in Latin as well as in vernacular translations into Middle English, Provençal, Flemish, and Old Norse among others. Christian monastic themes dominate the narrative, which basically concerns a quest for an earthly paradise. Scholars do not consider the *Navigatio* to be a genuine biographical account of St. Brendan's life. In many ways it is a religious version of the *immrama,* traditional sea journey tales of the Celtic world.

According to the *Navigatio,* a monk and kinsman named **Barinthus** visited the famous saint at his monastery and told of sailing westward and visiting the utopian **Land of Promise of the Saints.** After hearing this tale St. Brendan decided to visit the western paradise and invited 14 of his monks to accompany him. The monks agreed and a curach was constructed to make the journey. After 40 days at sea, stormy weather blew them to an island with steep cliffs (which some scholars identify as St. Kilda in the Outer Hebrides). They rested a few days and resumed their journey, reaching an island with huge sheep (possibly Streymoy in the Faeroes). An islander, later referred to as their steward, gave them food and encouraged them in their quest. Next they landed on what seemed to be a neighboring island, but which turned out to be a giant fish or whale that became aroused when they lit their cooking fires on its back. Fortunately St. Brendan knew the island was really a great sea creature, and he guided his followers to safety. They proceeded to a nearby island full of white birds that were actually fallen angels (this island would probably be Streymoy's neighbor Vagar).

After spending Easter on the island of birds, the travelers put to sea for three months, finally reaching the island of St. Ailbe. Possessing a mild climate, it was already inhabited by a community of monks whom God miraculously provided with food (St. Ailbe's Island is thought to be Madeira).

St. Brendan and his people spent the Christmas and Epiphany seasons among them. Setting sail once more, the monks exhausted their supplies after several weeks. In desperate straits, they propitiously sighted a lush green island replete with streams and springs full of fish. Unfortunately, drinking the water put the monks to sleep (the volcanic island of San Miguel in the Azores is the only Atlantic island with undrinkable springs). Upon waking, St. Brendan and his companions departed southward. Within three days they found themselves becalmed in a curdled sea (from this description it would appear that they had reached the Sargasso Sea). Once they escaped the area, the wind pushed them for 20 days until they found themselves once again at the islands of sheep and birds. The steward supplied them with more food, and prophesied that St. Brendan and his companions would reach the Land of Promise of the Saints after seven years of traveling. He foretold that they would remain at the Land of Promise of the Saints for 40 days and then return to their home monastery in Ireland. Before they attempted to fulfill the prophecy, St. Brendan and his monks rested for several weeks.

Beginning their voyage once more, St. Brendan and his companions sailed for 40 days. A fierce sea monster attacked them, but before it could destroy them, another sea monster intervened and killed their attacker. The next day they landed on a new island (this island has not been identified) and found some remains of the dead sea monster, which they ate. Bad weather forced them to remain there for three months, but when pleasant weather returned they resupplied their ship and resumed sailing southward. They reached a flat island covered with flowers but devoid of trees (identified as one of the Bahamas). The island was inhabited by three bands of people—one of boys, one of young men, and one of elders—who formed choirs and sang psalms praising God for the inspiration of the travelers. Leaving one of his monks to live on this island of steadfast men, St. Brendan continued his journey. Again the monks sailed until they depleted their supplies. Miraculously, a giant bird dropped a large bunch of grapes onto their ship, enabling the monks to survive 12 more days. Soon afterward, they reached the island from which the grapes had come. It was full of fresh springs and smelled of pomegranates (this island may be Jamaica, which is well known for its springs). The travelers returned to the island of St. Ailbe, although not before the giant bird that earlier befriended them defended them from a hostile griffin.

St. Brendan and his companions rested among the monks of St. Ailbe and spent Christmas and Easter there, after which they journeyed west once more. They discovered a sea of clear waters filled with strange fish (the clear waters of the Caribbean?), and a week later encountered a huge floating column of crystal in the sea (an iceberg?). For eight days strong winds carried them even farther north, where they came upon an island full of forges. The smiths who operated the forges attacked them by throwing big pieces of red-hot slag at St. Brendan's ship (it is suggested that what the travelers described was a volcanic eruption of **Iceland**). The next day they sighted a mountain spouting smoke and flames (the volcanic island of Jan Mayen). Afterward they visited Judas Iscariot on his island of eternal imprisonment and torment, and the island of Paul the Hermit, who prophesied that after the last six years of wandering St. Brendan would soon reach the Land of Promise of the Saints.

St. Brendan returned to spend Christmas and Easter on the island of sheep, then sailed westward for 40 days. His ship became enveloped in darkness (the fogs of the Newfoundland banks?), but broke through to daylight after an hour of sailing. The coast of the Land of Promise of the Saints appeared, and the travelers landed. It was a vast country, and 40 days of exploration failed to reveal its full extent. As St. Brendan and his companions neared the large river that Barinthus had described, a young man approached them. He revealed to St. Brendan that God had made him wander for the last seven years so he would discover the marvels of the sea. The young man then instructed St. Brendan to load his ship with precious stones and return home to his monastery. He also informed the travelers that God would disclose the location of the Land of Promise of the Saints at a future time when Christians would again be persecuted. St. Brendan returned to his monastery, where he died in a manner befitting a saintly Christian monk.

No one seriously believes that St. Brendan literally made the entire journey described in the *Navigatio*. Some scholars do believe, however, that the *Navigatio* is an imaginative tale that incorporates geographical knowledge held by the early medieval Irish. It is well known that Irish sailors went to the Faeroes and Hebrides on a regular basis and set up settlements on Iceland before the Vikings. If the identifications of other places mentioned in the *Navigatio* are correct, it would mean that the Irish reached the Azores and Madeira as well as various Caribbean islands and North America. These feats are theoretically within the capabilities of the primitive curachs, but irrefutable evidence has not been discovered in support of such speculations. See also **Irish Monks in America.**

Bibliography: Ashe, Geoffrey, *Land to the West: St. Brendan's Voyage to America*, 1962; Cameron, Ian, *Lodestone and Evening Star: The Epic Voyages of Discovery*, 1966; Farmer, D. H., ed., *The Age of Bede* (1965), includes a translation of the *Navigatio*; Severin, Timothy, *The Brendan Voyage*, 1978.

Brendan's Island

Also known as the Isle of St. Brendan, European sailors commonly held that this mythical island was the **Land of Promise of the Saints** visited by **St. Brendan** during his famous voyage, a belief that flourished in the Middle Ages and lasted as late as 1759, when it disappeared from the sea charts.

Medieval people believed St. Brendan literally made an Atlantic voyage and that the lovely Land of the Blessed Saints he visited was a real island. The island first appeared on a map of the world at Hereford Cathedral made around 1275. Brendan's Island appears as part of the Canary Islands, which were known in classical antiquity. In the 1339 map of Angelino Dulcert of Majorca, the location of Brendan's Island moved to the site of the present-day Madeira Islands, which Europeans discovered (or rediscovered) during the fourteenth century. A map dated 1367 by the Pizzigano brothers of Venice also identified Brendan's Island with the Madeiras. Brendan's Island moved

to the area of the Azores after their discovery in 1427. The Venetian mapmaker **Andrea Biancho** labeled the largest of the islands in the Azores as St. Brendan's Island on his map of 1448. By 1492, **Martin Behaim's** globe showed it as a large island located to the west of the Cape Verde Islands (where no such island exists). An English map from 1544 placed Brendan's Island in the middle of the Atlantic at about the same latitude as northern Newfoundland. Gerard Mercator, the great cartographer, adopted this location in 1567 and Abraham Ortelius followed him in 1571. There the peripatetic island remained until the middle of the seventeenth century, when it gradually disappeared from maps of the Atlantic. Some people continued to believe that Brendan's Island was a little-known island in the Canaries until at least 1759.

The belief in the existence of Brendan's Island was part of a general late-medieval notion that the Atlantic Ocean was sprinkled with islands such as **Antillia** and **Brazil**. Many were thought to be large, pleasant places that could be visited without much danger by the ships of that era. Such beliefs tended to encourage explorations of the Atlantic by the Portuguese and others.

Bibliography: Babcock, William H., *Legendary Islands of the Atlantic: A Study in Medieval Geography*, 1922; Ramsay, Raymond H., *No Longer on the Map: Discovering Places That Never Were*, 1972.

Bretons

Vague reports have circulated since the seventeenth century that Breton fishermen, along with **Basques** and Normans, sailed to Newfoundland and the Grand Banks well before 1492.

Bretons, particularly those from Saint-Malo, were famous for their seamanship during the medieval and early modern eras. Jacques Cartier (1491–1557), the great

French explorer of Canada during 1534–1542, was a native of Saint-Malo. After news of the voyages of Christopher Columbus in 1492 and John Cabot in 1497 circulated through Europe, the Bretons were quick to investigate reports of wonderful fishing grounds off Newfoundland. The first Breton fishing vessels arrived as early as 1504 and not later than 1506, some 20 years before the arrival of the Basques. The Grand Banks soon became a hub of activity for ships from Portugal and England, and for those of the Basques, Bretons, and Normans of France during the sixteenth century. When the great French historian André Thévet (1520–1590) published his *La cosmographie universelle* in 1575, he made no mention of pre-Columbian visits to the Americas by Bretons or anyone else from France. Neither did his contemporary, French historian and geographer François de Belleforest.

The first to suggest that Frenchmen, especially Bretons, Normans, and Basques, may have reached the Americas before Columbus was the early historian of New France Marc Lescarbot in 1609. Twenty years later, Pierre de Bergeron published his small history of French discoveries in America and elaborated on Lescarbot's story of Bretons, Basques, and other French fishermen having sailed to Newfoundland for centuries before Columbus. Unfortunately for supporters of the Bretons and Normans, in 1647 the great maritime legal scholar Etiènne Cleirac pared down Bergeron's account, leaving only the Basques as pre-Columbian visitors to America. From then on, stories of Breton and Norman fishermen sailing to pre-Columbian America were overshadowed by similar tales about the Basques. Of course, none of them had any basis in historical fact; they were merely Lescarbot's speculation evolving through repetition by later writers into the semblance of fact. Bretons arrived early on the coasts of North America, but they did not precede Columbus.

Bibliography: LeHuenen, Joseph, "The Role of Basque, Breton, and Norman Cod Fishermen in the Discovery of North America from the XVIth to the end of the XVIIIth Century," *Arctic* 37 (December 1984): 520–527; Scisco, Louis Don, "Precolumbian Discovery by Basques," *Proceedings and Transactions of the Royal Society of Canada* (3rd Series) 18 (1924): 51–61.

Bristol Voyages
(ca. 1481–1491)

There is a hypothesis that merchants and fishermen from Bristol, England, visited North America, probably more than once, before Christopher Columbus's first voyage in 1492.

The evidence supporting voyages to America by Bristol ships is rather ambiguous and vague. For instance, the **John Day letter**, written in late December 1497 and early 1498, reports John Cabot's voyage of 1497 to North America, which is identified as the **Isle of Brazil.** It also mentions, however, that ships of Bristol had already discovered Brazil "*en otros tiempos* (in times past)." Bristol records confirm that in the early 1480s ships searched for the Isle of Brazil. On 15 July 1480 a ship of John Jay and **Thomas Lloyd** sought but failed to find Brazil. Several merchants of Bristol, including Thomas Croft, sent out two ships, *George* and *Trinity*, on 6 July 1481 with Brazil as their destination. They appear to have completed their voyage, but between 1483 and 1490 there is no direct evidence for further western voyages.

Another significant piece of evidence is the letter of Pedro de Ayala, Spanish ambassador to England, that was written to Ferdinand and Isabella on 25 July 1498. This letter, like Day's, reported John Cabot's voyage of 1497 and also referred to annual Bristol voyages in search of Brazil begun seven years earlier. Unfortunately, the wording of Ayala's letter is vague. It is not certain whether the seven years refers to 1490–1496 or to 1491–1497. The letter also mentions a connection between John Cabot and the Bristol voyages, but does not clarify whether he was a participant or an observer. Furthermore, Robert Thorne the younger of Bristol claimed in 1527 that his father, Robert Thorne the elder, and Hugh Elyot discovered the "New Found Landes" before John Cabot. Geographer **John Dee** dated that voyage to 1494, but for no good reason. It might have taken place earlier and was certainly part of the annual voyages referred to by Ayala.

There is no scholarly consensus about the date of Bristol's discovery of North America. It is possible that a ship accidentally landed on North America before 1480, but no evidence survives. The most likely dates for the first successful Bristol voyage are 1481 or 1491, with the years in between and afterward being somewhat less likely. One certainty in all this conjecture is that Bristol merchants made western voyages before John Cabot's arrival in their city about 1494.

Besides the dating of those voyages, another puzzle is why the Bristol merchants were sailing west. Probably they were sailing to the Grand Banks for fishing. There had been serious conflicts between Bristol and the Hanseatic League of Germany over fishing in traditional Icelandic waters, with the Bristol fishermen losing. The Grand Banks provided them with a lucrative alternate fishing ground. Naturally they would try to keep new fishing grounds a secret, hence their failure to announce the finding of new lands across the western ocean. For the men of Bristol, the known riches in the water far exceeded any potential wealth they might find on the neighboring barren coastline. They also probably assumed that any land they saw was an island, not a continent, in accordance with the prevailing late-medieval concepts of the geography of the North Atlantic. A theory that the voyages to Brazil were simply a cover for trading voyages to

Greenland has not been confirmed by any archaeological evidence.

When John Cabot arrived in Bristol in 1494 or 1495, his intention was to sail west to reach China in the same manner as Columbus. The plan would have exposed the secret fishing grounds of Bristol, assuming they actually knew about them. Certainly Cabot's voyage did reveal the wondrous fishing off the Grand Banks, and many countries flocked to participate in its bounty. It seems highly likely that Bristol ships sailed west before Cabot, but whether they preceded Columbus remains merely an intriguing speculation in the absence of further evidence.

Bibliography: Quinn, David Beers, *England and the Discovery of America, 1481–1620,* 1974; Ruddock, Alwyn A., "John Day of Bristol and the English Voyages across the Atlantic before 1497," *Geographical Journal* 132 (June 1966): 225–233.

Buddhist Missionaries in Ancient America (458)

According to the narrative of **Hoei-shin,** five mendicant Buddhist monks from the kingdom of Kipin traveled to **Fusang** (the Chinese name for an eastern land that some scholars think may have been North America) and converted the inhabitants to Buddhism in 458, some 40 years before Hoei-shin's visit.

During the early centuries of Buddhism, it was common for missionaries to carry their religion to faraway lands. The kingdom of Kipin was a great center of Buddhist devotion and piety that has been variously identified as Kashmir, Afghanistan, or Bokhara. Its missionaries frequently participated in the spread of Buddhism, but whether some of them reached the Americas is highly problematic. If Buddhists did reach some part of the Americas and convert the inhabitants, no definite traces of this religion survive to prove it.

study reveals interesting correspondences of attributes, functions, or meanings between these cultures.

Other scholars, such as prominent Mexican archaeologist Alfonso Caso, find Kirchhoff's cultural parallels between Indian and Mexican religious traits to be forced or simply more apparent than real. They argue for independent invention or **parallel evolution** as the explanation for the development of Mexican religion and its calendar. Others, such as English scholar Nigel Davies, are not so quick to reject Kirchhoff's findings. Although Davies feels that Kirchhoff's methodology is flawed, he also thinks it may reveal some genuinely significant evidence for Indian and Chinese contacts. The religious similarities are too great to be dismissed as independent inventions but also too subtle to allow for definite assertions of trans-Pacific contacts. Kirchhoff's case is symptomatic of the growing acceptance of this possibility by professional scholars.

Bibliography: Davies, Nigel, *Voyagers to the New World,* 1979; Kirchhoff, Paul, "The Adaptation of Foreign Religious Influences in Pre-Spanish Mexico," Diogenes 47 (1964): 13–28 with a reply by Alfonso Caso: 29–35; Kirchhoff, Paul, "The Diffusion of a Great Religious System from India to Mexico," Proceedings of the 35th International Congress of Americanists (1964): 73–100.

Canaanites in Ancient America

According to the Old Testament of the Bible, the Children of Israel (or **Hebrews**) conquered Canaan, the promised land. After their defeat, the Canaanites made their way to America.

Several sixteenth- and seventeenth-century European writers speculated that Native Americans were the descendants of Canaanites. The first to suggest this theory was Mexican writer Juan Suárez de Peralta

Calendar and God List Parallels

Various anthropologists and archaeologists suggest that **Chinese** and **Hindus** visited Central America shortly after the second or third century. They point to striking parallels in the god lists and calendars of India, China, Java, and Mexico as evidence.

Paul Kirchhoff is the leading scholar promoting the methodology of using these parallels to prove trans-Pacific contacts between India and China and Central America. Focusing on the Hindu material, in 1964 Kirchhoff constructed a matrix of the animal names of the 28 Chinese and 27 Hindu lunar days with their correspondences to the 12 animal-day names used by both the Chinese and Mexican civilizations, for example, tiger, dog, or rabbit. His (ca. 1536–1591). His *Tratado del descubrimiento de las Indias*, written in 1580 but not published until 1878, suggested multiple origins for Native Americans, including the **Ten Lost Tribes, Carthaginians,** Ethiopians, and **Egyptians** as well as Canaanites. The importance of a Canaanite origin theory was that, due to the biblical curse on Ham and Canaan, it provided a justification for Spanish enslavement of the Native Americans. In his *History of New France* (1609), early–seventeenth-century French historian Marc Lescarbot considered the possibility that Canaanites fled from their Israelite conquerors and settled in America. In 1612 English writer William Strachey reached the same conclusions. Both writers cite idolatry and the practice of cannibalism among the natives of North America as evidence of Canaanite ancestry, since the Canaanites had engaged in, or were alleged to have engaged in, such practices. At the same time, both Lescarbot and Strachey thought that **José de Acosta's** theory of a narrow strait separating North America from Asia explained how the larger and more dangerous animals entered the Americas in prehistoric times. Finally, **Cotton Mather,** in his book *The Serviceable Man* of 1690, also suggested that the Canaanites came to America to escape the invasion and conquest of their land by Joshua and the Children of Israel. He also argued that as descendants of Ham and Canaan, Native Americans were subject to the biblical curse. Therefore, the wars of the English settlers against and their displacement of the tribes of New England were justified.

In the twentieth century, supporters of the Canaanite origin theory have rightly tended to merge it with the **Phoenician** origin theory. That merger is quite appropriate because the peoples of Canaan and Phoenicia were the same ethnic and cultural group. Still, the usage of Canaanite rather than Phoenician occasionally appears in the literature. Needless to say, the biblically based Canaanite origin theory has no basis in archaeological evidence.

Bibliography: Huddleston, Lee Eldridge, *Origins of the American Indians: European Concepts, 1492–1729,* 1967; Lescarbot, Marc, *History of New France,* 3 vols., 1907–1914; Rosenstein, N., "How Wide the Biblical World? A Challenge for Recognition and Preservation," *Biblical Archaeologist* 41 (Summer 1978): 84–85 and a reply by Marshall McKusick, "Canaanites in America: A New Scripture in Stone?" *Biblical Archaeologist* 42 (Summer 1979): 137–140.

Carthaginians in Ancient America

Many theories credit the Carthaginians, a North African trading people, with accidental or planned visits to the Americas in the era before their destruction by the Romans in the Punic Wars (264–146 B.C.).

The Carthaginians are one of the better-known ancient peoples because of their monumental struggle with the Roman Republic. But their defeat resulted in the destruction of their archives and libraries, so detailed knowledge about Carthage tends to be limited. Furthermore, as a trading nation, they tended to be secretive about their commercial activities.

According to tradition, colonists from the great **Phoenician** city of Tyre founded Carthage in 814 B.C.; however, archaeological evidence indicates a slightly later date. Although not the first Phoenician colony in the western Mediterranean Sea, it became the most important thanks to its superior location and harbor. By around 600 B.C. the Carthaginians were actively striving to establish and maintain a monopoly over the sea lanes of the western Mediterranean and the Atlantic Ocean. They defeated their Greek rivals at sea by 500 B.C., but the struggle for control of the strategic island of Sicily continued for centuries. Events there ultimately brought Carthage into conflict with Rome, resulting in the three Punic Wars with Rome the victor.

Carthage existed for over 600 years, during which time its people conducted explorations into the Atlantic Ocean. Carthaginian ships reached Britain, sailed as far south as Sierra Leone in West Africa, and possibly landed on the Azores and Madeira islands. Some writers suggest they also made accidental or even intentional voyages to the Americas.

During the sixteenth century, Spanish scholars tried to explain the origins of Native Americans, a people previously unknown to Europeans. One of the earliest and most persistent theories claimed that Native Americans were descendants of Carthaginian colonists. **Gonzalo Fernández de Oviedo y Valdés** first proposed it in 1535, basing his contention on the mistaken belief that **Aristotle** credited the Carthaginians with the discovery of a great island in the Atlantic Ocean about 590 B.C. Oviedo's theory quickly attracted other Spanish supporters such as Alejo Vanegas de Bustos, whose *Primera parte de las differencias de libros q̃ ay in el universo* (1540) claimed that Carthaginian settlers were responsible for populating the Americas. Francisco López de Gómara, secretary to Hernán Cortés and chronicler of the early Spanish empire in the Americas, added a new aspect to the theory in his *Historia general de las Indias* (1552). He suggested that the Carthaginian explorer **Hanno** discovered the Americas during his explorations down the west coast of Africa around 490 B.C.

The Carthaginian theory proved popular among Spanish writers. Florián de Ocampo, a historian of Spain, repeated Gómara's story of Hanno in his own book published a year later. In 1559 Vicente Palatino de Curzola used the Carthaginian theory to prove the primacy of Spain's claims to possession of the Americas. Mexi-

can scholar Juan Suárez de Peralta (ca. 1536–1591), writing about 1580, also believed that the Carthaginians reached the Americas, but credited them only with populating the islands of the Caribbean Sea. Other writers such as Mexican Dominican priest Augustín Dávila Padilla (1562–1604) in 1596, Spanish historian Antonio de Herrera y Tordesillas (ca. 1549–1625) in 1601, and Spanish Dominican priest Reginaldo de Lizárraga (ca. 1540–1612) in 1602 all supported the Carthaginian theory. Needless to say, **Gregorio García,** the undiscriminating enumerator of theories about pre-Columbian visitors, included the Carthaginian theory in his *Origen de los indios del nuevo mundo, e Indias occidentalies.*

During the seventeenth century some Spanish scholars began to question the Carthaginian theory. Spanish Franciscan historian **Juan de Torquemada** rejected it in 1613, as did Peruvian Augustinian priest Antonio de la Calancha (1584–1654) in 1638 and Pedro Cubero Sebastián in 1684. Their basic objection was doubt as to whether the ancient peoples of the Mediterranean world had any knowledge of the Americas. These ideas show the growth of a more sophisticated, critical approach. At the same time, many Spanish writers continued to support the Carthaginian theory.

Non-Spanish writers, such as French scholar Robert Comte in 1644, also began to support the Carthaginian theory. In 1671 English geographer John Ogilby (1600–1676) repeated Comte's assertions. Another Englishman, the traveler John Josselyn (fl. 1638–1675), gave the Carthaginian Hanno credit for reaching America, although Josselyn was a strong supporter of the theory of **Tartars** discovering and populating the Americas.

The Carthaginian theory broadened into a Phoenician theory during the seventeenth century. In some cases, writers appear to have imprecisely or incorrectly used the terms Carthaginian and Phoenician interchangeably, which persists into the twentieth century. When writers properly distinguish between the Phoenicians and Carthaginians, the general pattern is to attribute any supposed voyages to America before 600 B.C. to the Phoenicians and those after 500 B.C. to the Carthaginians. Carthage barred all other ships of Mediterranean origin from the Strait of Gibraltar about 509 B.C., and that blockade may have included ships from the Phoenician mother country. After that date, only Carthaginian ships would have had access from the Mediterranean to the Atlantic and the Americas.

Modern theories of Carthaginian contact with the Americas take two basic approaches. In one case, the Carthaginians came to the Americas by accident after being swept west by storms and the prevailing winds and currents. Such contacts were supposedly rare and never followed up. Another approach suggests that the Carthaginians reached the Americas either by accident or as part of a systematic program of exploration. Either way, they continued to return for trade, and their presence significantly influenced the development of Native American civilizations.

Charles M. Boland, in his popularly written account *They All Discovered America* (1961), claims that the Carthaginians (he refers to them as Phoenicians) first reached North America accidentally sometime before 480 B.C. using a northern approach via **Greenland.** According to Boland, in 480 B.C. a second group of Carthaginians arrived who were committed to the continuation of the religious ritual of human sacrifice. When Carthage signed a treaty with its Greek enemies agreeing to give up the practice, this group refused to give up their religion and fled to what is now New England for religious freedom. Another defeat at the hands of the Greek Agothocles of Syracuse in 311 B.C. compelled a third group to settle in present-day Virginia. Finally, in 146 B.C., a fourth group fled from the fall of their city to Rome and traveled to South America. Unfortunately, Boland bases this last migration on the fraudulent Paraíba Stone, which if authentic would be dated 534 B.C. (See also **Phoenicians in Ancient America.**) In fact, Boland's evidence is all flimsy and circumstantial.

Frederick J. Pohl, in his *Atlantic Crossings before Columbus* (1961), presents a less ambitious and somewhat better documented argument for Carthaginian visits to North America in the fourth century B.C. His case is also unconvincing since it attributes the construction of stone structures at North Salem, New Hampshire, to Carthaginians when other reliable research convincingly shows them to date from the seventeenth century A.D. In her *Fair Gods and Stone Faces* (1963), Constance Irwin writes that the Carthaginians traveled to the Americas, although she believes they were only following earlier Phoenician voyagers. **Cyrus Gordon** takes the same basic position in his *Before Columbus* (1971), as does James Bailey in *The God-Kings and the Titans* (1973) and **Barry Fell** in *America B.C.* (1976).

Like their Phoenician forebears, the Carthaginians are a potentially good candidate to have reached the Americas in the era before Christ. Their ships were capable of making an oceanic crossing and their intrepid trading ventures probably included one or more circumnavigations of Africa. Compared to such a voyage, an Atlantic crossing would have been relatively easy. No authentic evidence has yet appeared to prove that any Carthaginians reached America, making it unlikely that such contacts occurred.

Bibliography: Fingerhut, Eugene R., *Who First Discovered America? A Critique of Pre-Columbian Voyages*, 1984; Huddleston, Lee

Eldridge, *Origins of the American Indians: European Concepts, 1492–1729*, 1967; Warmington, B. H., *Carthage*, rev. ed., 1969.

Celts in Ancient America

Barry Fell's theory claims that ancient Celtic peoples from western Europe, particularly Iberia and Ireland, visited North America repeatedly between 3000 B.C. and A.D. 500.

According to Fell, during ancient times the Atlantic Ocean was a crowded highway for commerce and travel between North America and western Europe and the Mediterranean. Celts first reached America sometime after 3000 B.C. By 2000 B.C. they mined copper and took it back to Europe. One of the most important groups of later Celts came from Iberia, labeled Celt-Iberians by Fell. They supposedly had close associations with the **Phoenicians** and **Carthaginians**. Their presence in the New England and eastern Canadian coastal regions had a significant impact on the language and institutions of the Algonquian Indians by 1500 B.C. Even as late as A.D. 500, Celtic Christians from Ireland continued to visit North America.

Fell's evidence consists of linguistic comparisons, inscriptions, and monuments. The Algonquian vocabulary of law, medicine, and navigation supposedly derives from Celtic visitors. Various alleged Celtic inscriptions have been located in North America, particularly in New England. Many are written in the ogam script, which uses sticklike characters. Megaliths or dolmens and various other stone structures, especially those at Mystery Hill, New Hampshire, are also attributed to the wandering Celts. However, professional archaeologists and anthropologists do not consider Fell's evidence credible. Experts on Celtic and Algonquian languages deny any connection between them. Many of the Celts' supposed inscriptions are markings and petroglyphs produced by Native Americans of the pre-Columbian or colonial eras. Furthermore, ogam is a form of writing that developed in Ireland in the fourth century A.D. It was not used in Spain by either ancient Celtic peoples or Phoenician colonists. To suggest otherwise is anachronistic and without foundation in European archaeological evidence. Other inscriptions appear to be scratches produced by nature. Some of the stone structures attributed to ancient Celtic visitors are not what Fell and others claim. Historical and archaeological evidence points to the Mystery Hill site being a colonial root cellar rather than the "American Stonehenge" that Fell and others claim. Professional archaeologists find the idea of prehistoric and ancient Celtic migrations to North America to be absurd and without legitimate evidence.

Bibliography: Feder, Kenneth L., *Frauds, Myths, and Mysteries: Science and Pseudoscience in Archaeology*, 1990; Fell, Barry, *America B.C.*, [1976], 1989; Williams, Stephen, *Fantastic Archaeology: The Wild Side of North American Prehistory*, 1991.

Chhin (Qin) and Han Voyages (ca. 300–100 B.C.)

Before and during the dynasties of the Chhin and Han, **Chinese** ships made many voyages into the Pacific Ocean searching for the magical islands of immortality. One or more of these expeditions may have reached the Americas, particularly that of **Hsü Fu.**

Taoism (or Daoism) was and is an important religion in China. Alongside its better-known religious and philosophical principles, Taoism also displays a strong belief in magic and alchemy, especially during the fourth, third, and second centuries B.C. One particular alchemical belief stated that three magical islands named Phêng-Lai, Fang-Chang, and Ying-Chou were located in the sea. On these islands lived supernatural beings called genii, who possessed a drug capable of conferring immortality; under the right conditions they might be persuaded to part with some of it. Early traditions located these islands in the Sea of Po (Gulf of Chihli) off the Yellow Sea. By the time of the first emperor Chhin Shih Huang Ti (or Qin Shi Huangdi), who reigned from 246–210 B.C., their supposed location had shifted to somewhere in the vast Pacific. Near or far, the magical islands were almost impossible to visit. From a distance they looked like clouds, but when a curious ship attempted to approach them, winds would arise and blow the ship away. If the winds failed to stop the intruders, the islands would sink beneath the sea. Still, the ancient Chinese believed that some people could manage to reach these islands. Descriptions stated that many immortals lived on them in palaces of gold and silver, and that the birds and animals of the islands were completely white.

Ssuma Chhien (Si-ma Qian, 145–? B.C.), the great historian of the Former Han era and author of the *Shih Chi* (or *ShiJi*, i.e., Historical record) completed in 90 B.C., is the chief source of information about the magic islands and efforts to find them. He recorded that these attempts occurred well before the unification of China in 221 B.C. Two kings of the coastal kingdom of Chhi named Wei (reigned 378–343 B.C.) and Hsüan (reigned 342–324 B.C.), as well as Chao (reigned 311–279 B.C.), the king of another coastal kingdom called Yen, sent out obviously unsuccessful expeditions.

Repeated failures did not dampen the desire of China's rulers to locate the magic islands and so gain immortality. The best-known and most persistent hunter was the fearsome first emperor of unified China, Chhin Shih Huang Ti. Ruthless in his conduct of war and government, he was reluctant to accept his own inevitable mortality. Meanwhile various rumors circulated, claiming that several Taoist scholars had achieved immortality. Given such an intel-

lectual atmosphere, other Taoists managed to convince the first emperor that they could obtain the drug of immortality. The practical Chhin Shih Huang Ti wanted to lead the expedition personally, but worry about the possibility and consequences of failure caused him to reconsider and send others in his place.

Chhin Shih Huang Ti's search fared no better than those of his predecessors. Some of his explorers returned empty-handed but claimed they had sighted the three islands. Contrary winds, however, prevented them from landing. Others complained that attacks by great sharks hampered their efforts, so they asked the emperor to protect them by providing soldiers armed with crossbows. Chhin Shih Huang Ti agreed, and even developed a personal interest in hunting sea monsters. When he died in 210 B.C., he was on a tour of the coastal provinces of China that included sea monster hunting in its itinerary.

Little detail survives about these expeditions. Only one commander's name is known: Hsü Fu, a magician. When he first approached the emperor in 219 B.C., several expeditions had already failed. Hsü Fu managed to gain imperial support on a very large scale, but he too failed to secure the drug of immortality his emperor so desired. By 219 B.C. the first emperor began to complain about both the lack of success and the great expense involved in the hunt. The clever Hsü Fu managed to stave off Chhin Shih Huang Ti's wrath by claiming to have reached the islands. Once he arrived there, the wizards of the islands informed him that the emperor's presents were too poor. They demanded young men and women and artisans in exchange for the drug of immortality.

Chhin Shih Huang Ti quickly supplied Hsü Fu with 3,000 young people, many artisans, and an ample supply of grain. With this large complement, Hsü Fu sailed off, never to be seen again. Han historian Ssuma

Chhien thought Hsü Fu fooled the emperor into providing him with the means to found his own kingdom in some distant land that he had discovered. Hsü Fu's final destination is not known, but he could have sailed to Japan or the Americas.

Despite the continuing lack of success, search voyages continued into the period of the former Han dynasty (206 B.C.–A.D. 8). The most active Han sponsor of Pacific explorations was the great emperor Wu Ti (or Wu Di, reigned 140–87 B.C.). Around 133 B.C. his court included the alchemist Li Shao-Chun, who sailed the seas so he could converse with the immortals. Li claimed to have visited the islands of immortality but apparently failed to bring any of its precious drug home with him. That same year a government official named Khuan Shu led another expedition in search of the magic islands. Predictably he failed to find them, but that did not affect Wu Ti's decision to give him the important appointment of minister of sacrifices. A later voyage left China in 113 B.C. under the leadership of scholars specializing in the interpretation of clouds. Again, no positive results ensued. In the same year another magician, Luan Ta, prepared to depart with great fanfare, but never even dared to sail. Understandably he soon fell from favor. By 98 B.C. Wu Ti and the Han government appear to have lost interest in further explorations of the Pacific. Repeated failures to reach the islands had worn down their resolve.

Surviving records are too vague to determine exactly how many expeditions were sent out or how many failed to return. The eminent historian of China Joseph Needham has speculated that Hsü Fu or some of the other Han voyagers actually reached the Americas. Some archaeologists also believe that certain Native American artifacts show evidence of Chinese contact. But if Chhin or Han voyagers did reach the Americas, none of them returned to tell of it.

Bibliography: Davies, Nigel, *Voyagers to the New World*, 1979; Needham, Joseph, *Science and Civilization in China*, vol. 2: *History of Scientific Thought*, 1962; Needham, Joseph, *Science and Civilization in China*, vol. 4: *Physics and Physical Technology*, pt. 3: *Civil Engineering and Nautics*, 1971.

Chinese Visits to America

Numerous theories about pre-Columbian Chinese visits to the Americas have been promulgated by both scholars and popular writers. The dates for these visits range from the legendary past before 2000 B.C. to as late as around A.D. 900.

It has been claimed that the ancient Chinese geographical treatise titled *Shan Hai King* (Classic of mountains and seas) describes a number of places in the western part of North America, therefore indicating early Chinese visits. The *Shan Hai King* is the oldest known geographical work in the world. It supposedly dates back to 2550–2505 B.C., the reigning years of Emperor Shun, the last ruler prior to the semilegendary Xia (or Hsia) dynasty. According to tradition, Shun ordered Yu, his minister of public works, to compile a geography of the world. The result was the *Shan Hai King*. Yu later succeeded Shun and founded the Xia dynasty. This history is based solely on written traditions dating from the Han era over 2,000 years later.

The *Shan Hai King* originally consisted of 32 books and is one of the few to survive the great book burning by Chhin Shih Huang Ti, the first emperor of China, in 213 B.C. Only 18 partial books of the complete work survive. From as early as 300–100 B.C., Chinese scholars considered the *Shan Hai King*'s geographical descriptions to be fantasies or a geography of the spirit world, and that judgment remained the overwhelming scholarly consensus. But in 1885 American Edward Vining treated the *Shan Hai King* as a genuine geographical description that included

North America. In the twentieth century Henriette Mertz repeated Vining's contentions in a book titled *Pale Ink,* privately published in 1953. In 1972 a second edition, retitled *Gods from the Far East,* was published as a mass-market paperback, the latter sporting a cover reminiscent of Eric von Daniken's gods-from-outer-space books.

Vining and Mertz were primarily concerned with **Hoei-shin's** voyage to **Fusang,** but Mertz attempted to link some of the descriptions in the *Shan Hai King* with places in the western parts of Canada, Mexico, and the United States, including the Grand Canyon (supposedly the "great luminous canyon" of Chinese legend). Mertz believes that Chinese visitors to America were common well before Hoei-shin's visit, bringing their calendar and skills in metallurgy, writing, weaving, and ceramics to the Native Americans. They were also responsible for the classic oriental features found among many Native Americans and the source for the various **white god legends.**

Some professional prehistorians and archaeologists theorize that significant contacts did occur between China and the Americas, but not as early as 2000 B.C. The realm of the Emperor Shun was an early Bronze Age culture barely past the Stone Age culture of the Neolithic. It is hard to believe that people at that stage of civilization regularly crossed back and forth over the vast Pacific to the Americas. Mertz's geographical identifications for the descriptions in the *Shan Hai King* are mere speculation. The scholarly consensus that the *Shan Hai King* is simply an imaginary geography seems far more likely then Mertz's extension of Edward Vining's theories that it referred to North America. Furthermore, Mertz damages her credibility by espousing multiple theories of pre-Columbian visitors to the Americas including the **Ten Lost Tribes, Ulysses, Atlantis,** and early Christians. Finally, despite

the passage of time and Chhin Shih Huang Ti's destruction of books, it stretches credulity to believe that a great civilization of record keepers like the Chinese would almost completely forget about these visits to the Americas.

The Shang dynasty ruled over the original core of Chinese territory from 1766 to about 1100 B.C. Those dates make Shang culture somewhat senior to the sophisticated Olmec civilization of Mexico that flourished from 1200 to 600 or 500 B.C. Olmec culture was the first of the higher civilizations to appear in pre-Columbian Mexico, and it arose with relative suddenness. This led many people to speculate about the possibility of outside stimulation. The leading advocate of the Olmec culture receiving such impetus from Shang-era Chinese is Betty Meggers, a Smithsonian Institution scholar. In a 1975 article, she described the various traits shared by the Shang and Olmec such as writing, jade artifacts, batons as symbols of rank, similar architectures, cat-gods in the form of tigers and jaguars, and the deformation of skulls as a mark of beauty. Meggers' position was quickly attacked by another anthropologist, David C. Grove, who claimed the similarities were coincidental. Certainly geography is on Grove's side, since the Olmec lands are located on the Gulf of Mexico. Shang Chinese travelers would have had to work very hard to make their way across prehistoric Mexico to reach their erstwhile pupils.

Visitors from other Chinese dynasties supposedly continued to arrive over the centuries. The next dynasty was that of the Chou, which flourished from 1000–770 B.C. but diminished from 770 until 256 B.C. According to a series of articles written between 1949 and 1966 by archaeologist Robert Heine-Geldern, visitors from the late Chou period after 800 B.C. exerted significant influence on art and pottery motifs of the Lowland Maya after 400 B.C. and on the

Chavin culture of Peru, which arose about 900 B.C. and lasted until 250 B.C. In 1964 Gordon Ekholm, another respected archaeologist and an associate of Heine-Geldern, added the late Han dynasty (A.D. 24–220) to the list. Their beneficiaries were the people of the early Teotihuacán culture (300 B.C.–A.D. 200). Finally, in 1976 art historian Paul Shao argued for contacts between the Chinese Tang dynasty (618–909) and the last Classic Maya of Uxmal and Palenque (600–900). Among the shared artistic styles cited by these authors are the lotus and dragon motifs, tripod pottery, and human/animal/plant interfaces. Taken in isolation, these arguments seem to provide overwhelming evidence for a long sequence of Chinese visits to the Americas from the Shang through Tang eras.

Other scholars are unconvinced and remain faithful to the concept that the civilizations of the Americas are truly native. Robert L. Rands demonstrated that the lotus motif, supposedly shared by east Asians and the Maya, was almost certainly an independent invention. In 1964 Mexican archaeologist Alfonso Caso deeply undercut the methodology of comparing artistic motifs to prove trans-Pacific contacts. He paired examples of nearly identical artifacts from cultures that could not possibly have been in contact with one another, such as the Monte Albán culture with Bronze Age Palestine, Roman Pompeii, and the France of Louis XVI. According to Caso, stylistic similarities on their own mean nothing. Caso also argues against Shang contacts because the Chinese lacked a sufficiently developed marine technology at that time. Another argument against prolonged Chinese contact is that no exchanges of useful plants and animals resulted. Claims of pre-Columbian **maize** or corn in China have been proven to have no foundation. Finally, the Chinese were meticulous record keepers. Their historical treatises, geographical works, and encyclopedias are detailed and exist in unbroken sequences going back to the Qin (Chin) dynasty from 256–206 B.C. Some writings date back to the first appearance of primitive writing in Shang China. With such a wealth of historical documentation, it is hardly credible that the Chinese could have maintained periodic but significant contacts with the Americas without leaving a trace of that knowledge in their records. Only one-way drift voyages would have left no records. Some drift voyages undoubtedly took place, but could not possibly have the cultural impact that Meggers, Heine-Geldern, Ekholm, and Shao claim.

Bibliography: Caso, Alfonso, "Relations between the Old and New World: A Note on Methodology," *Proceedings of the 35th International Congress of Americanists* (1962): 55–71; Davies, Nigel, *Voyagers to the New World*, 1979; Ekholm, Gordon, "The Possible Chinese Origins of Teotihuacan Cylindrical Tripod Pottery and Certain Related Traits," *Proceedings of the 35th International Congress of Americanists* (1962): 39–45; Heine-Geldern, Robert, "The Problem of Transpacific Influences in Mesoamerica," *Handbook of Middle American Indians*, vol. 4, 1966; Heine-Geldern, Robert, "Representation of the Asiatic Tiger in the Art of Chavin Culture: A Proof of Early Contact between China and Peru," *Proceedings of the 33rd International Congress of Americanists* (1958): 321–326; Meggers, Betty, "The Transpacific Origin of Mesoamerican Civilization: A Preliminary Review of the Evidence and Its Theoretical Implications," *American Anthropologist*, 77 (1975): 1–27; Mertz, Henriette, *Pale Ink: Two Ancient Records of Chinese Explorations in America*, [1953], rev. ed. 1972; Rands, Robert L., "The Water Lily in Maya Art: A Complex of Alleged Asiatic Origin," *Smithsonian Institution, Bureau of American Ethnology Bulletin* 151 (1953): 75–153.

Cobo, Father Bernabé
(1580–1657)

Priest and historian Cobo's unpublished *Historia del Nuevo Mundo* (History of the New World), completed in 1653, represents the finest example of early-modern Spanish scholarship on the native peoples of the Americas. It followed **José de Acosta's** theory that the ancestors of Native Americans came from Asia via a land bridge somewhere in the then-unexplored northwest of North America (see also **Bering Land Bridge/ Strait Theory**).

Born in 1580 at Lopera, Spain, Cobo traveled to Seville in 1595 after completing his elementary education. From there he sailed to the New World where he would spend the rest of his life. Cobo lived in the West Indies for over a year before proceeding to Lima, Peru, in 1599. He completed his secondary education and in 1603 took the first vows leading to entry in the Jesuit order. Cobo performed wide-ranging missionary work among the natives of Peru and later lived in New Spain (Mexico) from 1629–1642. After 1620 he worked primarily in the larger cities of Lima and Mexico City, which provided him with access to the main archives of the Americas. Besides documentary research, Cobo also employed casual observations and interviews with various informants. His methods, however, were not nearly as systematic as those of **Bernardino de Sahagún.** Cobo completed his monumental but unpublished *Historia del Nuevo Mundo* in 1653 and died in 1657.

Basically Cobo reached the same conclusions on the origins of Native Americans as his great predecessor José de Acosta. In Cobo's opinion, the first Native Americans came across a northern land bridge or narrow strait from Asia while still in a primitive stage and within a few centuries after the great flood of Noah (Bk. 1, chs. 12–13). Cobo dealt with the problem of explaining the unique fauna and flora of the New World by suggesting that, just as angels helped Noah to gather various plants and animals into the Ark before the flood, they helped to redistribute them to their former homes afterward (Bk. 1, ch. 13). Besides arguing for the Acostan land bridge theory, Cobo also convincingly argued against the assertion that the biblical land of **Ophir** was Peru or Mexico, and that the **Hebrews** traded with them. He further denied that Hebrew settlers were the ancestors of Native Americans (Bk. 1, chs. 15–20). Cobo's scholarship maintained Acosta's high standards and anticipated the modern Bering Land Bridge theory of Native American origins. Because Cobo failed to publish his monumental study, it remained a little-known or used manuscript until it was finally published in four volumes between 1890 and 1893.

Bibliography: Cobo, Bernabé, *History of the Inca Empire*, 1979; Cobo, Bernabé, *Inca Religion and Customs*, 1990; Huddleston, Lee Eldridge, *Origins of the American Indians: European Concepts, 1492–1729*, 1967.

Coin Finds

Forty-one reports document the finding of Old World coins with pre-Columbian dates in the Americas, particularly North America, and there may be others. This evidence is used to argue for pre-Columbian visits by **Canaanites, Phoenicians, Hebrews,** Greeks, **Romans,** and Norse sailors, although only the Norse find stands up to scholarly scrutiny.

In 1553 Lucio Marineo Siculo (1460–1533), a somewhat credulous Italian humanist, reported the finding of a Roman coin from the time of Caesar Augustus in a gold mine in Panama. He concluded that its presence proved the Romans had reached the Americas before the Spanish. **Gonzalo Fernández de Oviedo y Valdés** touched on Siculo's story in his *Historia general y natural de las Indias* of 1535, and showed that it was ridiculous. Significantly, no one found any more pre-Columbian coins in the Americas until several Roman coins from the Imperial era turned up in the Fayetteville area of Tennessee between 1818 and 1823. The early archaeologist Caleb Atwater was immediately skeptical and suspected that the coins were deliberate plants. Tennessee antiquarian John Haywood considered the find authentic, but even he reported that, after a certain Mr. Colter (a man known to possess Roman coins) left Tennessee for Alabama in 1823, no more coins were found in Tennessee. Modern archaeologists generally agree with Atwater's original assessment, and think the Tennessee coins were a hoax.

Only one other documented coin find took place in the nineteenth century. In 1880 on an Illinois farm a Seleucid Greek coin from around 173–64 B.C. was found. The remaining 32 finds took place in the twentieth century; of that number, 24 were found after 1945. With the exception of the Norse penny found in Maine, these coins appear to have been brought to the Americas after 1492. Some coins turned out to be forgeries, such as the three Bar Kolchba coins found at various places in Kentucky in 1932, 1952, and 1967. Other finds are poorly documented. Staunch **diffusionists** Constance Irwin and Cyrus Gordon reported the finding of a massive cache of Roman coins in Venezuela containing some ninth-century Arabic coins. They claim that Mendel Peterson of the Smithsonian Institution is preparing a study of this Venezuelan find, but their claims are 20 and 30 years old and no such study has appeared. Perhaps the Venezuelan coin find was an archaeological will-o'-the-wisp.

Other genuine ancient coins have been located in archaeological situations that indicate they may be losses from modern collections rather than remains from the distant past. Many have been found on the surface of the soil rather than dug up. The natural

tendency for a coin would be to sink into the soil rather than work its way up. It is estimated some 1 million Roman coins are held in modern collections in the United States, most of them brought back from Europe after World War II. Many are worth less than $10, and therefore not looked after carefully. Accidental loss appears to be the source in most of these twentieth-century finds.

The geographical distribution of these coin finds neither proves nor disproves transoceanic contacts. Coastal states have been the sites of 18 finds, while interior states have produced 20. The eastern United States reports 27 coin finds, with only 11 in the western states; the south reports 24 finds compared to only 14 in the north. Diffusionists would argue that it is only to be expected that coin finds are more common in the east and especially the south, given the prevailing winds and **ocean currents** from Europe. But the roughly equal number of coin finds in interior and coastal states is an unexpected anomaly. Some writers suggest that the coins found along beaches may have been mixed with ballast dumped on the shoreline by post-Columbian ships. Diffusionists claim these coins washed onto the shore from pre-Columbian shipwrecks. Basically the geographical distribution of the coin finds supports no particular conclusion about the possibility of pre-Columbian contacts.

Jeremiah F. Epstein's 1980 study of coin finds basically concludes that none provides legitimate evidence for pre-Columbian contacts, with the possible exception of the Norse penny found in Maine in 1957. Initially identified as a medieval English coin, in 1978 it was reexamined and found to be from the reign of Olav Kyrre (1066–1093) of Norway. Tests establish that it is genuine, but the question remains—how did it get to Maine? Was it lost by a medieval Norse visitor, did Native Americans trading with the Norse in **Greenland** bring it south and lose it, did a modern visitor lose it, or is it a deliberate modern plant? If a medieval Norse visitor lost it, it would mean they visited North America far later and ventured farther south than most scholars think. The suggestion that Native Americans brought the coin south seems too implausible. But the basic anomaly relating to all the theories is the nature of the coin itself. It is an extremely rare medieval coin that circulated very briefly. No others have been found in Greenland, meaning that the chances of the coin being carried west by Norse traders is slight. On the other hand, the extreme rarity of the coin indicates it was probably not lost casually during the modern period. Furthermore, no prankster would knowingly use such a rare and valuable coin in a hoax. Anyone who knew the coin was Norse would be aware of its value. The specialized reference books needed for that purpose were not yet published when the coin was found in 1957. It would seem that the Norse penny is genuine archaeological evidence for a Norse visit to Maine. But why the Norse came remains a mystery. Scholars Marshall McKusick and Erik Wahlgren advise caution and suggest waiting for additional Norse artifacts to appear in Maine before drawing any definite conclusions.

Bibliography: Epstein, Jeremiah F., "Pre-Columbian Old World Coins in America: An Examination of the Evidence," *Current Anthropology* 21 (February 1980): 1–20; McKusick, Marshall B., and Erik Wahlgren, "The Norse Penny Mystery," *Archaeology of Eastern North America* 8 (1980): 1–10.

Côrte-Real, Voyage of João Vaz (ca. 1472 or 1476)

Portuguese historians consider Côrte-Real to be the true discover of America rather than Christopher Columbus, citing his par-

ticipation in the supposed **voyage of Diderik Pining and Hans Pothorst** in 1472 as evidence.

A shadowy figure who flourished during the 1470s, Côrte-Real was the father of northern voyagers Gaspar and Miguel Côrte-Real. The nature of his role in the Pining-Pothorst voyage is not clear, although some sources credit him with being commander. It is more likely that he merely served as an observer for the king of Portugal. Contemporary sources fail to mention the existence of any Côrte-Real voyage, but the true believers explain that silence as the result of the **Portuguese Policy of Secrecy.** Initially, those who believed in the actuality of the voyage considered it to be a solely Portuguese expedition. In 1920 Sophus Larsen, a Danish historian and librarian, first postulated the existence of a joint Portuguese-Danish voyage to America in 1472. Larsen reached that conclusion by piecing together a handful of scattered references. The voyage included the mysterious **Johannes Scolvus** as its pilot. Supposedly the explorers sailed beyond **Greenland** to Labrador and Newfoundland, where they observed the rich fishing in the Grand Banks. But they failed to locate their main objective—a Northwest Passage to China.

Evidence for connecting Côrte-Real to the northern voyage of Pining and Pothorst comes from three sources. A Portuguese historian named Antonio Cordeiro mentioned that in 1474 Afonso V of Portugal appointed Côrte-Real and Alvaro Martins Homens as cogovernors of Terceira in the Azores as a reward for their participation in a voyage of discovery to *terra do bacalhao* (i.e., stockfishland, another name for Newfoundland). Professional historians tend to discount this report since it was based on information derived from Gaspar Frutuosa, a highly unreliable Azorean antiquarian of the sixteenth century. Another piece of evidence is the association of the name João Vaz with a bay or land in Labrador on a number of sixteenth-century maps. Finally, Gaspar (d. 1501) and Miguel (d. 1502), the sons of João Vaz Côrte-Real, also made several journeys to the Arctic waters of North America in search of the Northwest Passage. These voyages, which cost them their lives, are cited as evidence of a family tradition of Arctic exploration.

Obviously, the evidence for João Vaz Côrte-Real's voyage to America is quite thin and ambiguous. Even most of its proponents do not believe that Alvaro Martin Homens accompanied Côrte-Real on any voyage to America. They explain the inclusion of Homens as an error by Cordeiro and Frutuosa. Others claim the voyage took place in 1476 and is mentioned in several relevant historical documents. Again they argue that any discrepancies are mistakes by Cordeiro and Frutuosa. Records show that Côrte-Real received the governorship of Terceira as a reward for military service against the Moors in North Africa well before Afonso V asked him to sail north. One Portuguese historian even contends that Côrte-Real and Johannes Scolvus, the so-called Polish pilot, were the same person. Professional historians (except the Portuguese) consistently find claims for the reality of Côrte-Real's voyage to be unfounded. In the last half of the nineteenth century, the respected historians Ernesto do Canto and Henry Harrisse wrote biographies of the Côrte-Real family that disbelieved or demolished, respectively, the existence of João Vaz's discovery of America. That did not stop Sophus Larsen from reviving the tale for use in his own complex version of the Pining-Pothorst expedition. Ethnic pride among Danes, Portuguese, and Poles, along with the efforts of people who love off-beat history, has kept the story alive and in the popular consciousness despite the best efforts of reputable historians such as Samuel Eliot Morison to refute them.

Bibliography: Boland, Charles M., *They All Discovered America*, 1961; Cameron, Ian, *Lodestone and Evening Star: The Epic Voyages of Discovery*, 1966; Morison, Samuel Eliot, *The European Discovery of America: The Northern Voyages*, 1971.

Cosa, World Map of Juan de la (1500)

This beautiful manuscript map by a shipmate of Christopher Columbus is the earliest to illustrate the new geographical knowledge acquired by Columbus's first three voyages and John Cabot's voyage of 1497. Some writers argue further that its seemingly accurate depiction of supposedly unexplored parts of Central America, combined with its presentation of the Americas as a landmass separate from Asia, proves the existence of secret Portuguese voyages to the Americas before 1492.

Mapmaker Juan de la Cosa (d. 1509) accompanied Columbus on his second voyage to the New World, serving as an able seaman on the *Nina* and on Columbus's explorations of Cuba and Jamaica in 1494. He even signed Columbus's declaration that Cuba was part of China's mainland province of Mangi and not an island. Yet when la Cosa later made his world map, he correctly depicted Cuba as an island, something Columbus would never admit, and a fact not yet known in 1500. His map was the first to present the results of Columbus's first three voyages; it also used a now-lost map of John Cabot's voyage of 1497 as a source.

For centuries la Cosa's world map lay in private hands, lost to the world of cartography, until it was spotted in a Parisian antique shop in 1836. It is now the property of the Museo Naval in Madrid. La Cosa apparently approached the emerging geography of the Americas with a far more open mind than Columbus. La Cosa sidestepped the issue of whether the New World was connected to Asia by neglecting to show the east coast of Asia on his world map. Most professional historians of cartography credit la Cosa with the simple combination of good guessing and caution when they evaluate the contents of his world map.

Supporters of a secret Portuguese discovery of the Americas before 1492 feel la Cosa's map reflects a knowledge of those clandestine voyages. For instance, la Cosa correctly shows the coastline of the New World as a solid line of land. They particularly feel that the outline of the Central American coastline is far too accurate to be the result of mere guessing. As they point out, none of this information was known in 1500. The original goal of Columbus's fourth voyage of 1502–1504 was to find a sea route to India by sailing through the area where Central America is located. On the

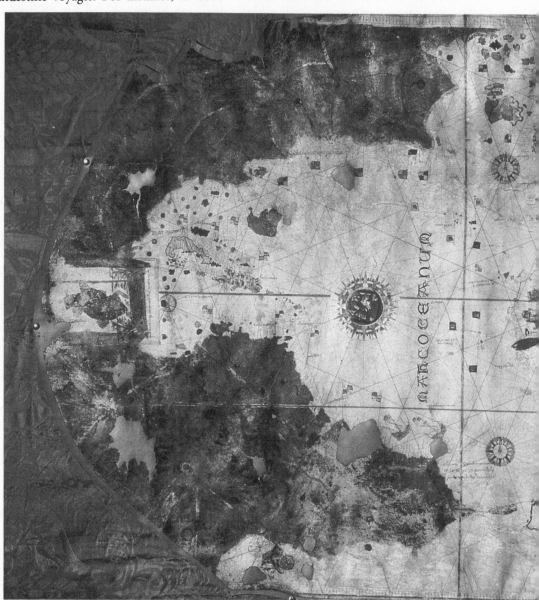

Map of Juan de la Cosa.

other hand, the outline of la Cosa's coastline for much of the New World is so vague and lacking in detail as to cast doubt on the arguments for a Portuguese discovery. Moreover, historian George Nunn plausibly suggests that the la Cosa map really dates from 1508, not 1500, which if true would eliminate any incongruities.

Juan de la Cosa continued to explore the New World, visiting South America with the expedition of Alonso de Ojeda and Amerigo Vespucci during 1499–1500. He died in a skirmish with Native Americans while attempting to establish a permanent settlement on the South American mainland in 1509.

Bibliography: Cameron, Ian, *Loadstone and Evening Star: The Epic Voyages of Discovery,* 1966; Nebenzahl, Kenneth, *Rand McNally*

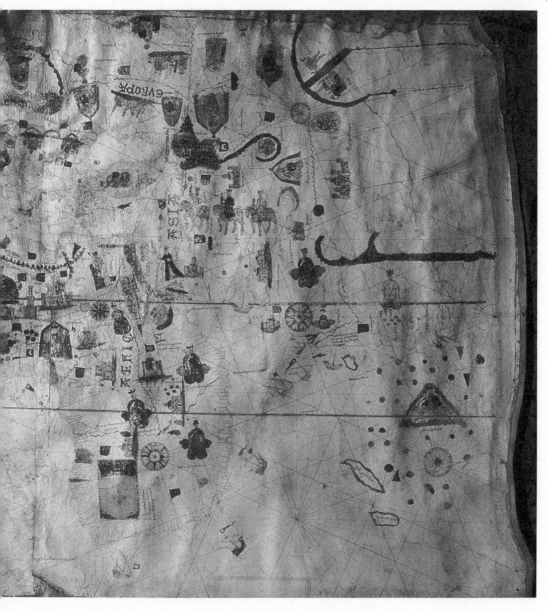

Atlas of Columbus and the Great Discoveries, 1990; Nunn, George E., *The Mappemonde of Juan de la Cosa: A Critical Investigation of Its Date*, 1934.

Cotton

Many writers and scholars speculate that the distribution of various species of the domesticated cotton plant is evidence of transoceanic contacts between the Americas and the Old World.

There are over 20 species of cotton, of which four are cultivated for their fibers. Two of the cultivated species, *Gossypium arboreum* and *Gossypium herbaceum*, have 13 chromosomes in their cells and are known as the Old World cottons. The other two species, *Gossypium hirsutum* and *Gossypium bardadense*, possess 26 chromosomes and are known as the New World cottons. Genetically the two cultivated New World cottons are hybrids that contain the 13 chromosomes of another wild species of New World cotton and the 13 chromosomes of the cultivated Old World cottons. The wild New World cottons are not capable of producing useful fibers, but combining these two sets of chromosomes creates a cotton plant that produces lush clumps of usable fibers. Obviously somehow and sometime, the cultivated Old World cottons came into contact with the wild New World cottons resulting in these hybrids. The mystery is whether this process occurred naturally or was assisted by humans.

Archaeologists have found remains of cotton at Mohenjo-Daro in the Indus River valley dating from 3000 B.C. In the Americas, cotton fabrics dating from 3000–2000 B.C. have been recovered from archaeological sites at the Tehuacán Valley in Mexico. Obviously the creation of *Gossypium hirsutum* and *Gossypium bardadense* took place in the distant past—so distant, in fact, that human assistance through transoceanic contact between the Old World and the Americas

seems very unlikely. Instead, natural means seem to have produced the cultivated New World cottons. Scholars developed two possibilities for how this process occurred. The first theory proposes that cultivated Old World cottons once grew in the Americas but became extinct sometime before 1492; no archaeological evidence supports this idea. The second theory suggests that unopened Old World cotton bolls were capable of floating across the oceans, and that prolonged exposure to salt water would not always destroy the seeds' ability to germinate successfully. Either scenario brings Old World cottons into contact with wild New World cottons without depending on human travelers to carry the seeds.

So the mere appearance of the hybridized New World cottons does not provide evidence for pre-Columbian contacts between the Americas and the Old World. But two anomalies in the distribution of cultivated cottons still remain. It appears that cultivated New World cottons may have reached the Cape Verde Islands off West Africa before 1492. Unfortunately, the vaguely documented post-Columbian introduction of various cultivated plants from the Americas confuses this issue and no definite conclusions have yet been reached. New World domestic cottons also grew on the Marquesas Islands of Polynesia before Christian missionaries tried to introduce an organized cotton industry during the nineteenth century. The first European visits to the Marquesas began with Alvaro de Mendaña de Nehras's discovery of those islands in 1595, but no further European visits occurred until Captain James Cook's in 1774. It is unlikely that either of these expeditions or subsequent European visitors would have introduced the cultivated New World cottons. An alternate and somewhat tentative explanation of the presence of New World cotton on the Marquesas is that **Polynesian-American contacts** took place during the pre-Columbian era. Otherwise, contrary to what some **diffusionist** writers maintain, the distribution of cultivated cottons does not support the various theories of pre-Columbian contacts between the Americas and the Old World.

Bibliography: Baker, Herbert G., *Plants and Civilization*, 2nd ed., 1970; Fingerhut, Eugene R., *Who First Discovered America? A Critique of Pre-Columbian Voyages*, 1984; Stephens, S. G., "Some Problems of Interpreting Transoceanic Dispersal of the New World Cottons," in *Man across the Sea: Problems of Pre-Columbian Contacts*, edited by Carroll L. Riley, et al., 1971.

Cousin, Voyage of Jean (1488)

This French sea captain from Dieppe in Normandy supposedly discovered South America some four years before Christopher Columbus's historic first voyage.

The city of Dieppe was the primary site of French seafaring during the fifteenth century. Its sailors served variously as merchants, privateers, and regular navy. Jean Cousin was one such merchant and privateer who engaged in trade along the coast of West Africa, trade that was also an illegal encroachment on the rights and territories of Portugal. According to surviving accounts, Cousin departed Dieppe for Africa in a single vessel. Instead of taking the usual route by way of the Canary Islands, he struck for the high seas in the company of Vincent Pinçon. Some writers claim that Pinçon was Vicente Yáñez Pinzon, the future companion of Columbus. Ocean currents and the trade winds carried Cousin's ship westward for two months before the Frenchmen finally reached land. They found flowing into the sea a river of such vast proportions that it was certain they had reached no mere island. Those who believe Cousin's voyage actually took place identify this great river as the Amazon. Naming the river Maragnon, Cousin

took careful note of its position, gathered specimens of the unfamiliar birds and plants, and sailed east for the African coast.

Trouble occurred after the French landed on Africa. During a trading session with the natives, Vincent Pinçon provoked a quarrel and seized their goods. In the fighting, Cousin could save his men only by firing on the natives. Trade came to an abrupt end, and the French had to return home in 1489 with part of their cargo lost. The Dieppe city council was outraged because Pinçon jeopardized their profitable African trade. They banished him and forbade his employment on any French ship. Meanwhile Cousin's discovery of the Maragnon was virtually ignored in the face of this threat to the lucrative African trade.

Three years later Christopher Columbus made his monumental voyage of 1492, permanently revealing the existence of the Americas to the rest of the world. In 1500, the Portuguese flotilla of Pedro Cabral accidentally disclosed the existence of Brazil while en route to India. With these two voyages, Cousin's neglected western discovery, if it occurred at all, became moot.

The oldest surviving account of Cousin's discovery appears in David Asseline's *Antiquitez et chroniques* published in 1688. Admiralty papers and manuscripts from the archives of Dieppe formed the basis of this work. It is impossible to check the authenticity of Asseline's assertions; an English force destroyed Dieppe, including its archives, in 1694. Jean-Antoine Samson Desmarquets in his *Mémoires chronologiques pour servir à l'histoire de Dieppe* of 1785 also related the Cousin story but did not identify his sources. Unfortunately, both books are separated by 200 to 300 years from the event they describe. No materials contemporary to Cousin's voyage survive to corroborate its occurrence. Certainly the voyage had no discernible impact on the great Age of Discovery unless it is accepted that Cousin's Vincent Pinçon was also Columbus's Vicente Yáñez Pinzon. If so, Vicente Pinzon and his brother led Columbus to the Americas rather than the other way around. The silence of the Pinzons on this aspect of their priority over Columbus, let alone that of Cousin and others from Dieppe, render the actuality of Cousin's discovery of South America highly doubtful.

Bibliography: Gambier, James William, "The True Discovery of America," *Fortnightly Review* 61 (no. 325, 1894): 49–64.

Cretans in Ancient America

Also known as Minoans, this ancient seafaring people became a candidate for consideration as pre-Columbian visitors to the Americas only after archaeologists discovered their existence at the beginning of the twentieth century.

Knowledge of the existence of this civilization remained lost to history until Sir Arthur Evans began his famous archaeological excavations in 1900. His discoveries revealed a sophisticated Bronze Age civilization that flourished from about 3000–1200 B.C. It was located on the island of Crete in the Mediterranean Sea and based its economic foundations on overseas trading. Since these predecessors of the **Phoenicians** were such good seafarers, many popular writers speculate that they reached the Americas in their travels, possibly in partnership with the Egyptians. The **diffusionist** writers Pierre Honoré's *In Quest of the White God* (1963), Constance Irwin's *Fair Gods and Stone Faces* (1963), Cyrus Gordon's *Before Columbus* (1971), and James Bailey's *The God-Kings and the Titans* (1973) all include the Cretans among the Old World peoples visiting the Americas. But many details are lacking; the who, when, where, and why of the Cretans making such long voyages is never discussed. Professional archaeologists and ancient historians consider the evidence cited by supporters to be extremely weak to nonexistent.

Bibliography: Davies, Nigel, *Voyagers to the New World,* 1979.

Cronus and the Isle of Cronus, Legend of

According to legend, Zeus, the victorious king of the Greek gods, assigned an island as the place of exile for his defeated father Cronus, the Titan. Since this island lay to the west of the British Isles, the prominent scholar of North Atlantic mythology Geoffrey Ashe suggests that the legend may represent a vague ancient awareness of the existence of North America.

About A.D. 75 the Roman Plutarch wrote a short book called *The Face in the Orb of the Moon;* it contained a description of a pilgrimage that left Britain every 30 years and sailed through the northern seas to study and meditate at the island of Cronus. The island was a beautiful place with a holy cave in which Cronus lay sleeping, attended by a mysterious court, while birds brought him ambrosia for food. While he slept, Cronus experienced dreams that served as oracles. The pilgrims came to the island to study such things as philosophy and astronomy.

Ashe's contention is that while the literal island of Cronus is a myth, the legend reflects a vague awareness of the North Atlantic's true geography. The region around the Gulf of St. Lawrence corresponds reasonably well to the area of the island of Cronus. Ashe also suggests that Plutarch's story was based on an unknown Celtic god and that, in typical Greek and Roman fashion, Plutarch substituted Cronus's name for that of the god. Other scholars are skeptical of Ashe's theory. Classical scholar J. V. Luce is of the opinion that speculations about western lands beyond the Atlantic Ocean were very common in the ancient world. But he believes they were just that—speculations—and not based on geographical knowledge derived from actual voyages.

Bibliography: Ashe, Geoffrey, "An Analysis of the Legends," in *The Quest for America*, edited by Geoffrey Ashe, 15–52, 1971; Graves, Robert, *The Greek Myths*, 2 vols., 1955; Luce, J. V., "Ancient Explorers," in *The Quest for America*, edited by Geoffrey Ashe, 53–95, 1971.

Curach

Also spelled currach or curragh, this Irish sailing vessel used skins or hides as its outer covering. Small rowing curachs are still in use in modern Ireland, but larger curachs equipped with sails and capable of long-distance voyages on the high seas of the stormy North Atlantic flourished between 500 and 800. The Irish who settled on **Iceland** and **St. Brendan,** and the alleged settlers of **Great Ireland,** would have used large sailing curachs in their travels.

The skin-covered curach dates back to prehistoric times in northern Europe. Like its analogues, the kayak and umiak of the **Eskimos,** the curach is ideally suited for sailing in stormy Arctic waters. Reports that curachs are fragile and clumsy to maneuver are not true. They are flexible, light, highly buoyant, and fully capable of weathering a gale on the open seas. The sailing curach of the early medieval era was relatively large, having a keel, ribs, and a wicker hull covered by skins. A mast with square-rigged sails could be mounted on the keel, and some sort of rudder was used for steering. Unfortunately, the perishable nature of the materials used means that no physical remains survive from the early Middle Ages, and historians are forced to rely on patchy descriptions from written records. St. Brendan made his legendary voyages in a curach capable of carrying 17 people with supplies for 40 days. Similar curachs would have carried the **Irish monks** and their sheep to the Faeroe Islands and Iceland.

The heyday of the sailing curach lasted from 500–800 and corresponded with the great age of Irish monasticism. Both eras ended with the onset of Viking raids on Ireland and the Norse occupation of the Faeroes and Iceland during the eighth century. The Irish of the curach era were great sailors capable of navigating the high seas using the stars and other signs such as the flight paths of birds. Sailing curachs were the ships of the heroes of the *immrama* stories as well as of the monks of Iceland and the Faeroes. Whether or not such curachs actually carried either St. Brendan or the monks of Great Ireland to America, experts feel that sailing curachs could have reached America just as easily as the long ships and knorrs of **Leif Ericsson** and the Norse. Tim Severin, an imitator of **Thor Heyerdahl's** methods, showed just how seaworthy curachs were by recreating Brendan's voyage in 1977.

Bibliography: Marcus, G. J., *The Conquest of the North Atlantic*, 1981.

St. Brendan in his curach atop a giant fish.

Americans degenerated into the Stone Age hunter/gatherer peoples found by European explorers and settlers of the post-1500 era.

Archaeology had only gradually emerged as a professional scholarly discipline in the late nineteenth century. Its ranks included many amateurs, some working alone and others in groups. Davenport, Iowa, with a population of 30,000 in 1871, boasted one such group of amateur scientists—the Davenport Academy, a body founded in 1867 and dominated by white Anglo-Saxons of the community. However, a substantial population of Germans also lived in Davenport. Jacob Gass (1842–1924), pastor of the First Lutheran Church, was an amateur archaeologist. In 1874 Gass got very lucky. Digging in mounds located on the Cook farm at the edge of Davenport, he discovered some very unique sculpted stone pipes and copper axe heads with their cloth covers still partially preserved. His find was quite rare and, as a result, in 1876 he was invited to join the Davenport Academy even though he was rather unpopular. Many people found Gass to be arrogant, dishonest, and a braggart. They also probably envied his lucky discovery of significant Mound Builder artifacts.

A conspiracy to humiliate Gass developed among certain members of the Davenport Academy. As a joke they obtained three roofing slates, possibly procured from the local bordello. On them they scratched a zodiac scene, a cremation scene with writing, and a hunting scene to simulate Mound Builder artifacts. If genuine, these artifacts would have shown that the ancient Mound Builders were literate and so ancient that they would have been contemporaries with the mastodons. The group deposited the fake tablets in an unexcavated portion of a mound that Gass was exploring. In January 1877, Gass discovered the fraudulent tablets. The digging site showed clear signs of recent disturbance, the drawings were crude, and the tablets themselves showed obvious signs

Davenport Tablets and Conspiracy

Archaeological artifacts found in January 1877 in the vicinity of Davenport, Iowa, these tablets supposedly contain symbols and a picture of a mastodon or elephant. They allegedly show the high civilization of the **Mound Builder** culture.

Late–nineteenth-century American archaeologists engaged in a heated debate over the relationship between the builders of the myriad mounds dotting the eastern United States and the historic Native Americans or Indians. Many people asserted that the two groups were separate peoples or races. Others believed the Mound Builders were an extinct white race destroyed by the Red Indians and that, without the ability to sustain the higher culture, the remaining Native of their roofing-slate origin; nevertheless, Gass and others readily accepted them as authentic. Having succeeded only too well, the pranksters planted a crude limestone tablet depicting a Mound Builder in a manner that definitely indicated tampering, and even led Gass to the right place and helped him find it—but to no avail. To their consternation, Gass's reputation as an archaeologist had grown so great that the limestone tablet was also accepted as genuine. Increasingly anxious to end the hoax, the pranksters made one last attempt by planting five fake tablets in a mound in nearby Cleona Township. Significantly, this time Gass and the Davenport Academy quietly suppressed these unmistakable fakes.

The exact nature and extent of the conspiracy may never be known. According to Marshall McKusick, the historian of this affair, Gass and other members of the Davenport Academy initially thought the slate and limestone tablets were genuine. They wrote up their discoveries in the academy's *Proceedings* and sent their finds to the Smithsonian Institution for further study. After an initially favorable reception, the experts at the Smithsonian began to express doubts. In 1883 one Smithsonian scholar, Henry Henshaw, wrote a report that branded the tablets as fakes, using very good archaeological methods to reach his conclusions. But the tone of Henshaw's report was so disparaging that Charles Putnam (1825–1887), president of the Davenport Academy, took offense. Putnam, a lawyer, accused the Smithsonian of engaging in a conspiracy to suppress all amateur scientific academies and defended the authenticity of the tablets by using the courtroom standard of reasonable doubt. Such techniques were quite successful in staving off the skeptics for a while, especially since Putnam had tapped into a nationwide reservoir of amateur scientific resentment against the supposed elitism of the Smithsonian scholars.

McKusick contends that even Putnam and Gass soon realized the tablets were fakes, but Putnam wanted to protect the Davenport Academy's reputation by any means—including blackmail, intimidation, and outright expulsion of dissidents. Meanwhile Gass, a man of elastic ethics, used his fame to enrich himself by selling his own fake artifacts. Just as a conspiracy created the fake tablets, another developed to protect their supposed genuineness. A fierce debate over their authenticity raged in such prestigious journals as *Science, Nature,* and *American Antiquarian.* Ultimately the scholarly findings of the Smithsonian Institution's professional staff prevailed over the tablets' supporters when the great archaeologist Cyrus Thomas published his mammoth study on the Mound Builders as the *Twelfth Annual Report of the United States Bureau of Ethnology* in 1894. It swept away the entire basis for the speculative mania surrounding the Mound Builders, including the Davenport tablets. But the nasty furor over the tablets made professionals wary about directly confronting hoaxes for many decades afterward.

Oddly enough, the Davenport tablets reappeared in archaeological controversies in 1976 when epigrapher **Barry Fell** cited them as genuine artifacts in his best-selling *America B.C.* According to Fell, the tablets were evidence for the existence of a combined **Egyptian,** Libyan-**Phoenician,** and Iberian-Phoenician colony in Iowa about 800 B.C. He claims that the cremation tablet is inscribed with writing from all three groups. It is strange that Fell chose to call the Davenport tablets authentic. Officials of the Putnam Museum, the successor to the Davenport Academy, warned him about the tablets' fraudulence. Fell also studiously ignored the first-rate debunking scholarship of Marshall McKusick regarding the background of the tablets, and he is unfortunately not alone. Although frequently used as evidence for pre-Columbian visits to the Americas, the Davenport tablets are fakes, pure and simple, and cannot be used to prove any of Fell's theories.

Bibliography: McKusick, Marshall, *The Davenport Conspiracy*, 1970; McKusick, Marshall, *The Davenport Conspiracy Revisited*, 1991; Williams, Stephen, *Fantastic Archaeology: The Wild Side of North American Prehistory*, 1991.

Day, Letter of John (ca. late 1497)

This mysterious letter is a report made to a Spanish admiral concerning John Cabot's voyage to North America in 1497 as well as other earlier western voyages by sailors of Bristol who supposedly discovered the legendary **Island of Brazil,** possibly indicating that they had visited the Americas before Columbus (see also **Bristol Voyages**).

Dr. Louis-André Vigneras discovered the John Day letter in the archive of Simancas, Spain, in 1955. It was written by Englishman John Day (who at other times in his life used the name Hugh Say) to the Almirante Mayor (great admiral), which most scholars think refers to Christopher Columbus. The letter indicates that Day was working for the admiral and familiar with Atlantic seafaring and geographical lore. Although the writer did not date the letter, internal evidence indicates it was written in late December 1497 or January 1498. In it Day reported that he had failed to locate a copy of the *Inventio fortunata,* a geographical treatise much discussed in the fifteenth and sixteenth centuries. He did acquire a copy of Marco Polo's book, and also included an account of John Cabot's recent discoveries. Day seemed to think Cabot may have discovered the island of the **Seven Cities** (see also **Antillia**) or Brazil.

John Day's letter is certainly authentic, and he or Hugh Say was a real person. Day was an adventuresome merchant of London with both a good education and useful social connections in the late fifteenth century's world of international trade. But his hard work and intrepid spirit failed to bring him wealth or fame; he died on the edge of poverty in late 1517 or early 1518. Although he was not a success, Day was certainly in a good position to know what he was talking about in his letter to the Spanish admiral. Unfortunately, the wording of Day's letter is not always clear, making it impossible to base a definitive interpretation on it.

The letter's importance lies in its revelations about the involvement of merchants of Bristol in voyages to the western Atlantic prior to the arrival of John Cabot. Some historians go so far as to claim that the Bristol voyages successfully reached America well before Columbus, but they disagree on the details. Professor D. B. Quinn suggests that fishermen of Bristol secretly visited the Grand Banks of Newfoundland as early as 1481. In contrast, Professor A. A. Ruddock believes they found the Grand Banks prior to 1480 but lost contact and were unable to reestablish it until Cabot's voyage of 1497.

Bibliography: Quinn, David Beers, "John Day and Columbus," *Geographical Journal* 133 (June 1967): 205–209; Ruddock, Alwyn A., "John Day of Bristol and the English Voyages across the Atlantic before 1497," *Geographical Journal* 132 (June 1966): 225–233; Vigneras, Louis-André, "The Cape Breton Landfall: 1494 or 1497," *Canadian Historical Review* 38 (1957): 219–229.

De Costa, Benjamin Franklin (1831–1904)

This American Episcopal clergyman and social reformer also established a reputation as the leading historian of pre-Columbian voyages to the Americas in the nineteenth century.

Descended from Huguenots with Portuguese ancestry, De Costa was born in Charleston, Massachusetts, on 10 July 1831. Graduating from the Biblical Institute of Concord, New Hampshire, in 1856, he entered the ministry in 1857. He soon developed an avid interest in historical research that resulted in the publication of *The Pre-Columbian Discovery of America by the Northmen* (1868), a collection of Norse sagas in English that was not superseded until 1890. Other publications followed, mostly 8 to 28 pages in length, covering historical explorers such as Verrazano and Henry Hudson as well as the problematical medieval Welsh and Irish visitors to America. The College of William and Mary recognized his scholarship in 1881 by conferring the honorary degree of D.D. on him. From 1882–1883 De Costa edited the *Magazine of American History*. He also wrote two chapters for Justin Winsor's *Narrative and Critical History of America*: "Norumbega and Its English Explorers" in volume 3 (1885) and "Jacques Cartier and His Successors" in volume 4 (1885). De Costa privately published a bibliography of his own writings in 1899 entitled *The Titles of 55 Separately Printed Works, with Some Other Matters, Covering a Half-Century.*

Twentieth-century historians characterize De Costa's work as showing "an amiable weakness for rescuing characters and events from the neglect or disparagement of historians." In the late nineteenth century, however, his contemporaries considered him one of the foremost experts on pre-Columbian voyages and the Age of Discovery in the New World. Largely forgotten in the twentieth century, those historians who know of De Costa respect his vast learning, although they also consider him overly credulous.

Bibliography: *Dictionary of American Biography*, 22 vols., 1927–1938; *National Cyclopedia of American Biography*, 62 vols., vol. 22: 1892–1984.

Dee, John
(1527–1608)

This Elizabethan scholar made important contributions to antiquarian studies, geography, and mathematics. A staunch imperialist, he justified British overseas expansion on the basis of legends of the great northern empires of the British kings Arthur and Malgo and the voyages of the Welsh **prince Madoc.**

John Dee was born in London, the son of a minor official in the court of Henry VIII, although both parents originally came from Radnorshire, Wales. The young Dee went to St. John's College, Cambridge, in 1543. Working very hard (he claimed to study 18 hours a day), Dee was rewarded with a fellowship in 1547 at Henry VIII's newly founded Trinity College. In 1548 he studied geography and mathematics at Louvain University in what is now Belgium. Moving to Paris in 1550 to lecture on mathematics, Dee's academic abilities were becoming widely recognized by other scholars throughout Europe. He returned to England in 1551, and soon entered the service of John Dudley, the duke of Northumberland, as a tutor. Dee survived Northumberland's fall from power at the beginning of the reign of Queen Mary, but was arrested in 1555 on the charge of attempting to enchant the queen. The reputation as a sorcerer stuck to Dee for the rest of his career, and in 1583 a fearful mob sacked his house at Mortlake and burned its great library.

Mary's successor Elizabeth and her councillors valued Dee's expertise, particularly on geographical matters. Dee also advised the great sailors Martin Frobisher, Sir Humphrey Gilbert, and Sir Francis Drake in planning their voyages to Cathay, raids against Spain, and the establishment of American colonies. In 1577 he wrote the multivolume *General and Rare Memorials Pertayning to the Perfect Arte of Navigation.* The first volume argued for the establishment of a royal navy of 60 ships to protect the embryonic British empire. A fourth volume, entitled *Great Volume of Famous and Rich Discoveries,* appeared later in the same year and discussed the possibility of using a northeast passage to reach Cathay. The *Great Volume* also included a historical justification for a British empire in the North Atlantic based on the legendary empire of King Arthur and the lesser-known British king Malgo. The book used the supposed voyages of the **Zeno brothers** during the fourteenth century for the same purpose. All of these shadowy events predated Columbus's voyage of 1492, which supplied the primary basis for Spain's claims to its American empire.

Dee provided further evidence for the primacy of English claims to the east coast of North America in two unpublished treatises written in 1578. These treatises, which have been lost, added to the arguments in favor of Sir Humphrey Gilbert's plan for raids on Spanish America and the establishment of colonies that would serve as bases for those raids. King Arthur's northern empire formed the cornerstone of Dee's arguments justifying British expansion up to 1580. He not only insisted that Arthur was a historical figure, despite the doubts expressed by some Renaissance historians such as Polydore Vergil, he also greatly expanded the size of Arthur's empire to include **Iceland, Greenland,** and possibly parts of North America.

Dee's basic argument shifted significantly when he presented Queen Elizabeth I with his "Her Majesty's Title Royal to Many Foreign Countrys, Kingdoms, and Provinces" in 1580. At the top of its list of justifications for a British empire appeared the western voyage of the Welsh prince Madoc in 1170 or 1171. Although King Arthur's empire, the voyages of the Zenos, and other earlier claims were still cited, Madoc now took precedence. Using the Madoc legend presented a direct challenge to Spain's colonies, because Madoc supposedly visited the Florida area and even Mexico. As presented by Dee, Madoc's voyage provided such strong justification for English imperialism that, from 1580 onward, it superseded the actual historic voyages of John and Sebastian Cabot in 1497 as the foundation of England's claims. It is not certain how or when Dee came across the story of Madoc's voyages. A plausible source is a manuscript history of Wales completed in 1559 by Welsh antiquary and geographer **Humphrey Llwyd.** After Llwyd's death in 1568, his manuscript came into the possession of Sir Henry Sidney, president of the Council in the Marches of Wales. Sidney's chaplain, **David Powel,** was a friend of Dee's, and made a copy of the manuscript for him. Powel himself added to Llwyd's manuscript and published it in 1584 as *The Historie of Cambria,* which included the Madoc legend.

Dee's initial connection of Madoc with the discovery of America took place earlier in 1577 as a result of correspondence with the great Flemish cartographer Gerard Mercator. In his letter, Mercator related stories of some long-lost descendants of Arthur's Britons visiting Norway hundreds of years after his death. Dee found this tale confusing and concluded that Mercator's information was erroneous. But if the descendants of Madoc's voyagers were substituted, the story made better chronological sense to Dee. In this way, Welshman John Dee moved another Welshman, Madoc, ahead of the Briton king Arthur as a justification for a British empire.

Ever the polymath, Dee lost interest in imperialism in 1583. Instead his interest turned to seeking ways to talk with angels. From 1583 to 1589 he traveled through

Europe in an effort to learn that heavenly language. During that time he visited the occultist Holy Roman Emperor Rudolph II. After Dee returned to England, he spent the last 20 years of his life in relative obscurity.

Bibliography: French, Peter, *John Dee: The World of an Elizabethan Magus,* 1972; Williams, Gwyn A., *Madoc: The Making of a Myth,* 1979.

Diffusionism

This anthropological concept seeks to explain cultural change on the basis of unilateral or reciprocal borrowing among different cultural groups that occurs as a result of trade, migration, or conquest. All theories that explain the rise of higher civilizations and their various cultural traits primarily on the basis of supposed contacts with the Old World are inherently diffusionist.

Anthropologists generally accept the phenomenon of diffusion as a partial explanation for cultural change. Uncounted historical and contemporary examples of one society

Hyperdiffusionists see Greek influences in the crested helmets of Hawaiian chiefs.

exchanging cultural traits with another are cited as evidence for diffusion. Such cultural exchanges have actually accelerated in the modern world. In the era of prehistory, however, the existence and degree of cultural diffusion become conjectural and controversial.

Traditional Judeo-Christian beliefs in a single creation (monogenesis) necessitated the concept that humanity and culture spread from one place of origin throughout the earth. The discovery of the Americas in 1492 confronted early–sixteenth-century Europeans with the realization that radically different societies of Native Americans existed in seeming isolation from the Old World. To explain this situation, some people turned to concepts of **multiple creation** (or polygenesis) and/or **parallel or independent evolution.** By the middle of the nineteenth century, Charles Darwin's evolutionary theories provided a greater scientific basis for theories of parallel evolution and independent invention of cultural traits, and dominated the emerging discipline of anthropology.

By the beginning of the twentieth century, a strong reaction developed against the evolutionary school's tendency to seek explanations in the formulation of general laws of human behavior (nomothetic principles). Franz Boas (1858–1942) represented one alternative to nomotheticism: cultural relativism or historical particularism, which basically contends that every society is unique and not subject to general laws of cultural development. Convergent evolution provided a corollary to Boas's ideas by suggesting that different societies might follow dissimilar paths of development but still end up with relatively similar cultures.

Diffusionism, particularly extreme or hyperdiffusionism, was another alternative to nomothetic theories of cultural evolution. In Scandinavia Jacob Worsaae and Oscar Montelius first developed moderate diffusionist ideas during the late nineteenth century. But they did not go far enough for some. Hyperdiffusionists denied that parallel evolution or independent invention took place to any great extent throughout prehistory. They claimed humans were remarkably uninventive and that history never repeated itself. Ironically the two main schools of hyperdiffusionist thought in England and Germany developed largely independent of each other during the early twentieth century. The more influential and scholarly of the two, the German school of hyperdiffusionism used the concept of *kulturkreise* (culture circles) to explain the spread of various complexes of cultural traits. Fritz Graebner was its leading exponent, particularly through his book *Die Methode der Ethnologie* (Method of ethnology) (1911), which supplied criteria for tracing cultural diffusion.

W. H. R. Rivers founded the less influential British school; he advocated a relatively moderate diffusionism as part of the general scholarly reaction against the evolutionists' nomotheticism. His pupil W. J. Perry and anatomist Grafton Elliot Smith took the diffusionist theory to its ultimate extreme by tracing all higher civilizations throughout the world back to one source: ancient Egypt. During the early twentieth century these two men wrote numerous books and articles postulating the influence of ancient **Egyptian** culture on various societies. While such hyperdiffusionist theories never dominated anthropological and archaeological thinking in the early twentieth century, moderate diffusionism did. Under these circumstances, it is not surprising that various fringe theories postulating visits to the New World by one or another group from the Old World (e.g., the **Ten Lost Tribes of Israel, Mongols**) or the lost continents of **Atlantis** or **Mu** found support in the rise of diffusionist concepts. After all, Smith's theory was simply a somewhat more restrained version of **Augustus Le Plongeon's** theories about Mayan-Egyptian contacts.

The development of radiocarbon dating after 1946 and its calibration using correlations with tree-ring datings (dendrochronology) during the 1960s completely undermined both the moderate and hyperdiffusionist reconstructions of prehistory. These techniques revealed that cultures once thought to be the beneficiaries of diffusion from ancient Egypt were actually as old or older than the oldest Egyptians. Archaeological thinking was revolutionized. The independent invention of various cultural traits obviously took place far more frequently than diffusionists had supposed. At the same time, archaeologists and anthropologists no longer gave credence to the parallel evolutionists' scheme of uniform and rigid stages for all cultural change. They replaced such thinking with the idea of convergent evolution, in which cultural changes occurred in many different ways. Still, diffusion was not totally rejected as an agent of cultural change. In 1940, even before the advent of radiocarbon dating, anthropologist A. L. Kroeber developed the subtle concept of stimulus diffusion. Stimulus diffusion goes beyond the old-style diffusionism's concentration on merely the direct borrowing and exchange of cultural traits among societies. Instead it investigates how contacts between cultures could engender or stimulate the realization of new possibilities, for example, Sequoyah's development of a unique alphabet for the Cherokee instead of simply borrowing the Roman alphabet of the European-Americans. As a result of these new developments in archaeology and anthropology, the chronology of prehistory has a firmer basis, providing a more reliable framework for interpretation. Another consequence of these changes was to render pointless the rancorous debate between evolutionists and diffusionists that dominated the late nineteenth and early twentieth centuries.

71

Bibliography: Elkin, A. P., and N. W. G. MacIntosh, eds., *Grafton Elliot Smith: The Man and His Work*, 1974; Harris, Marvin, *The Rise of Anthropological Thought*, 1968; Renfrew, Colin, *Before Civilization: The Radiocarbon Revolution and Prehistoric Europe*, 1973; Rowe, John Howland, "Diffusionism and Archaeology," *American Antiquity* 31 (January 1966): 334–337; Trigger, Bruce G., *A History of Archaeological Thought*, 1990.

Drogio

Sometimes spelled Drogeo or Droceo, this land appears in the **Fisherman of Frislanda's story,** which forms part of the **narrative of the Zeno Voyage.** Drogio was inhabited by a very primitive and cannibalistic tribe. Some writers identify Drogio with Nova Scotia and its natives as some sort of Algonquian tribe. Professional scholars, however, generally reject Drogio's existence since its origin lies in the suspect and almost certainly fraudulent Zeno narrative.

Durán, Fray Diego (1537?–1588)

Spanish missionary and historian of sixteenth-century Mexico, he wrote three surviving works describing the religion and history of preconquest Mexico. Although he was generally a fine ethnohistorian, his sixteenth-century worldview caused him to hypothesize about earlier contacts between the Aztecs and **Hebrews,** and possibly the early Christians, with **St. Thomas the Apostle** being the source of the myths about **Quetzalcoatl.**

Durán was born in Seville into a family of modest social standing. His family moved to Mexico when he was a young child and settled at Texcoco, where the young Durán learned the major native language of Nahuatl. His family moved to Mexico City when he was about 10 or 12 years old. He may have attended one of its many schools operated by religious orders. In 1556 the

19-year-old Durán became a novice of the Dominican order. He completed his religious training, and in 1561 began missionary work among the natives of Mexico, particularly those living in the Marquesado, a region corresponding to the present-day state of Morelos.

Durán quickly proved to be an astute observer and a ready student of the Aztecs' ancient beliefs, customs, and history. It became apparent to him that Christianity was often a veneer covering what he considered was the heathenism of the preconquest era. By the mid-1570s, Durán became convinced that he needed to organize and write down the vast amount of information he had accumulated on aboriginal religion and preconquest history. He hoped his work would aid other priests and missionaries to minister more effectively to the Native Americans. He also realized that their varied history and customs were of great interest to readers in Spain.

Durán completed *The Book of Gods and Rites*, his first manuscript, between 1576 and 1579, followed by *The Ancient Calendar* in 1579. Between 1580 and 1581 Durán composed his great *Historia de las Indias de Nueva España y islas de Tierra Firme* (History of the Indies of New Spain and the islands of the Terra Firma), his third surviving work. Throughout these works, Durán puzzled over supposed similarities between Aztec and Hebrew customs and rites such as food prohibitions and Sabbath-keeping. He noted that the same observation applied to many Christian and Aztec beliefs and ceremonies. Paralleling European Catholics, the Aztecs observed a season analogous to Lent, venerated holy relics, and staged religious dramas reminiscent of the Corpus Christi plays. Certain figures in Aztec mythology also seemed to correspond to persons from Hebrew or Christian history. In particular, Durán identified Quetzalcoatl/Topiltzin as simply the ancient Aztec name for St.

Thomas. During the sixteenth century, that apostle was widely believed to have visited the Americas during the course of his missionary work. Initially Durán merely speculated that such contacts were possible, but speculation soon evolved into a firm belief that such contacts had occurred between the Americas and the ancient Hebrews and early Christians. Needless to say, Durán did not originate these pre-Columbian contact theories, as they already had a wide circulation in the sixteenth century.

Durán's works were not published until the mid-nineteenth century or later. Unfortunately, he completed them at a time when Spanish officials were not interested in having the deficiencies of their missionary program revealed. Many modern scholars consider his work to be the best ethnohistory of Mexico written during the sixteenth century, superior even to **Bernardino de Sahagún's** superb writings, despite Durán's questionable ideas about pre-Columbian Hebrew and Christian contacts with the Americas.

Bibliography: Durán, Diego, *The Aztecs: The History of the Indies of New Spain*, translated by Doris Heyden and Fernando Horcasitas, 1964; Durán, Diego, *Book of the Gods and Rites and the Ancient Calendar*, translated by Fernando Horcasitas and Doris Heyden, 1971.

E

Easter Island

Also called Ilsa de Pascua, this isolated Polynesian island is located almost 2,000 miles from the coast of South America and 1,200 miles from the nearest inhabited island. Easter Island is best known for its mysterious *moai*, the great carved stone heads that stand and lie scattered across its landscape.

Easter Island is about 100 square miles in area with a population of 2,000, and belongs to Chile. Polynesian peoples were the first to settle there sometime between 300 and 500. Jacob Roggeveen of Holland in 1722 was the first European to visit. According to **Thor Heyerdahl's** theory, which he first published as *Aku Aku: The Secret of Easter Island* in 1958, two races inhabited Easter Island—the long ears and the short ears. The long ears migrated from

the Lake Titicaca area of Bolivia and were part of the mysterious Tiahuanaco culture. They formed the social and political elite of the island, and the *moai* were made in their image. Eventually their harsh oppressions of the short ears precipitated a successful social revolution resulting in the destruction of the long ears and the overthrow of their hated *moai*. Heyerdahl cites supposed similarities between the monumental and sacred architectures of Easter Island and Tiahuanaco, along with linguistic parallels, as evidence for his theory that Easter Island was a colony of ancient South America. He even suggests that the Easter Islanders developed a form of writing.

In the world of Easter Island studies, Heyerdahl's theory is actually fairly tame, even if other professional anthropologists do not find it convincing. Some people consider Easter Island to be a surviving outcrop of the lost continent of **Mu** or **Lemuria**. The mysterious *moai* are relics of the ancient Lemurian religion and bear witness to the existence of an ancient supertechnology. Eric Van Daniken considers Easter Island to be an abandoned space base built by extraterrestrial visitors. These alien astronauts erected the massive *moai* using their advanced technology. Archaeological evidence, needless to say, does not support either theory, especially since the remains of half-finished *moai* give archaeologists a clear indication of how the natives carved them out of basalt and then moved them to their sites.

Archaeological and linguistic evidence does not bear out Heyerdahl's theory either. The language of the Easter Islanders is closely related to the Marquesan dialect of the Polynesian language, a strong indication that they came from the Marquesas Islands and not Tiahuanaco. In addition, the culture and artifacts of Easter Island show strong parallels with other parts of Polynesia. On the other hand, most scholars consider the supposed similarities between Easter Island

and South American architecture and monuments to be superficial, insignificant, and coincidental. Anthropological research shows that Easter Island was originally divided into many small tribes who incessantly warred with one another and practiced cannibalism on enemy prisoners. The *moai* were erected as containers for the spirits of dead chiefs and worshipped by the survivors. Victorious tribes threw down the *moai* of the vanquished. Easter Islanders built no new *moai* after 1722, although they continued to push over those that remained standing. When Christian missionaries arrived in 1866, none of the *moai* remained upright. Easter Island's writing, like its Christianity, was not a native invention; it was introduced by Europeans. This contention is borne out by the lack of any writing samples from before 1864. Easter Island and its people are obviously part of Polynesia despite their geographical isolation. Most scholars admit the possibility of rare, accidental contacts with South America, but they reject any suggestion that such contacts were culturally significant or sustained. The seafaring technology of Easter Island and the Americas was incapable of sustaining regular two-way communication between places so far apart.

Bibliography: Bahn, Paul, and John Flenley, *Easter Island, Earth Island,* 1992; Davies, Nigel, *Voyagers to the New World,* 1979; Feder, Kenneth L., *Frauds, Myths, and Mysteries: Science and Pseudoscience in Archaeology,* 1990; Heyerdahl, Thor, *Aku Aku: The Secret of Easter Island,* 1958.

Egyptians in Ancient America

The ancient Egyptians are popular and perennial candidates as pre-Columbian visitors to the Americas, and there are numerous theories claiming that such contacts occurred.

Egyptian civilization arose about 3100 B.C. During the Old Kingdom era of 2700–2200 B.C. the Egyptians developed a system of writing and built the famous pyramids. The height of Egyptian political power occurred during the time of the New Kingdom, 1575–1087 B.C. After the passing of this era, Egypt went into a decline during which it was sometimes an independent state and other times conquered by rival empires such as the Assyrians, Persians, and Macedonians. Finally in 30 B.C. the Roman empire absorbed the Ptolemaic kingdom of Egypt. By that time Egypt's history spanned a mind-boggling 3,000 years, fascinating people to this day. When the general public envisions the most ancient of civilizations, they often think of Egypt.

Egyptian civilization has always attracted attention thanks to Cleopatra, the Sphinx, mummies, the pyramids, and hieroglyphic writing. Until Jean-François Champollion (1790–1832) deciphered the hieroglyphics in 1821–1822 using the Rosetta Stone, the Egyptians were a people of mystery. Wild speculation surrounded them because they were commonly thought to be the oldest human culture and perhaps even the inspiration for all other civilizations. Initially, however, the early Spanish chroniclers of the Americas tended to ignore the Egyptians as possible colonizers and civilizers of the New World. Only the Mexican-born Juan Suárez de Peralta (ca. 1536–1591), in his *Noticias históras de Nueva España,* mentioned the possibility of Egyptian settlements in Mexico, along with several others such as the **Ten Lost Tribes** and the **Canaanites.** On the surface, Egyptian civilization appeared to be very similar to those of Mesoamerica, particularly the Maya with their own pyramids and hieroglyphic writing. Closer analysis proving such similarities to be superficial and meaningless does not prevent some people from believing in Egyptian contact.

Even before archaeologists and historians developed their modern time frames and chronologies using carbon-14 dating and dendrochronology, people knew that various ruins such as those at Chichén Itzá were old. Just how old was not certain. **Charles Étienne Brasseur de Bourbourg** and **Augustus Le Plongeon**, two pioneer nineteenth-century archaeologists of the Maya, suggested that the Mayan culture was older than the Egyptian, and that the latter were actually the descendants of Mayan colonists. Their theories never gained much support with other scholars or the general public.

By the late nineteenth century, archaeological research indicated that Egypt was the home of the world's oldest civilization. At the same time, the theory of **diffusionism** exercised more influence on archaeological and anthropological thinking. Diffusionism reached an extreme in the work of English scholar G. Elliot Smith and his disciples, who claimed that Egypt was the first and only civilization to arise independently. All others, including those of the Americas, developed as a result of the diffusion of Egyptian ideas and culture. Smith traced these influences across the globe through such practices as mummification. In his well-known book *Elephants and Ethnologists* (1924), he claimed that some stylized stone carvings of macaws were actually pictures of elephants, which then proved the existence of contacts between the Old World and the Americas.

Skeptical American scholars, particularly Roland B. Dixon of Harvard University in his book *The Building of Cultures* (1929), rallied to attack Smith's theories. Dixon demolished Smith's evidence and convincingly proved that no contacts such as Smith envisioned had occurred. Although Smith's ideas faded in popularity, they did not die. Among others, the popular archaeological writers A. Hyatt and Ruth Verrill continued to accept them into the 1950s.

The idea of Egyptians visiting ancient America revived once more during the early 1970s. **Thor Heyerdahl's** *Ra* expeditions in 1969 and 1970 showed that simple reed boats, similar to those used by the ancient Egyptians, were capable of crossing the Atlantic Ocean from Africa to Barbados. He was soon joined by the Indian writer Rafique Ali Jairazbhoy and his books *Ancient Egyptians and Chinese in America* (1974), *Ancient Egyptians in Middle and South America* (1981), and *Ancient Egypt, Mexico, and the United States* (1992). Despite the breadth indicated by his titles, most of Jairazbhoy's research deals with Egyptian influences in ancient Mexico. According to Jairazbhoy, the Egyptians made contact during the reign of Ramses III (1195–1164 B.C.) and stimulated the growth of the Olmec civilization. The problem is that recent archaeological discoveries push the beginning date of Olmec civilization back to 1400 B.C. Jairazbhoy admits that this new information requires him to make some adjustments in his chronology. Nigel Davies, a historian of ancient Mexico, points out that many of Jairazbhoy's claimed cultural parallels are much too superficial. These include the practice of wrestling, a phallic cult, the use of incense burners, and dwarfs at royal courts. Davies does find one aspect of Jairazbhoy's research intriguing and worthy of further study and consideration—the 21 parallels Jairazbhoy found between Egyptian and Mexican religion. Davies cautions that the validity of these parallels is tentative since they are based on the supposition that sixteenth-century Spanish accounts of Mexican religion can be applied 2,500 years back to the time of the Olmecs, a dubious assumption. The Spanish accounts of Native American religion are useful historical documents, but they also contain significant errors and misunderstandings as well as deliberate distortions. Furthermore, it is inconceivable that the beliefs of Mexican religion remained static over such a long period of time.

Following Jairazbhoy's lead came **Barry Fell** in 1976 with his best-selling *America B.C.*

He too believes that ancient Egyptians reached North America, although he touches only lightly on that topic. Needless to say, evidence for Fell's claims is almost nonexistent.

New theories about Egyptians coming to pre-Columbian America continue to appear despite a lack of valid evidence, representing an idea that seemingly cannot die. As Robert Wauchope, the great anthropologist and archaeologist from Tulane University put it, "The theory of Egypt in America, or vice versa, . . . is here to stay. For some reason difficult to fathom, people become emotionally attached to it and will not believe the most convincing arguments against it that professional scholars can provide."

Bibliography: Davies, Nigel, *Voyagers to the New World,* 1979; Fingerhut, Eugene R., *Who First Discovered America? A Critique of Pre-Columbian Voyages,* 1984; Wauchope, Robert, *Lost Tribes and Sunken Continents,* 1962.

Eric (or Erik) the Red (ca. 950–1001)

Also known as Eirik the Red, Eirik Rauda, or Eirik Thorvaldson, this Norse seaman first pioneered the settlement of **Greenland** and was the father of **Leif Ericsson,** the first Norse to land in North America.

Eric the Red, the son of Thorvald Asvaldson, was born in Norway. As his name implies, he had red hair and a red beard. His family was a particularly quarrelsome lot and overly prone to violence even for the harsh tastes of the medieval Norse. After Thorvald and Eric the Red committed some murders, the resulting blood feud forced them to leave Norway for **Iceland.** By the time they arrived, all the good land had been claimed, and the competition among Icelanders simply to make a living was fierce. Eking out a living on marginal land was difficult for Eric, especially after his father died. He managed to move to richer land, but again became involved in feud and murder. Moving once more, Eric soon engaged in the same activities. Too violent for his fellow Icelanders, they banished him for three years.

Eric the Red used his banishment as an opportunity to explore. Gathering some faithful friends, in 982 he sailed in search of the mysterious western land sighted by Gunnbjorn Ulfsson sometime between 900 and 930. Greenland's barren eastern coast soon came into sight. With plenty of time on his hands, Eric followed the coastline

south. After he passed the southern tip of Greenland at Cape Farewell, he came upon some pleasant meadows as good as any found in Iceland. Eric explored further, spending two winters in Greenland, and gathered the skins of seals and walruses as well as walrus ivory. In 986 he returned to Iceland.

Eric talked about the riches of this western land, which he purposely named Greenland in order to make it sound more attractive. He advocated establishing a Norse colony there, to enthusiastic response. Many Icelanders were land-hungry and therefore eager to settle in the empty but pleasant lands of Greenland. Later that same year, Eric gathered 25 shiploads of colonists and sailed back to Greenland. Adverse winds and storms plagued the expedition, and only 14 ships landed. The rest were either forced to return to Iceland or lost at sea. The new settlement quickly grew and flourished.

Eric the Red settled at Brattahlid and was the unofficial leader of the Greenland Republic. His family converted to Christianity, but not Eric. His wife built a small church near Brattahlid and refused to sleep with her pagan husband. One story claims that it was Eric's son Leif who brought Christianity to Greenland, although more reliable accounts contradict this. By the time Leif Ericsson sailed on his western voyage to North America, Eric the Red was old. Although he was invited and would have liked to join his son, he remained behind. Eric died shortly after Leif's return to Greenland, possibly of a disease raging through the Norse colony that winter.

Bibliography: Jones, Gwyn, *The Norse Atlantic Saga,* 2nd ed., 1986.

Ericsson, Leif
(ca. 980–1020)

Also spelled Erikson, Ericson, or Eiriksson, he was the first Norse explorer to land on North America. His voyage took place in 1001 or later.

Leif was the son of **Eric the Red**, the leader of the Norse settlement on **Greenland.** Various surviving sources agree that Leif was a pleasant and brave man. The two **Vinland Sagas,** the *Greenlanders' Saga* and *Eirik's Saga,* vary significantly on the details of his role in Norse exploration of North America. *Eirik's Saga* credits the accidental discovery of America to Leif rather than to **Bjarni Herjolfsson** as the *Greenlanders' Saga* states. Storms supposedly drove Leif to the new land while he was on his way to bring Christianity to Greenland at the request of King Olaf Tryggvason. Unlike Bjarni, when Leif sighted the unknown land, he went ashore and took samples of the grapes and wild wheat growing there. He did not name the new land **Vinland,** nor did he make any settlement; **Thorfinn Karlsefni** did that on a later expedition. During the nineteenth century, historians considered *Eirik's Saga* the most authentic tale; hence Leif Ericsson was and still is credited with the Norse discovery of America by the general public.

However, by the twentieth century, historians considered the *Greenlanders' Saga* the more historically reliable of the two. It tells a considerably different version of the story. Bjarni Herjolfsson is the one who accidentally discovered Vinland in 986. Some years later, probably in 1001 or later, Leif decided to look for Bjarni's discovery. Buying Bjarni's ship, Leif gathered a crew of 35 and persuaded his father, the aging and reluctant Eric the Red, to lead the expedition. But during the final preparations, Eric's horse threw and injured him, so command fell back on Leif.

Reversing Bjarni's route, Leif and his crew reached a land of rock slabs and glaciers. They named that inhospitable place **Helluland,** which means "slab" or "flatstone land." They landed, but in their eyes it was a worthless place. Sailing south they sighted a second land, flat and wooded, that they named **Markland**, meaning "forest" or "woodland." After landing briefly they put back to sea for two days and spotted more land, a pleasant place of rolling meadows, forests, and rivers and lakes full of salmon. The climate appeared to be mild enough that there was no need for winter fodder. This was important to the Norse of Greenland and **Iceland** since they practiced cattle and sheep husbandry under the very difficult conditions of long, cold winters.

Deciding to winter in the third land, Leif and his crew built shelters (probably the buildings located by archaeologists at **L'Anse aux Meadows** at the northern tip of Newfoundland). Meanwhile the Norse explored the new land. One interesting incident involved Tyrkir, the German member of the crew, who located some wild grapes and got drunk. As a result Leif named the third land Vinland, which means wine land and refers to finding grapes. Leif chose

grapes and timber as the cargo they would carry back to Greenland. The next spring Leif's ship sailed directly back with fair winds all the way. After reaching the Greenland coast, Leif rescued the wrecked ship of Thorir the Norwegian, earning him the title Leif the Lucky. Unfortunately, the shipwrecked crew carried a disease that killed Thorir along with many Greenlanders, possibly including Eric the Red.

Leif Ericsson never returned to Vinland. He loaned his ship for voyages to Vinland first to his brother **Thorvald Ericsson** and then to his other brother **Thorstein Ericsson.** Later he gave Thorfinn Karlsefni permission to use his houses in Vinland but would not sell them. When Leif's sister **Freydis** and her husband Thorvard of Gardar asked to buy the Vinland houses, he again refused but granted them permission to use the buildings. After Freydis returned to Greenland, Leif uncovered the story of the cruel murders she committed in Vinland. He refused to

A painting of Leif Ericsson's discovery of America by Christian Krohg, 1893.

punish her, but he cursed her for her crimes. Apart from these episodes, nothing more is known of Leif's later life. He probably died in Greenland about 1020, leaving a reputation for daring and fairness that the sagas perpetuate to this very day.

Bibliography: Jones, Gwyn, *The Norse Atlantic Saga*, 2nd ed., 1986; Magnusson, Magnus, and Hermann Pálsson, trans. and eds., *The Vinland Sagas: The Norse Discovery of America*, 1966; Phillips, J. R. S., *The Medieval Expansion of Europe*, 1988.

Ericsson, Thorstein

He was the son of **Eric the Red** and the brother of **Leif Ericsson**, according to both the *Greenlanders' Saga* and *Eirik's Saga*.

Thorstein attempted to visit **Vinland** with his wife Gudrid but failed. Foul weather prevented his ship from sailing west all summer. Eventually he gave up and returned to **Greenland,** where he died. His widow later married **Thorfinn Karlsefni,** another would-be colonizer of Vinland. According to the *Greenlanders' Saga*, Thorstein's motive for going to Vinland was to recover the body of his brother **Thorvald Ericsson,** who had been killed by the **skraelings,** or Native Americans. *Eirik's Saga* states that Thorstein wanted to follow up his brother Leif Ericsson's discovery of Vinland, but makes no mention of Thorvald. It implies that Eric the Red may have accompanied him. If so, neither managed to set foot on North America, unless one includes Greenland as part of North America.

Bibliography: Magnusson, Magnus, and Hermann Pálsson, trans. and eds., *The Vinland Sagas: The Norse Discovery of America,* 1966.

Ericsson, Thorvald

Son of **Eric the Red** and brother of **Leif Ericsson,** he was killed by Native Americans, or **skraelings,** while exploring the **Vinland** region of North America.

Many discrepancies exist between the *Greenlanders' Saga* and *Eirik's Saga* concerning the details of the Norse explorations of North America. The role of Thorvald Ericsson is a case in point. According to the *Greenlanders' Saga,* after Leif's return from Vinland, Thorvald wanted to explore it further. Leif accommodated his brother's wish by providing both advice and the loan of his ship. After recruiting a crew of 30, Thorvald sailed for Vinland and found Leif's camp or houses. The Norse wintered there, and in spring sent a boat party west to scout out the new land. All along the way, the explorers observed forested coastlines with white sandy beaches. Although they met no people, they did come across a wooden corncrib. The modern historian Gwyn Jones speculates they traveled down the western coast of Newfoundland. After spending a second winter at Leif's houses, Thorvald journeyed east and then north the next summer. A fearsome storm drove his ship ashore, breaking its keel. The stranded Norse repaired the damage while Thorvald placed the broken keel on a point of land he named Kjalarness, or keelness. Continuing down the coast, Thorvald discovered two fjords. Landing on the promontory between them, he chose the site for his own future settlement. There the Norse encountered nine natives sleeping under their skin boats. They brutally killed all the natives but one, who managed to escape. Looking farther down the fjord, the Norse observed what they thought was a possible settlement. An inexplicable drowsiness came over them and they fell asleep. A mysterious voice wakened the slumbering Norse and warned them to take refuge on their ship. A large number of skin boats approached with the obvious intention of attacking them. Thorvald ordered his men to set up their shields as defensive breastworks along the gunwales of their ship. His strategy was to force the natives to attack a fortified position and thereby discourage them. It worked. The skraelings approached and shot arrows at the Norse but did not press their assault. After a while they withdrew or fled from the area. The Norse were unhurt except for Thorvald. A chance arrow passed between his shield and the gunwale and mortally wounded him. The dying Thorvald asked his men to give him a Christian burial on the land between the two fjords, which was named Krossaness for the crosses placed over his grave. Many scholars feel that the most likely site for this episode is Hamilton Inlet in Labrador. The survivors returned to Leif's houses for the winter. In spring they gathered a cargo of grapes and returned to **Greenland** with the news of Thorvald's death.

In contrast with the above account, *Eirik's Saga* states that Thorvald Ericsson was a member of the expedition led by **Thorfinn Karlsefni.** Karlsefni also sailed north past Kjalarness and up a river or fjord. Instead of meeting Native Americans, Karlsefni and Thorvald encountered a uniped, or one-legged man. The creature attacked them, killed Thorvald with an arrow, and made its escape unharmed. It is quite obvious that *Eirik's Saga* glosses over Thorvald's own expedition and possibly merges it with Karlsefni's later expedition. Most scholars consider the *Greenlanders' Saga* account to be the more complete and reliable of the two. See also **Vinland Sagas.**

Bibliography: Jones, Gwyn, *The Norse Atlantic Saga,* 2nd ed., 1986.

Eskimos

Also known as Inuit, they are the most recent of the Native Americans to cross over the **Bering Land Bridge or Strait** from Asia and are limited to the Arctic region of North America.

Although commonly known as Eskimos, the people of this Arctic cultural and ethnic group call themselves Inuit, which simply means "people" in their language. Anthropologists and prehistorians readily agree that the Eskimos, along with the closely related Aleuts, constitute the last significant prehistoric migration from Asia to North America. Physically and linguistically, Eskimos are quite distinct from the other groups of Native Americans sometimes referred to as American or Red Indians. However, Eskimos are fairly closely related physically, culturally, and linguistically with certain tribal peoples of far-eastern Siberia. Just when the Eskimos' ancestors crossed into North America is a disputed topic among anthropologists. The earliest arrival date for the Eskimos and Aleuts is thought to be about 9000 or 8000 B.C. Unfortunately, many of the probable archaeological sites in **Beringia** lie submerged beneath the Bering Sea as a result of rising sea levels caused by melting of the great glaciers of the last ice age. Other scholars place their arrival as late as 3000–1000 B.C. Starting out in Siberia at this relatively late date, the Eskimos moved across the Arctic in several stages.

The first indisputably Eskimo culture to emerge is called the Arctic Small Tools Tradition; it flourished from 2000–800 B.C. It appears to have developed in Siberia and then spread to America, although some scholars believe it may have arisen in Alaska. The Arctic Small Tools Tradition had, as its name suggests, many tools to aid in hunting and gathering, particularly the bow and arrow. Thanks to their efficient technology, the people of the Arctic Small Tools Tradition spread into the previously uninhabited eastern Arctic of Ellesmere Island and **Greenland.**

About 550 B.C. the Dorset or Paleo-Eskimo culture evolved out of the Arctic Small Tools Tradition, apparently in response to a cooling of the Arctic climate that forced the Eskimos to switch from hunting caribou to seals. Oddly, Dorset culture was not as technologically sophisticated as its predecessor, and even lost the knowledge of the bow and arrow. Still, it spread through the Arctic, and it was probably Dorset remains that **Eric the Red** found when he first settled Greenland. Dorset Paleo-Eskimos occupied the islands of Ellesmere and Baffin and northern Labrador when the Norse first arrived in North America about A.D. 1000. They would have been the **skraelings** the Norse encountered in those regions.

After 1000, the Thule culture of Alaska spread rapidly into the eastern Arctic. The Thule Eskimos, or Neo-Eskimos, had a highly efficient complex of tools including kayaks, umiaks, harpoons, and dog sleds. Hunting whales became possible with these tools, particularly the large skin boats called umiaks that were capable of carrying a number of rowers and harpooners. Whaling greatly increased their food supply, and the Thule population grew rapidly. Their success was possibly the undoing of the neighboring Dorset Paleo-Eskimos, in decline because of increased hunting competition with the Thule. The onset of a new phase of colder weather after 1250 completed the extinction of the Dorsets, while the highly adaptable Thule peoples expanded into northern Labrador. The Thule also moved into the territory of the Norse Greenlanders, who were suffering badly from the deteriorating climatic conditions. Thule Eskimos were the skraelings encountered by the Norse in southern Greenland. Modern Eskimo culture is basically the Thule culture adapted to the renewed appearance of Europeans after 1500.

Bibliography: Fagan, Brian M., *Ancient North America: The Archaeology of a Continent,* 1991; Fagan, Brian M., *The Great Journey: The Peopling of Ancient America,* 1987.

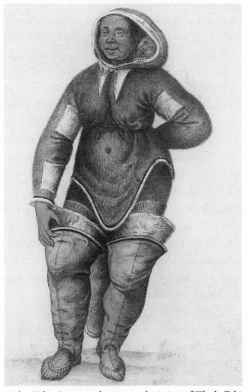
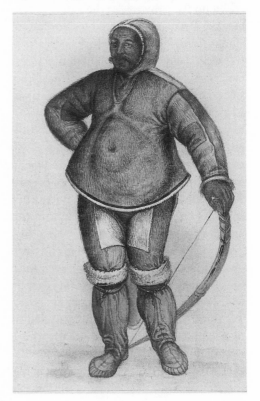

John White's sixteenth-century depiction of Thule Eskimos.

Estotiland

This mysterious island located in the north-western Atlantic is sometimes identified as Newfoundland. Supposedly it was first visited about 1370 by the **Fisherman of Frislanda,** or Orkney islands, who appears in the spurious narrative of **Nicolò and Antonio Zeno.**

The derivation of the name Estotiland is unclear. One theory holds that it was a contraction of the English phrase "East-Out-Land." Another suggests that the name originated in the Latin phrase *esto fidelis usque ad mortem* (I am faithful unto death). Proponents of an early **Irish** discovery of America believe that Estotiland is actually a corruption of Escotiland, for example, Scotland, since *Scotus* was the early medieval term for the Irish. Finally, Estotiland may be a corruption of Estofiland, which means stockfish (codfish) land, a reference to the excellent fishing off the Grand Banks of Newfoundland. By at least the sixteenth century the Portuguese referred to Newfoundland as *terra do bacalhao,* which translates as stockfish land. This explanation for the name Estotiland has even greater plausibility since the first European to visit that land was a fisherman.

According to the narrative of the brothers Nicolò and Antonio Zeno, around 1370 an unnamed fisherman reported finding an island, which he named Estotiland. A great storm blew four fishing boats, including his, about 1,000 miles across the Atlantic to this unknown island. He described it as a civilized place with cities and writing, and ruled by a king. The Estotilanders traded with **Greenland** and appeared to have had contact with Europe in the past.

Estotiland is most often identified as Newfoundland, and that is certainly its approximate location on the Zenos' map. Believers in the unnamed fisherman's visit feel that he reached a lost Norse settlement in **Vinland** that had survived long after those described in the **Vinland sagas.** In some sixteenth- and seventeenth-century Scandinavian maps, Estotiland indicated the location of either the **Markland** or the **Helluland** of the Norse. Modern scholars generally feel, however, that the Zeno narrative was merely a futile hoax designed to acquire some of the glory of the discovery of the New World for Venice and the Zeno family. So while Estotiland sometimes appeared on maps of the early modern era, it had its genesis in a fraud.

Bibliography: Babcock, William H., *Legendary Islands of the Atlantic: A Study in Medieval Geography,* 1922; Ramsay, Raymond H., *No Longer on the Map: Discovering Places That Never Were,* 1972.

Etruscans in Ancient America

Also known as Etrurians, Tyrhennians, or Tyrsenoi, this ancient Italian people were supposedly among the many Mediterranean peoples who visited America.

The Etruscans occupied approximately the same area as modern Tuscany in northern Italy. Their origins are obscure. Originally it was thought that they had migrated from Lydia in Asia Minor. Their mysterious language is not part of the Indo-European family, or any other. By the seventh century B.C., the Etruscans formed a single nation that reached the height of its power about 500 B.C. Successful on both land and sea, they even occupied Corsica. But the Etruscans were surrounded by many enemies—the Greeks of Campania and Syracuse, the Samnites, the early Romans, and the Gauls. Defeats became more frequent; by the third century B.C. the Romans conquered the Etruscan homeland.

The Etruscans were not among those whom Spanish writers in the Age of Discovery credited with pre-Columbian visits; too little was known about them during the sixteenth century. Archaeological discoveries in the nineteenth century changed the situation, and Etruscans began to appear on many lists of Mediterranean peoples who supposedly visited ancient America. The Etruscans fulfilled the right criteria: they were exotic, mysterious, and seafaring. No Etruscan or any other documents credit them with extensive Atlantic voyages, but historian Diodorus Siculus (fl. 60–30 B.C.) told how the Etruscans tried to colonize a western land newly discovered by the Phoenicians but had been blocked by the Carthaginians. Despite that setback, various **diffusionist** writers feel the Etruscans made many trips to America on the evidence of artistic motifs and religious practices. For example, Constance Irwin based her argument on pictures found in ancient America of people wearing shoes with pointed, upturned toes. Since Etruscans wore such shoes and were skillful seafarers, she concluded they must have traveled to America, possibly in association with the **Hittites.** The prominent diffusionist writers **Cyrus Gordon,** Pierre Honoré, Alexander von Wuthenau, and **Barry Fell** agree that the Etruscans reached the Americas. The evidence is basically broad artistic and linguistic parallels that most other professional archaeologists, anthropologists, and historians find weak and unconvincing.

Interestingly enough, there is one theory claiming that the Etruscans came from America to Europe. In 1969 Natalia Rosi de Tariffi wrote *America cuarta dimensión* (Fourth dimension America), in which she claims to have discovered supposed similarities among the Peruvian languages of Quechua and Aymara and such languages as English and Magyar. An Etruscan migration from Peru to Italy provided the connection. The linguistic basis for her theory is completely without scholarly support, but no more so than the idea that Etruscans regularly visited the Americas.

Bibliography: Davies, Nigel, *Voyagers to the New World*, 1979; Gordon, Cyrus, *Before Columbus: Links between the Old World and Ancient America*, 1971; Irwin, Constance, *Fair Gods and Stone Faces*, 1963.

Evolution of Culture (Parallel and Convergent)

Parallel evolution explains cultural change on the basis of fixed stages or steps following general laws of development (nomotheticism). Convergent evolution explains cultural change by viewing it as a process that follows many unique series of stages not amenable to classification by general laws of development. During the nineteenth and early twentieth centuries, archaeology and anthropology experienced a great debate between proponents of parallel evolution and **diffusionism.**

Cultural change or evolution is a phenomenon accepted by all students of human society since the archaeological and historical record makes its existence indisputable. Explaining how and why cultural change occurs, particularly in prehistoric societies, is much more controversial. Initially, parallel evolutionary thought dominated anthropological theory. In the early nineteenth century both Auguste Comte (1798–1857) and Georg W. F. Hegel (1770–1831) proposed theories to explain cultural change and human history based on general laws and fixed steps of development. According to this thinking, completely independent and separate societies would develop in exactly the same general way. The appearance of Charles Darwin's evolutionary theories in 1859 gave further impetus to the dominance of parallel evolutionist thought. Among the leading anthropologists supporting this theory were Englishman Edward B. Tylor (1832–1917) and American Lewis Henry Morgan (1818–1881). Neither scholar denied the importance of diffusion as a cause of cultural change; however, Tylor and other parallel evolutionists postulated that humanity had a psychic unity that accounted for independent inventions and fixed stages of cultural development. Parallel evolutionists attempted to impose as much order as possible on prehistory and cultural changes by discovering the true nomothetic principles or general laws.

Other anthropologists led by Franz Boas (1858–1942) protested the overemphasis parallel evolution theories placed on discovering general laws. These dissidents argued that human activity was far too disordered to be subject to general laws. Boas and his supporters advocated the approach of historical particularism or cultural relativism, in which each society's development is seen as unique. Convergent evolution, which postulates that separate societies could follow different stages of development to reach similar results, is closely related to historical particularism.

The other branch of anthropological thought to challenge parallel evolutionism was diffusionism. Whereas parallel evolutionists saw cultural change or innovations as common occurrences following general laws, diffusionists considered them unique and rare events in the rise of most civilizations. For diffusionists, most cultures evolved as a result of borrowings or exchanges from a higher civilization.

Supporters of theories of parallel evolution and convergent evolution generally do not consider prehistoric or ancient transoceanic contacts between the Old World and the Americas common or significant, if they believe they occurred at all. In the late twentieth century, convergent evolutionary thinking dominates the theories and methodological assumptions of professional anthropology and archaeology. As a result, these disciplines offer little support to advocates of various theories about pre-Columbian visitors and their influences on the ancient civilizations of the Americas.

Bibliography: Harris, Marvin, *The Rise of Anthropological Theory,* 1968; Trigger, Bruce G., *A History of Archaeological Thought,* 1990.

F

Fell, Barry
(1917–)

This controversial best-selling **diffusionist** author from New Zealand claims that various Old World peoples, particularly those from the Mediterranean and western Europe, visited and settled in pre-Columbian North America.

Howard Barraclough Fell's original doctoral training at the University of Edinburgh and his research was in marine biology, in which he enjoyed considerable success. Author of many scientific publications, he became a professor and eventually curator at the Museum of Comparative Zoology at Harvard University. Fell brought out *America B.C.* (1976), which became a best-seller. As a result of his book's success, he took an early retirement in 1977 to pursue his inter-est in the alleged visits of Old World peoples to North America in ancient times. His first book was followed by *Saga America* in 1980 and *Bronze Age America* in 1982. Fell also helped establish the Early Sites Research Society in 1973 and the Epigraphic Society in 1974. Both groups consist of supporters of hyperdiffusionist theories about contacts between the Americas and the Old World. According to Fell's theory, **Celts**, **Egyptians**, **Libyans**, Greeks, **Phoenicians**, and **Hebrews** visited, conquered, or settled in different parts of North America before the birth of Christ. He believes that most of the more advanced aspects of the various Native American tribal cultures are borrowings or survivals from these Old World visitors.

Professional archaeologists, anthropologists, historians, and prehistorians almost universally reject Fell's theories. In reviewing *America B.C.* for the *New York Times Book Review* of 13 March 1977, the eminent British archaeologist Glyn Daniel asked, "Why do responsible and accredited professors write such ignorant rubbish?" His review provoked many letters of protest from Fell's supporters. The Smithsonian Institution's Department of Anthropology received so many queries about the authenticity of the book's contents that two of its staff, Ives Goddard and William S. Fitzhugh, prepared a written critique. Their analysis was published under the titles "Barry Fell Reexamined" in *Biblical Archaeologist* 41 (1978) and "A Statement Concerning *America B.C.*" in *Man in the Northeast* 17 (1979).

The Goddard and Fitzhugh critique was a devastating indictment of Fell's flawed methodology. Fell based his theories on three basic types of evidence. First, he claimed that various Native American languages, place-names, and writing systems show Old World influences and antecedents. Second, he claims to have found and translated various stone inscriptions made by Old World visitors to North America.

Third, he claims that certain stone structures and artifacts are relics left behind by these visitors.

Fell's evidence received systematic examination by Goddard and Fitzhugh. Where Fell claimed that Micmac writing was descended from Egyptian hieroglyphics, they show that it has no structural relation to the Egyptian writing system. Instead, French missionaries created it to serve as a mnemonic device for Micmac converts learning the Roman Catholic catechism and liturgy. Regarding Fell's claim of finding loan words from Egyptian, Gaelic, and Semitic languages in the vocabularies of the Abenaki, Pima, and Zuni languages, Goddard and Fitzhugh convincingly demonstrate that he is mistaken. They also point out that Fell's contention that certain Native American place-names have Old World derivations is based on completely unreliable linguistic evidence and methods. The stone inscriptions Fell uses as evidence of contact are rejected by Goddard and Fitzhugh. They show that these so-called inscriptions are either accidental or random marks made by glaciation or plows, or are fakes such as the Paraiba stone of Brazil (see also **Phoenicians**) and the **Davenport Tablets**. Fell ignores the fact that some of his archaeological evidence consists of long-discredited hoaxes. The same observations apply to Fell's theories that the structures at Mystery Hill and the Newport Tower were built by pre-Columbian Old World visitors. Painstaking and well-accepted research proves that these sites are post-Columbian. Similar dubious practices abound throughout Fell's dealings with archaeological evidence. Goddard and Fitzhugh's basic conclusion is that Fell's linguistic, archaeological, and historical methodologies are too flawed to produce valid results.

Fell apparently did not take these criticisms of *America B.C.* to heart because his next book, *Saga America* (1980), was essentially a carbon copy. Reviewing the book for the magazine *Archaeology* in 1981 (vol. 31, no. 1: 62–66), Marshall McKusick found Fell's scholarly methods as deficient as ever. As McKusick bluntly and scathingly put it, "That such a book as *Saga America* could be perpetuated upon a naive reading public as authentic prehistory represents a scandal deserving censure of the issuing press and author alike. . . . In my opinion Barry Fell, late of Harvard, is the Typhoid Mary of popular prehistory." *Bronze Age America*, appearing in 1982, fared no better at the hands of professional archaeologists and prehistorians since it repeated the same egregious errors of method and fact. As Harvard archaeologist Stephen Williams points out, even the title of Fell's third book is misleading since no pre-Columbian bronze artifacts have ever been found in North America. Numerous other debunking studies of Fell and his followers by professional archaeologists continue to appear, but to no avail. Fell's ideas or similar ones, no matter how fallacious, will always attract a core of true believers. It is simply an unfortunate by-product of the general public's genuine fascination with history and archaeology.

Bibliography: Cole, John R., "Anthropology beyond the Fringe," *Skeptical Inquirer* (Spring/Summer 1978): 62–71; Cole, John R., "Barry Fell, *America B.C.*, and a Cargo Cult in Archaeology," *Bulletin of the New York State Archaeological Association* 74 (1978): 1–10; Cole, John R., "Cult Archaeology," *Early Man* 2 (1980): 9–12; Cole, John R., "Cult Archaeology and Unscientific Method and Theory," *Advances in Archaeological Method and Theory* 3 (1980): 1–33; Cole, John R., "Inscription Mania, Hyper-Diffusionism, and the Public; Fallout from a 1977 Meeting in Vermont," *Man in the Northeast* 17 (1979): 27–53; Little Turtle, "The Fell Trilogy: Synopses & Commentary," *NEARA Journal* 19 (1985):

79–95; McKusick, Marshall, "The North American Periphery of Antique Vermont," *Antiquity* 53 (1979): 121–123; Williams, Stephen, *Fantastic Archaeology: The Wild Side of North American Prehistory*, 1991.

Fisherman of Frisland's Story (ca. 1370)

This unnamed fisherman from the Faeroe or Orkney islands accidentally visited and lived in the previously unknown lands of **Estotiland** and **Drogio** for 26 years. When he returned home, he informed his ruler **Prince Zichmni** (see also **Sinclair, Voyage of Prince Henry**) of his adventures, which later appeared in the **Zeno Narrative** of 1558. Some writers claim Estotiland is Newfoundland, which would make the Fisherman a pre-Columbian visitor to the Americas.

The story of the unnamed Fisherman is contained within the narrative of the adventures of Nicolò and Antonio Zeno in the far northern Atlantic. Sometime in the mid-1390s the Fisherman returned home to Frislanda (the Faeroe Islands) after a 26-year absence. His adventure started during a fishing trip when four ships of Frislanda encountered a great tempest. It blew them 1,000 miles westward, where they sighted an island they named Estotiland. One ship wrecked on its coast, but the natives proved to be kindly and hospitable. They took the six survivors to a "fair and prosperous city." The king of Estotiland gathered many interpreters in an effort to talk with the fishermen. One interpreter finally succeeded when he spoke to them in Latin, and it turned out that he was also a castaway.

The king of Estotiland commanded them to stay, so for five years they lived there and learned the language and customs. They found Estotiland to be a rich and fertile country, only slightly smaller than **Iceland**. Its inhabitants practiced the same skills and crafts as the Europeans, including metallurgy and wheat farming. They had a written language, and the king had a library that included Latin books. The Fisherman concluded that they must have been in contact with Europe sometime in the past; in fact, they still traded with **Greenland**. The Estotilanders sailed in small boats and did not have the compass. Their seamanship was considerably inferior to that of the sailors of Frisland. As a result they held the Frislanders in great respect and asked them to provide instruction in the art of sailing.

One day the king of Estotiland sent the Fisherman with a fleet of 12 boats to the neighboring land of Drogio. Storms forced a landing and they were taken prisoner by Drogio's savage and cannibalistic inhabitants. Most of the expedition were killed and eaten, but a few, including the Fisherman, managed to save themselves by showing the natives of Drogio how to fish with nets. Once again, the Fisherman's skills gained him respect. Unfortunately, a nearby rival chief desired the Fisherman's skills for his people and warred on the Fisherman's captors until they agreed to turn him over. That was not the end of the matter. Drogio and the lands beyond abounded with warlike and jealous tribes, all of whom coveted the skills of the Fisherman. Over the course of 13 years he was passed among the various tribes 25 times.

During his long captivity, the Fisherman observed that "it was a very great country, and, as it were, a new world." The inhabitants of Drogio were quite primitive. They hunted with bows and wooden lances tipped with sharpened points, but they did not know how to make animal skins into clothing, and so went about naked. Although they had chiefs and some laws, they fought savagely among themselves and ate their captives. Farther south, however, the Fisherman learned that people lived in cities, built temples, and worked in gold and silver. They also practiced human sacrifice and ate the victims.

After many years of captivity, the Fisherman decided to escape. Heading back to his original landing in Drogio, he found he was still welcome. After living there another three years, he was rescued by a boat from Estotiland. Because of his knowledge of the language of Drogio, the Estotilanders employed him as an interpreter in trading expeditions to that region. It was lucrative employment, and after a few years the Fisherman became quite wealthy. He acquired his own ship and sailed home to Frislanda. The Fisherman reported his adventures to his lord, Prince Zichmni. The prince decided to investigate for himself and made his own western voyage during the mid- to late 1390s accompanied by Antonio Zeno. But they failed to find Estotiland.

Professional scholars such as Samuel Eliot Morison generally dismiss the Fisherman of Frislanda's story because it forms part of the Zeno Narrative, which is almost certainly a fraud. Other more credulous writers accept the story as a description of actual events. They identify Estotiland as Newfoundland and Drogio as Nova Scotia. Furthermore, they claim that Estotilanders were the descendants of Norse colonists in **Vinland.** This claim creates serious problems of evidence. First, if by the late fourteenth century the Estotilanders had been thriving for several centuries, why had they vanished without a trace by the time of the late–fifteenth-century explorations? Second, how could such an extensive community fail to leave any definite archaeological remains? Despite such problems, in 1964 the respected historian of geography E. G. R. Taylor gave credence to the Fisherman's story (although dating it incorrectly to 1354, well over ten years too early if one accepts the basic accuracy of the Zeno Narrative), as have other popular writers such as Frederick J. Pohl.

Bibliography: Lucas, Frederick W., *Annals of the Voyages of the Brothers Nicolò and Antonio Zeno*, 1898; Taylor, E. G. R., "The Fisherman's Story, 1354," *Geographical Magazine* 37 (1964): 709–712; Taylor, E. G. R., "A Fourteenth-Century Riddle—and Its Solution," *Geographical Review* 54 (1964): 573–576.

Fortunate Isles

Also known as Islands of the Blessed, they are variously identified as Madeira or the Canaries.

Many ancient Mediterranean cultures believed that the blessed dead went to live in some paradise located beyond the Strait of Gibraltar far off in the Atlantic Ocean. The belief in a western paradise formed an important component of Egyptian religion. Among the Greeks such beliefs took the form of the Elysian Fields, a winterless land of plenty. Another related mythological paradise was the Garden of the Hesperides, which was also located in the far west and existed under idyllic conditions. In it the daughters of Hesperis guarded a tree that bore golden apples. Although remote, it could be visited, and Hercules made his way there during his labors. By the time of the **Romans,** the islands were known as the Insulae Fortunatae, or the Fortunate Isles. Plutarch identified Madeira as their location, but most geographers considered the Canary Islands to be the true Fortunate Isles. Such a widespread belief in the existence of lands in the western Atlantic, particularly paradisiacal lands, would have been a great encouragement to early explorers. Some writers cite the belief as evidence that ancient seamen actually reached the western hemisphere and returned to describe it as a paradise. No satisfactory archaeological or historical evidence corroborates such visits. See also **Avalon** and **Blessed Isles.**

Bibliography: Cassidy, Vincent H., "More Fortunate Islands—and Some That Were Lost," *Terrae Incognitae* 1 (1969): 35–40.

Freydis

She was the illegitimate daughter of **Eric the Red** and sister of **Leif Ericsson,** who accompanied **Thorfinn Karlsefni** in his attempt to settle **Vinland** and later returned to make another attempt at settlement that ended in tragedy.

Both the *Greenlanders' Saga* and *Eirik's Saga* depict Freydis as brave or ruthless and given to violence. In possessing such a character she was a true daughter of Eric the Red, even though an illegitimate one according to *Eirik's Saga.* Both sagas have her married to Thorvard of Gardar, a farmer of **Greenland,** after which they differ significantly. *Eirik's Saga* tells how Freydis and Thorvard joined Thorfinn Karlsefni's expedition to establish a permanent Norse settlement in Vinland. Freydis also accompanied Karlsefni during his attempt to establish the new settlement of Hop farther to the south, where she exhibited great bravery during an attack by the natives. Although pregnant, she came out and loudly berated the Norsemen for not defeating the **skraelings.** When some of the natives turned on her, she snatched up a dead Norseman's sword to defend herself. In true **Viking** spirit she tore open her dress and exposed one of her breasts. Such behavior terrified the skraelings, who retreated to their boats and fled. Freydis's actions won her the admiration of Karlsefni and the other men. Afterward the Norse returned to Straumfjord, Karlsefni's northern settlement, and spent the winter there before giving up and returning to Greenland. If Freydis carried her baby to term, it must have been born in America, although the sagas are silent on that point.

The *Greenlanders' Saga* tells of another voyage to Vinland by Freydis that took place the year after Thorfinn Karlsefni's return. Since the Greenlanders considered such trips to be both lucrative and prestigious, Freydis persuaded two Icelandic brothers named Helgi and Finnbogi to be her equal partners on a Vinland voyage. She also received her brother Leif's permission to use the houses he had built in Vinland, called Leifsbudir.

Two ships sailed with a combined complement of over 70 men and women. Trouble arose immediately upon their arrival. The brothers' ship arrived first and they occupied some of Leif's houses. When Freydis arrived she ordered them out and refused to share the buildings, forcing the brothers to build their own houses. Hard feelings between the two companies grew worse over the winter. One morning Freydis walked over to the brothers' camp and asked Finnbogi to trade ships so that she and her people could move to another place. Finnbogi readily agreed. When Freydis returned home, she claimed the brothers had mistreated her, and demanded that her husband Thorvard avenge her. After she threatened to divorce him, Thorvard gave in and led his men against the company of Helgi and Finnbogi. While the brothers and their companions slept, Thorvard and his men entered the house and tied them up. As they brought their prisoners out one by one, the bloodthirsty Freydis executed them. She even used an axe to kill the five women, whom everyone else had refused to harm. Turning on her companions, Freydis threatened death to anyone who talked about the murders back in Greenland. When spring arrived, Freydis and her company loaded the two ships with a rich cargo and sailed home. But word of Freydis's horrible crimes leaked out despite her dire threats. A horrified Leif Ericsson investigated the rumors and found them to be true. Unable to punish his own sister, Leif prophesied that Freydis's descendants would never prosper. Thus ended the last known Norse attempt to establish a permanent settlement in Vinland. Settlers may have been massacred, but it was not by hostile natives. Of course, Freydis's mass murdering may never have happened given the amount of fiction mixed in with the facts in the **Vinland Sagas.** It is a problem that eludes a definitive and convincing answer from scholars.

Bibliography: Jones, Gwyn, *The Norse Atlantic Saga*, 2nd ed., 1986; Magnusson, Magnus, and Hermann Pálsson, trans. and eds. *The Vinland Sagas: The Norse Discovery of America*, 1965.

Fukienese Sailors, Story of (507)

Records from the Six Dynasties period in **Chinese** history briefly mention that a great storm blew a Fukienese ship into the far-eastern Pacific in 507. The crew found an island inhabited by dog-faced men who lived primarily on a diet of small beans. Similar stories appear in medieval European travelers' accounts such as those by the fictional Sir John Mandeville and **Aethicus of Istria.** Some people considered the story of the dog-faced men to be another instance of a pre-Columbian visit to the Americas by the Chinese. They perhaps were aided in reaching this conclusion because the story appears in the *Liang Shu* (ca. 629), a history of the Liang dynasty (502–557) right after the narrative of **Hoei-shin's** visit to **Fusang.** Details are too sparse to connect the island of dog-faced men with a specific part of the Americas or to be sure that the Fukienese visit actually took place.

Bibliography: Needham, Joseph, *Science and Civilization in China*, vol. 4, *Physics and Physical Technology, pt. 3, Civil Engineering and Nautics*, 1971.

Fusang

The ancient **Chinese** gave this name to a land located to the east of Asia in the Pacific Ocean. It was visited by the **Buddhist missionary Hoei-Shin** in 499. The name refers to a plant growing there that resembled a tree the Chinese called fusang. In 1761 French sinologist Joseph De Guignes identified the country of Fusang as California or Mexico. He asserted that the so-called fusang plant was the century plant or Mexican aloe. It has been claimed, however, that even before De Guignes's time, stories of the eastern land of Fusang prompted the Russian tsar Peter the Great to sponsor the Arctic explorations of **Vitus Bering** in the 1720s. Modern sinologists reject the identification of Fusang as America, pointing out that the name Fusang had a long career in Chinese cosmography as that of a fictional eastern land. The usage first appeared in the late Chou and early Han periods (ca. 400 B.C.–A.D. 9) as a reference to a marvelous eastern otherworld. Later the name was used as a poetic reference to Japan. Other stories involving Fusang could refer to the islands of the Ainu, Sakhalin, Kamchatka, or simply some fantasy land in the eastern Pacific. Obviously Fusang was not a specific place. Despite these scholarly objections, De Guignes's thesis continues to find supporters, although some of them locate Fusang in Peru rather than Mexico or California.

Bibliography: Needham, Joseph, *Science and Civilization in China*, vol. 4, *Physics and Physical Technology, pt. 3, Civil Engineering and Nautics*, 1971.

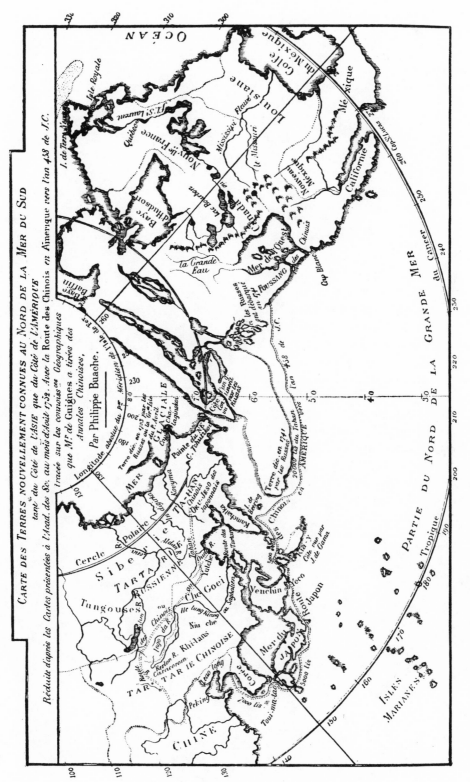

An eighteenth-century French concept of the Chinese voyage to Fusang.

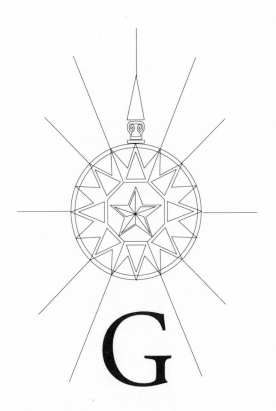

García, Father Gregorio (d. 1627)

This Spanish Dominican cataloged the various theories of Native American origins and concluded they were all true.

García came to Peru in the 1590s to do missionary work among the natives. During his nine years there he developed a keen interest in all the new and wonderful things he observed. In particular, he was fascinated by the native peoples and the question of their origins. As a result in 1607 he published his *Origen de los indios del nuevo mundo, e Indias occidentales* (Origins of the Indians of the New World and the West Indies). This large book lists 11 major theories of Native American origins and pre-Columbian visitors, offering detailed arguments for and against each of them. The first two theories advocate that ancient peoples came to the Americas by sea, either purposely or accidentally. **José de Acosta's** theory of a land bridge is the third theory. The eight remaining theories involve people from various historical or legendary nations making their way to the Americas: Carthage, Israel, **Ophir, Atlantis,** Spain, Greece, **Phoenicia,** and East Asia. Despite the great diversity of these theories, García accepted all of them as true.

García's book was one of the most frequently cited on this subject in the seventeenth century. It also reflects the confused state of historical and ethnographic studies during that time. García and most of his contemporaries believed that all cultures developed from a common source that could be traced to Noah and Adam (monogenesis). Except for a few outstanding individuals like José de Acosta, most early modern scholars denied that independent cultural evolution was possible. Therefore, scholars like García relied on the comparative method for identifying connections among individual cultures and societies. Similar cultural traits were eagerly recorded and listed, while divergent and incompatible traits were largely ignored. Using such an uncritical method, it is not surprising that García found all the theories of Native American origin to be true.

Despite its scholarship defects, Spanish historian **Andrés González de Barcía Carballido y Zúñiga** judged García's *Origen de los indios* to be the best work on the subject. In 1729 Barcía published a second edition of the book that included his own extensive additions. Both García and Barcía failed to use the systematic and critical approach to the ethnographic study of cultures that the brilliant early anthropologist Acosta pioneered. Instead, García and Barcía's work became an important and popular source for the advocates of various fringe theories on Native American origins and pre-Columbian visitors to the New World.

Bibliography: Huddleston, Lee Eldridge, *Origins of the American Indians: European Concepts, 1492–1729*, 1967.

Garcilaso de la Vega (el Inca) (1539–1616)

Prominent mestizo and the first historian born in the Americas, he was the first to name **Alonso Sánchez** as the **Unknown Pilot of Columbus**. His historical writings were used indirectly to bolster various fringe theories of Native American origins.

Garcilaso was the illegitimate son of Sebastian de la Vega, a Spanish soldier, and his concubine, an Incan princess. Fortunately for Garcilaso, his father acknowledged him as his son, and in 1560 the 20-year-old moved to Spain to live with paternal relatives. Upon completing his education, Garcilaso served with the army of Philip II of Spain from 1564–1574. After military service he took minor religious orders and resided in Cordoba, where he lived off a pension established by his father and the income derived from his writings.

As a mestizo, Garcilaso had roots in both the Spanish and Incan cultures and could speak the main Peruvian language Quechua. He was proud of his racial duality and took a great interest in the preconquest history of Peru. His first published work appeared in 1595, a translation from Italian of Leon Hebreo's neo-Platonic treatise, *The Philosophy of Love*. In 1603 Garcilaso began working on *La Florida del Inca* (The Florida of the Inca), a well-written narrative history of the De Soto expedition, which was brought out in 1605. The first part of the *Comentarios reales de los Incas* (Royal commentaries of the Incas) appeared in 1609; the second part was published in 1617 shortly after Garcilaso's death. These works were also well written, but unlike *The Florida*, the *Royal Commentaries* were based on both Garcilaso's personal observations and contacts and extensive documentary re-search. Given his family background, the *Royal Commentaries* understandably showed a greater sympathy for Native Americans than most early Spanish histories dealing with the New World and the establishment of the Spanish empire. The high quality of the scholarship in the *Royal Commentaries* brought him general recognition as the leading authority on Peruvian history.

Unlike many early historians of Spanish America, Garcilaso did not speculate about Old World origins of the Native Americans. His one direct contribution consists of his account of Alonso Sánchez as the Unknown Pilot of Columbus. Otherwise, Garcilaso's history of preconquest Peru with its accounts of native myths and legends has been used only indirectly as a corroboration for various speculative theories about pre-Columbian visitors to the Americas.

Bibliography: Crowley, Francis G., *Garcilaso de la Vega, el Inca, and His Sources in the "Comentarios reales de los Incas,"* 1971; Pupo-Walker, Enrique, "El Inca Garcilaso de la Vega (1539–1616)," in *Latin American Writers*, 3 vols., 1989; Varner, John Grier, *El Inca: The Life and Times of Garcilaso de la Vega*, 1968.

Geographical Concepts: Ancient, Medieval, and Renaissance

The geographical concepts and knowledge held by various ancient peoples would have had a big impact on attempts to make trans-oceanic voyages to the Americas. Many peoples simply did not have the geographical concepts and knowledge to envision such voyages, let alone attempt them.

Ancient peoples commonly viewed the world as a disk or bowl floating on a vast ocean and bounded on its edges by a canopy or firmament that held up the stars, planets, moon, and sun. Various versions of this basic cosmography existed among the peoples of the Near East such as the **Egyptians,**

Hebrews, Sumerians, Phoenicians, and **Hittites.** All these groups supposedly visited the Americas according to various writers. Their lack of geographical knowledge, not to mention (with the exception of the Phoenicians) poor nautical skills, makes such voyages implausible.

The Homeric Greeks believed their world was a disk or plate surrounded by the vast River Ocean. Beyond the River Ocean lay a great Outer Continent that encircled everything. The known world consisted of the three continents of Africa, Asia, and Europe, although some Greek writers counted only two because they combined Africa and Asia as one. About the fifth century B.C. the Pythagorean philosophers theorized that the world was a sphere. In time people devised ways of measuring the earth's sphericity and thereby proving it. Although this belief was common knowledge among educated Europeans, the decline and fall of the Roman empire during the third, fourth, and fifth centuries A.D. saw its hold temporarily weaken.

Aristotle and other Greek writers divided the spherical earth into five zones of climate—the two polar regions, the northern and southern temperate regions, and the torrid zone of the equator. Only the temperate zones were capable of sustaining human life. The torrid zone was impassable because of great heat. The Greeks also divided the earth into four quarters. The Pythagoreans created the concepts elaborated on later by Crates of Mallus. The Greeks called their quarter of the world the oikoumene, consisting of the three continents of Africa, Asia, and Europe. According to Crates, encircling oceans running east and west along the equator and north and south along the meridian divided the oikoumene from the other three quarters. The quarter located south of the oikoumene was called the antoikoi. In the western hemisphere, the **antipodes** lay to the north and the antichthones in the south.

Long-lasting speculation arose about the existence of a southern continent named **Terra Australis** and a western continent named **Terra Occidentalis.** As the latter two names indicate, the **Romans** shared the geographical concepts of the Greeks.

The theoretical boundaries of the Greek and Roman geographical concepts extended well beyond their firsthand knowledge. Some scholars believe that about 700 B.C., the age of Homer, such knowledge was limited to the eastern Mediterranean Sea, although others include the western Mediterranean. **Solon,** around 594 B.C., definitely would have known of the vast ocean beyond the Strait of Gibraltar, the full extent of the Black Sea, and the existence of the Red Sea. **Plato's** world in 400 B.C. was a bit larger and included all of the Red Sea, the Caspian Sea, the edge of India, and the entire coastline of the Iberian Peninsula. By 300 B.C., Alexander the Great campaigned in India and Pytheas of Massilia visited the British Isles and Scandinavia.

For many years the Greeks' activities in the western Mediterranean were hampered by the rise of the **Carthaginian** empire. This Phoenician colony outshone its founding city of Tyre before its final destruction by Rome in the three Punic Wars from 264–146 B.C. Little is known about either Phoenician or Carthaginian geographical concepts. Being traders, geographical knowledge was a jealously guarded commodity in both societies. The Greek historian Herodotus mentioned that Phoenician sailors successfully circumnavigated Africa about 600 B.C. while in the employ of the Egyptian pharaoh Necho. He added that he personally doubted the truth of the story. A century later the Carthaginian brothers **Hanno** and Himilco explored the Atlantic coastlines of Europe and Africa, respectively. Carthaginian traders were soon regularly bringing tin back from Britain. During this same era they may have visited the Canary, Madeira, and Azores islands as well. Some writers speculate that they reached the Americas, but their evidence is weak and unconvincing to most scholars.

The Romans inherited the Greeks' and Carthaginians' geographical discoveries. Their empire encompassed the entire Mediterranean basin along with parts of Britain and both western and central Europe. The Canary Islands were the **Fortunate Isles** of the Romans, but they did not know about the Azores or the Madeira Islands. Roman traders sailed the Indian Ocean and knew of China, but they did little else to expand the geographical knowledge of the west. The first significant Roman geographer was Strabo of the first century B.C. Pliny the Elder (A.D. 23–79) added to the geographical store of knowledge with his *Natural History*. The greatest Roman geographer, however, was Claudius Ptolemy from the second century A.D., who recorded the accumulated geographical knowledge of the Roman world in his great treatise *Geography*. Despite claims to the contrary, the Romans did not engage in pre-Columbian voyages to the Americas. The writings of their chief geographers make it clear that they did not know of any lands to the west.

The decline and fall of the Roman empire brought about an impoverishment of European geographical knowledge. Cosmas Indicopleustes (fl. 540–550) was an Alexandrian merchant and geographical writer who revived the concept of a flat earth in his book *Christian Topography*. The encyclopedist Bishop Isidore of Seville (ca. 560–636) had rather confused geographical ideas, as did the English monk and scholar the Venerable Bede (ca. 673–735). But unlike Cosmas, both men believed in the sphericity of the earth.

Among educated people during the Middle Ages, most of the Greek and Roman geographical concepts survived, including the idea of a spherical earth, the zonal theory of climates, and the existence of the antipodes.

By the time of Marco Polo (1254–1324), Europeans had traveled to China and India for trade on a number of occasions. The rest of Europe either did not know it or ignored it, but the Norse had long before discovered and settled **Greenland** and visited **Vinland**/North America (see also **Geographical Concepts: Norse**). The problem was that Vinland/North America did not fit into the traditional Greco-Roman scheme of three continents—Africa, Asia, and Europe. Despite their speculations about the existence of antipodes and Terra Occidentalis, when Europeans actually encountered an unknown western continent they could not comprehend it intellectually. As a result, the Norse discovery never became general geographical knowledge in medieval Europe.

During the fifteenth century, European geographical knowledge again expanded dramatically, although some of the inherited traditional but incorrect concepts also survived. A copy of Claudius Ptolemy's forgotten *Geography* made its way to western Europe from Constantinople in 1406. Ptolemy had constructed an atlas that employed coordinate lines in an attempt to portray the spherical earth on a flat world map. His example inspired similar activities by various Renaissance cartographers, ultimately resulting in Gerard Mercator's successful world map of 1569 that introduced the famous Mercator projection.

Ptolemy also contributed, although inaccurately, to the fifteenth-century debate over the true size of the earth. Eratosthenes (b. 280 B.C.), the librarian of Alexandria, provided a somewhat accurate measurement of 250,000 stadia, which is only one-seventh larger than the earth's actual circumference of 24,902 miles, making it the most accurate estimate of the earth's size made in antiquity. Ptolemy, however, chose to accept the far less accurate measurement of Marinus of Tyre (fl. A.D. 100), who estimated 180,000 stadia, or about 18,000 miles. Thanks to

Ptolemy's great prestige and scholarship, various fifteenth-century geographers including **Paolo Toscanelli dal Pozzo,** Christopher Columbus, and **Martin Behaim** also accepted the erroneous figure. This error made the earth so much smaller that sailing west across the Atlantic Ocean to Asia, with a rest stop at the island of **Antillia,** seemed quite feasible. Only several decades of exploration after 1492 would reveal the full magnitude of this error—the existence of the Americas and the vast Pacific Ocean.

Slowly but surely, geographical knowledge expanded during the fifteenth century, largely due to the efforts of the Portuguese. They rediscovered the Madeiras in 1418 and the Azores in 1427, and worked their way down the west coast of Africa until Bartolomeu Dias reached the Cape of Good Hope in 1487. There is little evidence that the Portuguese made any pre-Columbian visits to America or that they had any influence on European geographical concepts. On the eve of Columbus's historic voyage of 1492, Europeans had no place for unknown continents in their geographical thinking, although they were happy to incorporate such fictional islands as **Antillia, Brazil,** and **St. Brendan.**

Bibliography: Beazley, C. Raymond, *The Dawn of Modern Geography,* 3 vols., 1897–1906; Bunbury, E. H., *A History of Ancient Geography,* 2 vols., [1883], 1959; Phillips, J. R. S., *The Medieval Expansion of Europe,* 1988; Russell, Jeffrey Burton, *Inventing the Flat Earth: Columbus and Modern Historians,* 1991; Tozer, H. F., *A History of Ancient Geography,* 1897; Wright, John Kirtland, *The Geographical Lore of the Time of the Crusades,* [1925], 1965.

Geographical Concepts: Norse

The medieval Norse had two conceptions of the world. Both encouraged the belief that unknown lands lay to the west of **Iceland** and **Greenland.**

Around the year 1000 the Norse believed in the notion of a world circle, a hybrid of pagan Norse and classical concepts. The world was a platter surrounded by the Ocean Sea or Mare Oceanum. Dry land consisted of the traditional three continents of Africa, Asia, and Europe. The Atlantic Ocean, however, was an inland sea like the Mediterranean Sea. North of Scandinavia lay an extension of Europe that eventually became Greenland at its farthest tip. To the south, Africa extended westward and then northward, with **Vinland** located at its tip. In the gap between the promontories of Vinland and Greenland were the two islands of **Helluland** and **Markland.** Beyond them to the west lay the great Ocean Sea and the primeval Chaos known as the ginnungagap.

The idea that Vinland was part of Africa was very common among Scandinavian writers. Modern readers many find the idea ridiculous, but given the premise of the world circle it makes perfectly good sense. It also accounts for the story of the uniped, or one-footed man, that appears in *Eirik's Saga.* Medieval people believed unipeds lived in Africa. Therefore visitors to Vinland, which was supposed to be part of Africa, would naturally encounter unipeds.

Gradually the idea of the world circle gave way to the concept of a spherical earth. In that worldview Asia and Europe were connected in the far north by a land bridge. Below the land bridge, Asia formed the mainland that connected the various peninsulas of Greenland, Helluland, Markland, and Vinland. Thus a continuous coastline supposedly existed between Vinland and Europe, which would have been a great comfort to cautious Norse seaman navigating in the treacherous waters of the far north. Oddly enough, even in the late medieval conception of the world, the ginnungagap of pagan Norse mythology remained. It was commonly located in the sea between Vinland and Greenland, although some accounts placed it in the vicinity of the present-day Hudson Strait, the St. Lawrence estuary, or the strait of Belle Isle between Newfoundland and Labrador. By this later era, the ginnungagap was apparently thought of as a whirlpool or maelstrom.

Both concepts stated that unknown lands were located in the western Atlantic Ocean. By the time these concepts were fully formulated, Vinland had already been reached. Surviving evidence indicates that the early medieval Norse firmly believed that the western part of the North Atlantic was strewn with islands, beginning with Iceland. Such an idea provided a great incentive for exploration.

This Skalholt map from 1579 illustrates the Norse concept of the Atlantic Ocean as an inland sea. Skalholt was an Icelandic bishopric and center of learning.

Bibliography: Jones, Gwyn, *The Norse Atlantic Saga*, 2nd ed., 1986.

George and *Trinity*, Voyage of (1481)

This voyage was the second documented attempt by sailors of Bristol to locate the **Island of Brazil** in the western Atlantic Ocean. Records of the Exchequer of England indicate that Thomas Croft, a customs official of Bristol, was part owner of the ships *Trinity* and *George*. Croft loaded 40 bushels of salt on his ships, but claimed it was not merchandise for trade but rather supplies for the expedition during its search for Brazil. It is not stated whether the voyage was successful because the only purpose of the inquiry was to determine if Croft had engaged in trade—an illegal conflict of interest for a customs official. Some scholars speculate that the large amount of salt indicates sailors of Bristol were already engaged in secret fishing expeditions to the Grand Banks of Newfoundland, therefore anticipating Columbus's voyage to America by at least ten years. See also **Bristol Voyages.**

Bibliography: Quinn, David Beers, "The Argument for the English Discovery of America between 1480–1494," *Geographical Journal* 127 (1961): 277–285; Williamson, J. A., *The Cabot Voyages and Bristol Discovery under Henry VII*, 1962.

Gladwin, Harold S. (1883–1983)

This former stockbroker and amateur archaeologist's iconoclastic and controversial ideas about the origins of Native American civilizations and **diffusionism** included a lost fleet of **Alexander the Great** traveling across the Pacific Ocean to civilize Peru.

Harold S. Gladwin was born in New York City but educated in England. From 1908–1922 he owned a seat on the New York Stock Exchange and became quite wealthy. Tiring of his life in finance, he moved west. In 1924 Gladwin met Harvard archaeologist Alfred V. Kidder, who sparked his interest in southwestern archaeology. In a few years Gladwin founded his own research institute in Arizona, Gila Pueblo, which sponsored digs and published studies. Much solid and respectable research came out of Gladwin's early labors.

Campbell Grant's caricature of how professional archaeologists, or Dr. Phuddy Duddies, would really like to dispose of the defiant and iconoclastic Gladwin.

At the age of 64, Gladwin published his fantastical *Men out of Asia* (1947), in which he argued that the presence of humans in the Americas was far older than most professional archaeologists were willing to admit. Unfortunately, Gladwin set up and attacked an outdated straw man for the professional archaeologists' position. He proposed that it was people of the Australoid race who first crossed the **Bering Land Bridge** in about 25000 B.C. Four more migrations followed. The second was by a Negroid race that crossed the land bridge between 15000 and 2500 B.C. Gladwin associated that group with the recently discovered Stone Age Folsom culture, who stayed in North America. They were joined between 2500 and 500 B.C. by a third migration, the

Algonquin culture, whose ancestors Gladwin traced to Mediterranean Europe! The Algonquins also remained in North America and formed the various Algonquin tribes. **Eskimos** constituted the fourth migration, which occurred about 500 B.C., and they stayed in the Arctic regions. Finally, the fifth migration was by Mongoloids pushed out of Asia about 300 B.C. in a chain reaction of conflicts brought on by Alexander the Great's conquests. These people settled in both North and South America, and formed the Pueblo, Caddo, Toltec, Mayan, and Peruvian ethnic groups. They did not, however, create the sophisticated cultures and civilizations commonly associated with their ethnic groups.

Gladwin strongly rejected the theory that the ancient civilizations of the Americas developed in isolation through **parallel evolution.** He credited diffusion from the eastern hemisphere with stimulating the development of those civilizations. Various historical sources mention that Alexander the Great had assembled a huge fleet for exploration and colonization when he died unexpectedly in 323 B.C. His admiral, Nearchus, left the fleet to join forces with Antigonus, one of Alexander's successors, in Asia Minor. The great fleet then disappeared from history, but not from Gladwin's imagination.

According to Gladwin, the fleet sailed east and passed through Oceania, leaving behind some of its company, who became the Polynesians. Finally a remnant of the fleet reached South America and brought civilization to the natives it encountered. The white leaders of Alexander the Great's fleet became the inspiration for the various **white god legends** that developed among many Native American tribes. Needless to say, Gladwin's theory is based largely on pure speculation and has no support from most diffusionists and hyperdiffusionists, let alone from academic archaeologists and historians. Archaeologist Stephen Williams

suggests quite convincingly that *Men out of Asia* might actually have been written as some sort of complex joke.

In 1957, Gladwin published another archaeological work titled *History of the Ancient Southwest.* Its interpretations were also unorthodox. Even stranger, although it deals with some of the same cultures as *Men out of Asia*, it makes no reference to the chronology of prehistory advocated by the earlier volume. That omission lends even more weight to the idea that *Men out of Asia* was a parody of archaeological theory rather than a serious study. In his last book, *Mogollon and Hohokam A.D. 600–1000* (1979), Gladwin returned to hyperdiffusionism. One of his genuine contributions to archaeology was his earlier discovery of the existence of the Mogollon and Hohokam cultures. He spoiled that achievement by suggesting that the two cultures were a Libyan colony. Once again, he ignored his theories from *Men out of Asia*. Like the earlier archaeologist **Étienne Brasseur de Bourbourg,** Gladwin sullied his scholarly reputation with preposterous diffusionist theories and combined genius with being a crackpot.

Bibliography: Gladwin, Harold S., *Men out of Asia*, 1947; Williams, Stephen, *Fantastic Archaeology: The Wild Side of North American Prehistory,* 1991.

Gnupsson, Expedition of Bishop Eric (1121)

Several Icelandic annals record that Bishop Eric Gnupsson went on a quest to find **Vinland.** It is not certain that he ever left, let alone returned.

Bishop Eric Gnupsson and his trip to Vinland are very mysterious aspects of Norse contacts with pre-Columbian America. The surviving primary sources are laconic and simply state that he went looking for Vinland. They do not say why, how many people went with him, if he was successful, or if he returned. Enthusiasts for pre-Columbian transoceanic contacts such as Charles M. Boland and Hjalmar R. Holand state that Gnupsson led a large expedition to minister to thriving Norse colonies in America.

Boland, Holand, and others wrongly insist that Gnupsson was the first bishop of **Greenland.** Ecclesiastical records, however, show that the first diocese established in Greenland was at Gardar in 1124, and its first bishop was Arnald. Several other scholars, including the eminent historian Gwyn Jones, suggest that Eric Gnupsson was a bishop *in partibus infidelium,* which means he was a missionary bishop to the North

Atlantic region rather than bishop of Greenland. The crusading Norwegian king Sigurd (1106–1123) had Gnupsson appointed bishop about 1112 or 1113 by Pope Paschal II (1099–1118). Given his missionary status, it seems likely that Gnupsson's true assignment was to convert the heathen. Since the Norse were already Christians, he may have been sent to minister to the **skraelings,** or Native Americans, rather than any supposed Norse colony in Vinland.

No details of Gnupsson's activities survive. Some scholars claim that Bishop Eric left one memento of his visit—the Newport Tower in Rhode Island. Carl Rafn, the nineteenth-century Danish scholar, first

This seventeenth-century tower in Newport, Rhode Island, is frequently cited as evidence for Norse settlements in lower New England.

suggested that Gnupsson was its builder. Only Boland continues to credit Gnupsson; others put forward candidates such as the **Phoenicians** and members of **Paul Knutson's** expedition. Most modern scholars think the tower was built in the colonial era, sometime during the latter half of the seventeenth century. Bishop Eric left no trace of his mysterious mission to Vinland. The Icelandic annals and their references to Vinland demonstrate only a continuing awareness of the existence of Vinland a century after the voyages of **Leif Ericsson** and **Thorfinn Karlsefni**.

Bibliography: Boland, Charles M. *They All Discovered America*, 1961; Holand, Hjalmar R., *Explorations in America before Columbus*, 1956; Jones, Gwyn, *The Norse Atlantic Saga*, 2nd ed., 1986.

Gómara, Francisco López de (1511–1566?)

Spanish priest and secretary to Hernán Cortés, he was the first to propose **Atlantis** as the place of origin for Native Americans.

Gómara was born on 2 February 1511 in the town of Gómara, Castile, and entered the priesthood before the age of 20. From about 1530–1540 he served in the household of Diego Hurtada de Mendoza, the sometime Spanish ambassador to Venice. Returning to Spain around 1541, Gómara was chaplain to Hernán Cortés until the conquistador's death in 1547. Gómara wrote a history of the Spanish empire in the Americas focusing on Cortés, which appeared in 1552 as *La historia de las Indias y conquista de México* (History of the Indies and the conquest of Mexico). As the title indicates, it was two books under one title. The first dealt with the history of Spanish discoveries in the New World and gave a description of those lands and peoples. The second book focused on the history of the conquest of Mexico, but was in fact more a biography of Cortés.

Gómara's history proved controversial. **Bartolomé de Las Casas,** an early missionary and historian of Spanish cruelty in the Americas, despised it for its harsh attitudes toward Native Americans and worked to have it suppressed. Las Casas found an ally in Prince Philip (the future Philip II), who did not appreciate the derogatory portrayal of his father, Emperor Charles V. Gómara also aroused the ire of Bernal Diaz del Castillo, an old comrade-in-arms of Cortés, who resented the overemphasis on Cortés's leadership of the expedition. These complaints, however, largely concerned the second half of Gómara's history. The first half contained the material about pre-Columbian visitors to the New World.

Like a number of his contemporaries, Gómara told the story of the **Unknown Pilot of Columbus** and mentioned its several variants. Gómara did not take the story too seriously, however, since he also stated that Columbus was seeking the **antipodes** of East Asia and Japan rather than an unknown land in the western Atlantic. At the same time, Gómara felt that Mediterranean peoples of ancient times had some vague knowledge of the Americas. He was the first to propose that the Native Americans were descendants of colonists and refugees from Atlantis. He also adhered to the common opinion that **Hanno**, a **Carthaginian**, visited Cuba or Hispaniola. Furthermore, he insisted that Seneca's (d. A.D. 65) frequently cited prophecy from the tragedy *Medea* (ca. A.D. 49–62) about unknown lands in the western Atlantic indicated he knew about the Americas. He rejected the tale that Spanish refugees from the Moorish conquest of Iberia in 711 settled in the New World and added to the Native American population. Gómara also accepted the possibility that trans-Atlantic contacts could go both ways, and repeated a medieval story he heard from Olaus Magnus about Native Americans reaching Germany using a northwest passage. Unlike many people in 1550, Gómara correctly believed that America was not connected to Asia, but was separated by a body of water in the northwest.

Gómara's major contribution was the Atlantis story, which would be frequently repeated over the centuries. He also helped to propagate the stories of the Unknown Pilot and Hanno, making him an important link in the historiography of pre-Columbian visitors. It is also important to remember that Gómara stood in the mainstream of sixteenth-century scholarship. His contemporaries considered his ideas perfectly respectable and believable, and so they would remain until the dramatic advances in historical and archaeological scholarship of the nineteenth century.

Bibliography: Huddleston, Lee Eldridge, *Origins of the American Indians: European Concepts, 1492–1729*, 1967; Simpson, Lesley Byrd, ed., *Cortes: The Life of the Conqueror by His Secretary Francisco López de Gómara*, 1964; Wagner, Henry R., "Francisco López de Gómara and His Works," *Proceedings of the American Antiquarian Society* (October 1948): 263–282.

Gordon, Cyrus
(1908–)

A professor of **Hebrew** and Semitic languages who has held teaching positions at Brandeis University and New York University, he is a leading advocate of the **diffusionist** theory that many ancient Mediterranean peoples, particularly the **Phoenicians,** made voyages to the Americas. Although most of his academic writing deals with Ugaritic literature, Old Testament studies, and the ancient Near East, he has also written two books and a number of articles on the subject of trans-Atlantic contacts in ancient times. His books are titled *Before Columbus: Links between the Old World and Ancient America* (1971) and *Riddles in History*

(1974). Neither work was particularly well received by academic archaeologists or historians, but popular diffusionist writers cite them frequently and with great approval.

Great China

Also known as Great Han, Tahan, or Tuhan, this country lay to the northeast of China and was inhabited by the so-called painted people. The narrative of **Hoei-shin** mentioned passing through Great China on the way to **Fusang.** Some writers identify Alaska as Great China and tattooed **Eskimos** as the painted people. Professional sinologists, however, regard the Buriat region of Siberia as the correct location of Great China within the traditional geographical concepts of ancient China.

Great Ireland

Also known as **Hvítramannaland, White Man's Land,** and **Albania Superior,** Great Ireland is the name for the legendary settlement that Irish monks supposedly made on the east coast of what is now the United States during the early Middle Ages. It has been located as far north as the Gulf of St. Lawrence and as far south as the Carolinas. Many supporters place it in the vicinity of Haverhill, Massachusetts, and North Salem, New Hampshire, citing stone ruins as evidence of Irish habitation. See also **Irish Monks in America.**

Green Sea of Darkness

The **Arabic** name for the Atlantic Ocean or Western Ocean reflects the fear with which they regarded that formidable and dangerous body of water. According to geographer Abū-l-Hasan 'Ali ibn al-Husayn ibn Ali al-Mas'ūdī (d. 956; the common Western form of his name is al Massoudy), it was not possible to sail past the Strait of Gibraltar. As he described the Atlantic, "no vessel sails on that sea; it is without cultivation or inhabitant, and its end, like its depth, is

Greenland

unknown." That belief persisted though the time of Abū 'Abd Allāh Muhammad al-Idrīsī (1099–1180; the common Western form of his name is Edrisi). In his great geographical treatise *The Book of Roger*, Edrisi described how a permanent darkness hung over the Atlantic, whose waters were thick and black. Frequent storms and high winds swept over this unpleasant sea, making it impossible to navigate.

Al Massoudy and Edrisi represented the best in geographical thought of the medieval Islamic world, indicating that Arabs did little sailing on the Atlantic. Both men admitted that people had successfully sailed the Green Sea of Darkness, although their knowledge appears to be the hearsay of distant legends and rumors (see also **Arabic Voyages to the Americas**). The bold Arabic seafaring traditions exemplified by the legendary Sinbad the Sailor in the Indian Ocean had no counterpart in that portion of the Islamic world bordering the Atlantic. This circumstance argues strongly against claims that Arabic sailors reached the Americas well before Columbus, as does the lack of convincing archaeological evidence.

Bibliography: Beazley, C. Raymond, *The Dawn of Modern Geography*, 3 vols., [1897–1906], 1949.

Greenland

This large island in the Arctic waters of the North Atlantic was the westernmost permanent Norse settlement from 986 until about 1450–1500. Norse Greenlanders may have traded with the natives of Newfoundland, Labrador, and Baffin Island in the years after **Leif Ericsson's** voyage about 1001.

Gunnbjorn Ulfsson first sighted Greenland sometime between 900 and 930 when a storm drove him too far west while traveling from Norway to **Iceland**. Because he had sailed to Greenland's desolate and heavily glaciated eastern coast, Gunnbjorn made no attempt to land or return to explore his discovery. In 982 another Norse named **Eric the Red** decided to sail west from Iceland in search of Gunnbjorn's discovery. Upon reaching Greenland, Eric sailed south and rounded Cape Farewell, where he found meadows capable of sustaining a community. After spending several years there, Eric returned to Iceland in 986 singing the new land's praises. He called it Greenland to make it even more attractive to settlers. The ploy worked, and that same year Eric sailed from overcrowded Iceland with 25 ships carrying several hundred people. Only 14 reached Greenland; the rest either perished in stormy seas or turned back. Still, there were enough people to give the new colony a good start.

The Norse quickly formed two main settlements. The largest was called the Eastern Settlement, located just west of Cape Farewell. At its height it may have had 5,000 inhabitants. Three hundred miles farther up the west coast lay the Western Settlement. Considerably smaller, it numbered no more than 1,500 people at its high point. In between the two was a minor Middle Settlement with several hundred residents. It probably regarded itself as more of an outlying part of the Eastern Settlement than a separate colony.

The Norse found southern Greenland empty of people, although they discovered abandoned stone buildings and skin boats. Some attribute these remains to **Irish monks** fleeing from **Viking** raids on Ireland. Archaeological evidence indicates that the remains belonged to **Eskimos** of the Dorset culture, who abandoned the area as the climate warmed. A warming climate during the eleventh and twelfth centuries calmed the seas and made sailing to Greenland easier, thus making the Norse settlement possible. The milder climate also permitted the successful grazing of cattle and sheep, and aided the hunting of harp seals, walruses, and caribou. The Norse appear to have traded for furs, walrus ivory, and wood with the various Native American groups inhabiting northern Greenland and Labrador. Although able to make a living comparable to that of the Icelanders, the Norse had insufficient resources to colonize any farther west, as the failures of **Thorvald Ericsson** and **Thorfinn Karlsefni** in **Vinland** show.

Greenland was very much a part of the wider world of the medieval Norse. When Iceland adopted Christianity in the year 1000, Greenland soon followed suit, although Eric the Red remained incorrigibly pagan. The pope consecrated Arnald as the first bishop for Greenland in 1124; his cathedral was located at Gardar in the Eastern Settlement. **Bishop Eric Gnupsson,** said to have sailed to Vinland in 1121, was probably a missionary bishop without an established diocese. In 1261 the Greenlanders gave up their republic and accepted the sovereignty and protection of the king of Norway, as did Iceland a few years later. This decision ultimately contributed to the demise of the isolated colony.

The climate began to cool in the late thirteenth century, and things got even worse in the fourteenth and fifteenth centuries. The Norse grazing and hunting economy became less productive, and communication with Europe more and more difficult. The better-adapted Eskimos of the Thule culture began moving south. For many years relations between the Norse and the Eskimos had been a mixture of cautious trading and sporadic hostility. Although some writers suggest that Eskimo raiders wiped out the declining Norse settlements, a reduced economy and dwindling food supplies appear to have led to malnutrition, followed by disease, depopulation, and ultimate extinction. In 1448 Pope Nicholas V mentioned a heathen fleet attacking the Norse in Greenland, but archae-ological evidence shows the Norse settlements simply faded away. Eskimos occupied the Western Settlement by 1341 and the Middle Settlement by 1380. The Eastern Settlement expired sometime between 1450 and 1500. Eskimo folktales tell of the hunting and killing of Olaf, the last survivor of the Eastern Settlement. The best judgment on the extinction of these settlements blames it on the Norse failure to adopt an Eskimo-style economy in the face of a changing climate rather than defeat in battle with the Eskimos.

Bibliography: Jones, Gwyn, *The Norse Atlantic Saga,* 2nd ed., 1986; McGovern, Thomas H., "The Economics of Extinction in Norse Greenland," in *Climate and History,* edited by T. M. L. Wigley, et al., 1981; McGovern, Thomas H., "The Lost Norse Colony of Greenland," in *Vikings in the West,* edited by Eleanor Guralnick, 1982.

Grotius–De Laet Controversy (1641–1652)

The first literary controversy concerning the origins of Native Americans involved Dutch scholars Hugo Grotius (1583–1645), the father of international law, and Johan De Laet (ca. 1582–1649), a historian and geographer.

The origins of Native Americans provoked numerous speculations by Europeans from 1492 onward. During the first half of the seventeenth century, distinguished scholar Hugo Grotius found current explanations unsatisfactory. While serving as the Swedish ambassador in Paris, in 1641 he presented his own theory in a 15-page pamphlet titled *De origine gentium Americanarum* (Of the origins of the people of America). He suggested that Native Americans living north of the Isthmus of Panama were descendants of Norwegians arriving via **Iceland** and **Greenland.** Linguistic and cultural similarities formed the basis of his evidence. One exception to his Norwegian origin theory was the Yucatán people, whom Grotius claimed came across the Atlantic Ocean from Ethiopia. The Maya practiced circumcision and supposedly used crosses; the Ethiopians were Christians who also practiced circumcision. In South America, Grotius credited China as the source of the aboriginal peoples; since he believed the Peruvians were very civilized and had a writing system similar to the **Chinese,** they must surely be of Chinese descent. Grotius did not believe the theory of the **Ten Lost Tribes.** He also rejected **José de Acosta's** theory that the Native Americans came across a narrow strait from Asia. In his opinion the Americas were settled quite late—after the time of Christ in the case of the Ethiopians, and after the Norse settlement of Greenland at the end of the tenth century in the case of the Norwegians.

Grotius sent Johan De Laet, an acknowledged expert on America, a copy of his *De origine* while it was in manuscript and asked for comments. De Laet complied and gathered a number of notes on the topic. He suggested Grotius rethink his supposed geographical connections between the Old World and the Americas and the distribution of animals in the Americas. He also sent a copy of Acosta's *Historia natural y moral de las Indias* (Natural and moral history of the Indies). De Laet was a staunch adherent of Acosta's theory that the ancestors of Native Americans followed an Arctic strait route from Asia. Grotius ignored his advice and published *De origine* as originally written, an act that insulted and angered De Laet.

De Laet decided to reply to what he considered were Grotius's erroneous ideas. In 1643 he published his *Notae ad dissertationem Hugonis Grotii de origine gentium Americanarum. . . .* This work began with a condemnation of Grotius's assertion that no one had carefully studied the origins of Na-

tive Americans prior to his *De origine.* Next De Laet attacked Grotius's rejection of Acosta's land bridge theory. Grotius had incorrectly assumed that Acosta claimed **Scythians** as the people who came across the land bridge. Since the customs of Native Americans bore no resemblance to those of the Scythians, and because the Scythians relied heavily on horses while the Native Americans had no horses, Grotius concluded that no connection was possible. De Laet challenged Grotius's conclusion on two grounds. First, he pointed out that Native Americans were very likely the descendants of an Asian people displaced by the Scythians rather than direct descendants. Second, even if Native Americans were descendants of the Scythians, quite possibly some of them migrated to America prior to domestication of the horse. De Laet also asserted that the original inhabitants arrived far earlier than Grotius allowed; the diversity of languages and the large aboriginal population led De Laet to conclude that more time would have been needed to settle those lands. De Laet claimed that the migration to the Americas must have taken place, not after the time of Christ, but right after the confusion of languages at the Tower of Babel about 2200 B.C. Although he thought Acosta's Asian origin theory accounted for most of the aboriginal peoples, he was willing to concede that later immigrants also arrived by sea—but mostly in pre-Christian times and only rarely. For example, De Laet believed that Spaniards may have drifted to the Americas from the Canary Islands, that **Madoc** and the Welsh probably reached America, and that **Polynesians** may have sailed to America.

Grotius quickly responded in the same year with *De origine gentium Americanarum dissertio altera adversus obtrectatorem opaca quem bonum facit barba* (Of the origins of the people of the Americas: Another dissertation). The book was a bitter personal attack on De Laet, but added nothing to

Grotius's theories. Not to be outdone, De Laet just as quickly composed a rejoinder, which he published in 1644 as *Responsio ad dissertationem secundum Hugonis Grotii . . .* (Response to the second dissertation of Hugo Grotius . . .). After dealing with Grotius's personal attacks, De Laet again criticized his ideas. He pointed out that it was absurd for Grotius to divide the peoples of the Americas at Panama since there was nothing to prevent the inhabitants of North and South America from mixing. He wrote that Ethiopia did not border on the Atlantic Ocean and was not a maritime nation, so how could its people have sailed to and settled the Yucatán? As to Grotius's Peruvian theory, De Laet showed that they did not have a real system of writing, let alone a sophisticated one like that of the Chinese. With that said, Grotius and De Laet declined to continue the controversy, although it did not end. Works by Jean Baptiste Poisson and Robert Comte in 1644 commented on the controversy, although neither added much of substance. In 1645 De Laet persuaded Georg Horn, a professor of history from Gelderland, to write a refutation of Grotius, but Grotius died and Horn did not publish his study until 1652. It was a lengthy work titled *De originibus Americanis libri quatour* (Of the origins of the Americans: Four books), in which Horn supported the positions of De Laet and Acosta, arguing that the Native Americans had come across a land bridge from Asia. However, he also believed that **Phoenicians, Carthaginians,** and Chinese reached the Americas by sea at later dates.

One interesting aspect of the Grotius–De Laet controversy is the strong early support shown for Acosta's theory, the ancestor of the modern **Bering Land Bridge/Strait theory.** At the same time, the controversy also indicates how little progress occurred in the state of knowledge about Native American origins; not until the rise of modern archaeology in the late nineteenth century

would progress be made. Grotius's erroneous theories were not considered particularly implausible by many scholars until the beginning of the twentieth century.

Bibliography: Huddleston, Lee Eldridge, *Origins of the American Indians: European Concepts, 1492–1729*, 1967; Wright, Herbert F., "The Controversy of Hugo Grotius and Johan De Laet on the Origins of the American Aborigines," in *Some Less Known Works of Hugo Grotius*, edited by Herbert F. Wright, 1928.

Gunnlangsson, Voyage of Gudleif (ca. 1025–1030)

The *Eyrbyggia Saga* contains the story of a supposed pre-Columbian visit to North America by Norse sailors.

During a trading voyage between Dublin and **Iceland,** storms drove the ship of Gudleif Gunnlangsson of Iceland west to an unknown land. The natives, who appeared to speak Irish, took the Norse prisoner and

debated whether to kill the captives or enslave them. A group of horsemen approached under the leadership of a tall old man. The white-haired man greeted the Icelanders in Norse and asked about news from there. Later he persuaded the natives to release their captives, and advised the Norse to sail away immediately. When asked for his name, he refused to answer, but Gudleif recognized him as a man named Bjorn, forced to flee from Iceland for engaging in an adulterous affair. Bjorn sent back a gold ring as a gift for his former lover, but forbade anyone to come looking for him. The Norse departed and made their way to Ireland.

Some scholars identify the unknown land in the *Eyrbyggia Saga* with the **Great Ireland** of the legendary **Irish monks** who settled in America. Unlike some other sagas, the *Eyrbyggia Saga* never refers to its unknown land as Great Ireland or any of its other names. Scholars of the saga agree that its historical accuracy has always been quite high when it could be checked against other sources. Written as early as 1200 and not later than 1350, it describes events that supposedly occurred after the **voyages of Bjarni Herjolfsson** in 986 and **Leif Ericsson** in about 1001. Its author does not seem to know about the legend of Great Ireland even when he compares the natives of the unknown land with the Irish. Therefore, the saga does not prove a widespread belief in the existence of Great Ireland among the Icelandic Norse of the thirteenth and fourteenth centuries. See also **Irish Monks in America.**

Bibliography: Schach, Paul, trans., *Eyrbyggia Saga,* [1959], 1977.

H

mon legends, and religious parallels as evidence for Polynesian descent from the Native Americans. The possibility of Polynesian origins in Asia is rejected by Mormon scholars. Most professional anthropologists reject the Mormon ideas on Polynesia just as vehemently as they do those of Heyerdahl, even though some will admit that occasional Polynesian-American contacts took place in pre-Columbian times.

Bibliography: Petersen, Mark E., *Those Gold Plates!* 1979; Sorenson, John L., *An Ancient American Setting for the Book of Mormon*, 1985.

Hanno, Voyage of (ca. 490 B.C.)

This **Carthaginian** explorer and colonizer of West Africa was widely believed during the sixteenth century to have visited America.

Around 500 B.C. the Carthaginian government decided to promote exploration and the systematic establishment of trading posts beyond the Strait of Gibraltar. Large expeditions were sent out both north and south along the Atlantic coastline. The leaders of the two expeditions were the brothers Himilco and Hanno, governors of the Carthaginian settlers in Andalusia. Himilco commanded the northern expedition, which may have reached Britain, and marked the beginning of the Carthaginian takeover of the Atlantic tin trade.

Hanno's expedition sailed south along the west African coast. Its most important accomplishment was the foundation of the colony of Cerné (probably Herne Island at the mouth of the Río de Oro), which served as a post for the trans-Saharan gold trade. Some expedition members continued to sail south; after three weeks they encountered dense coastal forests and mysterious natives. Supplies began to run short, however, and they were forced to turn back. Most scholars think Hanno reached as far south as Sherbo

Hagoth the Shipbuilder

Mormons traditionally believe that Polynesia was populated by people from the Americas, specifically the white **Nephites,** based on the story of Hagoth found in the book of *Alma* 63: 5–8 in *The Book of Mormon.*

Hagoth built a number of ships on the shores of the Western Sea (Pacific Ocean) to carry settlers into the northern lands. Several of his ships sailed off and were never heard from again. It has been assumed that they settled in Polynesia, but *The Book of Mormon* does not sustain this contention. Needless to say, Mormons are very supportive of the theories of **Thor Heyerdahl** concerning **Polynesian-American contacts.** They list the presence of the **sweet potato** and **cotton,** similar fortifications, stone statues, com-

Sound near the western border of present-day Liberia.

Knowledge of Hanno's African voyage is preserved in a Greek translation of the original Punic document, which was a heavily censored account. After Columbus's voyage to America in 1492, many believed that Hanno had also visited the New World during his great expedition to Africa; several Spanish historians referred to such a visit. The first published mention of the Hanno story occurred in 1540 in the work of Alejo Vanegas de Bustos. He was followed by Florián de Ocampo in 1544 and **Francisco López de Gómara** in 1552. In 1559 **Humphrey Llwyd,** the first historian of **Madoc's** journey to America, also credited Hanno with visiting America. That story was later repeated by Richard Hakluyt in his widely read *Principall Navigations* (1589).

Belief in Hanno's discovery of America was not universal. Both Antonio Galvão, the Portuguese author of *Discoveries of the World* (1555), and Spanish scholar **José de Acosta** refer only to Hanno's African journey. Writing in 1582, another Spanish historian, Miguel Cabello de Valboa, directly attacked Vanegas's suggestion. Despite considerable scholarly skepticism, the story of Hanno's discovery of America persists into the twentieth century. The source for these speculations appears to be Hanno's reference to an inhabited island of forests far out in the western Atlantic. That reference, however, probably refers to a forgotten Carthaginian discovery of the Azores rather than America.

Bibliography: Huddleston, Lee Eldridge, *Origins of the American Indians: European Concepts, 1492–1729,* 1967; Kaeppel, C., *Off the Beaten Track in the Classics,* 1936; Luce, J. V., "Ancient Explorers," in *The Quest for America,* edited by Geoffrey Ashe, 1971.

Hebrews in Ancient America

Also known as the Israelites, the Children of Israel, or the Jews, in the sixteenth century many theories claimed that these biblical people were the ancestors of all or some of the aborigines of the Americas.

There are several variations on the Hebrew theory. One contentious aspect concerned the extent of the role played by Hebrew immigrants. Some writers claimed that all Native Americans were descendants of Hebrew settlers, but more commonly, others believed the Hebrews settled among a preexisting population of aboriginal peoples and were assimilated. For example, one theory pointed out that servants of King Solomon traveled to **Ophir** for gold and claimed that Ophir was in America. Some of these Hebrews remained behind and either completely populated the land of Ophir or merged with the original inhabitants. Most supporters of the Ophirite theory favored the latter view.

Other theories claimed that various Hebrew groups fled to the Americas as refugees from war and persecution. The most famous theory involved the **Ten Lost Tribes of Israel** as the ancestors of Native Americans. The biblical kingdom of Israel consisted of 10 of the 12 tribes of Israel. The Assyrian king Shalmanesar V invaded Israel in 724 B.C. and besieged its capital of Samaria. He died in 722, but his successor, Sargon II, completed the siege that same year and carried away close to 30,000 captives. According to 2 *Kings* 17: 6 and 23, "the king of Assyria captured Samaria and he carried the Israelites away to Assyria, and placed them in Halah, and on the Habor, the river of Gozan, and in the cities of the Medes. . . . So Israel was exiled from their own land to Assyria until this day." For many people, this event marked the end of the Ten Lost Tribes. The neighboring peoples of Media and Assyria simply absorbed them into their own population, and the exiles lost their religious and ethnic identity. The apocryphal book of 2 Esdras 13: 40–45, however, supplied the following intriguing information, indicating that the Ten Lost Tribes were not finished at all.

> These are the ten tribes that were led away from their own land into captivity in the days of King Hosea, whom Shalmaneser the king of the Assyrians led captive; he took them across the river, and they were taken into another land. But they formed this plan for themselves, that they would leave the multitude of the nations and go to a more distant region, where mankind had never lived, that there at least they might keep their statutes which they had not kept in their own land. And they went in by the narrow passages of the Euphrates river. For at that time the Most High performed signs for them, and stopped the channels of the river until they had passed over. Through that region there was a long way to go, a journey of a year and a half; and that country is called Arzareth.

According to 2 Esdras, the Ten Lost Tribes would reappear during the last days of the world. Endless speculation arose as to where the Ten Lost Tribes were and what they were doing. *Arzareth* literally means another land, but what land? Various places in Africa, Asia, and Europe have been suggested as possible sites. The European discovery of the Americas provided yet another possible candidate for Arzareth—that "more distant region, where mankind had never lived." The Ten Lost Tribes theory remains the most popular of the Hebrew origin theories from the sixteenth century on.

Other theories focused on the surviving remnant of the 12 tribes of the Hebrews, the kingdom of Judah and its successors. Jeru-

salem, the capital of Judah, fell in 586 B.C. to the besieging armies of Nebuchadnezzar of Babylon and its inhabitants carried away. Most of the captives eventually managed to return to their homeland, but some writers suggest that some refugees fled to the Americas and became the ancestors of Native Americans. That belief is the foundation of *The Book of Mormon* and its narrative of the tragic histories of the **Nephites, Lamanites, and Mulekites.** Mormons traditionally believe that the peoples described in *The Book of Mormon* populated all of the Americas, becoming the ancestors of all Native Americans. Recent Mormon scholarship scales back those claims and only credits them with populating Mexico's Isthmus of Tehuantepec. Other writers suggest that Hebrew or Jewish refugees came to America after the fall of Jerusalem to the Romans in A.D. 70. Another possibility involves survivors of the Bar Kochba revolt in 135. Other traumatic events that might have transformed some Hebrews into refugees are the various barbarian invasions of the Roman empire during the fifth century or the Islamic conquests of the eastern and southern Mediterranean coasts during the seventh century. Generally, the later in time a Hebrew group supposedly reached the Americas, the less it would be responsible for populating those continents. These later Hebrew immigrants would have formed enclaves or colonies within the existing societies of Native Americans.

One question that arises is why the Hebrews have been such popular and perennial candidates. The eminent anthropologist Robert Wauchope attributes this popularity to the widespread knowledge of the ancient Hebrews that the Bible makes possible. Prior to the rise of modern anthropology, the Hebrews were by far the best-known ancient people in an ethnographic sense. Furthermore, as English writer John Ogilby pointed out in 1671, traumatic events of the ancient world scattered the Hebrews or Jews far from their ancestral homeland. European travelers grew accustomed to finding Jews in all sorts of seemingly out-of-the-way places, including the Americas. Therefore, when they encountered strange customs and practices among the indigenous peoples they visited, they naturally used their knowledge of the biblical Hebrews as the measure for comparison. Lacking valid theoretical concepts of anthropology, these European observers were unable to distinguish among shared cultural traits that were the result of **parallel evolution** and independent invention, or those that might have resulted from possible cultural **diffusion**. If a Native American tribe practiced a custom such as circumcision, it was commonly and erroneously assumed that they had Hebrew antecedents or contacts in the past.

Despite the high profile of the ancient Hebrews in European consciousness, the first Europeans to explore or settle in the Americas after 1492 did not turn to Hebrew theories. They looked to the literature of classical Greece and Rome for the **Carthaginians** or survivors from **Atlantis**. During extensive research into the history of theories about Native American origins, historian Lee Eldridge Huddleston "was unable to locate any early explorers and historians who expressed the idea [i.e., the Hebrew theory] in writing." He concluded that the Hebrew theory was discussed but not accepted during the first decades of Spanish-American history. The earliest known reference may be in *The Decades of the New World* by Peter Martyr de Anglería (ca. 1455–1526), who stated that Christopher Columbus thought Hispaniola was the land of Ophir. This suggestion opened up the possibility that some of its inhabitants were descended from Hebrew visitors. There is no other evidence that Columbus thought he had found Ophir, and his Spanish contemporaries did not support the Ophirite or any other version of the

Hebrew theory until the last quarter of the sixteenth century.

The first person definitely to advocate the Ten Lost Tribes version of the Hebrew theory was Joannes Fredericus Lumnius of the Low Countries in his *De extremo Dei Iudicio vocatione* of 1567 and his *De vicinitate extremi judicii Dei et consummationis saeculi* of 1594. Although not widely circulated, Lumnius established the theological foundations of the Ten Lost Tribes theory. Following 2 Esdras, he claimed that they escaped the Assyrians and settled in America. French scholar Gilbert Genebard followed Lumnius in the same year with his *Chronographia,* which also supported the Ten Lost Tribes theory.

Traditional accounts frequently and wrongly credit **Bartolomé de Las Casas, Diego de Landa,** and **Juan de Torquemada** with promoting the Hebrew theory. These men were quite skeptical about the occurrence of any Hebrew contacts with ancient America. Other Spanish scholars studying the Native Americans of Mexico, however, found that the theory was a reasonable explanation of supposed similarities between Hebrew and Native American customs. **Diego Durán,** Juan Suárez de Peralta (ca. 1536–1591), and Juan de Tovar closely studied the aborigines of Mexico and found interesting parallels with the Hebrews. Writing about 1580, both Peralta and Durán pointed out how similar the story of the Ten Lost Tribes' escape from the Assyrians to the land of Arzareth was to the Aztec legends of wandering from their homeland of Aztlan.

During the early seventeenth century, Spanish chroniclers Pedro Simón (1574–1630?) and Antonio Vazquez de Espinosa (ca. 1570–1630) adopted the even narrower theory that Native Americans were descended solely from the Hebrew tribe of Issachar. A more complete version of the Ten Lost Tribes theory reappeared in 1681 in the work *Tratado único y singular del origen de los indios occidentales de Perú, México, Santa Fé y Chile* (A unique and singular tract about the origin of the West Indians of Peru, Mexico, Santa Fe, and Chile). Diego Andrés Rocha (ca. 1607–1688), a Jesuit and canon lawyer, wrote it to show why the Native Americans behaved poorly. Although he believed that Native Americans had some ancestry from early Spanish visitors, he believed they were largely descended from **Tartars** and Hebrews, which accounted for their wildness.

From the sixteenth century on, many Spanish writers strongly opposed the Ten Lost Tribes theory. Beginning with Bartolomé de Las Casas and proceeding on to **José de Acosta**, the seventeenth-century Juan de Torquemada, and Pedro Antonio de la Calancha y Benavides (1584–1654), the best Spanish scholars rejected the possibility of Native Americans being Hebrews. Acosta sensibly asked the following:

> But what reason of conjecture is there in this, seeing the Jews are so careful to preserve their language and Antiquities, so that in all parts of the world they differ and are known from others, and yet in the Indies [Americas] alone, they have forgotten their lineage, their law, their ceremonies, their messiahs; and finally their whole Judaism?

Good-sense arguments have never stopped absurd theories, and the Hebrew origin theory was no exception. Instead, it spread to northern Europe.

In 1644 the Jewish community of Amsterdam was rocked by the report that Antonio de Montezinos (Aaron Levi) had discovered the Ten Lost Tribes in the Spanish province of Peru. Montezinos claimed that while traveling in the region of Quito, he and his Native American guide Francisco confided to each other that they were prac-ticing Jews. Emboldened by this information, Francisco led Montezinos on a seven-day journey into the wilderness. At an unknown river, Francisco made a signal and some white people started to cross the river. Although the cautious white people would not allow Montezinos to cross the river into their land, he learned that they were Hebrews of the tribe of Reuben. The whites were on friendly terms with the native tribes in the area and had converted many of them to Judaism. Together they were plotting to overthrow the Spaniards. Needless to say, Montezinos's news was greeted with enthusiasm and apocalyptic musings. Menasseh Ben Israel, the great rabbi of Amsterdam, used Montezinos's story to persuade Oliver Cromwell and other Puritan leaders of the short-lived English Republic to allow Jews back into England. More importantly, Montezinos's story spread far more widely than any of the earlier Spanish theories about Native Americans being descendants of the Ten Lost Tribes. From that point the Ten Lost Tribes theory firmly entered the popular consciousness of Western society and has remained strongly ensconced ever since.

James Adair, the eighteenth-century historian of North American Indians, was another great popularizer of the Hebrew theory, and others followed in the early nineteenth century. Both Elias Boudinot and Ethan Smith were early–nineteenth-century American writers who accepted the truth of the Ten Lost Tribes version of the Hebrew theory. They also probably deeply influenced the thinking of **Joseph Smith, Jr.**, the founder of Mormonism. Other writers, such as Anne Simon in her *The Ten Tribes of Israel Historically Identified with the Aborigines of the Western Hemisphere* (1836), accused the early Spanish priests and officials of suppressing evidence that the Native Americans were of Hebrew ancestry. **Edward King, Viscount Kingsborough**, also supported the Hebrew theory and agreed with Simon's suspicions. The Ten Lost Tribes theory has managed to find committed backers ever since.

Other versions of the Hebrew theory have not had such long careers or such large followings, with the exception of the adherents of *The Book of Mormon.* One interesting theory concerns the burial site and supposed Hebrew inscription found at Bat Creek, Tennessee, during the late nineteenth century. In 1894 Cyrus Thomas, the Smithsonian archaeologist, identified the Bat Creek site as a Cherokee burial ground. That identification has been challenged in the twentieth century by various writers including **Cyrus Gordon,** a professor of Semitic languages. They claim that the Bat Creek inscription is Hebrew and relates to the Bar Kochba rebellion of A.D. 135 in Roman Judea. Gordon attempted to bolster his theory by pointing out that the Bat Creek inscription ties in quite nicely with various finds of Roman and Bar Kochba coins in the Kentucky and Tennessee area. Unfortunately, experts do not consider these **coin finds** to be genuine. Gordon's willingness to also consider the possibility that these inscriptions were made by refugees from the defeat of the Jewish Revolt in A.D. 70 does not help his case because the arguments against it are almost as strong as those against the Bar Kochba rebellion.

The Hebrew theory continues to attract new supporters. Professional archaeologists and anthropologists, on the other hand, completely dismiss the Hebrew theory and all its versions. They insist that no convincing evidence of pre-Columbian Hebrew visitors has yet been found, and strongly feel that none will, because no such visits took place. Still the romance and mystery associated with the Ten Lost Tribes as well as other aspects of the history of the Jewish people have made the Hebrews prime candidates for being pre-Columbian visitors to the Ameri-

cas—at least, in the realm of popular culture. It is an odd fate for an ancient people never well known for being seafarers.

Bibliography: Gaddis, Vincent H., *American Indian Myths and Legends,* 1977; Godbey, Allen H., *The Lost Tribes a Myth—Suggestions towards Rewriting Hebrew History,* [1930], 1974; Gordon, Cyrus H., *Before Columbus: Links between the Old World and Ancient America,* 1971; Huddleston, Lee Eldridge, *Origins of the American Indians: European Concepts, 1492–1729,* 1967; Katz, David, *Philo-Semitism and the Readmission of the Jews to England, 1603–1655,* 1982; Sanders, Ronald, *Lost Tribes and Promised Lands: The Origins of American Racism,* 1978; Vogel, Dan, *Indian Origins and the Book of Mormon: Religious Solutions from Columbus to Joseph Smith,* 1986; Wauchope, Robert, *Lost Tribes and Sunken Continents,* 1962; Weiner, George, "America's Jewish Braves," *Mankind* 4 (October 1974): 56–64.

Helluland

Meaning flatstone land or slab land in Norse, this is the name that Norse explorers of North America gave to the heavily glaciated land of stone they first sighted after leaving **Greenland.**

The **Vinland Sagas** describe it as lying either two or four days sail west of Greenland. Scholars generally agree that Helluland was Baffin Island, although nineteenth-century Danish scholar Carl Rafn and his followers, such as Hjalmar Holand, thought it was Newfoundland. According to the *Greenlanders' Saga,* it was the third and last land sighted by **Bjarni Herjolfsson,** although he did not land on it or name it. **Leif Ericsson** landed there later and named it Helluland. The Norse considered it a worthless country. *Eirik's Saga* credits **Thorfinn Karlsefni** with naming this stony country Helluland. It is described as being full of stone slabs, hence the name, and foxes. Given the nature of Helluland, the Norse made no attempt to settle there, although they appear to have traded with Dorset and Thule culture **Eskimos** who lived on Baffin Island and the surrounding areas. See also **Markland** and **Vinland.**

Herbert, Sir Thomas (1606–1682)

This English traveler was the author of a book popular among the reading public in seventeenth-century England, *A Relation of Some Yeares Travaile . . . into Afrique and the Greater Asia* (1634), which included an account of **Madoc's voyage** to America.

Herbert was born into a well-to-do merchant family of Welsh ancestry that had settled in York. He began attending Oxford University in 1621 but did not graduate. Thanks to the influence of his relative William Herbert, third earl of Pembroke, in 1627 he gained a place in the retinue of Sir Dodmore Cotton, who was going on an embassy to the king of Persia. Sailing around Africa on a type of ship known as an East Indiaman, the party arrived at Gombroon (now Bandar 'Abbās, Iran) on the Persian Gulf on 10 January 1628. They traveled overland to the Persian court at Qazvin where, on 23 July, Ambassador Cotton died of dysentery. The remainder of the embassy secured the Persian shah's permission to travel around his country. Departing 12 April 1629 for the voyage home, they visited the Coromandel coast of India, Ceylon, and various islands of the Indian Ocean. The party reached Plymouth by the end of 1629.

Herbert published an account of his travels in the east in 1634 titled *A Relation of Some Yeares Travaile, Begunne Anno 1626. Into Afrique and the Greater Asia, especially the Territories of the Persian Monarchie: and Some Parts of the Orientall Indies and Iles Adiacent,* followed by a greatly expanded second edition in 1638. Proving

quite popular, the book was reprinted a number of times over the years, and translated into Dutch in 1658 and French in 1663. During the English Civil War of the 1640s, Herbert fought on the side of Parliament. Appointed to attend the captive King Charles I, he performed his duties with great kindness until the king's execution in early 1649. After the Restoration in 1660, Charles II rewarded those good deeds with a baronetcy. For the remainder of his life, Herbert lived as a country gentleman and pursued his antiquarian interest.

Sir Thomas Herbert from an engraving by Joseph Halfpenny.

As a nostalgic Welsh expatriate, Herbert tended to find linguistic evidences for early Welsh visitors in most of the places he visited, including the Cape of Good Hope, Madagascar, and Mauritius. In the first edition of his travel narrative, he devoted a brief section to Madoc's discovery of America; in the second he increased it. Herbert's account of Madoc's journeys and settlement is more detailed than the earlier ones by **John Dee, David Powel,** and other sixteenth-century writers. Apparently Herbert may have used sources not available to the earlier historians and which were subsequently lost again. Even so, some details of the story remained vague. For instance, Herbert could not decide whether the Welsh landed in Canada, Florida, or Mexico. Citing the familiar speech of Aztec Emperor Moctezuma (Montezuma) II regarding visits by white sea voyagers, Herbert claimed that Mexican sources said they arrived in **curachs.**

It is impossible to know for certain whether Herbert had better sources than his predecessors or simply a better imagination for embroidering a story. What is certain is that the Madoc story became far better known because of Herbert's popular travel book, which he continued to revise until his death in 1682.

Bibliography: "Herbert, Sir Thomas," in the *Dictionary of National Biography*, 22 vols., 1908–1909; Williams, Gwyn A., *Madoc: The Making of a Myth*, 1979.

Herjolfsson, Voyage of Bjarni (986)

He was the first Norse seafarer to sight the mainland of North America.

The story of Bjarni Herjolfsson appears only in the *Greenlanders' Saga* (see also **Vinland Sagas**). That account tells how Bjarni's father Herjolf Bardarson farmed in **Iceland,** while Bjarni was a successful merchant in the carrying trade between Iceland and Norway. It was Bjarni's practice to spend the winter on his father's farm. During the spring of 986, Herjolf decided to sell the farm and move to the brand-new settlement of **Greenland.** In the fall, a surprised Bjarni arrived with his cargo to find that his father had left Iceland. Undaunted, Bjarni persuaded his crew to sail on to Greenland. Three days after leaving Iceland, foul weather and fog came up, driving Bjarni's ship west.

After many days at sea with no idea of their location, the storms abated and the Norse sighted land. Sailing in close to shore, they saw well-wooded land with low hills.

But they did not land; instead, they put out to sea for two days and sighted more land. It was also wooded, but it was flat. The absence of glaciers meant that it was not Greenland. The crew wanted to land and take on more water and firewood but Bjarni refused. Putting out to sea once more, they sailed another three days and again made landfall. This time the land was mountainous and glaciated, but again Bjarni refused to land, citing its worthless nature. Returning to sea, Bjarni's ship sailed another four days. This time they sighted a land that he thought was Greenland. Bjarni was willing to land, and it just so happened that they had reached his father's new home, called Herjolfness.

Bjarni decided to give up trading, and he worked the farm with his father. But he did not give up talking about his discovery of land to the west. Some years later, around the year 1000, he visited the court of Earl Eirik Hakonarson, who ruled Norway from 1000–1014. While his story provoked a great deal of interest, Bjarni's failure to land and explore drew much criticism. Nevertheless, the earl made Bjarni one of his retainers. Bjarni returned to Greenland the next summer and **Leif Ericsson** bought his ship in order to make his own western voyage. That voyage resulted in the first Norse landing and settlement on North America.

Bibliography: Jones, Gwyn, *The Norse Atlantic Saga*, 2nd ed., 1968; Phillips, J. R. S., *The Medieval Expansion of Europe*, 1988.

Hespérides, Islands of

Also known as the Islas Hespérides, this group of islands was discovered and settled by the legendary Spanish king **Héspero** about 1700 or 1100 B.C.

The sixteenth-century Spanish historian **Gonzalo Fernández de Oviedo y Valdés** claimed that those islands were actually the West Indies, thus giving Spain a very ancient primacy in the discovery of the Americas. His Hesperian theory was vehemently rejected by, among others, Fernando Columbus, the son of Christopher Columbus.

Héspero
(fl. 1700 B.C.)

Also known as Hesperus, this legendary Spanish king supposedly flourished around 1700 or 1100 B.C. and discovered the **islands of Hespérides** in the western Atlantic Ocean. Later sixteenth-century Spanish historians such as **Gonzalo Fernández de Oviedo y Valdés** identified them as the West Indies.

As a patriotic Spaniard, Oviedo was anxious to increase Spain's credit for the discovery of the Americas and to diminish that of Christopher Columbus, a Genoese foreigner. In his *Historia general y natural de las Indias*, Oviedo claimed that the first person to settle the Americas was the Spanish king Héspero and his followers. Héspero, not to be confused with the Hesperus of classical mythology, lived 650 years after Noah's flood, which was about 1700 B.C. according to the Hebrew chronology of the Bible, or 1100 B.C. according to St. Augustine's chronology. By sailing west, the Spanish king discovered the Isles of the Hespérides, which his people settled and populated. Contact with the colony was lost after his death and the whole episode was forgotten. According to Oviedo, the Hespérides were the West Indies, and the natives of the Americas were descendants of Spanish settlers with some **Carthaginians** added later. Oviedo's source for this story of Héspero was a Hellenistic historian of dubious reputation named Berosus (fl. ca. 290 B.C.).

While Oviedo's Hesperian story appealed to Spanish vanity, it also attracted some critics. The harshest was Fernando Columbus, the son of the discoverer, who took exception to Oviedo's attempt to diminish his father's achievement. In the tenth chapter of Fernando's biography of his father, he rejects Oviedo's claims by pointing out that the sources cited by the Spaniard did not bear out his claims. Fernando confused the historian Berosus with Roman geographer Sebosus, who lived about 50 B.C. Sebosus did not refer to Héspero as the ruler of Spain. Fernando also pointed out that another of Oviedo's sources, the astronomer Hyginus (ca. 65 B.C.–A.D. 17), placed the Hespérides in the east, not the west. Basically Fernando contended that Oviedo both faked his sources and misunderstood them.

The Portuguese historian Antonio Galvão (1503–1557) in his *The Discoveries of the New World*, first published in 1563, also rejected Oviedo's identification of the Hespérides as the West Indies. Galvão suggested that they were the islands of São Tomé and Príncipe off the west coast of Africa. He reasoned that ancient mariners tended to hug the coastline, so an African identification for the Hespérides made more sense than a West Indian one requiring a high seas journey. Oviedo's story of Héspero's discovery did not gain acceptance outside Spain; even within Spain, the theory's weak documentary basis meant that other more plausible theories quickly pushed it out of the mainstream of scholarly discourse.

Bibliography: Galvão, Antonio, *The Discoveries of the New World* (Hakluyt Society), 1962; Huddleston, Lee Eldridge, *Origins of the American Indians: European Concepts, 1492–1729*, 1967; Keen, Benjamin, ed., *The Life of the Admiral Christopher Columbus by His Son Ferdinand*, 1959.

Heyerdahl, Thor
(1914–)

This Norwegian anthropologist and archaeologist is the leading advocate of oceanic travel as a means for widespread cultural change among early human societies (see also **Diffusionism**). Heyerdahl's theories concentrate mainly on the problems of

119

Thor Heyerdahl and the reed boat Ra II.

Polynesian-American contacts, the origins of the **Easter Island** culture, and the feasibility of ancient **Egyptians** reaching the Americas in reed boats.

Born in Norway, Heyerdahl studied zoology at the University of Oslo. From 1937 to 1938 he lived on Fatu-Hiva in the Marquesa Islands of the Pacific Ocean. After returning to Norway he published *Fatu-Hiva: Back to Nature* in 1938, a book whose profits allowed him to live among and study the Bella Coola Indians of British Columbia. The German invasion of Norway in World War II trapped Heyerdahl in Canada, where he joined the Free Norwegian Forces. After the war ended he returned to his anthropological studies and formulated his theory that Polynesia had been settled by people from the Americas and not Asia as traditionally thought. When other scholars rejected his theories as preposterous or simply ignored his ideas, Heyerdahl decided on a practical demonstration. In 1947, he and some fellow Norwegians put together a reproduction of an ancient Peruvian balsa raft that they named *Kon Tiki* after the Andean sun king/god Kon Tiki (or Con Tiki), more commonly known as **Viracocha**. According to legend, when driven out of his kingdom, Kon Tiki sailed west into the vast ocean.

The *Kon Tiki* sailed from Callao, Peru, on 28 April 1947 using the Humboldt and South Equatorial currents, and on 30 July sighted land, the island of Puka Puka. Unable to steer, the Norwegians drifted past and finally ran aground on the reef of Raroia Island on 7 August. Heyerdahl quickly published a book about the voyage, also titled *Kon Tiki,* in 1948 that quickly became quite popular. *Kon Tiki* was eventually translated into 60 languages, including English in 1950, and became an international bestseller. Heyerdahl's name became a household word and *Kon Tiki* is still in print over 40 years later. In 1952, Heyerdahl followed up *Kon Tiki*'s success with a related academic study— *American Indians in the Pacific: The Theory behind the* Kon Tiki *Expedition,* which was not so well received by other scholars.

Heyerdahl turned his attention to the mysterious culture of Easter Island in 1954 and formulated a theory that people from the Lake Titicaca region in Bolivia and Peru had settled there about A.D. 200 rather than 1200, the date traditionally assigned by archaeologists. A popular version of this theory appeared in 1957 as *Aku Aku: The Secret of Easter Island,* with an English translation in 1958. An academic account, *The Archaeology of Easter Island,* appeared in 1961 but again other archaeologists and anthropologists greeted it with skepticism. Still, Heyerdahl's ideas gained some recognition and respect, and in 1961 the University of Oslo awarded him an honorary doctorate.

Heyerdahl's interest in **diffusionism** and transoceanic contacts by early humans continued unabated, and in the late 1960s his attention shifted to the Atlantic Ocean. This time he set out to prove that the reed or papyrus boats used in ancient Egypt and the Americas were capable of safe oceanic travel. Tribesmen from Lake Chad constructed a reed vessel for Heyerdahl that he named *Ra* after the Egyptian sun god. Sailing from Safi, Morocco, in 1969 with the types of provisions that would have been available to ancient Egyptians, the *Ra* reached open water. Its rudder broke, but even though it was drifting rather than sailing, the ship made good progress toward South America because it had entered the Canary and North Equatorial currents. Unfortunately, Heyerdahl failed to copy the ancient designs for reed boats exactly, and the *Ra* began to break apart. After traveling 2,700 miles, Heyerdahl and his companions abandoned the *Ra* only 600 miles from Barbados. He tried again the following year with the properly constructed *Ra II.* This time Heyerdahl reached Barbados with relative ease. He published an account of the two voyages that same year titled *The Ra Expeditions* (1970). The *Ra II* had vindicated papyrus as a suitable material for oceangoing vessels.

After the *Ra* voyages, Heyerdahl turned to the Middle East and the Indian Ocean. In 1977 another reed vessel was constructed on the Tigris River using the style of ancient **Sumerians**. That vessel sailed out of the Persian Gulf and south across the Arabian Sea to Djibouti at the mouth of the Red Sea. Heyerdahl's point was to demonstrate the wide geographical area the ancient Sumerians could contact simply by using the sea travel technologies available to them. More recently, in 1982 to 1983, Heyerdahl investigated the mysterious trading society that supposedly occupied the Maldives Islands before the rise of Islam. Most of Heyerdahl's career has been devoted to proving that transoceanic contacts and diffusion were possible using the technology available to many early cultures. Given the successes of the *Kon Tiki*, *Ra*, and Sumerian voyages, he feels that he has amply proven his point. In his opinion, it is time for mainstream archaeologists and anthropologists to stop being cultural isolationists and antidiffusionists and start taking diffusion and a certain level of early transoceanic contact as a serious possibility. On the other hand, continued research, much of it stimulated by Heyerdahl's work and theories, tends to undermine his theories about Polynesian-American contacts and the origins of Easter Island's culture. New linguistic and archaeological research ultimately supports the traditional theories. Still, Heyerdahl deserves much recognition for being an innovative scholar, a bold sailor, and a great popularizer of archaeology and anthropology.

Bibliography: Heyerdahl, Thor, *Early Man and the Ocean*, 1979; Heyerdahl, Thor, "Isolationist or Diffusionist," in *The Quest for America*, edited by Geoffrey Ashe, 1971; Jacoby, Arnold, *Señor Kon Tiki*, 1967; Ralling, Christopher, *The Kon Tiki Man: Thor Heyerdahl*, 1990.

Hindus in Ancient America

From the nineteenth century on, various writers hypothesized that Hindus from India reached the Americas and were the ancestors of at least some Native American peoples. A number of respected professional archaeologists during the twentieth century also believe that Hindus reached the Americas and contributed various aspects to the native civilizations of Mexico.

Hinduism is a complex of religious beliefs that have existed on the Indian subcontinent since around 1000 B.C. and have profoundly affected the development of Indian culture and society. For many writers, particularly during the nineteenth century, Hindu and Indian were virtually interchangeable terms. However, Hindus or Indians did not rank as high as peoples such as the **Hebrews** and **Phoenicians** or even the **Chinese** in the historical and cultural consciousness of Western nations. As a result, they were long ignored as potential candidates for being the ancestors of Native Americans or as pre-Columbian visitors. That situation changed in the nineteenth century.

One of the first writers to suggest that Hindus visited and settled in America was the American lawyer and amateur archaeologist Caleb Atwater (1778–1867). His study *Descriptions of the Antiquities Discovered in the State of Ohio and Other Western States* appeared in 1820 as part of the first volume of the *Transactions* published by the American Antiquarian Society. In this work, Atwater identified Hindu settlers as the mysterious **Mound Builders** of North America. The artifact that convinced Atwater of this Hindu connection was a Native American vase with three faces on it called the Triune

Vessel. Atwater claimed that the three faces were the Hindu gods Brahma, Vishnu, and Shiva. Soon after, Judge John Haywood of Tennessee echoed Atwater's Hindu theory in his own study, *The Natural and Aboriginal History of Tennessee,* in 1823. Because Hindu immigrants were not really the Mound Builders and no evidence accumulated to sustain the theory, it died out in the face of competition from more plausible theories.

The Hindus were not permanently retired as pre-Columbian visitors to the Americas. The great German traveler, naturalist, and anthropologist Alexander von Humboldt (1769–1859) noted strong resemblances between the Hindu and Mexican calendars. In 1866 French architect Eugene-Emmanuel Viollet-le-Duc (1814–1879) pointed out similarities between the design of ancient Mexican buildings and the architecture of certain buildings in southern India. These and other writers saw correspondences between the trio of Mexican gods Ho-Huitzilopochtli-Tlaloc and the three Hindu deities Brahma-Vishnu-Shiva.

The leading twentieth-century exponents of Hindu contacts are Gordon Ekholm of the American Museum of Natural History and Robert Heine-Geldern. Both men are respected prehistorians and supporters of the theory that various contacts took place between ancient America and East and South Asia, particularly China. They believe that the Hindus learned of the existence of the Americas from Han Chinese merchants, who had already visited Mexico. Hindu merchants, besides trading with Southeast Asia, followed the Chinese to the Americas. After the Hindus declined, other Southeast Asian peoples with a Hinduized culture also may have traveled to Mesoamerica. Ekholm and Heine-Geldern think that these Hindu visits probably took place around 700. They cite many cultural parallels as evidence, such as the lotus motif

used by both cultures in decoration, and the common shape of Mayan and Cambodian pyramids. Other scholars have long suggested that the similarities between the games of **patolli** in Mexico and **pachisi** in India provide another strong evidence for contact. The problem is that many of Ekholm and Heine-Geldern's parallels are too far apart chronologically to convince other scholars that **diffusion** of culture occurred. Skeptics suggest that independent invention or **parallel evolution** provides a more plausible explanation of these cultural similarities. These scholars also point to the curious selectivity of this supposed diffusion. No useful plants or animals were exchanged, and the Hindus failed to teach Native Americans to adopt the wheel for hauling heavy loads. Cultural exchanges were limited to art when many other useful items could easily have been exchanged. Given the weakness of such circumstantial evidence, most scholars believe that Hindus did not reach the Americans in the era before Columbus.

Bibliography: Heine-Geldern, Robert, "Traces of Indian and Southeast Asiatic Hindu-Buddhist Influences in Mesoamerica," *Proceedings of the 35th International Congress of Americanists* (1962): 47–54; Heine-Geldern, Robert, and Gordon Ekholm, "Significant Parallels in the Symbolic Arts of Southeast Asia and Middle America," *The Civilization of Ancient America,* edited by Sol Tax, 299–309, 1951; Wauchope, Robert, *Lost Tribes and Sunken Continents,* 1962; Williams, Stephen, *Fantastic Archaeology: The Wild Side of North American Prehistory,* 1991.

Hittites in Ancient America

This ancient culture was centered in Asia Minor and flourished from 2000–1200 B.C. Some of its members possibly visited early Mexico.

It was not until the twentieth century that archaeological discoveries revealed the Hittites as a prominent Near Eastern civilization rivaling their contemporaries, the **Egyptians**. The Hittites appear to have pioneered the widespread use of iron tools and horses. Between 1400 and 1200 B.C. they gained control of the Mediterranean coastal region known as Phoenicia, now modern Lebanon. Invasions by Indo-European peoples after 1200 B.C. destroyed all but fragments of the Hittite empire.

Early writers speculating about Mediterranean visitors to the Americas did not mention the Hittites because they were largely unknown to historians before the early twentieth century. Once known, they still did not become prime candidates because they were not a seafaring people. The **diffusionist** writer Constance Irwin changed that with her 1963 book *Fair Gods and Stone Faces*. She points out that figures wearing shoes with pointed and upturned toes have been depicted on the stone carvings decorating buildings and stelae at the Olmec site of La Venta. Rejecting the possibility that such unique footwear could have been independently invented, Irwin sought an Old World source. She found it in the Hittites, the most prominent wearers of pointed-toe shoes in the ancient Mediterranean world. Because they were not seafarers, she hypothesized the existence of a joint enterprise between the Hittites and **Phoenician** cities under Hittite rule to sail to the Americas. Such voyages would have taken place in the waning period of Hittite civilization from about 1200–800 B.C. Other writers also claim to see affinities between some ancient American and Hittite art and architecture, but such parallels are vague and highly problematic. Irwin's hypothesis is based on the supposed diffusion of pointed shoes. Most professional archaeologists and historians find such evidence mildly amusing but utterly unconvincing.

Bibliography: Davies, Nigel, *Voyagers to the New World*, 1979; Irwin, Constance, *Fair Gods and Stone Faces*, 1963.

Hoei-shin, Eastern Journey of (499)

Hoei-shin, also rendered as Hoei-sin or Hui-Shen, was a **Chinese Buddhist** monk who traveled far to the east and around a land called **Fusang**, which some scholars identify as various parts of the Americas.

The narrative of Hoei-shin appeared in the Chinese book *Liang Shu*, a history of the Liang dynasty (502–557), composed about 629. Hoei-shin lived during the period known as the Six Dynasties (220–589), a very confused time without a strong central empire. It was also one of the few times the Chinese showed much interest in learning about their neighbors. Buddhist monks supplied most of the surviving travel narratives, and Hoei-shin (whose name means "universal compassion") was one of their number.

Hoei-shin's narrative provides considerable detail about the land of Fusang, but tells little about the journey there and back. It may have begun at Japan and proceeded to Tahan or Tuhan (**Great China**), the land of the painted (tattooed) people. Some people identify Tahan as Alaska and the painted people as **Eskimos**. One prominent detail in the narrative was the fusang tree, which the natives used as a source of building material, linen, and paper. Because peace prevailed in Fusang, there were no fortifications or walled strongholds. There were two prisons for criminals: a northern location for the worst offenders and a southern location for petty offenders. Fusang's ruling elite had four ranks with the king, known by the title *ichi,* occupying the top of the social hierarchy. As a sign of rank, the kings of Fusang wore royal vestments of colors that changed according to a system of ten-year cycles. Below the king were three grades of nobility. The people of Fusang had oxen, horses, and deer for draught animals; the deer also supplied milk. Their metallurgical skills included the working of copper, gold, and silver, but not iron. Hoei-shin mentioned that he was not the first Asian to visit Fusang. Five Buddhist monks from Kipin (possibly Kashmir, Afghanistan, or Samarkand?) had already brought their religion to Fusang in 458 with considerable success. During his visit, Hoei-shin learned that a land inhabited by women only lay farther to the east, but he did not visit it. Appended to Hoei-shin's narrative was the brief mention of some **Fukienese sailors** visiting an island of dog-headed men in the far eastern Pacific in 507.

The early French sinologist Joseph De Guignes in 1761 was the first to identify Hoei-shin's narrative about Fusang as a description of a visit to ancient America. According to De Guignes, Fusang was located in present-day California. It was an exotic suggestion that invited controversy. Eventually German sinologist Julius Heinrich von Klaproth published a study in 1831 that systematically refuted De Guignes's interpretation and suggested instead that Japan was the real Fusang of Hoei-shin's narrative. But De Guignes had his defenders, of whom the most prominent were Gustave d'Eichthal of France and Carl Friedrich Neumann of Germany. In 1841 Neumann published Hoei-shin's narrative and used it to argue that Mexico was the true site of Fusang. D'Eichthal argued in 1862 to 1863 that America was more accessible to China than Japan because it could be reached without having to sail on the high seas. Some Americans also came out in support of Hoei-shin having visited America. Charles G. Leland published *Fusang or the Discovery of America by Chinese Buddhist Priests in the Fifth Century* in 1875. Leland's work was heavily based on Neumann's writings, which is not surprising because Leland made his living as a popularizer of various scholarly subjects.

However, he made an original contribution by suggesting that Fusang might have been Peru. Another American, Edward P. Vining, probably stretched the theory of Fusang to its limits by writing an 800-page book titled *An Inglorious Columbus*. Published in 1885, the book detailed all the evidence and returned Fusang's location to California or Mexico.

Supporters of Fusang's location in the Americas base their argument on several details of Hoei-shin's description. Working solely on the basis of the geographical directions Hoei-shin provided, California or Mexico are virtually the only possible locations for Fusang. Of course, the Chinese, along with most of their contemporaries, were notoriously careless about geographical details. Using Chinese records, De Guignes and his followers attempted to establish correspondences between the descriptions of the inhabitants of Fusang and various groups of Native Americans. A number of writers identify the fusang tree with the aloe or century plant, which has roughly similar characteristics. *Ichi,* the title for the king of Fusang, appears to some people to be a corruption of the Mayan Itzá or Peruvian Inca. Finally, it is argued that a voyage from China was quite possible given the geographical proximities and available naval technology.

Detractors point out that no traces of the supposedly quite successful missionary work of the Buddhists survive. The natives of Fusang had horses, cattle, and domesticated stags, but (with the exception of the llama in the Andean region) none of the Native American cultures developed any large domestic animals. Critics also point to the absurdity of Hoei-shin's descriptions of the land of women and the island of dog-headed men as discrediting the whole narrative. But his supporters counter that various European travel narratives from the Middle Ages also contained many of the same tall tales alongside accurate descriptions of existing foreign places. The most telling criticism, however, is the discovery that the name Fusang had a long history in Chinese cosmography as a fictional eastern land. It began between the late Chou and early Han eras (1000–100 B.C.) as the name for a marvelous eastern otherworld. Later the name was used as a poetic reference to Japan. Other stories mentioning Fusang could refer to the islands of the Ainu, Sakhalin, Kamchatka, or simply a fantasy land in the eastern Pacific. Fusang was simply not a specific place. As a result, professional sinologists do not believe that Hoei-shin's narrative records a Chinese visit to the Americas. At the same time, archaeologists and historians of both Asia and the Americas increasingly believe that significant periodic but unsustained cultural contacts occurred across the Pacific. The idea that Hoei-shin visited America occasionally enters into the consciousness of popular culture despite all the scholarly debunking, for example, Charles M. Boland's *They All Discovered America* (1961).

Bibliography: Leland, Charles G., *Fusang or the Discovery of America by Chinese Buddhist Priests in the Fifth Century,* [1875], 1973; Needham, Joseph, *Science and Civilization in China,* vol. 4: *Physics and Physical Technology,* pt. 3: *Civil Engineering and Nautics,* 1971; Vining, Edward P., *An Inglorious Columbus,* 1885.

Hsü Fu, Voyages of
(219 B.C. and after)

This **Chinese** magician made several voyages for the first emperor of China, **Chhin** Shih Huang Ti (or Qin Shi Huangdi), into the eastern Pacific Ocean in search of the magical islands containing drugs that conferred immortality. Since Hsü Fu never returned from his last expedition, some writers speculate that he may have reached and settled in the Americas.

Taoist alchemical beliefs in the existence of three magical islands that contained immortality drugs flourished in China during the Chhin (Qin) and former Han periods (206 B.C.–A.D. 8). Various rulers sent expeditions to locate these magical islands. However, Hsü Fu is the only leader of such an expedition whose name survives in the historical records.

The story of Hsü Fu appears twice in the great Ssuma Chhien's (or Si-ma Qian, 145–? B.C.) history, the *Shih Chi* (or *ShiJi*). According to that account, the first emperor, Chhin Shih Huang Ti (reigned 246–210 B.C.), had already sent out several unsuccessful expeditions in search of the magic islands of Phêng-Lai, Fang-Chang, and Ying-Chou. In 219 B.C., Hsü Fu and several others approached the emperor with a new proposal for yet another voyage of exploration. The emperor agreed to support their venture, which would involve several thousand people. Like the other voyagers before him, Hsü Fu failed to bring home the drug of immortality, causing the first emperor to complain of the great expense. As Hsü Fu well knew, Chhin Shih Huang Ti was a dangerous man to disappoint.

Unlike his predecessors, Hsü Fu claimed that he had landed on one of the magic islands. He met a great wizard who asked him if he represented the Emperor of the West (China). Hsü Fu replied that he did, and that he sought the drugs that allowed humans to live longer. The wizard refused to give him any because the emperor's presents were too poor. Sailing on to the island of Phêng-Lai, Hsü Fu visited a great palace guarded by a brazen dragon. He paid his respects to the sea wizard who lived there and asked what types of gifts would be required in exchange for the drugs of immortality. The sea wizard replied, "Bring me young men of good birth and breed, together with apt virgins, and workmen of all trades; then you will get your drugs." This exchange was quite acceptable to the first emperor, who had many subjects but only one life. He provided Hsü Fu with 3,000 young men and women, many artisans, and an ample supply of grain. Thus equipped, Hsü Fu again sailed off, never to return. Historian Ssuma Chhien speculated that Hsü Fu found an empty land suitable for colonization and fooled the first emperor into supplying him with settlers, and that he returned to this land and made himself king.

It is not certain where Hsü Fu went to escape Chhin Shih Huang Ti, who was one of the more cruel and tyrannical figures in Chinese history. Tradition has it that he settled in Japan, where he was known as Jofuku. His supposed tomb still exists at Shingu in Wakayama Prefecture. Archaeological evidence indicates a strong Chinese influence in Japan during the first century B.C., and therefore tends to support the story of Jofuku. It is possible, however, that Japanese scholars simply picked the story of Hsü Fu from the *Shih Chi* and embroidered it. The eminent historian of China Joseph Needham suggests it is just as likely that Hsü Fu settled somewhere in the Americas as any other place.

Bibliography: Davies, Nigel, *Voyagers to the New World*, 1979; Needham, Joseph, *Science and Civilization in China*, vol. 2: *History of Scientific Thought*, 1962; Needham, Joseph, *Science and Civilization in China*, vol. 4: *Physics and Physical Technology*, pt. 3: *Civil Engineering and Nautics*, 1971.

Hvítramannaland

From the Norse words *hvítir* meaning white and *manna* meaning man's, Hvítramannaland is the Norse name for **Great Ireland**, a legendary settlement of early medieval **Irish monks in America** that preceded the **voyages of Bjarni Herjolfsson** in 986 and **Leif Ericsson** about 1001.

I

Icaria

This unknown land in the western Atlantic Ocean was visited by **Prince Henry Sinclair** (or **Prince Zichmni**) and **Antonio Zeno** during the course of their search for **Estotiland.**

According to the narrative of the Zeno Voyage, the Icarians claimed to be ruled by kings called Icari, a derivation of the name of their first king and conqueror, Icarus, the son of Daedalus, a king of Scotland. The hostile Icarians would not allow Sinclair and his men to land. After clandestinely taking on fresh water, Sinclair continued his search for Estotiland.

There is no agreement over the geographical identification of Icaria, although most supporters of the authenticity of the Zeno Narrative think it refers to Kerry in Ireland. Some, like Frederick Pohl, identify

Icaria as Newfoundland. The sailing descriptions in the Zeno Narrative are too vague for any definitive conclusion. Most professional historians simply dismiss the Zeno Narrative and Icaria as a hoax concocted by some Venetians in 1558, well after the events it describes.

Iceland

This large island located in the eastern North Atlantic Ocean was first settled by **Irish monks** and later by Norse farmers during the early Middle Ages. It is well documented that the Norse or **Viking** settlers eventually went from Iceland to **Greenland,** and from there to **Vinland** in North America. Some writers also suggest, but on very little evidence, that the Irish monks made their way from Iceland to North America during this same period.

Iceland is sometimes identified as the Thule or Ultima Thule of ancient Greek and Roman geography. This identification is almost certainly incorrect, especially considering that Greek and Roman ships were not suited to survive in the dangerous northern waters around Iceland. The **curach** used by the Irish, however, made high seas voyaging to the Faeroe Islands and Iceland quite possible. Just when the Irish first reached Iceland is not known, but archaeological evidence indicates they were Iceland's first inhabitants. Iceland appeared in Irish sea voyage stories known as *immrama,* starting with the famous voyage of the mythological Irish hero Mael Dúin dating at least to the eighth century. Dicuil (fl. 825), an Irish geographer living in the court of the Frankish emperor Charlemagne, mentioned that a group of Irish churchmen visited Iceland in 795. This reference is the earliest date for an Irish presence in Iceland, but Dicuil does not call it a voyage of discovery or consider it out of the ordinary. The implication is that the Irish were well aware of Iceland by the time Dicuil wrote. Iceland was an ideal place for anchorite monks seeking seclusion, and they did so throughout the first two-thirds of the ninth century.

The blessed solitude of the Irish in Iceland was somewhat rudely interrupted after 860 by the unwelcome arrival of Norse settlers. Contrary winds blew a Norse vessel bound for the Faeroes to Iceland instead. Some sources give credit to Gardar Svavarsson, a Swede, while others point to Naddod the Viking or some unnamed merchants. Permanent settlers arrived under the leadership of Ingólf during the 870s according to the saga *Landnámabok* of Ari the Learned (Fródi). The arrival of the Norse immediately caused the Irish to abandon Iceland. It is commonly thought that the monks simply returned to Ireland. The *Landnámabók*, however, makes references to the mysterious Irish settlement of **Hvítramannaland**, located six days' sailing to the west, which some people think refers to North America.

Iceland quickly developed a substantial Norse population of 30,000 to 35,000 by 930. The unification of Norway by King Harold I Fairhair (ca. 860–930) caused many of those opposed to him to immigrate to Iceland. A general land shortage in Scandinavia also motivated many of Iceland's early settlers. The island remained an independent republic until its union with Norway under King Hakon IV during the years 1262–1264. Meanwhile Iceland continued to attract Norse settlers. **Eric the Red**, then 16 but later the father of **Leif Ericsson**, and his family left Norway to settle in Iceland because of a blood feud. A similar feud forced the adult Eric to leave Iceland and led to his discovery of Greenland in 982. Thus Iceland provided an important starting point for Norse explorations of the western North Atlantic and their discovery of North America.

Bibliography: Gelsinger, Bruce E., "Iceland," in *Dictionary of the Middle Ages*, edited by Joseph R. Strayer, 12 vols., 1982–1989; Marcus, G. J., *The Conquest of the North Atlantic*, 1981.

Immrama

This is a genre of early medieval Irish literature consisting of tales about sea voyages to strange or mythical islands. The *Navigatio Sancti Brendani Abbatis*, which describes the legendary **voyage of St. Brendan,** is closely related to the *immrama*.

Development of the highly seaworthy **curachs** by the early Christian Irish opened up the Atlantic Ocean for voyages of both fact and imagination. Curachs were particularly popular among the **Irish monks.** They engaged in many daring, long-distance sea pilgrimages, of which St. Brendan's voyage and the tales of **Great Ireland** were merely extreme and probably fictional examples. Furthermore, pre-Christian Celtic mythology was filled with heroes seeking the Otherworld across the seas. These two monkish and pre-Christian elements came together to form the *immrama*. The *Voyage of Bran*, written about 700, is the oldest surviving *immrama*. It tells how the god-hero Bran sailed to the two wonderful islands of Joy and Women in the Western Ocean. Returning to Ireland, Bran and his companion discovered that centuries had elapsed during their absence. A more fully developed *immrama* is the *Voyage of Mael Dúin*, which dates from 920 or earlier. If the earlier dating is correct, the *Voyage of Mael Dúin* is older than the *Navigatio Sancti Brendani,* which dates from 900–920. Other surviving *immrama* were composed later; over the years many were lost.

Some scholars consider the *Navigatio Sancti Brendani Abbatis* to be a Christianized *immrama*. Others argue, from the chronology of events, that it was the voyages of various Irish monks, including St. Brendan, that inspired the writers of the *immrama*. They point out the greater authenticity of the elements in St. Brendan's narrative and other stories of sea pilgrimages by Irish monks. These tales pay far more attention to such details as the direction of sailing and the length of time involved in a voyage than the secular *immrama*. Almost no scholar claims that the account of St. Brendan's voyage describes an actual journey. But many would argue that the story reflects knowledge of actual historical travels made by Irish monks in the Atlantic rather than being Christianized versions of purely fictional quests for the Otherworld as in the *immrama*. Certainly the *immrama* and the voyages of the monks show that the early Christian Irish traveled the Atlantic Ocean far more often and extensively than is generally recognized.

Bibliography: Ashe, Geoffrey, *Land to the West: St. Brendan's Voyage to America*, 1962; Ashe, Geoffrey, *Mythology of the British Isles*, 1990.

Ingram, David
(fl. 1567–1582)

An English seaman from Barking, Essex, he claimed to witness numerous marvels as a castaway in North America, including Native Americans using Welsh words. His story attracted the attention of many people in Elizabethan England, including **John Dee** and historian Richard Hakluyt.

Ingram accompanied the famous English seaman John Hawkins on his expedition to the Spanish West Indies in 1567. After Spanish forces destroyed much of the English fleet at San Juan d'Ullua, Hawkins was forced to maroon some of his company, including Ingram, near the Panuco River on the Gulf of Mexico. Heading north to escape capture by the Spanish, Ingram and two companions traveled 11 months and some 3,000 miles to Cape Breton, Nova Scotia, where a French ship rescued them. In 1582 Sir Francis Walsingham, the secretary of state under Queen Elizabeth I, summoned Ingram for questioning. Ingram's answers formed the basis for his "Relation," which Richard Hakluyt published as part of his *Principall Navigations* of 1589. Significantly, Hakluyt deleted the story from the second edition published in 1599, which indicates that he probably suspected Ingram's veracity.

Besides claiming to have seen great cities and elephants, Ingram reported that the natives called certain birds with white heads "penguins," which he thought was a Welsh word. He added, "and they haue also in use diuers other Welsh words." Ingram claimed to be the first to find evidence of a pre-Columbian Welsh presence in America. In effect, he originated the **Welsh Indian Legend.** John Dee and other proponents of British imperialism in the Americas were quick to utilize Ingram's "Relation" as supporting evidence for **Madoc's** discovery and colonization of America in 1170.

Bibliography: Ingram, David, *The Relation of David Ingram*, [1589], 1966; Unwin, Raynor, *The Defeat of John Hawkins*, 1960.

Inventio fortunata
(ca. 1365)

This lost geographical book of the Middle Ages supposedly described the Arctic region, including parts of North America. Various fifteenth- and sixteenth-century students of geography, including Columbus, mentioned its existence.

The *Inventio fortunata* is one of the Middle Ages' lost books, although some claim that a fragment survives. Richard Hakluyt asserted in 1589 that its author was **Nicholas of Lynn,** an English Carmelite of the late fourteenth century, but he seems to have no basis for his attribution. Some modern scholars suggest that Lynn's contemporary, the Franciscan Hugh of Ireland, wrote it, although that identification is extremely speculative. Generally scholars prefer to credit an unknown English Franciscan mathematician familiar with the astrolabe with authorship of the *Inventio*. One thing is certain—the unknown author did not visit North America as a member of the mythical voyage of **Paul Knutson** in 1355–1364 as has been claimed.

The earliest mention of the *Inventio* occurred in a 1497 letter by Englishman **John Day** to a Spanish admiral who was possibly Columbus. In the letter Day apologizes for not being able to acquire a copy of the *Inventio* for the admiral. Cartographer Johannes Ruysch referred to the *Inventio* four times in his world maps of 1507 and 1508. Both **Bartolomé de Las Casas** and Ferdinand Columbus mentioned it as one of the sources studied by Christopher Columbus. The great Flemish geographer Gerard Mercator cited it six or seven times in his Arctic chart of 1569. In 1577 he provided English geographer **John Dee** with a summary of its contents. Mercator also mentioned, however, that he derived his information indirectly from a fourteenth-century Flemish book by the obscure Jacobus Cnoyen (Knox?) of 's Hertogenbosch rather than directly from the *Inventio*. Apparently many people had heard of the *Inventio* and were familiar with its contents without actually having read it.

Mercator's summary of its contents indicates that its author had the same degree of geographical knowledge as medieval Icelandic colonists living on **Greenland.** The *Inventio* included extensive although confused information on the Canadian Arctic. Hudson Bay, Hudson Strait, and Fox Basin can all be recognized from its descriptions, along with other less clearly identifiable Arctic locations. It is not clear that the author knew about **Vinland.** Basically the *Inventio* described a geography that was common knowledge to Icelanders but not to the rest of Europe. The apparently confused organization of the *Inventio*'s Arctic descriptions indicates the author did not have firsthand knowledge. It has been suggested that the author may have borrowed his information from a book by Arctic traveler and clergyman Ivar Bardarson called *Det gamle Gronlands beskrivelse* (Description of Greenland) written between 1360 and 1380.

The *Inventio fortunata* was a relic of the geographical knowledge acquired by the **Vikings** during the course of their North Atlantic explorations. Medieval Europe never managed to assimilate this knowledge since it conflicted with the prevailing assumption that there were only three continents. The Viking discoveries contained in the Inventio were ignored or forgotten until Columbus's discoveries revived interest in them. But by then, perhaps only secondhand accounts of the elusive *Inventio* survived to tantalize Mercator, Dee, and others.

Bibliography: De Costa, Benjamin Franklin, *Inventio Fortunata. Arctic Exploration with an Account of Nicholas of Lynn*, 1881; Oleson, Tryggvi J., *Early Voyages and Northern Approaches*, 1964; Taylor, E. G. R., "A Letter Dated 1577 from Mercator to John Dee," *Imago Mundi* (1956): 56–69.

Irish Monks in America

A persistent legend held that Irish monks inhabiting **Iceland** fled west when Norse settlers arrived in 874. First they moved to **Greenland** and then to North America, where they founded the settlement known variously as **Great Ireland, Hvítramannaland, White Man's Land,** Albania, and **Albania Superior.** The neighboring tribes of Native Americans completely absorbed the Irish into their societies. There is no convincing archaeological evidence to substantiate a pre-Columbian Irish presence in North America.

Much of the unique character of Irish Christianity's monastic organization can be attributed to the *Celi Dei* (i.e., servants of God), whose name has been corrupted to Culdees. The Culdees were Irish Christians who antedated the mission of St. Patrick about 435. They practiced a version of Christianity that frequently borrowed from the old pagan Celtic rites. Like other Irish monks, the Culdees emphasized a particularly rigorous, ascetic form of monasticism. Irish monks constantly sought isolated and austere places to practice their religious vocation and often verged on being hermits. From Ireland, the monks spread to the Faeroe Islands in 725 and to Iceland sometime before 795. Viking raids on Ireland also began in 795 and were followed by permanent settlements, such as Dublin, in 835. As a result of these raids, the Irish monks abandoned the Faeroes and, along with more refugees from Ireland, moved to Iceland. That safe haven was lost in 874 when Norse settlers began arriving, and the Irish abandoned Iceland. But where did they go next? Most historians and archaeologists think they simply gave up and returned to war-torn Ireland. Supporters of the legend of Irish monks in America, however, maintain that they fled west, eventually settling in North America.

If the monks fled west, their first stop would have been Greenland. As before, they settled down and built stone houses, hoping they had finally distanced themselves from the hated Norse. But they were again disappointed. In 982 **Eric the Red** settled in Greenland, and the timid Irish moved even farther west. Eric the Red and his compan-

ions never even knew the Irish lived in Greenland, but as the Norse historian Ari the Learned (1067/1068–1148) later reported, they found abandoned stone buildings and hide boats. Supporters of the legend of Irish monks in America consider these to be remains left by the monks. Significantly, Eric the Red later believed that the owners of the boats and buildings were related to the inhabitants of **Vinland**—the **skraelings**. Modern historians and archaeologists contend that the remains were left by the Dorset Paleo-**Eskimos.**

According to the legend, the Irish sailed west to Labrador. A small group began a settlement on Sculpin Island in the Canadian Arctic, where stone ruins still exist. Most continued south and finally stopped at the Merrimack River, which flows into the Atlantic at Newburyport, Massachusetts. Some settled upriver at the site of present-day Haverhill, while others occupied Pattee's Cave at North Salem in southeastern New Hampshire. A number of fringe archaeologists claim that Pattee's Cave had been settled a thousand years earlier by **Phoenicians.** Of course, not every supporter of the existence of Great Ireland locates it in Massachusetts and New Hampshire. Modern historian Tryggvi Oleson places it on the Gulf of St. Lawrence; nineteenth-century Danish scholar Carl Rafn thought Hvítramannaland was in the Carolinas.

Wherever they stopped, the Irish found a land that agreed with them. They must have long abandoned the practice of celibacy, since too much time elapsed for the

original monks to still be alive. Supporters of the existence of Great Ireland claim that evidence of Irish settlements is scattered all along the eastern seaboard, with the greatest concentration in New England.

One of the biggest advocates of the Irish as the first European settlers of America was William B. Goodwin, an insurance executive from Hartford, Connecticut, and an amateur archaeologist and historian. Beginning in 1921, Goodwin's searches for evidence of Great Ireland focused on the sites around North Salem, New Hampshire. He tried to enlist the support of Harvard professor Hugh Henchen in 1939; instead, the academic community rejected his findings. Where Goodwin saw Irish buildings, professional archaeologists saw colonial-era root cellars. Where Goodwin saw Irish potsherds, they saw Native American artifacts. The academic community generally considers Goodwin's theories to be part of fringe archaeology, although he has a number of supporters and allies among other amateur archaeologists.

The Irish settlers of Great Ireland had not seen the last of the Norse. Storms brought Norse seaman **Ari Marson's** ship to their shores almost before the Irish had time to unpack. Other Norse groups were also blown to Great Ireland. But according to the legend, with no place farther west to hide, the Irish stood their ground. They captured the Norse castaways, baptized them, and forced them to join the settlement of Great Ireland, protecting its secret. Nevertheless, rumors of the Irish settlement began to circulate among the Norse and even made their way into the various Norse sagas.

Besides the story of Ari Marson, there is the tale of **Gudlief Gunnlangsson** and Bjorn in the *Eyrbyggia Saga*. Bjorn was an Icelander forced to flee west after an adulterous affair drew the wrath of the woman's family. He was never heard from again. A number of years later, around 1025–1030, a storm

drove Gudlief Gunnlangsson into a strange western harbor while he was sailing from Dublin to Iceland. Natives, apparently speaking Irish, appeared and took Gudlief and his crew prisoner. While they debated whether to kill the Norse or enslave them, a tall old man with a white beard appeared on horseback. The old man proved to be a leader of the natives. Speaking in Norse, he asked about events back in Iceland, then warned them to leave quickly or risk being killed. Although the old man would not give his name, Gudlief recognized him as the long-lost Bjorn. The old man sent a ring back with the Norse as a gift for his former lover. Another story of Hvítramannaland appears in *Eirik's Saga*. **Thorfinn Karlsefni's** expedition captured several skraeling boys. They told the Norse of people in a neighboring land who dressed in white, shouted a lot, and carried banners around, from which description the Norse concluded that the boys were talking about the Irish monks of Great Ireland. These stories, however, form the only evidence for Irish monks settling in America. No genuine early-medieval Irish artifact has ever been found anywhere along the eastern seaboard of the United States or Canada. Supporters speculate that, after a number of years, the local population of Native Americans assimilated the monks completely and without trace. For people like popular writer Charles M. Boland, the Irish or Culdees were the skraelings of **Leif Ericsson** and the Norse who followed him. Most professional historians regard the legend of Irish monks settling in North America as a myth or, at best, a theory lacking any convincing evidence.

Bibliography: Boland, Charles M., *They All Discovered America*, 1961; Goodwin, William B., *The Ruins of Great Ireland in New England*, 1946; Morison, Samuel Eliot, *The European Discovery of America: The Northern Voyages 500–1600*, 1971; Oleson, Tryggvi

J., *Early Voyages and Northern Approaches*, 1964.

Itzamná

This Highland or Quiché Maya god is sometimes identified with **Quetzalcoatl**, the Aztec deity frequently considered to be a **white god** and Old World visitor to pre-Columbian America. Itzamná was a sky god who taught the Maya how to grow corn or **maize**. Unlike the Lowland or Yucatec Maya god **Kukulcan**, the cult of Itzamná does not appear to be an adaptation from the cult of Quetzalcoatl. Like other alleged white gods, Itzamná apparently did not have white skin in the original legends. That trait appears to be a postconquest addition, therefore severing any link between Itzamná and supposed pre-Columbian contacts with the Old World.

Bibliography: Mercatante, Anthony S., *The Facts on File Encyclopedia of World Mythology and Legend*, 1988.

Ixtlilxochitl, Fernando de Alva (1577–1648)

Mestizo historian and colonial official, he wrote from a Native American perspective on the pre-Columbian and early colonial periods of Mexican history. Like other mestizo historians such as **Garcilaso de la Vega,** Ixtlilxochitl did not speculate about native origins, but later writers such as **Edward King, Viscount Kingsborough,** and various Mormon historians used his writings to prove their own theories.

Ixtlilxochitl was a grandson of the king of Texcoco on his mother's side. After graduating with honors from the Colegio de Santa Cruz de Tlaltelolco, he governed Texcoco in 1612 and the Tlalmanalco in 1617. In recognition of his royal lineage, Philip III of Spain later made Ixtlilxochitl a generous grant of land that allowed him to concentrate on his historical studies. Ixtlilxochitl gathered information by conducting extensive interviews with natives and by collecting Toltec and Aztec manuscripts. Many of his sources are no longer available to modern historians, making his writings an important primary source for the pre-Columbian history of Mexico.

Ixtlilxochitl provided reconstructions of the various creation myths and the early mythological histories of the various Native American nations. Besides being of great use for mainstream historical studies, this primary material was used by Lord Kingsborough to prove the Hebrew origin of the Native Americans and by various Mormon scholars to corroborate the historical narrative in *The Book of Mormon.*

Bibliography: Hunter, Milton R., and Thomas Stuart Ferguson, *Ancient America and the Book of Mormon*, 1950; Thomas, Jack Ray, *Biographical Dictionary of Latin American Historians and Historiography*, 1984.

J

American tribes. Most anthropologists consider contacts of this nature of little cultural significance.

The one important exception to the general vagueness of the Japanese pre-Columbian contact theories is the **Jumon/Valdivia** theory. This theory suggests that about 3000 B.C. castaway Japanese fishermen drifted to what is now Ecuador and taught the Valdivian people how to make elaborate pottery. Many professional archaeologists and anthropologists take this theory very seriously. Otherwise, the literature on Japanese pre-Columbian contacts with America is thin, especially compared to that on **Chinese** contacts. Of course, Japan developed its classic form of civilization much later than China.

Bibliography: Fingerhut, Eugene R., *Who First Discovered America? A Critique of Pre-Columbian Voyages*, 1984; Sorenson, John L., and Martin H. Raish, *Pre-Columbian Contacts with the Americas across the Oceans: An Annotated Bibliography*, 2 vols., 1990.

Jaredites

Mormons believe that this mysterious people came to the Americas sometime after God confused humanity's language at the Tower of Babel. The Jaredites created a great civilization, but they became evil and exterminated themselves in suicidal wars shortly before the arrival of Lehi and his sons in ancient America.

The account of the Jaredites is contained in the book of Ether in *The Book of Mormon*. It tells how Jared and his righteous brother asked God for guidance in the aftermath of the language confusion at the Tower of Babel about 2800 B.C., or about 2200 B.C. if the chronology of Bishop James Ussher (1581–1656) from the Authorized Version of the Bible is followed. Their faithfulness pleased God, who promised to reward them and their people with the richest land of all—the land where Noah lived before the

Japanese in Ancient America

The possibility that the Japanese reached America before 1492 is frequently but superficially referred to in the literature of transoceanic contacts.

Supposed similarities between the Japanese and some Native American groups in terms of language, armor and weapons, art, religion, or fishing techniques are frequently cited as evidence. But the when, why, and how of such contacts are seldom discussed. It is well known that during the eighteenth and nineteenth centuries, boatloads of Japanese fishermen were often carried accidentally to North America by the strong Japan (Kuroshio) current of the northern Pacific Ocean. European explorers of the Pacific Northwest coast of the Americas found Japanese castaways held as slaves by Native flood, which according to Mormon tradition was located in the Americas. After several years of traveling across a wilderness, the Jaredites reached a sea. They built eight rather strange ships supposedly patterned after Noah's Ark. The ships were floating capsules, carrying passengers on the inside, but with no outer deck for crew or passengers to go on top or sail the vessel. God provided Jared's brother with shining stones to illuminate the inside of the sealed-up ships while they were at sea. The Jaredites then entered and launched their ships; God provided a wind that blew them to their promised land.

In the geography of *The Book of Mormon* there is a Land Northward and a Land Southward, divided by a Narrow Neck of Land. The promised land of the Jaredites was located in the Land Northward. Once they settled in, the Jaredites prospered and their population grew. But problems appeared in Jaredite society as social conflicts grew and civil wars occurred. Prophets admonished the Jaredites, and periods of moral regeneration took place. But they did not last; the trend of Jaredite history was toward corruption and ultimate destruction.

The finale occurred during the reign of the warlike king Coriantumr, sometime between 600 and 400 B.C., with 580 B.C. the most likely date. Coriantumr fought a series of civil wars with rivals for his throne, culminating in the struggle with Shiz. The surviving Jaredites took up one side or the other and engaged in a war of mutual extermination. Millions died—men, women, and children—until only Coriantumr and Shiz remained alive on the bloody battleground of Hill Ramah. Even so, they continued fighting until only Coriantumr survived the holocaust. After he recovered somewhat from his wounds, Coriantumr wandered south and took shelter with the newly arrived **Mulekites** from Judah at their settlement of Zarahemla. The Jaredite

prophet wrote down the tragic history of his people on metal tablets that were later discovered by the **Nephite** king Limhi and delivered to the prophet Mosiah for translation. The tablets told how the Jaredites fell from their status as God's chosen people because of their wickedness. The Nephites became their successors as God's people in the ancient Americas.

Mormon historians and archaeologists generally identify the Jaredites with the Olmec culture, which was centered in Mexico's Veracruz state. They also include the Monte Albán culture in the state of Oaxaca as part of the Jaredite kingdom. Chronologically and geographically the Olmecs provide a good match with the Jaredites, since they also flourished between about 1200 and 600 B.C. Apart from these broad similarities, little is certain, since the book of Ether glosses over many of the kinds of detail that could make for firmer identifications. One respected Mormon scholar, Thomas S. Ferguson in his *One Fold and One Shepherd*, originally considered the Jaredites to be **Sumerians**, who first landed at Panunco in northern Mexico by sailing across the Atlantic Ocean. In contrast, another prominent Mormon, Hugh Nibley, suggests that the Jaredites were a nomadic herding people who migrated from the Middle East across Asia. After reaching the Pacific coast, they built ships and caught the Japan (Kuroshio) current, which carried them into the North Pacific current and across the Pacific Ocean to Central America. The most recent Mormon scholarship of John L. Sorenson and Bruce W. Warren agrees with Nibley. They identify Oaxaca as the Jaredite heartland of Moron.

Traditionally Mormons believe that the final wars of the Jaredites completely stripped the Americas of people with the exception of Coriantumr and Ether. The empty land, filled only with abandoned ruins and bare bones, awaited the Mulekites, Nephites, and **Lamanites,** who reached the Americas shortly after the last suicidal battle at Hill Ramah. John L. Sorenson suggests a different scenario in which the Jaredites did not annihilate themselves. Some survived and lived alongside the Nephites, Lamanites, and Mulekites, ultimately merging with them.

Non-Mormon archaeologists and prehistorians do not generally accept the book of Ether as a genuine historical document. They find its account fanciful, with little relation to surviving archaeological evidence. Its reports of millions of casualties in the Jaredite conflicts dwarf all modern wars. Even more serious are reports of Jaredites using steel and having horses and elephants. Pre-Columbian Native Americans did not know how to make iron, let alone steel. Horses were extinct in the Americas by 3000 B.C., and elephants never lived there. Attempts to identify mastodons and mammoths as the Jaredite elephants founder on sound archaeological evidence showing that these creatures were extinct thousands of years before the Jaredite era. Some claim that the Jaredite migration to America could serve as a cause for the apparently sudden rise of the Olmec civilization. Most professional archaeologists prefer to view the Olmec cultural florescence as a purely native affair or look to Shang China for its inspiration, if they admit to the possibility of transoceanic influence at all. Mormon archaeologists continue to predict that future research will eventually vindicate the narrative of Ether.

Bibliography: Davies, Nigel, *Voyagers to the New World,* 1979; Ferguson, Thomas S., *One Fold and One Shepherd,* [1958], rev. ed, 1962; Nibley, Hugh, *Collected Works of Hugh Nibley,* vol. 5: *Lehi in the Desert, The World of the Jaredites,* and *There Were Jaredites,* 1988; Sorenson, John L., *An Ancient American Setting for the Book of Mormon,* 1985; Warren, Bruce W., and Thomas S. Ferguson, *The Messiah in Ancient America,* 1987.

Jesus Christ in Ancient America

Members of the Church of Jesus Christ of the Latter Day Saints, along with other groups known collectively as Mormons, believe that in A.D. 34, Jesus Christ visited and preached to the people of the Americas shortly after his death and resurrection.

Europeans arriving in the Americas after 1492 were amazed at the prevalence of so-called **white god legends** and the supposed vestiges of Christianity in various Native American religions. It seemed as though the Maya and others used the cross as a sacred symbol, and rituals similar to baptism were practiced widely. Many sixteenth-century Spanish priests suggested that St. **Thomas** visited the Americas and that his evangelizing accounted for these Christian survivals. Such a situation was certainly consistent with Jesus's command in Matthew 28:19 to "Go ye therefore, and teach all nations." Later writers proposed that other Christian visitors such as **St. Brendan,** the monks of **Great Ireland,** or **Prince Madoc** might have been responsible for preaching to the Native Americans and thereby left traces behind.

The Mormons are unique in believing that Jesus Christ literally visited the Americas after his death and resurrection. Their belief is based on *The Book of Mormon,* which tells the history of God's chosen people and his church in pre-Columbian America. Jesus told his followers in Judaea, "And other sheep I have, which are not of this fold: them also I must bring, and they shall hear my voice and there shall be one fold, and one shepherd" (John 10:16). The "other sheep" were the people of the Americas; that passage from John was repeated verbatim by 3 Nephi 15:17 in *The Book of Mormon.* In fact, it is recorded in 3 Nephi 16:3 that Jesus also mentioned to the Native Americans that he would also be preaching to the **Ten Lost Tribes of Israel.** No indication is given as to where they were located.

The Book of Mormon is full of references predicting the coming of Jesus to the Americas. As that time approached, the signs grew more and more obvious. About 6 B.C. the hardy prophet Samuel the **Lamanite** preached repentance as preparation for Jesus's arrival. A few years later, the Star of Bethlehem appeared as a sign of Jesus's birth, and the prophet Nephi continued to preach of the coming of Jesus. Most of the Native Americans, however, remained unmoved and unrepentant. On the day of Jesus's death, dreadful storms and massive earthquakes occurred. Many cities were entirely destroyed and thousands of people died. Three days of thick darkness followed, completing the discomfiture of the survivors. Jesus spoke to those still alive and called on them to repent. Needless to say, the survivors were very contrite. Jesus physically came down from heaven in a white robe, established his church (led by 12 disciples), and returned to heaven. Two hundred years of peace followed. After the last of those who had actually seen Jesus died, the new generations backslid toward the evil of former days. Social injustice and war became rampant, and ultimately the Lamanites exterminated the **Nephites,** both the righteous and the wicked. The Christian church in America was extinct except for a few pale vestiges.

Mormon scholars have expended much effort to uncover evidence of Jesus's visit and ministry in the Americas. Many of the Christian survivals cited by early Spanish priests are also used by Mormons as evidence. Jesus in his white robe, as described by 3 Nephi in *The Book of Mormon,* was quite literally a white god come to earth. Therefore, Mormon scholars attempt to portray the deities **Quetzalcoatl, Kukulcan,** and **Viracocha** as blurred memories of Jesus's visit.

Traditional Mormon scholarship tries to locate signs of Jesus throughout the Americas, so Milton R. Hunter's *Christ in Ancient America* (1959) spends as much time discussing parallels between Jesus and the Peruvian deity Viracocha as it does on the Mexican god Quetzalcoatl.

Recent Mormon scholarship focuses almost exclusively on Mexico and Guatemala as the lands described in *The Book of Mormon,* and therefore concentrates on the parallels between Jesus and Quetzalcoatl. The name Quetzalcoatl is variously translated as "plumed serpent," "precious serpent," or "precious twin." Snakes have a relatively negative image in Judeo-Christian culture because of the snake's role in humanity's fall from grace in the Garden of Eden. But Mormon scholars point out that the snake was also used as a symbol of redemption during the incident of the Brazen Serpent described in Numbers 21 in the Bible. Numerous other parallels concerning astronomy, calendars, cosmography, the cross, and ethical teachings have also been marshaled as examples.

Mormon archaeologists are searching for evidence of the massive natural disaster they believe occurred at the time of Jesus's death in A.D. 34. Remains of cities damaged by volcanic eruptions have been found in excavations of various archaeological sites from Teotihuacán near Mexico City to Tres Zapotes in Veracruz, and south to Guatemala and El Salvador. Some ash layers may date to approximately A.D. 30. Underwater ruins have been discovered in Lake Atitlán in Guatemala, and recovered artifacts possibly date to the time of Jesus. Of course, non-Mormon archaeologists disagree with the interpretations Mormons place on these evidences, and suggest other interpretations. If Jesus Christ did come to the Americas, he would definitely rank as the region's most significant pre-Columbian visitor—or post-Columbian visitor, for that matter.

Bibliography: Ferguson, Thomas S., *One Fold and One Shepherd*, [1958], rev. ed., 1962; Hunter, Milton R., *Archaeology and the Book of Mormon*, vol. 2: *Christ in Ancient America*, 1959; Warren, Bruce W., and Thomas S. Ferguson, *The Messiah in Ancient America*, 1987.

Jumon/Valdivia Trans-Pacific Contacts (3000 B.C.)

This theory, closely associated with Smithsonian Institution archaeologist Betty Meggers, suggests that fishermen from the Jumon culture of prehistoric Japan accidentally drifted to Valdivia, Ecuador, where they taught the indigenous people how to make relatively sophisticated pottery.

Valdivia, Ecuador, is the home of some of the oldest pottery discovered in the Americas, dating as far back as 3000 B.C. Amateur archaeologist Emilio Estrada first discovered this pottery in 1956. Paradoxically, the earliest Valdivian pottery already used fairly advanced techniques, designs, and decorations. No artifacts from earlier initial and intermediate stages have been found so far. In fact, Valdivian pottery was not only more advanced than that of the neighboring cultures of Monagrillo, Panama; Puerto Hormiga, Columbia; and Guañape, Peru, it was also older. It was as though Valdivian pottery dropped out of nowhere.

By 1961, however, Estrada had managed to link Valdivian pottery with another time and place—the contemporary Jumon culture of prehistoric Japan. The link was the decorative castellation on the rim of a piece of Valdivian pottery found by Estrada. Such castellation was a design used almost exclusively by the Jumon peoples of early Japan about 3000 B.C. After comparisons, the Jumon and Valdivian pottery were found to be virtually identical. Jumon potters used 24 of the 28 pottery decorations used by Valdivians. The neighboring Puerto Hormiga and Monagrillo pottery shared only 11 and 7 types, respectively, with Valdivia. Archaeological evidence shows that the Valdivian potters did not learn their techniques from inferior contemporaries in the Americas, leaving either independent invention (also known as **parallel evolution**) or **diffusion** from the Jumon culture of Japan as explanations.

Betty Meggers rejects independent invention as an explanation. She argues that the similarities between the two pottery types are too great to be coincidental, and that direct contact must have occurred between Jumon Japan and Valdivia. In 1961 she and Estrada put forward the theory that fishermen of the Jumon culture were accidentally swept off by the powerful Kuroshio or Japan current. It carried them across the northern Pacific Ocean and down the west

coast of the Americas until they drifted ashore at Valdivia. According to Meggers, these fishermen, who were not modern **Japanese,** would have been physically and culturally similar to the Valdivians. They could have fit easily into Valdivian society, and could have taught the potteryless Valdivians the art and craft of pottery making, which had been in existence in Japan since about 7000 B.C. Thus Meggers explains the sudden appearance of Valdivian pottery and its striking resemblance to Jumon pottery. There are many cases of **Chinese** and Japanese fishermen carried by storms to the California coast in the nineteenth century. Meggers feels that Jumon fishermen were capable of the same trip and would arrive in even better condition.

Many scholars remain skeptical of Meggers' conclusions, much to her frustration. They insist that independent invention or parallel evolution is a more convincing explanation. Some suggest that, given the xenophobia of most primitive peoples, shipwrecked Japanese fishermen stood a far better chance of being killed than welcomed. Such fishermen would probably not have been potters, so how could they have taught

the Valdivians? Others suggest that early Valdivian pottery should be dated to 2000 B.C., not 3000 B.C., which would mean Jumon and Valdivia were no longer contemporaries. Finally, the California current along the west coast of North America completes its turn west about the middle of Mexico. How were the Jumon fishermen able to continue drifting south to Ecuador? Meggers considers these criticisms to be incorrect or insignificant. Furthermore, she now advocates further contacts between the Olmec culture of Mexico and the Shang dynasty in China (see also **Chinese Visits to America**). As can be seen, the theory of Jumon/Valdivian contact is one of the best-supported theories of trans-Pacific contact before 1492, and it still receives considerable criticism. The last word has not yet been written on the reality of Jumon/Valdivian contacts.

Bibliography: Davies, Nigel, *Voyages to the New World,* 1979; Meggers, Betty J., "Did Japanese Fishermen Really Reach Ecuador 5,000 Years Ago?" *Early Man* 2 (1980): 15–19; Meggers, Betty J., "A Transpacific Contact in 3000 B.C.," *Scientific American* 214 (1966): 28–35.

Karlsefni, Thorfinn

This Icelandic merchant led one of the expeditions to **Vinland** following **Leif Ericsson's**, variously dated to about 1010 or about 1020–1025.

When Thorfinn Karlsefni arrived in **Greenland**, he enjoyed the hospitality of either Leif Ericsson or **Eric the Red**. Spending the winter in the Ericsson home of Brattahlid, he met Gudrid, the widow of **Thorstein Ericsson**. A mutual attraction developed and the couple soon married. The Greenland Norse continued to talk about Vinland, and Karlsefni decided to go there.

According to the *Greenlanders' Saga*, Leif gave Karlsefni permission to use his houses in Vinland, also called the Leifsbudir. Sixty men and five women sailed west for Vinland in one ship. They brought along livestock, as they intended to establish a permanent settlement. The settlement had a favorable start. The capture of a whale provided plenty of food for the winter, and the cattle prospered in Vinland's lush meadows, although they became overly frisky. Winter passed uneventfully, but one summer day some **skraelings,** or Native Americans, appeared. Initially the cattle frightened them off, but soon afterward trade developed. The skraelings were particularly fond of milk and traded many furs for it.

After the skraelings departed, Karlsefni ordered the construction of a wooden palisade to fortify the Norse settlement. About the same time Gudrid gave birth to Snorri, the first European known to be born in the Americas. During the first stages of the next winter, the skraelings again returned to trade. All went well until one of Karlsefni's men killed a skraeling for trying to steal a Norse weapon. The skraelings fled, but Karlsefni realized they would be back in force and seeking revenge. Picking his battleground carefully, Karlsefni developed a plan that included the bull. His strategies worked and the skraelings were quickly driven off with heavy losses. However, the bloody encounter convinced Karlsefni that Vinland was not for him. In the following spring, he and his company gathered their timber, furs, and grapes, packed their belongings, and returned to Greenland.

Eirik's Saga gives a considerably different and more detailed account of Karlsefni's expedition. In this version, he and his partners gathered three ships and 160 people for the settlement. The party included Leif Ericsson's brother **Thorvald Ericsson** and his sister **Freydis**. Differing from the *Greenlanders' Saga*, Karlsefni is the first to reach Vinland after Leif Ericsson, and it is he who named the various regions: **Helluland, Markland,** and Vinland. Thorvald Ericsson dies on Karlsefni's expedition, but the killer is a uniped (one-footed man), not a skraeling.

Karlsefni established his Vinland settlement at a place called Straumfjord, which many scholars feel is the same as Leifsbudir. According to *Eirik's Saga*, the first winter was difficult and food ran short. The Norse killed a whale, but eating it made them sick and therefore was of no help.

By spring the Norse recovered, and after gathering food, Karlsefni decided to explore to the south. After sailing a long time, the Norse found a good site for a settlement. Since it was located on a tidal lake, they named it Hop, or Hope. Fish and game were plentiful, but after several weeks skraelings appeared. According to *Eirik's Saga*, this would have been the first Norse encounter with Native Americans. No fighting took place but neither did trade, and the natives departed. The Norse built a house for shelter, but winter came and went without snowing once.

The following spring, a large number of skraelings came in skin boats and traded furs for red cloth. The Norse's bull, snorting ferociously, charged out of the woods and frightened off the skraelings, with ominous results. Three weeks later they returned, but this time they sought war, not trade. The Norse tried to stand their ground, but their opponents' greater number compelled them to retreat. Freydis came out and berated the Norsemen for retreating from such a pathetic enemy. Grabbing the sword of a dead Norseman, Freydis turned to face some of the attackers. In Norse fashion she bared one of her breasts and beat it with her sword. This terrified the skraelings, and once more they fled. Karlsefni and the other men gathered around Freydis and congratulated her on her bravery. They surveyed their losses—a total of two men killed. Although this was not a heavy toll, Karlsefni decided to leave because the natives would never allow them to settle in peace.

Returning to Straumfjord, Karlsefni and his party rested, then headed north with one ship to search for the missing Thorhall the Hunter. During this excursion the Norse supposedly encountered the uniped who killed Thorvald Ericsson. Some scholars name Hamilton Inlet in Labrador as the location of this incident. After Thorvald's death, the party returned to winter at Straumfjord. By this time, the stress of isolation was beginning to tell. All sorts of quarreling broke out, and the single men began to annoy the married couples. So after three years, the party abandoned their settlement and sailed back to Greenland. Along the way they stopped at Markland and captured two skraeling boys who told them a story of the white man's country, or **Hvítramannaland** (see also **Irish Monks in America**). Karlsefni spent the next winter with Eric the Red, but soon returned home to **Iceland** with Gudrid. Three Icelandic bishops were descended from Karlsefni's family: Bjorn Gilsson, bishop of Holar, 1147–1162; Brand Saemundarson, bishop of Holar, 1163–1201; and Thorlak Runolfson, bishop of Skalholt, 1118–1133. Such descendants helped to preserve and even expand the story of Thorfinn Karlsefni's role in the explorations of North America as told by the **Vinland Sagas**.

Bibliography: Jones, Gwyn, *The Norse Atlantic Saga*, 2nd ed., 1986; Magnusson, Magnus, and Hermann Pálsson, trans. and eds., *The Vinland Sagas: The Norse Discovery of America*, 1966; Oleson, Tryggvi J., *Early Voyages and Northern Approaches*, 1964.

Kensington Rune Stone

This famous but fraudulent Norse artifact discovered in Minnesota in 1898 still has supporters of its authenticity despite considerable debunking scholarship.

Olof Ohman "discovered" the Kensington Rune Stone while clearing trees from his farm in Douglas County near the town of Kensington, Minnesota, in 1898. The exact date of his find is unclear; an official report supplies the date of 8 November, but Ohman's affidavit says it was August. There was an inscription on the stone written in runic characters, the ancient alphabet of Scandinavia. Unfortunately, the physical appearance of the inscription belied its supposed antiquity, its cuts showing none of the weathering associated with a stone carving over 300 years old. It has been suggested that the inscription was added after Ohman unearthed the stone.

The rune stone's inscription told of a party of Norse making its way through the wilderness in 1362 and suffering the loss of ten of its members from attacks by hostile natives. Such a find was of immense interest to the Scandinavian immigrant community of the upper Midwest. They were anxious to find proof of Norse precedence over Christopher Columbus in the European discovery of America. The World Columbian Exposition at Chicago in the 1890s aroused the ethnic ire of Scandinavian-Americans. They wanted to believe that the Kensington Rune Stone was authentic, so local support was strong.

The scholarly reception of the Kensington Rune Stone was negative from the start. Professors O. J. Breda of the University of Minnesota and George O. Curume of the University of Illinois quickly pronounced it a fake on the basis of anachronistic usages of both runic characters and Norse words. A search for the graves of the ten slain Norsemen turned up nothing. Enthusiasm for the rune stone stalled, and Ohman took it back to his farm where he used it as a stepping-stone. True believers in the Scandinavian community continued to claim that the Kensington Rune Stone was genuine.

In 1907 Hjalmar R. Holand came to Douglas County to gather material on Norwegian immigration to the United States. During his researches, the locals told him about Ohman's stone and the curious

Holand went to see it. Rejecting earlier scholarly opinion, Holand decided it was a true Norse artifact. Ohman gave the stone to him, and from 1908 through the rest of his life, Holand attempted to prove that the Kensington Rune Stone was a medieval Norse inscription. He succeeded in interesting the Minnesota Historical Society, so much so that they issued a report on the stone's authenticity. Ignoring scholarly

Kensington Rune Stone.

opinions to the contrary, they pronounced it genuine. Efforts by Holand in 1911 to secure favorable judgments from European scholars met with failure; they all considered it a hoax. Holand was undaunted. In 1932 he published his first book, *The Kensington Stone*, which defended the stone's authenticity and linked it to **Paul Knutson's** expedition of 1355–1363 or 1364. He sent the stone to the Smithsonian Institution in 1948 for further scholarly investigation, with negative results. Nevertheless, Holand continued to publish, citing the Kensington Rune Stone as a true medieval Norse artifact.

In the 1950s a wave of scholarly publications denied the authenticity of the stone. John A. Holvik of Concordia College in Morehead, Minnesota, had been actively opposed to Holand's theories since 1911. He brought Danish scholar Erik Moltke into the controversy, and Moltke published his own article-length attack in 1953. Books from Norse experts Erik Wahlgren in 1958 and Theodore C. Blegen in 1968 followed. These studies convincingly showed that the Kensington Rune Stone was a fake. Blegen suggested how Olof Ohman could have collaborated with his neighbor Sven Fogelbad to produce the inscription. None of this scholarly activity stopped the true believers. Neither did Holand's death in 1963; his role as chief defender was assumed by physicist and mathematician Ole G. Landverk. Landverk not only believed the inscription was genuine, he introduced an additional theory that its literal message was a cryptogram. These ideas appeared in books published in 1967 and 1974. The scholarly community remains unconvinced. The majority of historians and archaeologists consider the Kensington Rune Stone to be no more than one of the most persistent hoaxes in the history of American archaeology.

Bibliography: Blegen, Theodore C., *The Kensington Rune Stone: New Light on an Old Riddle*, 1968; Moltke, Erik, "The Ghost of the Kensington Stone," *Scandinavian Studies* 25 (1953): 1–14; Wahlgren, Erik, *The Kensington Stone: A Mystery Solved*, 1958; Williams, Stephen, *Fantastic Archaeology: The Wild Side of North American Prehistory*, 1991.

Kingsborough, Viscount (1795–1837)

Compiler and publisher of the massive and well-respected collection of ancient Mexican codices and Spanish documents titled *Antiq-*

uities of Mexico (1830–1848), he was also an adherent of the theory that Native Americans were descendants of the **Ten Lost Tribes of Israel.**

Kingsborough was the son of George King, third earl of Kingston. He inherited the courtesy title of Viscount Kingsborough in 1799. From 1814 to 1818 he studied classics at Oxford University. Early in 1815 he fell in love with the study of Mexico, a love that turned into an obsession. It is commonly believed that his passion for Mexican antiquities developed as a result of viewing colorful codices from pre-Columbian Mexico while touring the treasures of Oxford's Bodleian Library. That belief is contradicted by the testimony of Sir Thomas Phillipps, a close friend and fellow antiquarian, who had written his letter of introduction to the Bodleian. According to Phillipps, Kingsborough had already resolved to devote his energies to the study of ancient Mexico before his Bodleian visit.

Initially Kingsborough balanced his antiquarian interests with his responsibilities as a peer. In both 1818 and 1820 he secured election as the member of Parliament for County Cork in Ireland. In 1826 he resigned his seat in the House of Lords in favor of his younger brother, and the collection of Mexican antiquities became an all-consuming obsession. It took all Kingsborough's time as well as his fortune, which was not stable because he had inherited his father's substantial debts. Furthermore, the scope of Kingsborough's interest grew. He originally envisioned the publication of a three-volume compendium of facsimiles of pictorial manuscripts, then added a fourth volume of illustrations. Later he published Spanish documents dealing with ancient Mexico, such as the work of **Fernando de Alva Ixtlilxochitl.** Eventually the set reached nine fat volumes in length; there would have been a tenth if Kingsborough had lived longer.

Kingsborough's *Antiquities of Mexico* represented the best that nineteenth-century publishing had to offer in terms of paper, binding, and printing. Each volume was an imperial folio and weighed about 65 pounds. Estimates of publication costs range between £32,000 and £40,000, an enormous sum for that era. Its lavish production completed the bankruptcy of Kingsborough, who died of typhus in a Dublin prison on 27 February 1837 during his third incarceration for debt.

Kingsborough's belief that Native Americans were descendants of the Ten Lost Tribes of Israel motivated the ruinous extravagance of publishing the *Antiquities of Mexico*. The idea did not originate with him, and his comparisons between the Hebrew and Aztec cultures were, if anything, less persuasive than those of his predecessors. Unlike many adherents of the theory, Kingsborough was a resolute anti-Semite who considered Jews to be hard-hearted and enemies of Christianity. Despite his dubious motive and theory, he produced a compilation of historical documents that scholars still find valuable.

Bibliography: Goodkind, Howard W., "Lord Kingsborough Lost His Fortune Trying To Prove the Maya Were Descendants of the Ten Lost Tribes," *Biblical Archaeology Review* 11 (September–October 1985): 54–65; Graham, Ian, "Lord Kingsborough, Sir Thomas Phillipps, and Obadiah Rich: Some Bibliographical Notes," in *Social Process in Maya Prehistory,* edited by Norman Hammond, 45–55, 1977.

Knutson, Expedition of Paul (1355–1363/1364)

Also spelled Knudsson, this supposed Norse expedition was made for the purpose of preserving Christianity in **Greenland**. Some writers suggest that Knutson and his company continued on to America in search of lost Greenland colonists. They supposedly got as far as Minnesota, where they carved the **Kensington Rune Stone.** No serious scholars believe these details.

The fourteenth century was a time of decline for Norse settlements in Greenland. The increasingly cooler weather made traveling the North Atlantic more dangerous, while cattle and sheep husbandry on Greenland became ever more precarious. Colder weather also brought the **Eskimos** south, and competition placed additional pressure on the already beleaguered Norse. By about 1350 church official and chronicler Ivar Bardarson reported that the Western Settlement had been abandoned. This state of affairs greatly concerned King Magnus of Norway, a man devoted to the preservation and expansion of Christendom.

Fearful that true Christianity was in jeopardy, in 1354 King Magnus ordered Paul Knutson to take a party of men to Greenland and make sure that Christianity was safe. The king even loaned Knutson the royal ship for his journey. Unfortunately the letter commanding Knutson to undertake the mission is the only reliable documentary evidence that survives. Some writers are not even sure Knutson ever sailed. Others suggest he went to Greenland, departing in 1355 and returning in 1363 or 1364. They cite the Eskimo kayaks displayed in Oslo Cathedral as evidence of both his return and his missionary work among the heathen. If Knutson did sail farther west, no itinerary of his eight- or nine-year journey survives.

Lack of evidence has never stopped speculation about various pre-Columbian transoceanic contacts, and Knutson's expedition is no exception. The alleged discovery of the Kensington Rune Stone in Minnesota during 1898 added material for speculations about Norse expeditions and settlements in North America. The most elaborate hypothesis was that of Norwegian-American

Hjalmar R. Holand. In 1932 he defended the authenticity of the Kensington Rune Stone and connected it with Paul Knutson's expedition of 1355–1363 or 1364, on the basis of the Kensington Rune Stone conveniently bearing the date 1362.

According to Holand, in 1342 the remnants of the Western Settlement abandoned their homes and moved to **Vinland** rather than the Eastern Settlement. After Knutson arrived, he went in search of them. His expedition sailed to Vinland (which for Holand was located in Rhode Island), where they became one of the many builders of the Newport Tower (actually built during the late seventeenth century). (See also **Gnupsson, Expedition of Bishop Eric.**) Knutson sailed north into Hudson's Bay, where a party of 30 men traveled overland into the heart of the continent. Problems with hostile natives increased, and ten of the party were massacred, as recorded on the Kensington Rune Stone. The rest either perished soon after or were absorbed into more hospitable tribes. The supposedly light-skinned and blue-eyed **Mandans** are suggested as possible descendants of the lost Norse. The redoubtable Charles M. Boland, another popular writer on pre-Columbian contacts, basically agreed with Holand's reconstruction of the Knutson expedition, but he suggested they took a different route to Minnesota, via the eastern United States and Lake Superior. Other writers include the English Arctic traveler **Nicholas of Lynn** as a member of the Knutson expedition, but the evidence is unconvincing. Professional archaeologists and historians in America and Europe consider the Kensington Rune Stone a hoax. Without it, the Knutson expedition has only King Magnus's letter to document that it ever took place. There is no other evidence that the party reached Greenland, let alone the North American mainland.

Bibliography: Boland, Charles M., *They All Discovered America*, 1961; Holand, Hjalmar R., *Norse Discoveries and Explorations in America, 982–1362*, 1968, but originally published in 1940 as *Westward from Vinland*; Morison, Samuel Eliot, *The European Discovery of America: The Northern Voyages*, 1971.

Kon Tiki Expedition (1947)

Thor Heyerdahl made a voyage from South America to Polynesia on a balsa raft in 1947 to demonstrate the possibility that **Polynesian-American contacts** took place in an east-to-west direction.

During his residence on Fatu Hiva from 1937–1938 and through his studies of the Bella Coola Indians of British Columbia during 1939–1940, Thor Heyerdahl developed a theory that the Polynesians were descendants of two migrations of Native Americans. He based this unique and radical theory on several types of evidence. Currents in the central Pacific Ocean generally run in a strong east-to-west direction, which would make sea travel from South America to Polynesia relatively easy. Conversely, the traditional theory that Polynesians came from Asia in a west-to-east movement required travel against these same strong currents. He believed this sailing logic made it more likely that the Polynesians originated in the east. Another strong point of evidence was the presence of the **sweet potato** in Polynesia. The sweet potato, a plant of undoubted American origin, was definitely present in Polynesia well before 1492. It is not capable of floating across thousands of miles of ocean, so someone must have brought it to Polynesia from pre-Columbian America. Heyerdahl also suggested a number of significant cultural parallels that also argued for transoceanic contact. Both Polynesians and Peruvians built temples in the form of stepped pyramids and erected monolithic stone images. The war technology of Polynesians and Native American tribes of the Pacific Northwest was also very similar.

Linguistic parallels between the Polynesian and Peruvian languages, especially the Quechua of the Incas, appeared strong to Heyerdahl. In particular, he pointed out how the legend of **Viracocha,** a legendary sun god/king of the Peruvians, fitted quite neatly into his theory. The pre-Inca Peruvian name for Viracocha was Kon Tiki (or Con Tiki). According to the legend, the fair-skinned Kon Tiki and his followers were driven from their kingdom in the Andes by a rebellion. They sailed west from the Peruvian coast, never to be seen again. Many Polynesians are quite light-skinned, with beards and occasional red hair. Furthermore, there was a widespread legend among the Polynesians about a fair-skinned god called Tiki, who had come from across the eastern ocean and was associated with the sun. The complementary nature of the Kon Tiki and Tiki legends provided a compelling piece of circumstantial evidence.

According to Heyerdahl's theory, there were two different migrations from the Americas. He does not rule out the possibility that some peoples of Asian origin may have already been living in Polynesia before the arrival of the Native Americans. The first American migration was Kon Tiki and his peaceful followers, who spread across the different islands. Next came the more warlike Native Americans of the Pacific Northwest coast. The two groups merged and created the distinctive Polynesian culture that European explorers described from the sixteenth century on.

Heyerdahl's theory initially received little support from academic anthropologists and archaeologists. To dramatize his case, Heyerdahl built a reproduction of a Peruvian seagoing balsa raft, which he named the *Kon Tiki*. On 28 April 1947, he and his crew sailed from Callao, Peru, for Polynesia using the Humboldt and South Equatorial cur-

rents to carry them along. Three months later, on 30 July, they sighted Puka Puka in the Tuamotu Islands. By that time they were no longer able to steer the *Kon Tiki*, so they drifted past the island. On 7 August, the *Kon Tiki* ran aground on the reef of Raroia. Everyone survived and they even managed to save the *Kon Tiki*, which is now on display in a museum in Oslo, Norway. Heyerdahl quickly wrote an account of the expedition, which was published in 1948 and became the international best-seller *Kon Tiki*. The *Kon Tiki* expedition proved that primitive transoceanic navigation was possible.

Since 1947, scholarly research has not bolstered Heyerdahl's theories. Intensive research demonstrates that the Polynesian language derives from the Austronesian family of languages, which includes neighboring Melanesia and Micronesia. Recent archaeological digs in western Polynesia also reveal that the first settlements occurred far earlier than once thought. This information seriously conflicts with Heyerdahl's chronology. Furthermore, Polynesians had pigs and other Old World animals and plants that indicate far more sustained contact with Asia than the sweet potato indicates for the Americas. Most scholars admit that sporadic contacts and cultural exchanges took place between Polynesia and America, but they firmly reject Heyerdahl's contention that Native Americans were the ancestors and culture-bringers of that region.

Bibliography: Davies, Nigel, *Voyagers to the New World,* 1979; Heyerdahl, Thor, *American Indians in the Pacific,* 1952; Heyerdahl, Thor, *Kon Tiki,* 1950, first English edition with many subsequent printings.

Kukulcan

Also spelled Cuculcan, this is the Lowland or Yucatec Maya name for the Toltec and Aztec god **Quetzalcoatl,** the prototype of the Mesoamerican versions of the **white god**

legends. Gucumatz is the Lowland or Quiché Maya name for Quetzalcoatl/Kukulcan.

Kukulcan, like Quetzalcoatl, means "feathered serpent." The cult of Kukulcan came to the Yucatán Peninsula in 987 when Toltecs or some other related Central Mexican people invaded the region and conquered the city of Chichén Itzá. Some suggest that the historical Topiltzin/ Quetzalcoatl moved to the Yucatán after being driven from his original home of Tollan. The principal problem with that suggestion is that the Kukulcan cult demanded human sacrifice; Topiltzin/Quetzalcoatl condemned the practice when he ruled Tollan. It seems unlikely that the same person preached two such radically different beliefs.

As with Quetzalcoatl, there is no evidence from most authentic Native American sources that Kukulcan was white-skinned. Although Kukulcan may not literally have been a white god, his legend certainly prepared the Maya of the Yucatán for the return/appearance of unique and powerful strangers to rule over their land, thus easing the Spanish conquest. The legend of Kukulcan is almost certainly a Toltec import, and in no way reflects a vague memory of an actual civilizing visit by Old World peoples such as **Phoenicians, St. Thomas, St. Brendan, Prince Madoc,** or even **Jesus Christ.**

Bibliography: Carrasco, Davíd, *Quetzalcoatl and the Irony of Empire: Myths and Prophecies in the Aztec Tradition*, 1982; Mercatante, Anthony S., *The Facts on File Encyclopedia of World Mythology and Legend*, 1988.

God did not favor them. Instead God favored Nephi, further arousing Laman and Lemuel's jealousy and wrath. Numerous ugly incidents took place between the older brothers and Nephi; after Lehi died, Laman and Lemuel became completely estranged and refused to accept Nephi as God's chosen leader. Fearing for their lives, Nephi and his followers fled to a new land, which they named Nephi. Their flight did not end the troubles; instead, it marked the beginning of a millennium-long conflict between the Nephites and Lamanites.

The Book of Mormon states that God cursed the Lamanites with dark skin because of their wickedness. It also portrays the Lamanites as an uncivilized and lazy people who lived in tents and preferred hunting to farming. Further evidence of the low nature of the Lamanites was their propensity to go about half-naked, their lack of cleanliness, and the shaving of their heads. Being lazy, they preferred the easy way of robbery rather than working to accumulate wealth, so they made war on the industrious Nephites, who prospered as farmers and craftsmen.

Although the Lamanites lived as nomadic hunters, their population grew greatly, and soon they outnumbered the Nephites. They had their own kings and cities, which suggests that not all were nomadic hunters. Furthermore, the Lamanites were not always bad and certainly not naturally evil. Nephites tried to convert them to the true faith and sometimes succeeded. Ammon, the missionary son of the Nephite king Mosiah, permanently converted the Lamanite king Lamoni and his people about 90 B.C. Sometimes the Lamanites lived more uprightly than the Nephites. Approximately 6 B.C. Samuel the Lamanite prophet preached to the Nephites, calling on them to repent before the imminent coming of Jesus.

After the coming of Jesus Christ about A.D. 30, 200 years of righteousness passed in which the distinction between Lamanite and

Lamanites

According to *The Book of Mormon,* these people were a nation of ancient Americans consisting of the descendants of Laman and Lemuel (the sons of Lehi and older brothers of Nephi), along with the descendants of a companion, Ishmael. The Lamanites were unremittingly hostile to the **Nephites,** who were the descendants of Nephi, and eventually destroyed them in a huge battle by Hill Cumorah. Traditionally, Mormons believe that Native Americans are descendants of the Lamanites. *The Book of Mormon* also uses the term Lamanite to refer to anyone rejecting the gospel of **Jesus Christ.**

Laman and Lemuel were the oldest sons of Lehi, the leader of a Hebrew migration to America described in *The Book of Mormon.* They were rebellious and envious people, so

Nephite disappeared. But in 231 the Nephites and Lamanites separated once more. Nephites followed the gospel, while Lamanites rejected it. By 300 most of the Nephites had also backslid and become evil, leaving them open to attack by the numerically superior Lamanites. The Lamanites annihilated the last of the Nephites in 385 in the battle by Hill Cumorah. After their triumph, the Lamanites fought among themselves and remained brutish heathens.

Mormons traditionally identify Lamanites as the ancestors of the indigenous peoples living in the Americas in 1492. Such a broad identification becomes increasingly untenable in the light of archaeological discoveries made since the first publication of *The Book of Mormon* in 1830. As a result, recent Mormon scholarship suggests that the Lamanites and Nephites were simply a small part of a population that included not only **Mulekite** and **Jaredite** survivors but many other unnamed peoples. John L. Sorenson, an anthropologist of Brigham Young University, theorizes that the rapid Lamanite population growth was because the original Lamanites assumed leadership over primitive aboriginal peoples in the Guatemala and Yucatán regions of Central America. Such an interpretation better fits the archaeological record, but it also contradicts the literal words of *The Book of Mormon*—not a pleasing prospect to fundamentalist Mormons. Sorenson concludes by placing a figurative usage on the modern Mormon practice of referring to all Native Americans as Lamanites. As he explains it, a Lamanite is the descendant of any pre-Columbian inhabitant of the Americas who has not yet adopted the Mormon faith.

Sorenson's portrayal has the problem of convincingly reconciling itself to the archaeological record. So-called Lamanite archaeological sites in Guatemala do not appear markedly inferior to so-called Nephite archaeological sites. But *The Book of Mormon*

describes the early Lamanites as "an idle people full of mischief and subtlety, and did seek in the wilderness for beasts of prey" (2 *Nephi* 5:24) and "led by their evil nature that they became wild, and ferocious, and a bloodthirsty people, full of idolatry and filthiness; feeding on beast of prey, dwelling in tents, and wandering about in the wilderness with a short girdle about their loins and their heads shaven . . . and many of them did eat nothing save it was raw meat" (*Enos* 1:20). Sorenson contends that such descriptions are an exaggeration on the part of hostile Nephites, as was the "skin of blackness" that described the complexion of the Lamanites.

Bibliography: Ferguson, Thomas S., *One Fold and One Shepherd*, [1958], rev. ed. 1962; Sorenson, John L., *An Ancient American Setting for the Book of Mormon*, 1985; Vogel, Dan, *Indian Origins and the Book of Mormon*, 1986.

Land of Promise of the Saints

This is the name for a large island in the western Atlantic that both **St. Brendan** and the monk **Barinthus** visited, according to the account in the *Navigatio Sancti Brendani*. Many writers identify the Land of Promise of the Saints as North America, but no concrete historical evidence supports this contention. The Land of Promise of the Saints was large, and neither Barinthus nor St. Brendan managed to cross it despite journeys lasting 40 days. Both travelers came upon a great river flowing from east to west, which is identified as the Ohio. It appears that the Land of Promise of the Saints is simply another name for the legendary western paradise known as the **Blessed Isles** by Irish Christians. The Blessed Isles, in turn, were a Christian version of a western paradise, a widespread belief among the peoples of western Europe and the Mediterranean basin, as exemplified by stories of the **Fortunate Isles**.

Landa, Diego de (1524–1579)

Spanish Franciscan monk, bishop of Yucatán, and historian, he is notorious for his mass burning of Mayan codices as idolatrous and devilish materials. Some erroneously classify him as one of the writers who thought Native Americans were of **Hebrew** descent.

Landa entered the Franciscan order in 1541 and went to Yucatán as a missionary in 1549. Like many Franciscans and other Spanish clerics, Landa was an ardent supporter of the rights of Native Americans and a critic of their exploitation by the conquistadors. Anxious to convert his charges to Christianity, he diligently learned the Mayan language and customs, and zealously sought to keep his beloved flock from backsliding into their old pagan ways. In 1562 that concern compelled him to destroy their ancient sacred books and temples and imprison recalcitrant practitioners of paganism. His actions went too far for the tastes of other churchmen. Complaints were lodged and he was sent back to Spain to appear before the Council of the Indies and answer charges. While in Spain, he wrote his *Relación de las cosas de Yucatán* in 1566 as part of his effort to defend himself. This work, a survey of Mayan culture, religion, social institutions, and history, remained in manuscript form until **Charles Étienne Brasseur de Bourbourg** discovered it in Madrid archives in 1864. Landa was exonerated and in 1573 promoted to bishop of Yucatán. He died six years later.

Landa is frequently cited as an adherent of the Hebrew or Jewish theory of Native American origins. In fact, he said only that the Yucatán natives claimed their ancestors had come from the east with God's help, which if true meant they were of Jewish descent. Landa did not generally believe in the literal truth of native legends. Unlike some early Spanish chroniclers, such as **Diego Durán**, Landa did not take the Jewish theory seriously, and Jewish/Native American parallels were given no space in his book on the Maya. Nevertheless, he did not dismiss the Jewish origin theory out of hand. Overall, Landa was an extremely objective observer who gave the Yucatán people the credit for their cultural achievements.

Bibliography: Huddleston, Lee Eldridge, *Origins of the American Indians: European Concepts, 1492–1729*, 1967; Landa, Diego de, *Yucatan before and after the Conquest*, translated by William Gates, [1937], 1978; Wilgus, A. Curtis, *The Historiography of Latin America: A Guide to Historical Writing, 1500–1800*, 1975.

L'Anse aux Meadows

The only genuine Norse archaeological site so far found in North America, excluding **Greenland,** it was discovered by Helge Ingstad in 1960. Considerable controversy exists as to whether it is **Leif Ericsson's** settlement of Leifsbudir in **Vinland.**

Until this discovery, scholars debated whether the Norse had actually visited North America as described in the **Vinland Sagas.** If they accepted that, scholars then argued over the identity of Vinland, locating it from Florida to Hudson's Bay. Most scholars placed Vinland somewhere in New England because of the sagas' references to wild grapes. Norwegian scholar Helge Ingstad supported a more northerly location on the basis of his studies of Norse sites in Greenland. In his opinion, references to wild grapes were later additions to the text derived from the unreliable history of **Adam of Bremen.** Ingstad's method for locating Vinland was to search systematically the coasts of the eastern seaboard of North America by sea and air. Starting in Rhode Island, he worked his way to the northern tip of Newfoundland, where he located Norse remains near the isolated fishing village of L'Anse aux Meadows.

Ingstad and his wife, Anne Stine Ingstad, excavated L'Anse aux Meadows from 1961 to 1968. They uncovered seven buildings, along with a smithy and a row of boat sheds. Initially the site did not produce any definite Norse artifacts, but eventually the remains of iron nails, spindle whorls, and stone lamps of undoubted Norse origin were found. Radiocarbon dating of wood scraps proved consistent with the Vinland Sagas' dating of the Norse voyages to the early eleventh century. Archaeological evidence indicates that the site was occupied for a relatively brief period of no more than 25 years. The Norse were not the only occupants of L'Anse aux Meadows; Dorset **Eskimo** and Beothuk Indian remains were also uncovered.

Helge Ingstad contends that the discovery of L'Anse aux Meadows proves that Vinland was located in Newfoundland and that it is probably Leif Ericsson's settlement. The topography of L'Anse aux Meadows, with its lush meadows and bay, matches the descriptions in the Vinland Sagas, supplying strong evidence in favor of Ingstad's identification. Initially his identification met with much skepticism by scholars such as Magnus Magnusson. Their chief argument against L'Anse aux Meadows as the site of Leif's settlement was the absence of wild grapes and wheat. The site also lacked the protective wooden palisade **Thorfinn Karlsefni** built during his expedition. But as the authenticity of the site as Norse became certain, more people accepted Ingstad's identification of Newfoundland as Vinland. Others express strong doubts, including Brigitta Linderoth Wallace, director of Canada's L'Anse aux Meadows project. She argues that L'Anse aux Meadows lies in the extreme north of the region the Norse called Vinland. The discovery of plant materials from areas farther south among the Norse

Reconstruction of a Norse building at L'Anse aux Meadows.

remains at L'Anse aux Meadows shows that the Norse ranged well beyond Newfoundland, consistent with the sagas' mention of the southern settlement of Hop in Vinland. Wallace views L'Anse aux Meadows as a trading post and port for ship repair rather than a permanent agricultural settlement like the Eastern and Western Settlements of Greenland. Little evidence survives of the existence of trade between Norse Greenland and the inhabitants of **Markland** and Vinland. Still, archaeologists think that such trade did exist, and the discovery of L'Anse aux Meadows bolsters their assumptions. No other genuine Norse sites have been found in North America, although most scholars consider it likely that such discoveries will be made in the future. Further finds would place L'Anse aux Meadows and the Norse presence in America in a clearer historical perspective.

The Canadian government began administering the site in 1968. In 1977 it became a national historical park, and a permanent visitor center was added in 1985. It is the one direct evidence for an authentic pre-Columbian visit to the Americas apart from the Native Americans and Eskimos.

Bibliography: Ingstad, Anne Stine, and Helge Ingstad, eds., *The Norse Discovery of America*, 2 vols., 1985; Wallace, Brigitta Linderoth, "The L'Anse aux Meadows Site," in *The Norse Atlantic Saga*, by Gwyn Jones, 2nd ed., 1986.

Las Casas, Father Bartolomé de (1474/1484?–1566)

Priest and missionary to the Native Americans in the early years of the Spanish West Indies, Las Casas is wrongly credited with believing that the natives were descended from the **Ten Lost Tribes of Israel**. Instead, Las Casas thought they originated in eastern Asia. He repeated the story of the **Unknown Pilot of Columbus** in his *Historia de las Indias* (History of the Indies), but did not indicate whether or not he believed it.

A native of Seville, Las Casas or members of his family participated in Spain's exploration and settlement of the New World from its very beginning in 1492. When he departed for Hispaniola in 1502, he had probably already taken minor religious vows. After helping in the suppression of a native uprising, Las Casas was rewarded with land and native slaves. He continued his clerical career and in 1512 became the first priest ordained in the New World. Initially unsympathetic to Native Americans, in 1514 Las Casas became one of their most fervent defenders when he was confronted by their growing poverty and brutal exploitation by Spanish colonists. He joined the Dominican order in 1524 and, despite great opposition, urged the Spanish crown to require humane treatment of Native Americans. His efforts resulted in the more humane New Laws of 1542. Las Casas became bishop of Chiapas in Mexico in 1544, but continued to encounter resistance to his efforts to protect the natives. He returned to Spain in 1547 to defend his actions before officials of the church and crown, but was unsuccessful; he was never allowed to return to the New World.

Las Casas's most famous historical work is *Brevísima relación de la destrucción de las Indias* (A brief narration of the destruction of the Indies) of 1552. It was translated into several other languages, including English, during the sixteenth century, and greatly contributed to the formation of the infamous Black Legend of the Spanish conquest of the New World. His discussions of Native American origins and pre-Columbian explorers of the New World, however, appeared in two unpublished works. In the *Apologetica historia* (Apologetic history), completed in 1550, Las Casas stated his opinion that Native Americans were descended from East Indians or Asians, and

Las Casas, Father Bartolomé de

provided a detailed rejection of the **Hebrew** origin theory. Las Casas completed his main historical work, *Historia de las Indias,* in 1559 but left instructions that it was not to be published until 40 years after his death. In fact, it was not published until 1875–1876. In it he reviewed and rejected **Oviedo's** theories of **Carthaginian** and Spanish (**Héspero**) discoveries and settle-ments in the Americas. He also denied that the Americas were the biblical **Ophir.** Las Casas did not give his thoughts as to the true origins of Native Americans, but he felt that their residence in the New World was very ancient. He cited findings of artifacts buried deep in the strata of a riverbed as evidence, making himself an early practitioner of ar-chaeological methods.

Bartolomé de Las Casas.

Because his ideas remained unpublished until the late nineteenth and early twentieth centuries, they had little impact on the intervening debates. The same may be said of his opinions on the Unknown Pilot of Columbus. In telling the story, he mentions that the rumor was circulating widely throughout Hispaniola when he arrived in 1502. His ambiguous conclusion was that while the story was not true, it was certainly possible.

Bibliography: Hanke, Lewis, *Bartolomé de Las Casas, Historian: An Essay in Spanish Historiography*, 1952; Phelan, John L., "The *Apologetic History* of Fray Bartolomé de Las Casas," *Hispanic American Historical Review* 49 (1969): 94–99; Wagner, Henry Raup, and Helen Rand Parish, *The Life and Writings of Bartolomé de Las Casas*, 1967.

Le Plongeon, Augustus (1826–1908)

He was a controversial pioneer archaeologist who primarily worked on the Mayan ruins of Uxmal and Chichén Itzá during the 1870s and early 1880s. He and his wife Alice Dixon (1851–1910) accomplished much useful archaeological fieldwork, but their theory that the Maya were the originators of all human civilization, including Egypt and **Atlantis**, brought them into disrepute with the rest of the emerging archaeological profession.

Although Le Plongeon was the son of a French naval officer, he regarded himself as a citizen of the United States. During his early life he traveled widely, particularly in the Americas. He trained in medicine, which allowed him to adopt the title of doctor, and photography, which he used to good effect in his archaeological work. He developed an interest in American antiquities and archaeology. In early 1873 the 47-year-old adventurer married Alice Dixon, a 22-year-old English girl living in Brooklyn. The Le Plongeons began their joint archaeological

career in July by sailing for the ruins of Yucatán.

The Le Plongeons were assiduous recorders of the details of the Mayan ruins they visited. Their greatest discovery was in 1875 when they uncovered a statue they named Chaacmool (Mayan for powerful warrior) but later altered to Chacmool. Based on the Chacmool and other evidence from the ruins, Le Plongeon developed a version of Mayan history going back 10,000 or 11,000 years involving Queen Moo, Prince Coh, and others. This dating made the civilization of Queen Moo the oldest on earth and the source of all others, or so Le Plongeon reasoned. This belief classified Le Plongeon as an extreme **diffusionist** or hyperdiffusionist just at the time when diffusionism was coming under increasing attack in scholarly circles. Like many of his contemporaries, Le Plongeon believed Atlantis existed, but he was unique in that he considered it to be a colony of the Maya, and not the other way around. The same situation applied to Egypt, which according to Le Plongeon was visited regularly by the Maya in the prehistoric era. Such theories attracted much criticism to Le Plongeon, who stoutly defended his ideas. His spirited defense only caused the archaeological profession to ostracize him further.

Le Plongeon's flamboyant manner did not help his case. Many tales circulated that do him little credit. He liked to tell a story about how he convinced his Mayan workers that he was one of their ancestors returned to this world by comparing his profile to a bearded figure on a bas-relief. The story has been widely doubted from the time Le Plongeon told it, but in fact it seems to have been largely true. Persistent rumors that he used dynamite on archaeological digs are not true. It is claimed that he believed the ancient Maya had telegraphs; what he actually said was that they had prophesied the invention of telegraphy. Le Plongeon maintained, however, that on his cross **Jesus Christ** actually spoke Mayan, not Aramaic. This was to serve as a particularly dramatic example of the supposedly widespread Mayan influence on the ancient world. Instead, it made him look ridiculous.

Although the archaeological profession rejected the Le Plongeons' theories, other fringe groups did not. Later in life the Le Plongeons developed close ties with the leaders of **Theosophy**, which did nothing to improve their scholarly reputations. Augustus died in 1908 with his work ignored, and Alice, embittered about the way academics had treated them, died two years later. According to a recent (and sympathetic) biographer of the Le Plongeons, if they had limited themselves to their factual archaeological fieldwork, forgoing speculation about the origins of civilization, they would be well and respectfully remembered as fine archaeologists.

Bibliography: Brunhouse, Robert L., *In Search of the Maya: The First Archaeologists*, 1973; Desmond, Lawrence G., and Phyllis M. Messenger, *A Dream of Maya: Augustus and Alice Le Plongeon in Nineteenth-Century Yucatan*, 1988; Wauchope, Robert, *Lost Tribes and Sunken Continents*, 1962.

Lemuria

Or **Mu**, it is the name for a fabled lost continent in the Pacific Ocean. Many people, including **Theosophists** and **Rosicrucians**, consider Lemuria the home of humanity and the source of all civilizations, including those of Native Americans, particularly the Maya of Central America.

The origin of the name is attributed to two different sources. According to one account, a Scot named it after the Lemures. According to Roman mythology, they were the evil ghosts of the dead appeased during the Lemuria, a festival occurring in May. A more likely derivation connects the name to the theories of the German scientist and defender of Darwinian evolutionary theory Ernst Heinrich Haekel (or Jaekel; 1834–1919). During the 1860s and 1870s, various geologists and paleontologists postulated the prehistoric existence of different continents and land bridges to explain the distribution of similar fossil remains separated by great oceans. Haekel extended this theory into the evolutionary era of the Age of Mammals. He applied its implications to human evolution in two books—*Natural History of Creation* (1868) and *Origins and Genealogy of the Human Race* (1870). He suggested that a land bridge or island once existed, allowing lemurs to spread throughout both the Old World and the Americas. In fact, Haekel claimed that this lost land bridge or island was the point of origin for lemurs, and possibly for the human race as well. English scientist Philip L. Schlater was so impressed by Haekel's idea that he named the theoretical land bridge Lemuria.

Subsequent scientific research rendered Haekel's Lemurian theory obsolete, but not before some nonscientists got hold of it and turned it to their own purposes. Prominent among those nonscientific adherents was Madame Helena P. Blavatsky, a cofounder of the Theosophical Society in 1875. Madame Blavatsky presented her ideas on Lemuria in a two-volume work titled *The Secret Doctrine*, which claimed this lost continent of the Pacific Ocean as the ancient home of humanity's third root race. Later Theosophical writers elaborated on Blavatsky's ideas. Her somewhat simple-minded Lemurians had four arms and an eye in the back of their heads, were hermaphroditic, and presented a generally apish appearance. The far more advanced Atlanteans evolved from the Lemurians to form the fourth root race. Both races colonized other parts of the world including the Americas before the destruction of their homelands.

By 1890, William Churchward (no relation to the James Churchward who wrote about Mu), could write a letter to the *Brooklyn Times* complaining that **Atlantis** got all the public's attention when Lemuria deserved an equal share. Other prominent supporters of Lemuria include **Anthrosophists**, Rosicrucians, and the lost-continent expert and popular writer J. Lewis Spence. They all agree that civilization existed on Lemuria and spread to other parts of the world including the Americas. Spence considers the Polynesians survivors of the sinking of Lemuria; his contemporary James Churchward makes the same claim, but calls the continent Mu. Whether one uses Lemuria or Mu, the geological record shows no sign that such a Pacific continent ever existed. History and archaeology also offer no corroboration, since no one has ever discovered any reliable and legitimate documentation or artifacts from or about Lemuria. Lists of supposed shared Lemurian traits in cultures of both the Old World and the Americas are not at all convincing. Supporters of Lemuria and Mu fall back on occult sources such as Madame Blavatsky's secret Senzar language, James Churchward's Naacal Tablets, and communications by astral clairvoyance, none of which makes for good historical or archaeological conclusions.

Bibliography: de Camp, L. Sprague, *Lost Continents*, [1954], 1970; Wauchope, Robert, *Lost Tribes and Sunken Continents*, 1962; Williams, Stephen, *Fantastic Archaeology: The Wild Side of North American Prehistory*, 1991.

Libyans in Ancient America

This theory, advocated by **Barry Fell**, Cyclone Covey, and their followers, suggests that ancient and early medieval Libyans not only reached North America, they made their way deep into the interior for trade and settlement.

Barry Fell contends that sometime after about 400 B.C. Libyans reached North America and worked their way inland to the south-

western desert region of the present United States. His evidence for this somewhat unexpected migration is the claim that the language of the Zuni tribe is an offshoot of the Libyan language; what is more, an offshoot showing the linguistic influence of Greek colonies in that region from 800 B.C. onward. Fell's Libyan theory forms only one piece of his collage of ancient visitors to the Americas. It is directly contrary to long-standing and well-documented findings of the Smithsonian Institution's Bureau of Ethnology that no Native American language in North America has any meaningful affinities with Old World languages.

Closely related to Fell's Libyan migration theory is the episode of the Tucson Artifacts and Calalus, a supposed Roman-Jewish colony in Arizona founded by people from Libya. The Tucson Artifacts were a group of metal crosses discovered in 1924. A man named Charles Manier found the first cross in the desert. It weighed 65 pounds and bore the Latin inscription "Calalus the Unknown Land." Joined by his friend Thomas Bent, Manier eventually found 30 more artifacts between 1924 and 1930. By 1925 many scholars suspected the artifacts were a hoax. Nevertheless, Byron Cummings, dean and soon-to-be president of the University of Arizona, initially supported the artifacts as authentic, as did Andrew E. Douglass, the father of dendrochronology. Their support collapsed in 1928, and by 1930 the Tucson Artifacts appeared to be completely discredited. In 1975 Cyclone Covey, a professor of American history at Wake Forest University, revived the whole story in his book *Calalus: A Roman Jewish Colony in America from the Time of Charlemagne through Alfred the Great*. In 1980 his ideas were picked up by Barry Fell in *Saga America*. Basically they suggest that Calalus served as a place of refuge for Jews and Christians driven out of North Africa by the Vandal and Islamic invasions. Professional archaeologists and anthropologists still adamantly reject the idea of Libyan settlements in pre-Columbian America, particularly in the southwestern United States. Acceptance of the Tucson Artifacts is a good example of credulously accepting suspect and discredited archaeological finds as reliable evidence.

Bibliography: Fell, Barry, *America B.C.*, 1976; Fell, Barry, *Saga America*, 1980; Williams, Stephen, *Fantastic Archaeology: The Wild Side of North American Prehistory*, 1991.

Lloyd, Voyage of Thomas (1480)

This was the first documented attempt by sailors of **Bristol** to explore the western Atlantic Ocean in search of the **Island of Brazil.**

According to William Worcestre's *Itineraries*, on 15 July 1480 an 80-ton ship departed Bristol with expert seaman Thomas Lloyd as ship's master. Its goal was to locate Brazil somewhere to the west of Ireland. On 18 September word arrived in Bristol that after nine weeks at sea, Lloyd had been driven back to Ireland without finding Brazil.

Bibliography: Williamson, J. A., *The Cabot Voyages and Bristol Discovery under Henry VII*, 1962.

Llwyd, Humphrey (1527–1568)

This Welsh physician and antiquary completed a manuscript on Welsh history in 1559 that contains the earliest surviving mention of **Madoc's voyage** of discovery and colonization of unknown lands in the western Atlantic.

Born in Denbigh, Llwyd graduated from Oxford University with a B.A. in 1547 and an M.A. in 1551. He studied medicine and served as the personal physician of Henry FitzAlan, the earl of Arundel, and his

family for more than 15 years. He also served in Parliament twice, as the member for East Grinstead in 1559 and later for Denbigh in 1563–1567. In addition to these duties, he worked on studies that gained him a reputation as an accomplished antiquarian and geographer. He engaged in a friendly and scholarly correspondence with the famous Flemish geographer Ortelius (Abraham Oertel; 1527–1598). His promising career came to a premature end when he contracted a fever while traveling home to Denbigh from London.

Llwyd wrote or translated a number of works on antiquarian, geographical, or medical topics, but only published two of them. One of his unpublished works included an English translation of "Brut y Tywysogion," a history attributed to Caradoc of Llancarvan; a "Description of Cambria," by John Price; and extensive material written by Llwyd himself. A note in Llwyd's handwriting states that he completed the manuscript on 17 July 1559. Included in the manuscript is the account of Madoc's voyage. Unfortunately, Llwyd's sources, including the Madoc story, no longer survive.

After Llwyd's death, Sir Henry Sidney, the lord president of the Council in the Marches of Wales, obtained a copy of the manuscript, which he later shared with Welsh scholar **John Dee.** In 1583 Sidney gave the manuscript to his chaplain **David Powel** with instructions to prepare it for publication. Powel published it in 1584 as *The Historie of Cambria* with his own extensive additions, allowing access to Llwyd's work by other Tudor scholars of the exploration of the New World and the Madoc legend such as Richard Hakluyt. The original manuscript of Llwyd's history is in the collections of the British Library as the Cottonian Manuscript Caligua, A.vi.

Bibliography: "Llwyd, Humphrey," in *Dictionary of National Biography*, 22 vols.,

1908–1909; Williams, Gwyn A., *Madoc: The Making of a Myth*, 1979.

Lost Continent Legends, Scientific Basis for

The three major lost continents known to popular culture are **Atlantis, Mu,** and **Lemuria. Theosophists** also believe in the existence of an ancient Arctic continent of Hyperborea, and the spiritualist followers of John Ballou Newbrough believe that a continent named Pan once existed in the northern Pacific Ocean. No evidence of these lost continents exists; while so-called lost continents have existed in distant geological epochs, none was contemporaneous with modern humans.

Archaeological and scientific evidence clearly supports the contention that none of the legendary lost continents ever existed. Explorations of the ocean floors have not revealed any remnants of lost continents in either the Atlantic or Pacific. Ignatius Donnelly, the late–nineteenth-century scholar of Atlantis lore, suggested that Dolphin Ridge in the mid-Atlantic was a submerged remnant of Atlantis, while the Azores and Madeira islands were surviving mountains of Atlantis. Dolphin Ridge, however, is two to three miles below the surface of the sea, much too deep a geological subsidence to have occurred over a mere 10,000 years. Furthermore, while volcanoes and earthquakes have caused land to submerge, such losses were very localized and nowhere approached continent size. There is no trace of any natural disaster of a magnitude that could sink a continent.

Modern geology also accepts the theory of plate tectonics and the accompanying concept of continental drift. The continental drift theory claims that between 300 and 200 million years ago, all land was connected together in the one continent of Pangea. This supercontinent broke up and the various pieces moved slowly off to form the present-day continents. Such continental movement is responsible for the geological processes of mountain building and earthquakes. Alfred I. Wegener (1880–1930) first published the modern theory of continental drift in 1912. Although the circumstantial evidence for his theory was quite strong, he could offer no explanation as to why the continents moved.

Wegener's theory remained on the fringes of academic geology until the late 1950s, when the theory of plate tectonics provided an explanation for the phenomenon of continental drift. Plate tectonics suggested that the earth's crust consists of a number of plates floating on a plastic layer of hot mantle below the surface. Circulation of hotter or cooler portions of the mantle pushes or moves the solid plates. As a result of the plate tectonics theory, Wegener's once-rejected theory of continental drift is now the orthodoxy of modern geology. It is also a nemesis of lost continent theories, because with continental drift there is no room for sinking continents like Atlantis and Mu. Furthermore, no genuine archaeological evidence has ever been found to support the existence of Atlantis, Mu, or Lemuria.

Bibliography: Davis, Richard A., Jr., *Oceanography: An Introduction to the Marine Environment*, 1991; de Camp, L. Sprague, *Lost Continents*, [1954], 1970; Feder, Kenneth L., *Frauds, Myths, and Mysteries: Science and Pseudoscience in Archaeology*, 1990.

1169, he left numerous progeny (at least 19 and possibly 27) and a badly confused succession. Civil war broke out among some of the sons. But Prince Madoc (possibly an illegitimate son) wanted to avoid the turmoil. In 1170 he sailed across the western ocean and found an unknown land. Apparently he liked it because he left a settlement of 120 people and returned to Wales to recruit more colonists. He fitted out a fleet of ten vessels and returned to join the first group. Some people mention a third voyage. It was supposedly from these Welsh colonists that the legendary **Welsh Indians** were descended.

Details of the history of Madoc's supposed colony are fragmentary, confused, and contradictory. Various parties put forward a wide assortment of claims as to where Madoc landed: Mobile, Alabama; Florida; Newfoundland; Newport, Rhode Island; Yarmouth, Nova Scotia; Virginia; points in the Gulf of Mexico and the Caribbean including the mouth of the Mississippi River; the Yucatán; the isthmus of Tehuantepec, Panama; the Caribbean coast of South America; various islands in the West Indies and the Bahamas along with Bermuda; and the mouth of the Amazon River. Madoc's true route is, of course, unknown. Some think he followed a northern route similar to that of the **Vikings**. Most supporters of the Madoc story, however, propose a southern route, using the winds and currents that helped Columbus on his voyages.

What Madoc and his followers did once they reached the New World is almost pure speculation. They have been credited with being the source of the Aztec, Mayan, and Incan civilizations. According to early Spanish accounts, the Aztec emperor Moctezuma (or Montezuma) gave a speech repeating the legend that the original Aztec rulers came from an island across the great sea (see also **Viracocha**). Sixteenth-century Englishmen such as Richard Hakluyt and Sir Humphrey

Madoc, Voyage of Prince (ca. 1170–1171)

From the sixteenth to the twentieth century it was widely believed that Madoc, a Welsh prince and one of the sons of Owen Gwynedd, made two (and possibly three) voyages to America, where he founded a Welsh colony, more than three centuries before Columbus's first voyage in 1492.

At the middle of the twelfth century Wales was divided into three domains: Gwynedd, Powys, and Deheubarth, which corresponded to the northern, central, and southern parts of the country, respectively. These three states warred with one another in between beating off Irish raiders and resisting the imperialistic ambitions of England under the Normans. When the ruler of Gwynedd, Owen (Owain) Gwynedd, died in

Gilbert were quick to connect that speech to the Madoc legend. Madoc has also been identified with the white god **Quetzalcoatl** of Mexico. One marginal version of the Madoc story identifies the Welsh as the **Nephites** of *The Book of Mormon* rather than the **Hebrew** refugees mentioned in that document.

The most fully developed version of the Madoc story lands the prince and his followers at Mobile Bay in Alabama. Supposedly this accounts for the fortifications the Spanish explorer Hernando de Soto observed in Alabama. From Mobile Bay the Welsh moved northward to the region of present-day Chattanooga, Tennessee, where they built and abandoned more fortifications such as those at Fort Mountain, Georgia. The explanation for all this moving and fortifying is the implacable hostility of neighboring tribes of Native Americans. Continuing north, the beleaguered Welsh fought and lost a climactic battle at Sand Island in the Ohio River near Louisville, Kentucky. The greatly weakened remnant of the Welsh fled westward. Traveling up the Missouri River, they developed into the allegedly culturally and physically distinct tribe of the **Mandans.**

The historiography of the Madoc legend is a complicated affair. It first appeared in a manuscript history of Wales written by Welsh antiquary **Humphrey Llwyd** and completed around 1559. Llwyd had access to old Welsh chronicles and writings no longer extant, which makes his the oldest surviving account. Llwyd's manuscript went through several hands until another Welshman, **John Dee,** read it. Dee used the Madoc legend in his manuscript *Title Royal* of 1580 to help justify English claims to some of North America. That document, in turn, inspired Sir George Peckham to write his *True Reporte,* published in 1583. *True Reporte* was the first printed work to mention Madoc, and it also used the story to argue for the primacy of England's claims to

the Americas. **David Powel** quickly followed with *The Historie of Cambria* (1584), based largely on the manuscript work of Humphrey Llwyd.

A big problem for supporters of the historicity of Madoc's voyage is that no definite mentions occur before Humphrey Llwyd. Madoc's contemporaries are silent about his activities. One later Welsh poet, Maredudd ap Rhys, wrote a poem around 1440 in which he described Madoc, son of Owen Gwynedd, as a great sailor. While Maredudd's poem does not mention a voyage to a western land, it indicates that a seafaring Madoc tradition existed by the fifteenth century. Apparently, medieval Flemish visitors to Wales circulated an earlier (but now lost) romance of Madoc throughout western Europe, but whether it included a western voyage is not known. These lost tales are probably the source for claims by Dee, Peckham, and others that Madoc discovered America.

Although the sixteenth-century English were interested in the Madoc legend primarily as a means to strengthen their claims to territory in North America, interest continued into the seventeenth century and beyond. In 1634 **Sir Thomas Herbert** argued for the primacy of Madoc over Columbus as the discoverer of America in his *A Relation of Some Yeares Travaile, Begunne Anno 1626. . . .* Others followed with their own retellings of the Madoc legend. Supposed sightings of Welsh Indians kept interest in Madoc aroused through the eighteenth century. Even the revelation by John Evans's mission to the American west in 1792–1797 that no Welsh Indians seemed to exist did not seriously diminish belief in Madoc's voyage to America. Thomas Stephens's prize essay for a Welsh competition in 1858, *Madoc—An Essay on the Discovery of America by Madoc ab Owain Gwynedd* (later published in 1893) finally demolished the serious historical basis for the Madoc legend.

Despite Stephens's work, popular belief in the legend continued well into the twentieth century. Reuben T. Durrett (1824–1913), founder and president of the Filson Club of Kentucky, wrote *Traditions of the Earliest Visits of Foreigners to North America,* focusing mainly on the Madoc legend, in 1908 as a club publication. Although Durrett did not firmly endorse its historical truth, he was highly sympathetic to the possibility. His contemporary **Benjamin Franklin De Costa,** the leading authority on pre-Columbian explorers of the Americas, believed in the legend. In 1950, Zella Armstrong revived the cause with her *Who Discovered America? The Amazing Story of Madoc,* which argued forcefully for the existence of Madoc's voyage and colony. Inspired by such writings, the Virginia Cavalier Chapter of the Daughters of the American Revolution erected a marker in 1953 commemorating Madoc's supposed landing at the site of Fort Morgan in Mobile Bay, Alabama. Richard Deacon followed up in 1966 with *Madoc and the Discovery of America,* which provided another detailed defense of Madoc's historicity. Even Gwyn A. William's highly scholarly study of 1979, *Madoc: The Making of a Myth,* which maintained a sympathetic but skeptical tone throughout, concluded on a credulous note.

Bibliography: Deacon, Richard, *Madoc and the Discovery of America,* 1966; Williams, Gwyn A., *Madoc: The Making of a Myth,* 1979.

Maize

More commonly known in North America as corn, the scholarly world almost universally accepts that this important food plant originated in America and spread throughout the world after Christopher Columbus's voyage of 1492. At the same time, many **diffusionist** writers suggest that maize originated in Asia, or that it was of American origin but traveled to Africa, Asia, and Europe before 1492, thus indicating the existence of pre-Columbian contacts between the Americas and the Old World.

During the three and a half centuries following 1492, the true geographical origin of maize became confused. Although many respected herbalists and botanists correctly claimed that maize was an American plant, many equally eminent plant experts thought it was of Old World origin. The debate continued until 1857 when botanist Alphonse de Candolle, author of *Origin of Cultivated Plants,* presented an extremely convincing argument for American origin. His contention was bolstered in 1875 when another botanist, P. Ascherson, linked maize to the closely related American plant teosinte. Further archaeological and botanical research proved maize's descent from plants of the teosinte family. Archaeologists gradually reconstructed maize's domestication and evolution by Native American agriculturalists. This research eliminates any possibility that maize was first developed in either Southeast Asia or China. Efforts to prove an Asian origin for maize continue but fail to provide evidence as remotely convincing as that supporting the American origin theory.

Many people argue that American maize was transported from the Americas to other parts of the world in the era before 1492. George F. Carter, the distinguished geographer, made such claims for pre-Columbian maize in China. Extensive research into the voluminous and detailed botanical literature of pre-Columbian China failed to reveal any evidence of the cultivation of maize before the early sixteenth century. The archaeological and historical record for South Asia also provides no indication of the existence of maize in that region prior to 1492. Claims for pre-Columbian maize in the Philippines are based on a completely erroneous interpretation of some medieval **Chinese** geographical treatises.

Literature concerning pre-Columbian maize in Africa is extensive, and the chief exponent of that theory is South African anthropologist M. D. W. Jeffreys. Jeffreys believes that Arabic–black **African** contacts with the Americas took place about 900 and after. Maize appeared in the Ife region of present-day Nigeria between 1000 and 1100. Jeffrey marshaled linguistic evidence to support his theory of pre-Columbian African maize, but other scholars such as F. Willett and Marvin P. Miracle found it weak and unconvincing. Paul C. Mangelsdorf, the leading authority on the evolution and history of maize/corn, suggests that ambiguities in the terminologies used by Jeffreys' sources may be causing a confusion between maize and the similar sorghums that grew in pre-Columbian Africa.

Some people even suggest that maize arrived in Europe prior to 1492, and the possibility that Norse seafarers brought it back from **Vinland** is proposed by some scholars. The great geographer Carl O. Sauer argued that maize must have been introduced into Europe during the pre-Columbian era simply because it had spread too rapidly to have arrived afterward. Such an argument has no basis in historical documents. Maize first received notice in 1532 in a herbal written by Jerome Buck. Another early herbalist, Leonard Fuchs, included an illustration of maize in his herbal of 1542. During the rest of the sixteenth century, maize appeared regularly in European herbals and botanical works. No such mentions occurred in European botanical works written during the fourteenth and fifteenth centuries—an odd omission unless maize had not yet reached Europe.

Mangelsdorf pointed out another evidence for post-Columbian introduction of maize into the Old World: the total absence of pre-Columbian corncobs. Pre-Columbian corncobs are very commonly found in archaeological sites throughout the Americas. They survive readily under many climates and conditions, but so far none that can be convincingly dated prior to 1492 have been found in the Old World. Since pre-Columbian maize appears not to have existed in the Old World, maize cannot be cited as evidence that pre-Columbian contacts took place between the Old World and the Americas.

Bibliography: Crosby, Alfred W., Jr., *The Columbian Exchange: Biological and Cultural Consequences of 1492*, 1972; Fingerhut, Eugene R., *Who First Discovered America? A Critique of Pre-Columbian Voyages*, 1984; Mangelsdorf, Paul C., *Corn: Its Origin, Evolution, and Improvement*, 1974; Viola, Herman J., and Carolyn Margolis, eds., *Seeds of Change: A Quincentennial Commemoration*, 1991.

Mandans

Many tribes of Native Americans are identified as **Welsh Indians,** but the Mandans of the upper Missouri River valley in North Dakota are the tribe most consistently cited as being Welsh.

The now virtually extinct Mandans spoke an archaic form of the Siouan language group and, judging from their customs, originated in the Great Lakes or Ohio Valley regions of the eastern woodlands. Archaeological evidence indicates that between 700 and 900, various unrelated bands of proto-Mandans moved into the Missouri Valley along the Big Bend region and between the Bad and Cheyenne rivers. They built villages with permanent structures of timber and earth, and practiced large-scale bison hunting as well as sedentary agriculture on the floodplain of the Missouri River. About 1100 the Mandans began fortifying their villages against attacks by new groups of Native Americans moving into the area. Gradually, environmental conditions and enemy pressures contracted Mandan territory to the land between the Cannonball and Knife rivers of North Dakota by 1650. This was the historic homeland of the Mandans during their early contact with European civilization.

Pierre Gaultier de Varennes de La Vérendrye, the first European definitely to reach the Mandans, arrived on 3 December 1738. His mission was to establish direct trading relations between the Mandans and New France. At first La Vérendrye was disappointed by what he saw. Assiniboin Indians led him to expect that the Mandans were distinctively white and lived in European-style villages. Instead, he found that the Mandans differed little in appearance and culture from other tribes. They were pleasant hosts and sharp traders. At the time of La Vérendrye's visit the Mandans were at the height of their prosperity, which was based on being the middlemen of the Great Plains trading network.

After a visit in 1742 by La Vérendrye's son, direct contact between the Mandans and the French abruptly ended because of the renewal of the French and Indian Wars. European visits to the Mandans resumed on Christmas Day 1773, when a trader named Mackintosh of the Northwest Company arrived. Disaster struck the Mandans during the early 1780s in the form of a smallpox epidemic that devastated many Native American tribes. Smallpox reduced the Mandans' population from 3,600 to about 1,000 (some estimates credit the Mandans with a population as high as 8,000 to 15,000 in 1738). With such a reduced population, the Mandans could no longer adequately maintain their defenses against Sioux raiders. They fled north to the Knife River and allied with the Hidatsa tribe. This new location was where frontier trader James Mackey found the Mandans in 1787.

Engraving of Mandans in their alleged Welsh coracles after a nineteenth-century drawing by Karl Bodmer.

Sioux attacks continued throughout the 1790s but were repulsed. European visitors arrived in increasing numbers during that decade, including John Evans, who sojourned among the Mandans from 1796–1797 during his unsuccessful quest for Welsh Indians. Lewis and Clark's expedition visited the Mandans in the fall of 1804 and made detailed notes on their language and customs. Other European visitors continued to reach the Mandans, particularly U.S. government commissioners trying to bring peace to the warring tribes of the Great Plains. The last important European visitors were American painter George Catlin in 1832 and Alexander Philip Maximilian, a German prince of Wied-Neuwied in 1833–1834, accompanied by the painter Karl Bodmer. Both men published illustrated accounts of their journeys, including many accurate observations on Mandan culture and society. George Catlin (1796–1872) firmly believed the Mandans were descendants of Madoc's Welsh colonists. Prince Maximilian was more objective about what he saw, and Bodmer was a more realistic painter than Catlin. Prince Maximilian denied the Welshness and whiteness of the Mandans. These last two visitors' accounts came in the nick of time. A new smallpox epidemic in 1837 further reduced the Mandan population from 1,600 to as few as 31. The Hidatsas absorbed the survivors and moved to Fort Bertheld in 1845. They were joined by the Arikara in 1862, and in 1871 the U.S. government placed the three affiliated tribes on a permanent reservation.

Although Mandan traditions of moving up the Missouri River to escape relentless enemy attacks are consistent with legends of Madoc's Welsh colony, archaeological evidence indicates that the Mandans reached the upper Missouri well before 1170, the date of Madoc's voyage. Furthermore, linguistic studies of the Mandan and other Native American languages reveal no evidence of Welsh influence. The theory attributing the supposed light skin and blue eyes of the Mandans to a genetic infusion from Norse survivors of **Paul Knutson's** lost expedition in the fourteenth century has even less validity. A close reading of travelers' accounts of the Mandans reveals that most European eyewitnesses found them indistinguishable in coloration and culture from other Native Americans, despite expectations to the contrary.

Bibliography: Catlin, George, *Letters and Notes on the Manners, Customs, and Conditions of the North American Indians*, 2 vols., [1844], 1973; Meyer, Roy W., *The Village Indians of the Upper Missouri: The Mandans, Hidatsas, and Arikaras*, 1977; Newman, Marshall T., "The Blond Mandan: A Critical Review of an Old Problem," *Southwestern Journal of Anthropology* 6 (1950): 255–272.

Mandingos in Medieval America

Several writers promote the theory that Mandingo peoples, primarily from the empire of Mali in West Africa, visited or settled in the Americas about 1307 and after.

The Mandingos consist of three groups: Soninke, Soso, and Malinke (also known as Mandingo). During the early thirteenth century, the Malinke leader Sundiata undertook a series of conquests that led to the formation of the empire of Mali or Mande. By the beginning of the fourteenth century, the empire of Mali dominated West Africa. According to oral traditions, between 1307 and 1311 Emperor **Abubakari II** (or Abu Bakr) organized two expeditions to explore the western Atlantic Ocean. The first consisted of some 400 ships, of which only one returned to report the discovery of a great current in the middle of the ocean. Abubakari II took personal command of the second expedition of some 2,000 ships, which sailed west and was never heard from again.

The question becomes: What happened on Abubakari's voyage? Supporters of **African voyages to pre-Columbian America** suggest two possible answers. In *They Came before Columbus*, anthropologist Ivan Van Sertima contends that Abubakari and his people settled along the northern coast of South America and on various Caribbean islands. They took up gold trading, a traditional economic activity of West Africans, and did business in Mexico, where they became part of the association of merchants known as the *pochteca*. Gradually they merged with the aboriginal peoples through intermarriage. In contrast, Harold G. Lawrence hypothesizes that the Mandingos established a steady transoceanic trade with Mexico and the Caribbean that continued up to and through the time of Christopher Columbus's voyage of 1492. **Leo Wiener**, the twentieth-century progenitor of theories of Africans in ancient America, also advocates the idea that a steady trading relationship existed between the Mandingos and pre-Columbian America. These theories require acceptance of the idea that large and elaborate Mandingo fleets visited or settled in the Americas before 1492 but left significantly fewer traces than the paltry efforts of the Norse (see also **L'Anse aux Meadows**).

Supporters present various types of evidence: linguistic parallels; sculpted heads with Negroid features; reports of black-skinned peoples already living in the Americas when Columbus arrived; the presence of metal artifacts made of *guanin*, an alloy of African origin; pre-Columbian place-names of Mandingo origin; and plant migrations. In the opinion of skeptical scholars, this breadth of evidence has little depth. Linguistic experts generally find the parallels between Native American and Mandingo languages circumstantial or forced. Evidence of pre-Columbian Mandingo place-names also appear to be forced or of post-Columbian origin. No artifacts made of guanin have

been located in any pre-Columbian archaeological excavations. Most reports of black-skinned peoples already living in the early Spanish Caribbean are secondhand accounts and therefore suspect. Communities of free blacks existed in the Caribbean early in the era of Spanish settlement but traditionally were thought to be escaped slaves. Another strong possibility is that some pre-Columbian Native Americans were simply very dark-skinned. Although physical characteristics of Native Americans are commonly thought to be very homogeneous, wide variations exist. Leo Wiener's theory that tobacco was native to Africa and taken to the Americas in pre-Columbian times has been shown to be completely false. Similar assertions that **maize** (or corn) reached West Africa before 1492 also appear to be erroneous. Many scholars deny that various pre-Columbian sculptures and drawings depict supposed African visitors. The fact that these facial features have a supposed Negroid appearance only shows that some Native Americans (as well as some Caucasoids) have full lips and broad noses. If the Mandingos and the later **Songhay** were so active in the Americas, it prompts the question: Why did they disappear so quickly and completely from the post-1492 Americas after almost 200 years of profitable trading? How did the Portuguese, trading on the west coast of Africa through much of the fifteenth century, fail to observe the commercial ocean voyages of the Mandingos? Finally, if the Mandingos made such an impact on the pre-Columbian Americas, why is the evidence so sparse and ambiguous? The absence of convincing answers tends to leave most historians and archaeologists with grave doubts about a medieval Mandingo presence in America before 1492.

Bibliography: Feder, Kenneth L., *Frauds, Myths, and Mysteries: Science and Pseudoscience in Archaeology*, 1990; Lawrence,

Harold G., "Mandingo Voyages across the Atlantic," in *African Presence in Early America,* edited by Ivan Van Sertima, [1986], 2nd ed., 1992; Van Sertima, Ivan, *They Came before Columbus,* 1976; Wiener, Leo, *Africa and the Discovery of America,* 3 vols., 1920–1922.

Markland

Meaning forest land or woodland, Norse explorers of North America gave this name to the flat wooded land south of **Helluland.**

The **Vinland Sagas** describe the sailing time from Helluland to Markland as two or three days. Scholars generally identify Markland as southern Labrador, although nineteenth-century Danish scholar Carl Rafn and his followers, such as Hjalmar Holland, thought it was Nova Scotia. The *Greenlanders' Saga* tells how Markland was the second land sighted by **Bjarni Herjolfsson** when he got lost on his way to **Greenland.** During his explorations, **Leif Ericsson** named the land after its many trees. According to *Eirik's Saga*, it was **Thorfinn Karlsefni** who gave the heavily wooded country its name. Archaeological evidence indicates that Norse Greenlanders traded with Native American tribes living in Labrador such as the Beothuk, Point Revenge Indians, Montagnais, and Naskaupi, as well as Dorset Culture **Eskimos.** Given the scarcity of wood in Greenland and the proximity of Labrador's forests, such a pattern of trade would be sensible and fulfill a real need. See also **Vinland** and **Skraelings.**

Marson, Voyage of Ari (982)

This Norse seaman was blown off course while traveling from Ireland to **Iceland** and ended up a prisoner of the natives of **Great Ireland** or Hvítramannaland.

According to the Norse saga known as the *Landnámabók,* Ari Marson was traveling between Ireland and Iceland when storms drove him to Great Ireland, or Hvítramannaland, which lay six days' sail to the west. The natives took him prisoner and forcibly baptized him and his crew. The saga credits Hrafn, a merchant of Limerick, as the first person to tell this widely known story. Thorfinn, the earl of Orkney, also knew of Ari's captivity and cryptically reported that "Ari had been recognized in Hvítramannaland but failed to get away. He was held in high regard there." That was the last that was heard of Ari Marson.

Charles M. Boland, a popular writer on pre-Columbian visitors to the Americas, took the saga's few lines about Ari Marson and made the following detailed reconstruction of events. Early in 982 the **Irish monks** or Culdees supposedly living in **Greenland** fled when **Eric the Red** and the first Norse settlers arrived. Sailing west they stopped at the Merrimack River in Massachusetts and began to settle. Later that year Ari Marson's lone, lost ship suddenly arrived. Boland suggests that Marson's ship was probably blown west 16 days' sail rather than 6. The Irish did not flee this time; instead, they captured Marson and his crew, burnt his ship, and forcibly baptized the pagan Norse. Four years later more Norse ships were blown west while trying to settle Greenland. Some of the Norse were captured, but one ship apparently escaped. The crew of that ship recognized Ari, who may even have warned them off. The captive Norse eventually became part of the community of Great Ireland. Their presence is commemorated in the name **Norumbega** originally used for the New England region. Eventually both Irish and Norse were completely absorbed into the neighboring tribes of Native Americans. Unfortunately for Boland's theory, not one shred of archaeological evidence exists to corroborate the existence of Great Ireland or Ari Marson's voyage.

Bibliography: Boland, Charles M., *They All Discovered America,* 1961; Jones, Gwyn, *The Norse Atlantic Saga,* 2nd ed., 1986.

Mather, Cotton
(1663–1728)

Puritan minister and historian of New England, he supported several theories about Native American origins and pre-Columbian visitors—the narrow strait theory of **José de Acosta**, the Welsh theory (see also **Madoc, Voyage of Prince**), and the **Canaanite** theory. He explicitly rejected the **Preadamite** theory, the **Ten Lost Tribes**, and the supposed missionary visits of **St. Thomas**. Mather even suggested that the Devil brought the Native Americans to the Americas to keep them from the gospel.

Cotton Mather was the product of the union of two prominent families of Puritan Boston, the Cottons and the Mathers. He studied at Harvard University, graduated in 1678, and became a fellow in 1690. From 1685 until his death in 1728, he served as the minister of the Old North Church in Boston. A man of diverse interests, Mather wrote almost 500 volumes of sermons, theology, history, philosophy, and science. His reputation spanned the Atlantic Ocean; in 1710 Aberdeen University conferred an honorary degree on him and in 1713 the Royal Society of London elected him as one of its fellows. As a historian, one of his goals was to show how God's will operated in all events whether great or small. Another was to preserve and justify the godly work of the Puritan settlers of New England. Both goals led him to the problem of explaining the role of Native Americans in God's plan for Puritan New England, and from there to determining their origins.

Mather's first effort at explaining the origins of Native Americans appeared in the treatise *The Serviceable Man* (1690), in which he suggested they were the descendants of Canaanites. They fled from Palestine to America after Joshua and the Children of Israel drove them from their homeland. As Canaanites, they were subject to the biblical curse on Ham and Canaan, which in turn justified English Puritan attempts to conquer and displace them.

Twelve years later, Mather published his sprawling *Magnalia Christi Americana; or The Ecclesiastical History of New England* (1702). In this work he put forward more theories of Native American origins. His ethnic pride made him a strong supporter of the Welsh or British reaching America some 300 to 400 years before the Spanish, with languages and customs supposedly providing ample evidence for their presence. Nevertheless, he did not argue for better treatment of Native Americans on the basis of their being kindred of English Puritans. Mather also accepted Spanish priest José de Acosta's land bridge or narrow strait theory, which would soon evolve into the **Bering Land Bridge/Strait Theory**. In Mather's opinion, primitive hunters from Asia could easily have passed over the narrow Arctic seas to reach America. In the *Magnalia Christi* he flatly rejected the Ten Lost Tribes theory and made a joke about it by playing on the name of Thomas Thorowgood, a leading advocate of that theory. He put forward the suggestion that the Devil had brought the Native Americans to the Americas in order to hide them from the gospel. So, of course, he denied that St. Thomas or any other apostle or missionary reached the Americas before 1492.

India Christiana was Mather's last work to discuss the problem of Native American origins. He advocated the continuation of efforts to evangelize them, and included a repetition of his Devil theory and his rejection of the St. Thomas legends. Mather denied the possibility of the existence of Preadamites (people descended from a creation prior to Adam), but accepted the possibility that Old World peoples could have sailed to the Americas.

Like most of his writings, Mather's ideas on Native American origins were diffuse. He obviously never made up his mind as to their true origins. Certainly the Canaanite, Bering Strait, and **Welsh** theories did not fit very well with one another, or with intervention by the Devil. Properly skeptical of the Ten Lost Tribes theory and correct in his support of the Bering Strait theory, Mather's support for Welsh and Canaanite theories shows that one of the greatest intellectuals of colonial America could not always keep his credulity and prejudices in check.

Bibliography: Arndt, Murray, "Cotton Mather," in *Dictionary of Literary Biography*, vol. 30: *American Historians 1603–1868*, edited by Clyde N. Wilson, 1984; Huddleston, Lee Eldrige, *Origins of the American Indians: European Concepts, 1492–1729*, 1967; Vogel, Dan, *Indian Origins and the Book of Mormon*, 1986.

Melungeons

This isolated and mysterious community of dark-complected people lives in the mountainous region between Blackwater, Virginia, and Sneedville, Tennessee. Their origins are not known, although it has been variously suggested that they are descendants of wandering **Hebrews, Phoenicians,** or **Madoc's** Welsh followers. In fact, it is most likely that they descend from post-Columbian Portuguese castaways.

The derivation of the name Melungeon is not known. Some possibilities are the French *melange* for mixture, the Greek *melan* for black, and the Portuguese *melango* for shipmate. When the first Anglo-American settlers arrived in eastern Tennessee, they found the Melungeons already living there. Tall, swarthy, mostly grey-eyed, and with straight black hair, they call themselves Portuguese, which they pronounce "porterghee." Their white neighbors regarded them as a mixed community of renegade whites, Indians, and runaway slaves. Those with more imagination thought they might be descendants of the lost English colony of Roanoke whose inhabitants disappeared without a trace before 1590. Another theory following the same British theme suggested that the Melungeons were survivors of Prince Madoc's Welsh colony, supposedly in America during the Middle Ages. The problem was that the Melungeons themselves never claimed to be of English or Welsh ancestry. Some writers speculated that deserters from Hernando de Soto's expedition were their ancestors. After the Civil War, a Tennessee judge named Lewis Shepherd won a court case arguing that the Melungeons were descended from Phoenician or **Carthaginian** refugees who had escaped the Roman sack of Carthage. More

recently, **diffusionist** historian **Cyrus Gordon** suggests that they are connected to supposed Hebrew writing appearing on the Bat Creek Stone found in Tennessee in 1885. The Smithsonian Institution's scholars identified the stone as a Cherokee artifact, but in 1970 the diffusionist writer Joseph Mahan identified the writing on it as Hebrew inscription and informed Gordon.

All these theories ignore the rather sparse oral traditions among the Melungeons that claim they are Portuguese. Their assertion is actually quite plausible; many Portuguese pirates operated in American waters during the seventeenth century. Disputes often arose among the pirates, resulting in the losers being marooned. It is possible that a group of such castaways stole some Native American women and fled inland to their present location in Tennessee. Considerable circumstantial evidence supports this theory. The Melungeons have definite Latin features, venerate the cross, and commonly use the names Sylvester and Bragans. Genetic research on modern Melungeons also supports a strong probability of predominantly Portuguese ancestry. Such research makes it almost certain that the Melungeons are not a remnant of pre-Columbian settlement by Hebrews, Phoenicians, or Welsh, and so another intriguing legend dies.

Bibliography: Brewster, Paul G., "The Melungeons: A Mystery People," *Ethnos* 29 (1964): 43–48; Gaddis, Vincent H., *American Indian Myths and Mysteries*, 1977; Pollitzer, William S., "Ancestral Traits, Parent Populations, and Hybrids," *American Journal of Physical Anthropology* 30 (1969): 415–420.

Menasseh Ben Israel (1604–1657)

Also spelled Manasseh, this Jewish scholar and rabbi of Amsterdam publicized the purported discovery of the **Ten Lost Tribes** in South America as part of his effort to secure the legal readmission of the Jews into England.

Menasseh Ben Israel was born in Portugal to a Jewish family that outwardly conformed to Christianity. Later they moved to Amsterdam where Jews were allowed to practice their religion. The young Menasseh received an excellent education and became the rabbi of his congregation, Nevah Shalom, at a mere 18 years of age. His scholarship quickly earned him a Europeanwide reputation.

In 1644 Antonio de Montezinos, another Portuguese Jew, arrived in Amsterdam claiming to have encountered members of the Ten Lost Tribes of Israel while traveling in the Quito region of South America. After a careful examination, leaders of the Jewish community concluded that Montezinos was telling the truth. Word of his discovery spread, and many people wrote to the well-known Menasseh Ben Israel for more details. To meet this demand Menasseh prepared a *Relación,* which summarized the Montezinos story. The widespread interest in Montezinos's discovery lay in its apparent partial fulfillment of Christian and Jewish prophecies. Christians saw it as a sign of the approaching second coming of Christ, while Jews believed it was a sign of the coming of their messiah.

Menasseh Ben Israel certainly accepted the messianic implications of a reappearance of the Ten Lost Tribes. But he believed that one thing remained to be done to complete both the Jewish and Christian prophecies— the readmission of the Jews into England. He corresponded with the rulers of England, the radical Puritan leaders of Parliament, and Oliver Cromwell, the commander of their army. His argument was that, with the discovery of the Ten Lost Tribes, readmission of the Jews to England would complete their dispersal throughout the world. Thus the stage for Christ's second coming would be completely prepared. To bolster that point, he wrote *Spes Israelis* in 1650, which in 1652 was translated into English as *The Hope of Israel*. It claimed that only part of the Ten Lost Tribes traveled to the Americas by crossing the **Strait of Anian;** the rest scattered across Africa, Asia, and Europe. Menasseh's book aroused such interest that it was quickly reprinted in several editions.

In 1655 Menasseh Ben Israel went to England to present his case to a panel of Puritan clergy, which included John Owen and Hugh Peter, under the auspices of Oliver Cromwell. The panel's debates resulted in a pamphlet war over whether or not to readmit the Jews into England. The controversy forced Menasseh to write his *Vindiciae Judaeorum* in 1655 as a further defense of the readmission of the Jews. Apparently he and his allies were persuasive, because the Lord Protector Cromwell allowed the Jews to settle in England that same year. Cromwell was a firm believer in fulfilling biblical prophecies, but he also saw the Dutch Jews and their commercial skills as a resource that would greatly benefit the English economy. Menasseh Ben Israel did much to popularize the long-lived legend of the Ten Lost Tribes locating in the Americas with at least some of the Native Americans as their descendants.

Bibliography: Katz, David, *Philo-Semitism and the Readmission of the Jews to England, 1603–1655*, 1982; "Manasseh Ben Israel" in *Dictionary of National Biography*, reprinted in 22 vols., [63 vols., 1885–1901], 1908–1909; Weiner, George, "America's Jewish Braves," *Mankind* 4 (October 1974): 56–64.

Mongols in Medieval America

This unique early–nineteenth-century theory claims that Mongols conquered and civilized most of the Americas during the thirteenth century.

In 1827 Englishman John Ranking put forward a theory of Mongol invasion of the Americas in his book *Historical Researches on the Conquest of Peru, Mexico, Bogata, Natchez, and Talomeco, the Thirteenth Century, by Mongols, Accompanied by Elephants*. Based heavily on Peruvian legends and myths gathered by early Spanish settlers, Ranking's book began with Kublai Khan's attempted conquest of Japan in 1281. Ranking suggested that when a great typhoon sank or scattered the Mongol fleet, survivors were blown west until they reached the Americas. Aided by their elephants, they conquered the Native Americans and founded the Inca and Aztec empires. Manco Capac, the first Inca ruler, was a son of Kublai Khan, and the Aztec kings were descendants of a Mongol noble. Virtually all higher civilizations in the Americas derived from the Mongol conquest, even that of the **Mound Builders,** as Ranking's reference to Natchez in the book's title indicates.

The Ranking theory has many problems. A major one is a lack of convincing evidence for a Mongol presence. Another is that archaeology clearly shows the existence of many advanced civilizations prior to the arrival of the Mongols and long before the rise of the Incas and Aztecs. Ranking could not have known these things in 1827, but by the mid-nineteenth century, the antiquity of civilization in the Americas was obvious. Finally, Ranking's theory stretches credulity to the utmost. The Mongols have never enjoyed a reputation as great bearers of civilization. Why did they suddenly fill that role in the Americas? Furthermore, how could the remnant of a fleet that failed to conquer Japan go on to conquer most of the Americas? It would seem that Ranking considered Native Americans to be so weak and inferior that they were ripe for conquest and civilizing by anyone. Ranking's theory was never well received and was treated largely as a mildly amusing curiosity of scholarship.

Bibliography: Davies, Nigel, *Voyagers to the New World,* 1979; Wauchope, Robert, *Lost Tribes and Sunken Continents,* 1962.

Mound Builders

The myth that the Mound Builders of North America were a lost white race dominated popular and professional archaeological theories for most of the nineteenth century and was closely connected to many theories of pre-Columbian contacts between the Old World and the Americas.

Mound building was an ancient tradition among Native Americans of the eastern portion of what is now the United States, and continued for some time after 1492. Mounds are classified into two basic types: burial and temple. Burial mounds were piles of dirt raised over the bodies of a dead chief or nobleperson, corresponding to the pyramids of the Egyptians. Temple mounds were artificial hills with temples placed on the top, similar to the pyramids of Mesoamerica. Other mounds were calendrical or in the shapes of effigies.

Two basic traditions or cultures are associated with the burial mounds: the Adena and the Hopewell. The oldest is the Adena style, which flourished from 1000 B.C. to A.D. 100, and was centered in the river valleys of southern Ohio. This culture overlapped with the more elaborate Hopewell culture, which existed from 200 B.C. to A.D. 400. The Hopewell culture occupied much of the Ohio and lower Mississippi river valleys, with particular concentrations of settlements in Ohio and Illinois. A hiatus of mound building occurred between A.D. 400 and 900. At the end of that period the Mississippian culture began to build temple mounds. This culture lasted from 900 to 1500 and occupied much of the eastern half of the present United States. The Natchez tribe is an example of a late Mississippian culture that built and used temple mounds well into the era of European contact.

European settlers on the eastern seaboard of North America did not initially come into contact with mounds. Early explorers of the interior regions, however, reported their existence and described Native Americans building them. Most mounds were located west of the Appalachians in the greater Mississippi Valley. When Europeans began to settle there in the mid-eighteenth century, reports of mounds increased and even assumed startling proportions. Speculation over their origins became rampant. What were the purposes of the mounds? Who built them? What happened to the builders?

It was obvious that some mounds had been used for burial purposes; human remains and artifacts were frequently found in them. In fact, some tribes continued to use existing mounds for burial far into the period of European contact. Some people suggested that a few mounds were the mass graves of warriors slain in fierce battles. Others appeared to be fortifications connected to these wars, although some mounds seemed to have religious or ceremonial functions. But until the systematic methods of modern archaeology were applied to the mounds, all theories, both wild and rational, were pure speculation.

The basic debate centered on whether the Mound Builders were the ancestors of Native Americans or some other lost race. One of the first to suggest the lost race theory was Benjamin Smith Barton (1766–1815) of Philadelphia. In 1787 he wrote *Observations on Some Parts of Natural History,* which despite its title was largely a study of the mounds. He claimed that Danish **Vikings** built the mounds and then moved to Mexico, where they became the Toltecs, predecessors of the Aztecs. Other people, including Thomas Jefferson, thought the Mound Builders were simply the ancestors of the historic Indians or Native Americans. However, Barton's lost race theory touched a

ANCIENT AMERICAN BATTLE-MOUND.

(See Nott, page 310.)

Romanticized image of an ancient battle-mound.

romantic chord, and it soon had many imitators and competitors, particularly those theories suggesting that the lost race was white.

In its most fully developed form, the lost race theory stated that a civilized white race occupied North America in ancient times and built the mounds. After some time, savage hordes, the ancestors of Native Americans, invaded the land of the Mound Builders and destroyed them and their civilization in a series of bloody wars. Other variations of the lost race theory included the contention that the Mound Builders were colonists from the more civilized cultures of Mexico or that the Mound Builders first settled in North America but abandoned it to the savage invaders and relocated in Mexico, thereby bringing civilization to that region.

According to the lost race theory, all Mound Builders were part of one great civilization, which may even have been one great empire. White Americans generally thought that Native Americans were too lazy and primitive to have produced the mounds. They also argued that the mounds and their builders preceded the Native Americans. Some advocates claimed that the Mound Builders had the skill of writing and wrote in Old World scripts, proving both the existence of transoceanic contacts before Columbus and the cultural superiority of the Mound Builders over the Native Americans. The Mound Builders also had far more advanced metallurgical skills than Native Americans. It was also claimed that the surviving Native Americans knew or remembered nothing about the mounds and their builders. In his *American Antiquities and Discoveries in the West* (1833), Josiah Priest (1788–1851) put forward a plethora of candidates for the lost race of Mound Builders: **Polynesians, Egyptians,** Greeks, **Romans,** Israelites, Scandinavians, **Welsh,** Scots, and **Chinese.** Priest was merely cataloging the

existing and often wild speculations being bruited about by early–nineteenth-century Americans. In 1882 Ignatius Donnelly connected the Mound Builders to **Atlantis.** Such speculations even became connected to the creation of a new religion when **Joseph Smith, Jr.,** brought out his translation of *The Book of Mormon* in 1830. It claimed to be the historical record of a migration to the Americas by **Hebrews,** some of whose descendants built the mounds and were white-skinned.

For nineteenth-century Americans, the theory of a lost race of Mound Builders was a very convenient belief. It allowed them to regard Native Americans as irredeemable savages who had never possessed a high culture and never would. Furthermore, if their barbaric ancestors destroyed the civilization of the white Mound Builders, then it was only fair for them to be pushed aside, in turn, by the advancing white civilization of the United States. At bottom, the myth of the lost race of Mound Builders was a convenient, romantic fiction with very racist and deadly implications.

Although the lost race theory dominated mid–nineteenth-century concepts, not everyone accepted it. Ephraim G. Squier and E. H. Davis assumed the lost race theory was correct when in 1848 they published their classic *Ancient Monuments of the Mississippi Valley.* But John Wesley Powell (1834–1902), the first director of the Smithsonian Institution's newly created Bureau of Ethnology in 1879, had very serious reservations. He assigned a like-minded scholar, Cyrus Thomas, to conduct a systematic study of the mounds. Thomas's long-anticipated study appeared in 1894. Prosaically titled *Report on the Mound Explorations of the Bureau of Ethnology,* it basically demolished the lost race theory. It showed conclusively that the Mound Builders were of the same race as Native Americans. Mound building activity by Native Americans was documented into historical times. Thomas also clearly demonstrated that Mound Builders did not constitute a single nation or culture, but rather many different cultures. He discredited and rejected various artifacts purporting to show that the Mound Builders used advanced metallurgical techniques and alphabetic writing. Since the appearance of Thomas's iconoclastic study, professional archaeologists have refined and expanded his findings, although the basic conclusions remain intact. The destruction of this theory eliminates the need to connect the fictional lost white race to any of the various supposed transoceanic migrations from the Old World to the Americas. The demise of the mound builder myth, of course, did nothing to end speculations about the occurrence of pre-Columbian visitors to the Americas.

Bibliography: Feder, Kenneth L., *Frauds, Myths, and Mysteries: Science and Pseudoscience in Archaeology*, 1990; Silverberg, Robert, *Mound Builders of Ancient America: The Archaeology of a Myth*, 1968.

Mu

This legendary lost continent of the Pacific Ocean is also commonly known as **Lemuria**. Like **Atlantis** in the Atlantic Ocean, the supposed inhabitants of Mu peopled and brought civilization to the Americas in the distant past.

Opinions vary over the derivation of the name Mu. Some claim that it simply came from a shortening of Lemuria, the alternate name for the lost continent. Others credit the early Mayan archaeologist **Charles Étienne Brasseur de Bourbourg** with creating the name from an erroneous reading of two Mayan hieroglyphics in the *Troano codex*. Furthermore, Brasseur mistakenly translated the codex as talking about a cataclysmic earthquake. The indefatigable amateur archaeologist **Augustus Le Plongeon** composed a similar and equally erroneous

translation of the same *Troano codex*, complete with the catastrophic sinking of Mu and a loss of 64 million people some 10,000 years ago.

The most prolific supporter of Mu's existence was Colonel James Churchward (1850–1936), an English adventurer. Churchward's life, as reported by him, is a curious merging of fact and fiction. Just where the facts end and the fiction begins is not always too clear. Educated at Oxford and Sandhurst, Churchward claimed to serve in India as a colonel of the Lancers. During his time in India, he met and became friends with an old high priest of the Hindu religion after the priest discovered Churchward's interest in ancient cultures. The priest taught him a dead language that was supposedly the original language of humanity. Together they began to translate the sacred tablets of the Naacals, which were in the priest's custody. The Naacals were emissaries of the religion of Mu to its various colonies throughout the world. The tablets originated either from Mu or from Burma, an important Muvian center in earlier times. As Churchward and the priest worked their way through the tablets, they learned the forgotten history of Mu. Churchward's Mu was located in the Pacific Ocean, and stretched from the Fiji Islands east to **Easter Island** and north to Hawaii. Civilization arose on Mu 50,000 years ago and ended some 12,000 years ago with the continent's destruction in volcanic fire, floods, and submergence under the sea. Its civilization equaled that of Western Europe and North America in the early twentieth century but without the evils of war and social oppression. Churchward considered Mu the inspiration for the story of the Garden of Eden and other legends of earthly paradises. Several races lived on Mu, but the white race provided its benevolent ruling class, at least as told by Churchward, who was himself white. Mu's inhabitants sent out colonies that survived the cataclysm that destroyed their motherland and became the ancestors of the ancient civilizations of Egypt, Sumer, the Indus Valley, China, the Maya, and the Pueblos. However, those cultures were but pale reflections of the original glory of Mu; the destruction of the heartland sapped the vitality of the survivors and caused them to regress.

Churchward wrote three books presenting his reconstruction of Mu's civilization and history. *The Lost Continent of Mu* appeared in 1926, followed by *The Children of Mu* in 1931 and *The Sacred Symbols of Mu* in 1933. In addition to the Naacal tablets, Churchward gleaned information from archaeological and historical sources. He tended to ignore reputable scholars and gravitated to discredited authors and books. Augustus Le Plongeon's archaeological theories had long been rejected by other scholars, but not by Churchward. In particular, he enthusiastically incorporated the Mexican tablets that amateur archaeologist William Niven discovered in 1921. In Churchward's eyes, they were closely related to the Naacal tablets, and he proceeded to translate them. But to the archaeological profession, Niven's tablets were and are a crude although voluminous hoax.

Churchward claimed that Mu was the mother of all human civilization, and that the **Polynesians** are the survivors of the submergence of their homeland. Professional scholars from many different disciplines, both scientific and historical, vehemently reject all his contentions. Churchward's usual practice was to ignore reputable scholarship (since it tended to contradict his own ideas) while positing some very bad science of his own. One example was his geologically unsound belief that Mu sank as a result of the collapse of a gigantic network of subterranean gas pockets. No remotely reliable geological, archaeological, or historical evidence has been discovered to show that the

lost continent ever existed or that it sent out colonists who populated the rest of the earth, including the Americas. That lack, however, has not stopped Churchward's books from remaining in print and continuing to find enthusiastic readers.

Bibliography: Churchward, James, *The Lost Continent of Mu*, [1926], 1987; de Camp, L. Sprague, *Lost Continents*, [1954], 1970; Wauchope, Robert, *Lost Tribes and Sunken Continents*, 1962; Williams, Stephen, *Fantastic Archaeology: The Wild Side of North American Prehistory*, 1991.

Mu-lan-p'i

According to two **Chinese** geographers writing in the twelfth and thirteenth centuries, Arabic traders regularly visited this far western land in great ships. Although commonly thought to refer to Islamic Spain, several writers identify it as someplace in the Americas, indicating that Arabic visitors arrived several centuries before Columbus's historic journey.

Chou Ch'ü-fei, writing in 1178, and Chau Ju-kua, writing in 1225, produced treatises on the Chinese trade with **Arabic** lands and mentioned a land called Mu-lan-p'i. Both scholars derived their information from interviews with Arabic merchants visiting China. Mu-lan-p'i supposedly lay 100 days' journey by sea west of Ta-shih, the Chinese name for the lands of Islam. Arabic traders traveled there in great ships capable of carrying several thousand persons from their port of T'o-pan-ti. Some of the strange products of the far western land were a grain three inches long, a melon six feet around, and large sheep that were several feet high.

Sinologists Friedrich Hirth and W. W. Rockhill translated Chau Ju-kua's book, *Chu-fan-chi*, in 1911. They identified Mu-lan-p'i as the realm of the Almorvids in North Africa and Islamic Iberia, and T'o-pan-ti as the Egyptian port of Damietta.

Otherwise, Hirth and Rockhill dismissed the reports of Mu-lan-p'i's exotic plants and animals as mere fantastical embellishments about a distant land.

In 1961 sinologist Hui-Lin Li dissented from their interpretations. Arguing that the lands of the Almorvids formed a part of the Ta-shih and that the long journey of 100 days to Mu-lan-p'i did not fit travel in the Mediterranean, he suggested that Mu-lan-p'i lay in the Americas. Specifically Hui-Lin Li located Mu-lan-p'i around Lake Maracaibo and T'o-pan-ti as a port in Islamic Iberia, probably Lisbon. Furthermore, the various alien plants and animals were identified as species native to the Americas. He claimed that the three-inch-long grain was **maize** and that it may have been transported to Africa in pre-Columbian times, the six-foot-circumference melons were pumpkins, and the large sheep were llamas and alpacas. Hui-Lin Li's interpretation was incorporated by Africanist Ivan Van Sertima into his arguments for a pre-Columbian African presence in the Americas.

Unfortunately, Hui-Lin Li's identification of Mu-lan-p'i as America founders on the lack of any reasonable corroboration in the works of medieval Arabic geographers. No western lands appear in Arabic geographies, nor do the gigantic ships that supposedly traveled between T'o-pan-ti and Mu-lan-p'i. It appears that Hirth and Rockhill's judgment that the accounts of Mu-lan-p'i referred to the lands of the Maghreb and Iberia was correct, along with their assessment of the foreign products as mere exaggerations.

Bibliography: Hirth, Friedrich, and W. W. Rockhill, eds., *Chau Ju-kua: His Work on the Chinese and Arab Trade in the Twelfth and Thirteenth Centuries, Entitled Chu-fan-chi*, [1911], 1966; Li, Hui-Lin, "Mu-lan-p'i: A Case for Pre-Columbian Transatlantic Travel by Arab Ships," *Harvard Journal of Asiatic Studies* 23 (1961): 114–126; Van Sertima, Ivan, *They Came before Columbus*, 1976.

Mulekites

According to *The Book of Mormon*, they were the third group of immigrants to reach the ancient Americas. Some of the Mulekites formed the original population of Zarahemla, the ultimate home of the refugee **Nephites.**

Mulek was a son of Zedekiah, the last king of Judah. During 589–588 B.C., King Nebuchadnezzar of Babylon besieged and captured Jerusalem, captured and blinded Zedekiah, and carried the survivors off into the Babylonian Captivity. Mulek and his followers managed to escape the wrath of the marauding Babylonian army. With God's help, they passed through the wilderness and crossed the sea to the Americas. The Mulekites landed on the eastern coast of the Land Northward, which was also called Mulek since that was where Mulek and his people made their first settlement. Many Mormon scholars now identify this as the Mexican state of Veracruz. Wherever they landed, it was close to the recent and final apocalyptic battleground of the **Jaredites.** That immediate area was known, for obvious reasons, as the Land of Desolation. Soon some or all of the Mulekites moved into the Land Southward and founded the city of Zarahemla, which was named after another of their leaders. They encountered Coriantumr, the last surviving Jaredite, who told them the tragic history of his people. The Mulekites prospered and grew in population, but they failed to perpetuate their original **Hebrew** religion and language. Wars and social conflicts divided and agitated Mulekite society by the time Mosiah, the refugee king, and his righteous Nephites discovered the Mulekites sometime after 200 B.C. The directionless Mulekites immediately accepted the godly Mosiah as their king. The Nephite refugees retaught them proper Hebrew language and customs, and reintroduced social justice. Mulekites and righteous Nephites quickly merged into one united society of Zarahemla.

The Book of Mormon's account of the Mulekites in the book of *Omni* is very vague. The details of how they reached America are not stated. After they arrived in the Land of Desolation, it is not clear whether all or just some of the Mulekites moved to Zarahemla in the Land Southward. Passing references, however, indicate that some Mulekites remained behind and populated the Land Northward. Mormon scholars identify the archaeological site of Santa Rosa in the Mexican state of Chiapas as the ruins of Zarahemla, although not as yet to the satisfaction of non-Mormon scholars.

Bibliography: Sorenson, John L., *An Ancient American Setting for the Book of Mormon*, 1985.

Multiple Creation Theory

Also known as polygenesis, this theory suggests that God created human beings on two or more occasions, as opposed to the single creation of Adam and Eve described in the Bible. It was used to explain the presence of the large population living in the Americas when Christopher Columbus arrived in 1492. The multiple creation theory eliminated the need to postulate various ancient transoceanic contacts between the hemispheres.

Following the narrative in the Bible, traditional Christianity teaches that all human beings are descended from the single creation of Adam and Eve (also known as monogenesis). Furthermore, the occurrence of the universal flood of Noah meant that all peoples and cultures could ultimately trace back to one of Noah's three sons: Shem, Ham, or Japheth. The problem with these orthodox teachings is the relative shortness of the biblical chronology. God created the world around 4000 B.C. and destroyed it with Noah's flood 1,656 years later by Jewish reckoning, or 2,262 years later by the reckoning of St. Augustine of Hippo. This time frame left approximately 3,200 to 3,800 years for the formation of the earth's diverse cultures and races, including those long isolated in the Americas. Many people felt that this chronology did not allow sufficient time for such an accomplishment.

The alchemist Paracelsus (1493–1541) suggested that God created two Adams, one for the Old World and one for the Americas. Such **Preadamite** or Coadamite ideas received their fullest development in the writings of French scholar Isaac de La Peyrère (1594–1676). Using some vague passages in the Bible, he argued that God created the Preadamites on the sixth day of creation and only created Adam after the seventh day of rest. He also denied the universality of Noah's flood and limited its effects to Palestine and the **Hebrew** descendants of Adam. La Peyrère's ideas aroused a storm of controversy that only ensured their wider circulation. Scientists and scholars of the pre-Darwinian era debated whether monogenesis or polygenesis better explained the racial and cultural diversity of humanity and the peopling of the ancient Americas. Nevertheless, orthodox Christians, both Protestant and Catholic, continue to adhere to the ideas of a single creation and a universal flood.

Bibliography: Greene, John C., *The Death of Adam: Evolution and Its Impact on Western Thought*, 1959; Hodgen, Margaret T., *Early Anthropology in the Sixteenth and Seventeenth Centuries*, 1964; Huddleston, Lee Eldridge, *Origins of the American Indians: European Concepts, 1492–1729*, 1967.

N

Nephites

This nation of people living in ancient America forms the primary focus of *The Book of Mormon.* They were the descendants of Nephi, son of the prophet Lehi. Lehi fled with a group of **Hebrews** from the Kingdom of Judah in 597 B.C., the final days before the destruction of Jerusalem by Nebuchadnezzar of Babylon. After settling in America, the Nephites became quite prosperous, but after a while fell away from their original godly ways. Ultimately they suffered annihilation by the rival **Lamanite** nation in A.D. 385.

Nephi was the fourth son of Lehi, the Hebrew prophet who led his family out of sinful Jerusalem in 597 B.C. and ultimately to the new promised land of America around 585 B.C. Although Nephi was the youngest son, he was intellectually and morally the best. So God and Lehi picked Nephi to lead his family, the new chosen people, in the event of Lehi's death. That choice rankled the two eldest sons, Laman and Lemuel, and bitter confrontations occurred even while Lehi lived. After he died, Laman and Lemuel completely rebelled against Nephi's authority. They withdraw from the Hebrew colony and became the Lamanites, a nomadic hunting people. Nephi and his people became the Nephites, a hard-working agricultural people who built cities. God then cursed the wayward Lamanites with "a skin of blackness," while the Nephites continued to be "fair and delightsome."

Faced with the unremitting hostility of his older brothers, Nephi and his supportive family members moved from the original Hebrew settlement. By 570 B.C. they founded the city of Nephi, which Mormon scholars identify as the archaeological site of Kaminaljuyu in Guatemala. The Nephites prospered, but their very success proved to be their undoing—with wealth they became corrupt. Things got so bad that sometime between 279 and 130 B.C., a good man named Mosiah led the remaining godly people out of Nephi to start a new and purer life. Moving far through the wilderness, Mosiah and his people came across the unknown city of Zarahemla, which had been founded after 588 B.C. by the **Mulekites,** another group of refugee Hebrews. Some Mormon scholars claim that an archaeological site at Santa Rosa in Chiapas state in Mexico is the ruins of that city. The isolated people of Zarahemla had lost the knowledge of their Hebrew religion and culture, but they welcomed the Nephites and even made Mosiah their king. The Nephites in turn taught the people of Zarahemla the proper religion, language, and customs of traditional Jews, and eventually the two peoples merged.

Meanwhile the inhabitants of the city of Nephi suffered from both wicked rulers and

Lamanite attacks. Devastated by the Lamanites, the people of Nephi rebuilt but then came under the rule of the wicked King Noah. One group of righteous Nephites, led by the prophet Alma, fled from Noah's persecutions and established a new settlement at Helam. The Lamanites attacked again and captured the city of Nephi, causing Noah to flee. He was later killed by his own followers. The Lamanites enslaved the people of Nephi and made Limhi, the just son of Noah, a puppet-king. Faced with this bleak future, Limhi and his people abandoned Nephi about 121 B.C., sneaking away under cover of darkness while their Lamanite guards were drunk. They sought refuge at Zarahemla with the righteous Nephites. Alma's Nephites at Helam also faced serious problems. Lamanite armies discovered them, occupied Helam, and placed Amulon, an evil priest of King Noah, over them as king. Miraculously God caused the Lamanite garrison at Helam to fall asleep, which allowed Alma and his people to flee to Zarahemla. This migration in 120 B.C. completed the reuniting of the Nephite nation at Zarahemla.

Wars between Nephites and Lamanites continued in the years that followed. Cycles of righteousness and evil also occurred among the Nephites, but various prophets, particularly Samuel the Lamanite about 6 B.C., continued to predict the coming of **Jesus Christ.** Soon after, the Star of Bethlehem appeared to the peoples of the Americas and announced the birth of Jesus. Many Nephites still refused to lead just lives. When Jesus died on the cross about A.D. 34, storms and earthquakes in the Americas destroyed numerous cities and killed vast multitudes. Three days of darkness followed. Jesus then appeared to the survivors, preached the gospel, chose disciples, established his church, and returned to heaven.

Two hundred years of peace and prosperity followed, but this success only planted the seeds of destruction once more. Riches led to greed, greed to envy, and envy to violence throughout their society. The divisions between Nephites and Lamanites reappeared by 234, although by then the term Nephite could also simply mean those people who followed the gospel. By 300 most of the Nephites had become as wicked as the Lamanites. War broke out between the Nephites and the Lamanites in 322. Slowly but surely the numerically superior Lamanites wore down the Nephites as the renewed wars dragged on for years. The end came in 385 when the Nephites gathered at Hill Cumorah for a last stand against the hordes of advancing Lamanites. Thousands upon thousands died. All the Nephites were gone except for the prophet Moroni, who had the golden books of Nephite history. He managed to avoid marauding Lamanites, completed the history, and buried its precious records in 422. Centuries later Moroni appeared in angelic form to **Joseph Smith, Jr.** After leading Smith to the golden books, Moroni gave him the means to translate them. That translation was *The Book of Mormon.*

The story of the Nephites, as found in *The Book of Mormon,* is difficult to reconcile with the continuing archaeological discoveries of the twentieth century. Traditionally Mormons believe that *The Book of Mormon* tells the entire history of the ancient Americas. Lehi landed in South America and his descendants peopled both continents. The battle at Hill Cumorah took place in upstate New York. Such an interpretation was viable in the 1830s when little was known about the chronology and geography of the pre-Columbian civilizations. One increasingly popular theory or belief in the existence of an extinct white race of **Mound Builders** dovetailed nicely with *The Book of Mormon*'s account. Progress in archaeological studies discredited the myth of the Mound Builders by 1894. The same advances in knowledge tended to make traditional Mormon beliefs about the pre-Columbian history of the Americas more and more difficult to sustain.

Mormon scholars attempted to reconcile *The Book of Mormon* to these new findings of modern archaeology. By the beginning of the twentieth century, they focused on Central America, especially central and southern Mexico and Guatemala, as the setting for the events described in *The Book of Mormon*. In this revised interpretation, the Isthmus of Tehuantepec is the "Narrow Neck of Land," the city of Nephi is the archaeological site of Kaminaljuyu outside Guatemala City, and Zarahemla appears to have been located at Santa Rosa in the state of Chiapas in Mexico. Furthermore, Nephites and Lamanites were not the only peoples living in the Americas. **Jaredite** survivors and other groups were also present in Central America, with other more distant tribes and cultures remaining completely untouched by Nephite influences. Hill Ramah/Cumorah becomes the Cerro El Vigia in the Tuxtla Mountains near Veracruz, Mexico. This new interpretation is a radical change from traditional Mormon belief locating Hill Cumorah in upstate New York, where Joseph Smith, Jr., found the golden books of Moroni. Mormons even built a great monument there. Moving Cumorah to Mexico solves some of the problems in the narrative of *The Book of Mormon*, but it also creates new ones—such as explaining how Moroni transported the golden plates all those hundreds of miles from southern Mexico to New York. It is an improbable journey but, as Mormon scholars point out, not impossible. They cite the journey of **David Ingram** as an example of a lone man successfully traveling across the primitive North American continent. Ultimately, the explanation of divine intervention is enlisted. Mormons continue to work hard at reconciling *The Book of Mormon* to the advances in archaeological knowledge. While their scholars rightly claim a growing

sophistication and plausibility for their interpretations, non-Mormon archaeologists generally remain extremely skeptical about their claims.

Bibliography: Ferguson, Thomas S., *Cumorah—Where?* 1947; Sorenson, John L., *An Ancient American Setting for the Book of Mormon*, 1985; Vogel, Dan, *Indian Origins and the Book of Mormon*, 1986; Williams, Stephen, *Fantastic Archaeology: The Wild Side of North American Prehistory*, 1991.

Nicholas of Lynn's Arctic Journey (1360)

This English Carmelite friar supposedly traveled the Arctic and made his way to North America around 1360.

Little is known for certain about Nicholas of Lynn other than that he came from the seaport of Lynn in Norfolk, belonged to the Carmelite religious order, taught theology at Oxford, and in about 1386 composed the *Kalendarium* (almanac) referred to by Geoffrey Chaucer in his *Treatise on the Astrolabe*. In *Principall Navigations* Richard Hakluyt also identified this same Nicholas of Lynn as a mysterious Arctic explorer. Citing both Gerard Mercator and **John Dee**, Hakluyt told how an English friar made extensive journeys through the northern islands in 1360. During these travels the friar took extensive measurements with his astrolabe, encountered a giant whirlpool, and delivered a report on his findings to King Edward III of England in a book titled *Inventio fortunata*. According to Dee's testimony, the friar traveled to the northern islands and back five times. The modern chronicler of the **Viking** presence in America, Hjalmar R. Holand, goes even further, claiming that Nicholas of Lynn traveled to Hudson's Bay as a member of **Paul Knutson's** expedition.

Hakluyt's identification of Nicholas of Lynn as the Arctic-traveling friar seems to have no concrete basis. His informant Dee basically got his information from Mercator, and Mercator claimed to have read it in a lost work of the shadowy figure Jacobus (James) Cnoyen (Knox?) of Hartzevan Buske (i.e., 's Hertegenbosch or Bolduc). Mercator called the friar a Franciscan, whereas Nicholas of Lynn was a Carmelite. No confirmed copy of the *Inventio fortunata* is available for study, although an alleged fragment may be in private hands. Geographical writers of the late fifteenth and sixteenth centuries frequently referred to the *Inventio fortunata* and cited material indicating that a mysterious friar may have visited North America in the fourteenth century. Modern scholarship, however, rejects Hakluyt's identification of the historical Nicholas of Lynn with the mysterious Arctic explorer.

Bibliography: Eisner, Sigmund, ed., *The Kalendarium of Nicholas of Lynn*, 1980; Sarton, George, "The Mysterious Arctic Traveller of 1360: Nicholas of Lynn?" *Isis* 29 (1938): 98–99 and reply by Aubrey Diller, "The Mysterious Arctic Traveller of 1360, Nicholas of Lynn," *Isis* 30 (1939): 277–278.

Norse Naval Technology

The Norse are the only people known for certain to have reached the Americas by sea before 1492. That they were able to achieve this transoceanic contact is a tribute to their seamanship. They were definitely the greatest sailors of the Atlantic world of the Middle Ages, although it can be plausibly argued that the maritime skills of the **Polynesians** surpassed those of the Norse.

The **Vikings** and their sleek longships are quite familiar to many people since they have been the subject of many books and movies. But **Leif Ericsson** did not sail to **Vinland** in a longship. The classic longship (or *langskip*) was primarily a coastal vessel. It carried Viking warriors on raids to the western European coastline, but not across the stormy deeps of the Atlantic Ocean to colonize Ireland, the Faeroe Islands, **Iceland, Greenland,** or Vinland.

The ship that transported the Norse over the dangerous waters of the Atlantic Ocean was the *hafskip,* or seaship. Such seagoing vessels existed in primitive form by the year 800 and allowed the Norse to settle the Faeroe Islands. By the last half of the ninth century, the *knörr* form of the *hafskip* evolved. The *knörr* had a wider beam and deeper draught, and rode higher out of the water than a *langskip*. A *langskip* discovered at Skuldelev was 95 feet long and 13 feet 9 inches wide, while a *knörr* from the same site was less than 55 feet long but 15 feet wide. The *knörr* had far more cargo space and was capable of carrying between 30 and 50 people, supplies, livestock, and other bulky items for hundreds of miles. In comparison, a good *langskip* had room for 50 or 60 warriors but no bulky cargo. The *knörr* was a sailing vessel, while the *langskip* sometimes relied on its banks of oars when becalmed or maneuvering in tight waters. Both the *knörr* and the *langskip* used square-rigged sails, but some recent writers suggest that Norse ships were capable of sailing near the wind thanks to a tacking boom called a *beitiáss.*

It is important to keep in mind that the *langskip* and *knörr* were both capable of making an Atlantic crossing. Magnus Anderson sailed a reproduction of the Gokstad ship (a *langskip*) across the Atlantic in 1893. He reported very favorably on its sailing qualities. *Knörr* reproductions have also crossed the Atlantic Ocean during the twentieth century and received high praise for their seaworthiness.

The Norse were excellent navigators within the limits of their simple technology. Their basic limitation was an inability to determine longitude, which meant they were forced to use latitude sailing. The latitude sailing technique is demonstrated as follows. The crew of a ship wants to sail from point A to point B. The two points are separated by a large amount of open sea and are not located on the same latitude. The ship's crew knows, however, that point B is at the same latitude as point C, which can easily be reached by coastal sailing from point A. They sail from point A to point C, and then sail in a straight line across the open water to point B. Sailing in a straight line required that the Norse measure latitude at sea by observation of the sun and stars. Various historical records describe Norse sailors taking such measurements. Most high seas voyages were considerably more complicated than the above example and involved detailed sailing directions that were common knowledge among Norse seamen. The Norse also navigated by dead reckoning, which involved the estimation of the ship's location based on calculating the distance and direction the ship covered each day. Under normal conditions, a Norse ship could sail about 120–144 nautical miles, or about 138–166 English miles, in a 24-hour period.

Norse seamen employed navigational techniques based on the close observation of various natural phenomena. Much could be learned about the proximity of land from cloud formations and the color of the seawater. Flights of birds and driftwood also provided clues for locating land, as did the behavior of wind and sea currents. Flights of geese from Ireland to Iceland helped first the Irish and then the Norse locate Iceland. Despite their navigational skills, the Norse got lost at sea on occasion. According to the **Vinland Sagas,** the discovery of Vinland was accidental. Both **Bjarni Herjolfsson** and Leif Ericsson lost their way to Greenland and stumbled across a new land instead. These were not isolated incidents. The Norse even had a word for being lost at sea—*hafvilla,* which meant a state of disorientation.

All these sailing techniques were known to seamen of the Mediterranean world, but the Norse had far greater experience with long-distance sailing in a north-south direction. They were also more accustomed to longer trips over open water and rougher seas. By the second half of the fifteenth century, however, the Portuguese and others equaled the Norse in high seas sailing, particularly that accomplished sailor, Christopher Columbus.

Bibliography: Jones, Gwyn, *The Norse Atlantic Saga,* 2nd ed., 1986; Marcus, G. J., *The Conquest of the North Atlantic,* 1981.

Norumbega

Appearing in numerous variant spellings, Norumbega was the sixteenth-century name for the region of North America now known as New England, along with the state of New York. In addition, the name referred specifically to a supposed golden city located in that region and to the river that flowed through the city. The city was supposedly comparable to a sixteenth-century European city in its level of civilization.

The derivation of the name Norumbega is controversial, but the best authorities maintain that it comes from the Abenaki Indian word *Nolumbeka,* which means quiet waters between two series of rapids. Others claim a European origin for the name. It supposedly refers to Normandy, home of many of the men who sailed with explorer Girolamo da Verrazano in 1525. In 1891 Scandinavian-American professor Eben Norton Horsford advanced the theory that Norumbega was simply the local tribes' corrupt pronunciation of Norbega, the old Norse name for Norway. He located the **Vinland** of the Norse in Massachusetts and placed **Leif Ericsson's** settlement at Watertown. Several other Norse derivations were suggested, but none ultimately proved valid. In 1961 popular writer Charles M. Boland claimed that Norumbega was the name of the settlement of Norse castaways who had been taken prisoner by the Irish Culdee settlers of **Great Ireland.** (See also **Irish Monks in America.**) The actual location of Norumbega is uncertain, with some placing it on the Hudson River and others on the Penobscot River of Maine. Since the city of Norumbega did not exist, which river was the Norumbega will probably never be known. The Penobscot, however, seems to be the more likely candidate.

The name Norumbega first appeared on Verrazano's map of 1529, in which he recorded North American explorations he made in the service of France. The name was spelled Oranbega and referred to a river full of islands. Interestingly enough, Spaniard Diego Ribero's map of 1529 also showed the same river full of islands, but he named it the Rio de Las Gamas (deer). Later French visitors to that region sent back glowing reports. In 1539 Pierre Crignon described it as a "land most abounding in every kind of fruit." When Jean Allefonce visited the region in 1542, he claimed to have visited the town of Norumbega. According to his account, it was a fur trading center whose tall and handsome men dressed in sable, spoke a language that sounded like Latin, and worshipped the sun. That same year a new French map by Jomard called the region Auorobagra. Gerard Mercator's map of 1569 included the region and city, but spelled it Norombega. The maps of Jomard, Mercator, and other sixteenth-century geographers such as Abraham Ortelius basically copied most of their details from Ribero's map, but persisted in calling the region by some variant of the name Norumbega rather than Tierra de Estevan Gomez as Ribero had named it. Travelers continued to expect to find a great city there until the early years of the seventeenth century.

In 1582 the English castaway **David Ingram** claimed to have passed through a great city of crystal and gold in the course of his travels through eastern North America during 1568. Rumors about the wealth of Norumbega provided at least a partial motivation for a number of English voyages of exploration and colonization to North America between 1579 and 1603. That group included Sir Humphrey Gilbert's fatal voyage of 1583. The continued failure to locate Norumbega finally took its toll and produced skepticism. Samuel de Champlain, the French explorer, exemplified this new attitude. Traveling from St. Croix in Canada down the east coast of North America, Champlain looked for the great city of Norumbega on the Penobscot River but failed to find it. He concluded that reports of its existence were merely unsubstantiated and incorrect hearsay. He found the natives of the region to be just as primitive as those living along the St. Lawrence River. They had no material culture similar in any way to that of Europeans. In 1612 Marc Lescarbot, an early historian of French Canada, also expressed doubts about Norumbega's existence and questioned Jean Allefonce's truthfulness. The myth of a European-style city inhabited by supposed Latin speakers and located somewhere on the northeast coast of the present-day United States finally died. Norumbega as a place-name persisted for a few more years, but the arrival of Pilgrims and Puritans brought the region a new name—New England.

Bibliography: De Costa, Benjamin Franklin, *Ancient Norombega,* 1890; Diamond, Sigmund, "Norumbega: New England Xanadu," *American Neptune* 11 (April 1951): 95–107; Morison, Samuel Eliot, *The European Discovery of America: The Northern Voyages,* 1971; Ramsay, Raymond H., *No Longer on the Map: Discovering Places That Never Were,* 1972.

Nubian-Egyptians in Ancient America (ca. 751–654 B.C.)

This theory, espoused by anthropologist Ivan Van Sertima, claimed that during the time of the Nubian or twenty-fifth dynasty of Egypt, ships from that realm, either by design or accident, reached Mexico carrying Nubians, **Egyptians,** and **Phoenicians.** They deeply influenced the indigenous Olmec culture.

Ever since their discovery in the Mexican state of Veracruz in the mid-nineteenth century, the giant stone heads of the Olmecs, popularly called "babyfaces," caused some observers to speculate about pre-Columbian visits by Africans. Some **diffusionist** writers such as James Bailey and Constance Irwin definitely think the heads portray Negroid Africans, but they view these Africans as either mercenaries or slaves of Phoenician merchants. Van Sertima, however, turned that suggestion on its head and argued that it was the Nubian blacks who were in charge of the expedition rather than the already subjugated Egyptians or the hireling Phoenicians.

Olmec civilization developed about 1500 B.C., but Van Sertima contends that the great stone heads were not sculpted until after 800 B.C. He suggests that ships carrying Nubians, Egyptians, and Phoenicians reached Mexico around that time. With the assistance of the Phoenicians and Egyptians, the Nubian warriors took over and set themselves up as the kings and nobility of the Olmecs. In addition to the enigmatic stone heads, Van Sertima cites as evidence some smaller terra cotta heads with alleged African features, some supposedly pre-Columbian Negroid skeletal remains, and various shared traits of monarchy such as a double crown, the royal flail, the sacred boat of kings, the use of purple, false beards, feathered fans, and ceremonial umbrellas.

Other anthropologists, archaeologists, and historians do not find Van Sertima's evidence convincing. His skeletal evidence for a pre-Columbian Negro presence is either extremely inclusive or post-Columbian in origin. Negroid features on the stone heads and terra cottas are explained as stylistic conventions used in Native American portraiture. Furthermore, some Native Americans, like some Caucasoids and Mongoloids, show strong Negroid features without any recent heredity of Negroid genes. Tightly curled hair, broad noses, full lips, and dark skins are not the exclusive traits of Negroid Africans or their descendants. The shared monarchical features that Van Sertima lists could easily be independent inventions. As things stand, the evidence for a Nubian presence in Olmec Mexico is too weak to merit any serious revision or rejection of existing conventional theories suggesting that the Olmecs developed their civilization without the benefit of influences from the Old World, including Africa.

Bibliography: Feder, Kenneth L., *Frauds, Myths, and Mysteries: Science and Pseudoscience in Archaeology,* 1990; Van Sertima, Ivan, *They Came before Columbus,* 1976; Van Sertima, Ivan, "Egypto-Nubian Presences in Ancient Mexico," in *African Presence in Early America,* edited by Ivan Van Sertima, [1986], 2nd ed., 1992.

air and water contract. This circulation is further affected by the rotation of the earth in a phenomenon called the coriolis effect. All objects moving about the earth's surface are subject to this phenomenon, which deflects them from a straight path into a curved path. In the northern hemisphere, the coriolis effect deflects moving objects to the right, while in the southern hemisphere it deflects them to the left. Both the Northeast Trade winds of the northern hemisphere and the Southeast Trade winds of the southern hemisphere show such deflection to the right and left, respectively. The same observation generally applies to the ocean currents. In the North Atlantic, the Canaries current becomes the North Equatorial current, which then turns into the Gulf Stream and circles around to the right to meet the Canaries current. In the northern hemisphere, a vast amount of water moves round and round to the right, while in the southern hemisphere, it moves to the left. Continents, with different heating and cooling patterns from the oceans, can distort these neat patterns. Changing seasons also affect the currents and winds. The North Equatorial countercurrent, moving from west to east, exists only in the second half of the year. During the first half, water in that area moves in an east-to-west direction. Still, there is an amazing overall regularity about ocean currents and wind patterns, especially in the vast Pacific Ocean.

Sailing ships, particularly square-rigged or square-sailed vessels, were and are very much dependent on ocean currents and winds to carry them. Development by eighth-century Arabs of the triangular lateen sail and its spread to Europe allowed ships to sail closer to or against the wind. The adoption of a two-masted rig in the twelfth century allowed even closer sailing against the wind by using a zigzag course. However, no early sailing ship could ultimately sail against both wind and current. Oar-driven galleys

Ocean Currents and Winds

Prior to the appearance of vessels with mechanical engines, high seas travel took place in sailing ships. These ships were at the mercy of winds and ocean currents, which meant that some routes were feasible for crossing the oceans and others were impractical or impossible. Only certain transoceanic contacts between the Americas and the continents of Asia, Africa, or Europe would have been possible on the basis of these patterns of prevailing winds and currents.

General

Prevailing winds and ocean currents are caused by the uneven heating and cooling of the earth's atmosphere and water. Warmer and cooler air and water creates a circulation as warmer air and water expand and cooler were not an option for high seas voyages of any length. Their large crews consumed food and water in quantities too great for any galley to venture far from land. So which was more important for a sailing ship—winds or currents? Historians of the same mind as Samuel Eliot Morison tend to emphasize wind. They think that ancient, medieval, and early modern seamen really sailed their ships.

In contrast, **Thor Heyerdahl,** an anthropologist and a student of humanity's earliest seafaring, places emphasis on the role of ocean currents. He likens ocean currents to conveyor belts or escalators; a person traveling in the same direction as an escalator or conveyor will be carried along automatically. But if that same person walks with the escalator, they will move even faster. On the other hand, a person moving against an escalator or conveyor will have to work much harder to make any progress at all. Citing the example of his voyage in the *Kon Tiki,* Heyerdahl points out that 4,000 miles separates Peru from the beginning of Polynesia. Propulsion from the *Kon Tiki*'s sails accounted for only 1,000 miles of the trip; the South Equatorial current or Humboldt current carried the *Kon Tiki* the other 3,000 miles. In comparison, if Heyerdahl had tried to sail from Polynesia to Peru against the current, it would have been like sailing 7,000 miles, that is, 4,000 miles in geographical distance plus 3,000 miles added by movement of the ocean current. Obviously a journey going with the current would be infinitely easier than a journey moving against it. It is no wonder that Heyerdahl refers to the various ocean currents as conveyors. In his opinion, most voyages by early sailors were drift voyages primarily using currents, not winds.

Atlantic Ocean

The Atlantic Ocean, particularly in the north, is a stormy, unpredictable, and dan-gerous sea. The North Atlantic is dominated by the great circular ocean current consisting of the Canaries current, the North Equatorial current, and the Gulf Stream. It is the eddies of the powerful Gulf Stream that help to create the mysterious Sargasso Sea. Two wind systems dominate the northern half of the Atlantic Ocean: the Westerlies that blow in a northeasterly direction starting about 40° north latitude to beyond 60° north, and the Northeast Trades that blow toward the southwest around the Tropic of Cancer and merge with the Southeast Trade winds around the equator to form the Doldrums and the Intertropical Convergence Zone.

A similar but mirror-image pattern exists in the southern half of the Atlantic Ocean. The South Equatorial current meets with the Brazil current, eventually sweeping around to become the Benguela current, which flows north up the west coast of southern Africa. Southeast Trade winds blow toward the northeast from the Cape of Good Hope and the Tropic of Capricorn up to the equator where they merge with the Northeast Trades. Between 40° and 60° south, the powerful Roaring Forties blow from the northwest to the southeast. These patterns of wind and current shift northward or southward to a certain degree with the changing seasons.

The easiest Atlantic route for a sailing ship to follow from east to west is to use the North Equatorial current and the Northeast Trade winds, the route that carried Christopher Columbus to the Americas in 1492. In fact, Heyderdahl dubbed it the Columbus conveyor. The same Northeast Trade winds will also readily carry a ship to the coast of **Brazil** with a small southward correction. The ship can then enter the Brazil current and easily move down the coast of South America. Another feasible route lies in the far north. In the region of **Iceland** and **Greenland,** the great circular patterns of winds and currents are less dominant. It is possible to catch other favorable winds and currents and cross the far northern seas by the island-hopping method used by Norse seamen to reach **Vinland** in North America. Although this northern route is much shorter than the Columbus conveyor, it passes over far more dangerous seas. Heyerdahl dubbed it the Eiriksson conveyor, after **Leif Ericsson.**

Two potential routes are available for traveling from the Americas to the Old World. The route leading back to Europe involves catching the Gulf Stream and the Westerlies. It is the only feasible route for crossing the North Atlantic from west to east and is quite reliable. But dangerous storms occur along this path through the high seas. During his first voyage of 1492–1493, Columbus used the Gulf Stream and Westerlies for his return to Spain and barely survived two great storms at sea.

It is also possible to return to Africa from South America by using the Roaring Forties to cross the South Atlantic. But those winds are not called the Roaring Forties for nothing. They are very strong and make sailing conditions in the entire southern hemisphere extremely dangerous. Neither southern Brazil and Argentina nor southern Africa were home to any seafaring peoples during the pre-Columbian era.

There are only so many ways that a preindustrial people could have gotten back and forth across the Atlantic using sailing ships. The Portuguese learned this fact to their sorrow when their attempts to sail west from the Azores consistently ran into almost insurmountable difficulties from contrary winds and currents (see also **Van Olmen, Voyage of Ferdinand**). It was not until 1500 that Gaspar Côrte-Real managed to beat his way across the North Atlantic to Greenland. If ancient **Egyptians** or medieval **Africans** managed to reach the Americas by using the so-called Columbus conveyor, how did they

get back home? They would have had to come back via the Azores and the Iberian Peninsula, but there is no archaeological or documentary evidence that either of these groups came that way.

Pacific Ocean

The Pacific Ocean is a much larger body of water than the Atlantic and, as Ferdinand Magellan commemorated in its name, more peaceful. In fact, it is so much larger that its true vastness has been hard for people to comprehend throughout history. Its great size almost killed Magellan and his crew when they crossed it.

Because of its size, the Pacific Ocean's current and wind patterns are far more regular than those of the Atlantic. In the North Pacific, the great clockwise circulation of water is formed by the Kuroshio or Japan current in the west; it becomes the California current in the east and then, on its way back to Asia, the North Equatorial current. The great counterclockwise circulation in the South Pacific is made up of the Humboldt or Peru current in the east, which travels west as the South Equatorial current. When it turns south it becomes the East Australian current until it again turns east and becomes the West Wind Drift. There is also an Equatorial countercurrent that travels from west to east, although it is a seasonal phenomenon. Thor Heyerdahl denies that it could be used effectively by a sailing vessel or for a drift voyage, but others think he is wrong.

The Pacific Ocean's wind patterns are fairly similar to those of the Atlantic. It has Northeast and Southeast Trade winds that blow from the Tropics of Cancer and Capricorn to the equator, where they form the Doldrums. The Roaring Forties of the South Pacific are also quite strong and create areas with some of the world's most dangerous and nasty weather. Westerlies are much less pronounced in the North Pacific because

Asia and North America approach each other so closely at the **Bering Strait**. These two large landmasses create wind patterns that blow toward the continents in the summer and toward the ocean in the winter.

Sailing ships have three significant paths across the Pacific Ocean. In the North Pacific, the Kuroshio current is very strong. Many cases have been documented of nineteenth-century **Chinese** and **Japanese** fishermen unintentionally carried by this current across northern waters to the California coast. There is speculation that similar voyages occurred in pre-Columbian times, some accidental (see also **Jumon/Valdivia Trans-Pacific Contacts**) and others intentional (see also **Fusang**). Furthermore, the North Equatorial current and the Northeast Trade winds provided an easy way to return to Asia. In the South Pacific, the South Equatorial current made a ready path for traveling from east to west, complemented by the Southeast Trade winds. This was the route used by Thor Heyerdahl's *Kon Tiki* expedition. The route back to South America, however, was not at all good; the vicious Roaring Forties of the South Pacific make the West Wind Drift area one of the most dangerous sailing areas in the world.

The chief problem with these Pacific Ocean navigation paths is locating them. Spanish seamen following Magellan went through a dangerous trial-and-error process marked by many casualties. Alvaro de Saavedra Céron managed to locate the North Equatorial current route from Mexico to the Philippines in 1527–1528, but died in the attempt to find a way back. It was not until 1567 that Andres de Urdaneta found the proper way to sail from Asia to the Americas using the Kuroshio and California currents. Alvaro de Mendaña de Nehra successfully used the South Equatorial current in 1568 to search for legendary rich islands reported by the Incas. He found the Solomon Islands, but no riches, and died during a subsequent exploration. The experience of the Spanish and others shows that crossing the immense Pacific Ocean could be very dangerous. Many of the Chinese and Japanese fishermen swept off by the Kuroshio current arrived in California dead or dying from thirst or starvation. Even the Polynesians, in all probability the world's greatest sailors, suffered many fatalities on their epic voyages.

Trans-Pacific contacts between Asia and the Americas were possible although fraught with danger. Archaeological evidence indicates that contacts probably took place on a sporadic basis (see also **Polynesian-American Contacts** and **Chinese Visits to America**). But such contacts were not sustained nor were they particularly significant culturally. Our present knowledge of winds and currents also makes certain supposed pre-Columbian trans-Pacific contacts seem even less likely since the **Hindus, Alexander the Great's Fleet,** and the **Nephite/Lamanite** migration all seem to have sailed against prevailing winds and currents.

Bibliography: Davis, Richard A., Jr., *Oceanography: An Introduction to the Marine Environment*, 2nd ed., 1991; Fernández-Armesto, Felipe, *The Times Atlas of World Exploration*, 1991; Heyerdahl, Thor, *Early Man and the Ocean*, 1979; Leary, Colleen A., "Weather and Wind," and Philip L. Richardson, "Tides and Currents," in *The Christopher Columbus Encyclopedia*, edited by Silvio A. Bedini, 2 vols., 1992.

Ophir

This mysterious land is mentioned in the Bible as the home of King Solomon's gold mines, but its actual location remains unknown. Many writers since 1492 have tried to identify it with someplace in the Americas. Others claim that Native Americans were the descendants of Ophir, the great-great-great-grandson of Shem, the son of Noah.

According to I Kings 9: 26–28, the **Phoenicians** sailed with some servants of King Solomon from the port of Ezion-Geber on the Red Sea to Ophir and brought back much gold. Most biblical scholars place Ophir in the southern Arabian peninsula along with the more famous land of Sheba. Others locate Ophir in southern Africa, a theory that provided the basis for H. Rider Haggard's famous novel *King Solomon's Mines.* With the European discovery of the Americas, some people shifted Ophir's location to the Americas. In his *Decades of the New World* (1511–1530), Peter Martyr de Anglería stated that Christopher Columbus thought Hispaniola was Ophir, although nothing written by Columbus supports such a contention. Martyr also claimed that Solomon's fleet sailed to Ophir, but did not say if he believed Native Americans were descendants of those sailors. On the other hand, in *Historia de las Indias* (1559), **Bartolomé de Las Casas** found Martyr's location of Ophir on Hispaniola to be ridiculous. Las Casas thought the legendary Ophir was located in East Asia. His opinion had little impact since his history remained unpublished until the nineteenth century. In 1586 Spanish soldier and chronicler Miguel de Cabello Valboa (ca. 1535–1605) traced the history of human migrations in his *Miscelánea Antártica y origin de los indios y de las Incas del Perú.* He claimed that Ophir, the descendant of Shem, moved to East Asia after the confusion of languages at the Tower of Babel. His descendants became a seafaring race who then traveled to the Americas and populated them. According to Cabello Valboa, the name Peru derived from Ophir and the name Yucatán from Ophir's father, Joktan. He pointed out similarities between Native American and East Indian clothing as further evidence of relationship. Fernando Montesinos (ca. 1600–1652), a Jesuit scholar, took the Ophirite origin theory one step further in

hismanuscript *Memorias antiguas historiales y políticas del Perú,* completed in 1644. He claimed that the man Ophir personally settled in the Americas and not in East Asia. For some reason Montesinos thought Ophir was Noah's grandson rather than great-great-great-great-grandson as stated in the book of Genesis. His error pushed back the first settlement of the Americas to an earlier date. In 1684 another Spanish writer, Pedro Cubero Sebastián, published *Descripción general del mundo y notables successos dél,* which included the theory of Ophirite settlement in the Americas. But Cubero simply and egregiously plagiarized Miguel de Cabello Valboa. The Ophirite origin theory otherwise received little support in early modern Spain. The only northern European scholar to take the theory at all seriously was Samuel Purchas (ca. 1577–1628), the English historian of the Age of Discovery, in his *Hakluytus posthumus* of 1625.

The Ophirite theory of Native American origin did not die with the end of the seventeenth century. Twentieth-century adherents of the theory that Phoenicians visited pre-Columbian America also support the locating of Ophir somewhere in the Americas. Thomas Crawford Johnston in his *Did the Phoenicians Discover America?* of 1913 places Ophir in the Americas. In the concluding chapter of *In Quest of the White God* (1964), **diffusionist** writer Pierre Honoré made a passing reference to Ophir being in the Americas. **Cyrus Gordon,** another supporter of ancient Mediterranean peoples including the Phoenicians visiting the Americas, leaves open the possibility of Ophir being in the Americas. A footnote in his *Before Columbus* (1971) stated that Ophir was probably in Africa, but the main text hints at the possibility of an American location. The fact remains that the biblical scholars' placement of Ophir in southern Arabia is the identification most consistent with the biblical record. It also conforms to what is known of the ancient Red Sea trade.

Bibliography: Gordon, Cyrus H., *Before Columbus: Links between the Old World and Ancient America*, 1971; Huddleston, Lee Eldridge, *Origins of the American Indians: European Concepts, 1492–1729*, 1967; Johnston, Thomas Crawford, *Did the Phoenicians Discover America?* [1913], 1965; Montesinos, Fernando, *Memorias antiguas historiales y políticas del Perú*, 1920.

Oviedo y Valdés, Gonzalo Fernández de (1478–1557)

Courtier, colonial administrator, and holder of the office of chief chronicler of the Indies, Oviedo's history was the first literary work to discuss the origins of Native Americans. He proposed that they were descendants of ancient Spaniards of **Héspero** and **Carthaginians.** The work also contains the first published account of the story of the **Unknown Pilot of Columbus.**

Oviedo served as a page to Don Juan, the son of Ferdinand and Isabella of Spain, and acquired a good basic eduction in Renaissance humanism. Witnessing Columbus's return in 1493 from his first voyage to the New World, Oviedo himself traveled there in 1514. During the remainder of his career as an administrator, he crossed and recrossed the Atlantic eight times, spending 27 years in the Indies and 15 in Spain. In 1526 he published his *Summario de la historia natural de las Indias* (Summary of the natural history of the Indies), which was written for Emperor Charles V. Appointed as official chronicler for the Indies by 1532, he spent at least 35 years working on his great study, the *Historia general y natural de las Indias* (General and natural history of the Indies). The *Historia general* recorded the various events of Spain's empire in the New

World up to 1549. Although Oviedo began publishing it in 1535, the massive manuscript was not published in its entirety in his lifetime.

Oviedo strongly supported Spain's right to sovereignty over the New World and had little sympathy for Native Americans. That latter sentiment brought him into conflict with his contemporary and fellow historian **Bartolemé de Las Casas.** Eyewitness accounts and archival research formed the main basis of Oviedo's *Historia general*. In 1535, it became the first work to print the widely circulated tale of the dying Unknown Pilot who told Christopher Columbus about new lands located in the western ocean. Unlike other historians, Oviedo rejected the story as too unlikely to be true. In contrast, he accepted as true the story, attributed to **Aristotle,** that the Carthaginians discovered and temporarily colonized a large and pleasant island across the Atlantic that was, in fact, America. His favorite theory on the first discovery of America, however, patriotically attributed it to the Spanish king Héspero. According to legend, in 1658 B.C. Héspero discovered the **Islands of Hespérides,** which Oviedo identified as the West Indies. Héspero's settlers formed the foundation of the population of Native Americans, supplemented by the later arrival of Carthaginians. In this way Oviedo gave Spain a claim to the New World that was independent of Columbus. The Spanish government could use such a claim to undercut persistent claims by the heirs of Columbus to a greater share of the New World's treasure. The supposed antiquity of Héspero's colony also greatly predated most of the pre-Columbian visitors claimed by other European powers. Because these theories deprived Christopher Columbus of the credit for the discovery of the New World, his son Ferdinand Columbus wrote a biography of his father and a defense of his achievements. Oviedo's

Héspero theory received little support from other scholars, including the Spanish, but his Carthaginian theory attracted adherents in the sixteenth century and continues to find devotees far into the twentieth century.

Bibliography: Arocena, Luis A., "Gonzalo Fernández de Oviedo y Valdés (1478–1557)," in *Latin American Writers*, edited by Carlos A. Solé, 1989; Huddleston, Lee Eldridge, *Origins of the American Indians: European Concepts, 1492–1729*, 1967.

P

Patolli-Pachisi Parallels

A frequently discussed and superficially compelling evidence for pre-Columbian contacts between Asia and America is the similarity between the Aztec game of patolli and the **Hindu** game of pachisi.

Both patolli and pachisi are games in which the players move pieces around boards with cross-shaped tracks divided into segments. The number of moves a piece can make is determined by throwing lots; the Hindus used cowrie shells and the Aztecs used beans. Similarities between these and other games were noted as early as 1724. In 1879 the great English anthropologist E. B. Tylor (1832–1917) wrote a paper suggesting that patolli derived from pachisi as a result of ancient contacts between Asia and the Americas. In 1896 Tylor added to his

argument the authority of probability, as he considered it highly improbable that two such similar games could have been invented independently.

Tylor's contemporaries, American scholars Stewart Culin and Daniel Brinton, rejected his conclusion. They stressed that the game had been independently invented in the Americas without any Asian influences, and went on to cite evidence of geographical distribution and variations. But in the next generation of scholars, doyen of American anthropology A. L. Kroeber (1876–1960) supported Tylor's conclusions for many years. Kroeber employed the concepts of homologies and analogies from biological evolution to cultural evolution. A homology is a trait in an organism or culture that is definitely related to a similar trait in another organism or culture. An analogy is the case in which similarities between the traits of two organisms or cultures are only superficial and in which no true connection exists. A biological example of a homology would be the wings of bats and birds. Both organisms are vertebrate animals with very similar skeletal structures. On the other hand, bat wings and butterfly wings are analogous. They perform the same function but structurally and evolutionarily are completely unrelated. Homologs and analogs exist in human cultural evolution, but the distinctions between them are seldom so clear cut.

Other anthropologists have a theory of limited possibilities to explain similarities among different cultures. Basically this theory states that in many cases the realm of cultural choice is not that great. Therefore some seemingly complex and similar institutions and artifacts may develop independently because the probabilities against it are not all that great. In the case of patolli and pachisi, the dice or lots must have at least two flat sides to be functional, and the cross shape of the board is a rather common and universal shape. With cultures all over the world engaged in gaming, it is not surprising for similar games to appear independently. Anthropologist Charles John Erasmus cautioned against the facile calculating of possibilities or probabilities for the development of similar cultural traits. Large numbers of people at all times and all over the world are engaged in the process of cultural evolution. That variable, however, is seldom taken into consideration when the probabilities of independent invention are discussed. Furthermore, patolli is the only aspect of Aztec culture that shows any indication of possible Hindu contact. The absence of other cultural traits of probable Hindu origin is another strong evidence against any pre-Columbian contacts between Mexico and India.

Bibliography: Erasmus, Charles John, "Patolli, Pachisi, and the Limitation of Possibilities," *Southwestern Journal of Anthropology* 6 (1950): 369–387.

Phoenicians in Ancient America

This ancient seafaring people are a perennial candidate for having visited the Americas thousands of years before Columbus.

Phoenicia was a region of independent city-states in the ancient Mediterranean world that corresponds geographically to modern Lebanon. Its inhabitants considered themselves **Canaanites**, and their culture was almost identical to that of the Canaanite parent civilization. Phoenician society assumed its classic form after 1200 B.C. in its main coastal cities of Tyre, Sidon, Byblos, and Ugarit. It appears that by 1000 B.C. the Phoenicians engaged in seaborne trading. They definitely visited the western Mediterranean lands before 900 B.C. Greek and Roman traditions claimed that they founded, among others, the settlements of Cadiz (Gades) in 1100 B.C., Utica in 1087 B.C., and Carthage in 814 B.C. Some writers speculate

that Phoenicians reached the mines of Cornwall in Britain before their **Carthaginian** descendants. In the Bible it is recorded that King Hiram I (981–947 B.C.) of Tyre arranged for some of his people to sail with servants of King Solomon of Israel from the port of Ezion-Geber down the Red Sea to the mysterious land of **Ophir**. Other Phoenicians in 600 B.C. may have circumnavigated Africa for the **Egyptian** pharaoh Necho (610–594 B.C.).

Phoenician independence was threatened by the rising power of Assyria well before 853 B.C. Later the Assyrian king Sargon II (721–705 B.C.) conquered most of the coastal area of the eastern Mediterranean, but some Phoenician cities managed to survive. Another Assyrian ruler, Esarhaddon, sacked Sidon about 680 B.C., although Tyre continued to hold out. The constant threat of attack from first the Assyrians and then the Babylonians, which included an epic siege of 13 years duration, weakened the trading city. By the time of Nebuchadnezzar of Babylon's great siege of Tyre from 587–574 B.C., Carthage (originally a colony of Tyre) had grown strong enough to bar its trading rivals, including Tyre, from the western Mediterranean sea lanes. After the fall of Babylon, Tyre and the other Phoenician cities willingly submitted to the milder rule of the Persians under Cyrus the Great (559–530 B.C.) and even supplied the backbone of the Persian navy. By that time, the Phoenicians had declined from their former maritime greatness.

During the sixteenth and seventeenth centuries, Spanish chroniclers of the Americas did not always differentiate between the Phoenicians and Carthaginians. Even when they did, they tended to focus on the better-known Carthaginians as visitors and colonizers of America. In 1540 Spanish historian Alejo Vanegas de Bustos claimed that both the Carthaginians and Phoenicians settled and populated the Americas. Later Spanish historians ignored the Phoenicians as possible pre-Columbian visitors because it was generally believed that the ancients had no knowledge of lands in the western hemisphere. **Andrés González de Barcía Caballido y Zúñiga** significantly revived the Phoenician theory in his 1729 revision of **Gregorio García's** *Origen de los indios del nuevo mundo.*

From then on, Phoenician visitors and colonists became a standard part of the fringe scholarship of ancient American history. In 1781 French scholar Antoine Court de Gébelin theorized that Phoenicians were in cordial contact with Native Americans before 2000 B.C., a chronological impossibility in light of the accurate datings of modern archaeology. Other Phoenician theories followed in the nineteenth century, including Sir George Jones's *An Original History of Aboriginal America* (1843) and John B. Newman's *Origin of the Red Man* (1852).

In 1872 the most enigmatic of the supposed Phoenician artifacts came to light—the Paraíba Stone. A man named Joaquim Alves da Costa claimed to have found, "near the Paraíba" River in **Brazil**, a broken stone that had an inscription in a strange alphabet carved on it. After transcribing the inscription, Costa sent the copy to Rio de Janeiro for study. Brazil had no experts in ancient Semitic languages. But the conscientious naturalist Ladislau Netto took up the assignment, learned **Hebrew**, ultimately determined that the writing on the stone was Phoenician, and then translated it. His translation described how ten ships with Phoenicians from Sidon sailed from Ezion-Geber and around Africa in 534 B.C. Storms blew some of them west to the coast of Brazil, where they carved the inscription. Immediately French scholar Ernest Renan attacked the Paraíba inscription as a fake, and others soon joined him. By 1885 the hapless Netto felt compelled to publish a retraction of his original conclusions and

even suggested five possible suspects for composing the hoax. Despite this setback and the fact that Costa disappeared with the stone, some people continued to believe in its authenticity. No accredited scholar ever saw the stones firsthand. Even the original location of the find was in great doubt since Brazil had two different Paraíba regions. Still, the story of the Paraíba Stone continued to attract believers.

During the 1960s **Cyrus Gordon**, a professor of Semitic languages and ardent **diffusionist,** revived the Paraíba Stone's claims to authenticity. Basically Gordon asserted that the Paraíba inscription contained Phoenician grammatical constructions unknown in 1872. These same constructions were originally used to argue against the stone's authenticity. Subsequent research during the twentieth century, Gordon said, revealed that grammatical usages in the Paraíba inscription were genuine. Other equally qualified specialists in Semitic languages disagree with his conclusions and continue to declare the Paraíba Stone a hoax. That judgment is the opinion of archaeologists and prehistorians in general.

Most theories of Phoenician visits to the Americas had them crossing the Atlantic Ocean to get there, but not all. In 1892 Thomas Crawford Johnston joined the supporters of a Phoenician presence in the Americas. But he gave the theory a new aspect in 1913 with his book *Did the Phoenicians Discover America?* He claimed that the Phoenicians of King Hiram I sailed down the Red Sea, over the Indian Ocean, and across the Pacific Ocean to reach the Americas.

The Phoenician theory continued to attract many supporters during the twentieth century in addition to Cyrus Gordon. One was Joseph Corey Ayoob, who in 1951 privately published *Were the Phoenicians the First To Discover America?* That work reappeared in a second edition in 1964 and was followed by another study of the Paraíba Stone in 1971. Reaching a much wider audience was popular writer Charles M. Boland. In his book *They All Discovered America* (1961), he included a chapter that showed Phoenician visitors had come to America before 480 B.C. and in 480 B.C., 310 B.C., and 146 B.C. The problem is that he was actually talking about the closely related but distinct Carthaginians. Frederick J. Pohl, in his *Atlantic Crossings before Columbus* (1961), also conflates the Phoenicians with the Carthaginians. In contrast, Constance Irwin's *Fair Gods and Stone Faces* (1963) carefully distinguishes between Phoenician and Carthaginian voyagers to the Americas. Her theory is that Phoenician traders, accompanied by Negro slaves, reached Mexico about 800 B.C. and helped to stimulate the rise of the Olmec civilization. These same visitors also supplied the initial inspiration for the persistent **white god legends** found among the many Native American groups. Unfortunately, while 800 B.C. was the earliest date for artifacts from Olmec archaeological sites examined in 1963, subsequent research pushed back the beginning of Olmec civilization to 1500 B.C., well before any possibility of Phoenician influence. Irwin also suggests that refugees from Tyre, who fled during the siege by Nebuchadnezzar of Babylon from 587–574 B.C., came to the Americas and further stimulated the native civilizations of Mesoamerica. Cyrus Gordon's *Before Columbus: Links between the Old World and Ancient America* (1971) reached the same basic conclusions as Irwin and supplied further archaeological and linguistic evidence of Phoenician visits. A few years later, James Bailey in *The God-Kings and the Titans* (1973) followed Irwin in asserting the existence of Phoenician colonies in pre-Columbian America. **Barry Fell** also believes that Phoenicians visited the Americas and supplies supposed linguistic and archaeological evidences for their presence in his best-selling *America B.C.* (1976). Unfortunately, in Fell's case, the specifics of the arrival dates and the routes followed by these alleged Phoenician settlers and traders are much vaguer than in the theories of Irwin and Bailey. Still, all these writings show that the theory of Phoenician visits and colonies in the pre-Columbian Americas is very much alive and well.

The Phoenicians and Carthaginians were probably the greatest sailors of the Mediterranean. Their ships were capable of oceanic travel, and archaeological evidence has been discovered that indicates they reached the Azores, Madeira, and Cape Verde Islands. Knowledge of those places had been lost to the Mediterranean world as early as the time of the Roman empire and was not regained until the fifteenth-century explorations by the Portuguese. Just how much the Phoenicians really knew about geography and navigation will never be known for sure. Their jealously guarded secrets have been lost forever in the ravages of war and time. Technically it is possible that the Phoenicians reached the Americas, but no archaeological evidence has yet been discovered to prove the contentions of Irwin, Gordon, Bailey, and Fell. Since even the fleeting Norse presence in **Vinland** left definite archaeological remains at **L'Anse aux Meadows**, it seems logical that the Phoenicians would have left similar evidence of their presence. The absence of such remains is strong evidence that the Phoenicians never reached the Americas.

Bibliography: Cross, Frank M., "The Phoenician Inscription from Brazil: A Nineteenth Century Forgery," *Orientalia* 37 (1968): 437–460; Davies, Nigel, *Voyagers to the New World*, 1979; Doran, Michael F., "Phoenician Contact with America?" *Anthropological Journal of Canada* 12 (1974): 16–24; Moscati, S., *The World of the Phoenicians*, 1968.

Pining and Pothorst, Voyage of (ca. 1472 or 1476)

This supposed joint Portuguese-Danish expedition sailed the old medieval Norse route to North America in search of a northwest passage to China. Instead, they ended up visiting Labrador and Newfoundland. Other members of the expedition included **João Vaz Côrte-Real** and the mysterious **Johannes Scolvus** as pilot.

Medieval Europeans believed there was a northwest passage in the Arctic that would allow a ship to sail from Scandinavia to China and back. Claudius Clavus, the early–fifteenth-century Danish cartographer, accepted its existence and stated that the legendary fourteenth-century traveler Sir John Mandeville used it on his return trip from the Far East. Given this context, some twentieth-century historians speculate that Prince Henry the Navigator of Portugal (d. 1460) would also have been interested in exploiting this northwest passage, based on the assumption that Prince Henry's African explorations were primarily directed toward finding a sea route to India. Therefore, the Portuguese prince would have been just as interested in a northern route as a southern if the former showed a greater chance for success. But in fact, the best scholarship on Portuguese overseas expansion in the fifteenth century saw Prince Henry's primary motives as being directed toward controlling the sub-Saharan trade in gold and slaves, spreading Christianity, and defeating Islam in North Africa. Finding a sea route to India did not figure in his plans. This has not stopped some writers from postulating a cooperative venture between Portugal and Denmark in the early 1470s to locate a northwest passage.

According to this theory, Prince Henry initiated Portuguese-Danish cooperation by allowing a Danish nobleman called Vallarte (probably Wollart) to accompany a Portuguese voyage to Cape Verde in 1448.

Unfortunately, the Dane and several others fell into the hands of hostile natives and were never seen again. But Vallarte's misfortune did not end future joint ventures. After a gap of some 20 years, cooperation resumed in the early 1470s. The Portuguese crossed the Bight of Biafra in 1472, which is where the African coastline begins to curve sharply southward. As a result, previous hopes for quickly rounding Africa and reaching India were temporarily dashed. This setback may have caused Portugal's attention to shift northward to the quest for a northwest passage.

The history of Portuguese explorations in the western and northern Atlantic is confused by the widespread belief that numerous secret voyages took place during the fifteenth century (see also **Portuguese Policy of Secrecy**). Many places on the eastern coast of the Americas supposedly experienced visits by the Portuguese some years before the arrival of Christopher Columbus. Except in Portugal, most professional historians deny that Portugal conducted such secret explorations or was capable of keeping them secret for long. Despite these arguments, some popular writers continue to believe in and write about these secret voyages.

The most significant voyage was that of the Danes Didrik Pining and Hans Pothorst, who were accompanied by João Vaz Côrte-Real and Johannes Scolvus. Christian I of Denmark (ruled 1448–1481) organized the voyage, supposedly at Portugal's request. Just who commanded the expedition is unclear. Danish writers claim that Pining and Pothorst were the leaders. In contrast, Portuguese writers place Côrte-Real in command. Pining and Pothorst were seamen who made a living as freebooters, sometimes serving the king of Denmark and sometimes committing depredations for their own personal profit upon anyone with the bad luck to cross their path. Little is known about the complete careers of these two seamen. Initially the two started out lawfully employed as Danish naval commanders. Pining is sometimes described as a Norwegian nobleman and at other times as a German in the service of Denmark. For a period of time he served the Danish king as governor of part of **Iceland**. Pothorst was Danish, with a desire for respectability sufficient that he had his picture painted on a wall of the Maria Church in Elsinore, Denmark. By the 1490s, however, the two men turned to piracy, pure and simple, and all the northern kingdoms outlawed the pair. In 1494 they set up a base on an unidentified island named Hvítsark and constructed a carved stone navigator's compass on it. Eventually their wicked deeds caught up with them. According to one account, the authorities captured and hanged them. Other versions claim that the pair met their end by drowning or were murdered by other pirates.

Well before they met their bad end, Pining and Pothorst, at the command of Christian I and at the request of Afonso V of Portugal, led an expedition in search of unknown northern islands and continents. Nothing certain is known about this voyage. It took place in 1472 (assuming that it took place at all), despite other conflicting dates. Their fleet definitely reached **Greenland** since one of its objectives was apparently to punish the **Eskimos** for engaging in piratical activities. The fleet pushed on to Labrador and Newfoundland and observed the wonderful fishing off the Grand Banks. But Pining, Pothorst, and their companion Côrte-Real failed to locate the elusive Northwest Passage. Supporters of the occurrence of this voyage cite its failure as the reason for Portugal's renewed interest in exploring the African coast for a sea route to India. That effort was rewarded in a few years by Bartolomeu Dias's discovery of the Cape of Good Hope in 1487–1488.

All evidence for the existence of the Pining-Pothorst voyage is circumstantial and after the fact. Its advocates, however, avoid this difficulty simply by blaming the Portuguese policy of secrecy for the lack of direct evidence. In fact, the combined story of Pining, Pothorst, Côrte-Real, and Scolvus had no independent existence until Danish scholar and librarian Sofus Larsen put it all together in 1924. Nationalistic pride was quickly aroused in Denmark, Poland, and Portugal, which have provided enthusiastic supporters ever since. But even its supporters are not in agreement over some significant details. Certainly the date of the voyage is under dispute since some sources give it as 1476 rather than 1472. Other sources suggest that João Vaz Côrte-Real made a separate voyage from that of Pining and Pothorst. Some writers claim that Hans Pothorst and Johannes Scolvus were the same person. Professional historians simply reject the whole story as an imaginative reconstruction with no basis in actual events.

Bibliography: Cameron, Ian, *Lodestone and Evening Star: The Epic Voyages of Discovery,* 1966; Larsen, Sofus, *The Discovery of America Twenty Years before Columbus,* 1924; Morison, Samuel Eliot, *The European Discovery of America: The Northern Voyages,* 1971.

Piri Re'is Map
(1513)

This Ottoman Turkish world map provided a fairly accurate depiction of the Americas. It was based partially on information acquired from one of Christopher Columbus's sailors. Because of the map's delineation of an ice-free Antarctic coastline, it has been variously claimed that it derived from maps and charts from a lost higher civilization that existed during the last ice age or from satellite photographs made by extraterrestrial visitors.

In 1501, the admiral Kemal Re'is led the Ottoman Turkish fleet to war against Venice. During that campaign he captured a Spanish ship; its crew included a sailor who had participated in Columbus's first three voyages to the Americas. The sailor had charts of the lands Columbus discovered. Eventually those charts came into the hands of Piri Re'is (1470–1554), a nephew of Kemal. Piri also rose to be an admiral, and he gained a reputation as a cartographer and geographer. In 1513 Piri used the captured charts in his compilation of a world map. Unfortunately, he led an expedition in 1552 that failed to dislodge the Portuguese from their stranglehold on Hormuz in the Persian Gulf. When he returned to his base in Egypt, the disgruntled Ottoman Sultan Suleiman I had him beheaded. His papers and maps were placed in the collections of the Topkapi Palace, where they remained forgotten until 1929.

In the aftermath of World War I, Turkey rebuilt itself under the charismatic leadership of Mustafa Kemal the Ataturk. As part of the process, the government converted the Topkapi Palace into a national museum. As scholars sifted through the contents of the palace they discovered the Piri Re'is map. The map attracted much attention because it contained a lengthy note in Turkish by Piri Re'is that described Columbus's voyages; it also claimed that he used charts of the West Indies that had been personally composed by Columbus. A search of the Turkish archives failed to locate those charts. Still, the historical significance of the map's Columbus connection is very important because it provides a good indication of what the great explorer thought was the true geography of the western Atlantic. Some historians dispute Piri Re'is's claims about the Columbus charts and argue that he received only verbal information from his Spanish prisoner.

It is very important to remember that the Piri Re'is map is only the surviving part of a larger world map, and that it depicts only the mid- and southern Atlantic Ocean and its adjacent coastlines. Besides the Columbus material, Piri Re'is claimed to have used 20 other maps for his sources. Some of those maps dated back to the time of Alexander the Great and some used mathematical projections. In 1956 Arlington H. Mallery, an author who believed in the occurrence of various pre-Columbian contacts between the Americas and Europe, pointed out that the Piri Re'is map accurately depicted sections of the Antarctic coastline long concealed by ice. That created the problem of explaining how Piri Re'is could have known that information. Mallery suggested that such knowledge represents the intellectual remnants of some long-disappeared civilization of seafarers that thrived during the last ice age. In 1966 Charles H. Hapgood constructed a detailed argument for just such a lost civilization (see also **Sea Kings, Ancient**). Even this rather sensational theory did not retain its primacy for long. When Eric Van Daniken published his first ancient-astronaut book *Chariots of the Gods* in 1970, he claimed that the Piri Re'is map was based on information derived from photographs of the earth taken from outer space! The question had become, was it ancient sea kings or ancient astronauts who reached the Americas before Columbus? Of course, neither theory is backed by anything more than speculation over the contents and sources of the Piri Re'is map. Hapgood at least made detailed geographical and mathematical analyses of the map to support his arguments. Still, there is a definite lack of corroborating evidence to support Hapgood, let alone Van Daniken. Under such circumstances, the mainstream interpretation of the Piri Re'is map as the earliest map directly attributable to information provided by Columbus must stand.

Bibliography: Akcura, Yusuf, *Piri Re'is' Map*, 1935; Hapgood, Charles H., *Maps of the Ancient Sea Kings: Evidence of Advanced Civilization in the Ice Age*, [1966], rev. ed., 1979; Nebenzahl, Kenneth, *Rand McNally Atlas of Columbus and the Great Discoveries*, 1990.

Pizzigano, Map of Zuane (1424)

This map was the first to use the name **Antillia** and identify it with a large island in the western Atlantic. This depiction is thought by some scholars to be evidence that the Portuguese visited the Americas before 1424. (See also **Portuguese Policy of Secrecy**.)

Historians of cartography did not know of the existence of Zuane Pizzigano's map until 1946 when it came into the possession of London bookseller William R. Robinson. It had been part of a massive collection of books and manuscripts acquired by the antiquary Sir Thomas Phillipps (1792–1872), but how and where Phillipps acquired the map is not known. Scholars agree, however, that the map is genuine and that it was made in 1424 by a Venetian. Whether the cartographer was Zuane Pizzigano (apparently a descendant of fourteenth-century Venetian cartographers Francesco and Marco Pizzigano) is not certain since the original cartographer's signature was erased and rewritten.

The Pizzigano map is a portalan sea chart such as sailors used for navigation because they were more accurate than ordinary schematic maps. Besides depicting the coast of Europe and North Africa, the map includes four islands in the western Atlantic Ocean: Antillia, Satanazes, Saya, and Ymana. Armando Cortesão, a twentieth-century Portuguese historian of geography, claims that the names of the islands are Portuguese, but his etymological evidence could be applied equally well to any Romance language. Antillia is drawn larger than Portugal and is also identified as the island of the **Seven Cities**. In his *Historia de las Indias*, **Bartolomé de Las Casas** stated that Portuguese sailors were accidentally driven to the island of the Seven Cities by a storm during the time of Prince Henry the Navigator. They returned to Portugal, but refused to go back to the island despite the prince's order. This tale was apparently well circulated because sixteenth-century Portuguese historian Antonio Galvão told virtually the same story in his *Discoveries of the World* and dated it to 1447. However, that would place the supposed discovery too late to influence Pizzigano's map. The twentieth-century Portuguese geographer Armando Cortesão is not bothered by that; he claims there were several Portuguese voyages to the Americas during the fifteenth century. In fact, he believes there were many earlier voyages going all the way back to the **Phoenicians**. Cortesão does not claim to know which Portuguese were the first to reach the Americas or where they landed. In his opinion, the landing could have been anywhere from Trinidad to **Greenland**. As evidence, he points to ancient knowledge of the Sargasso Sea, which is located far to the west of the Azores Islands and is even depicted on **Andrea Biancho's map** of 1436. Armando Cortesão's ideas nicely complement those of his brother Jaime Cortesão and other supporters of the thesis of a Portuguese Policy of Secrecy.

Most historians of geography and exploration, such as Samuel Eliot Morison and Bailey W. Diffie, reject the idea that the Antillia on Pizzigano's map is part of the Americas. Late-medieval cartographers commonly placed rumored or legendary places on their maps. Doubters of Portuguese pre-Columbian visits to the Americas contend that Antillia and its Seven Cities are merely a legend that made its way onto a map. As they point out, there is no incontrovertible evidence that the Portuguese reached America numerous times before Christopher Columbus, undermining completely any claims for a Portuguese prediscovery of the Americas, including those based on the Zuane Pizzigano map of 1424.

Bibliography: Cortesão, Armando, *The Nautical Chart of 1424 and the Early Discovery and Cartographical Representation of America*, 1954; Diffie, Bailey W., and George D. Winius, *Foundations of the Portuguese Empire, 1415–1580*, 1977; Nebenzahl, Kenneth, *Rand McNally Atlas of Columbus and the Great Discoveries*, 1990.

Plato
(ca. 429–347 B.C.)

A famous Greek philosopher from Athens, he created the story of the lost continent of **Atlantis.**

Plato introduced the story of Atlantis in his dialogue *Timaeus* (or *Timaios*). It was one of his last dialogues and was directed toward demonstrating the pervading rationality of the world. In the course of making this point, Plato tells how his narrator Timaeus's distant ancestor **Solon** traveled to Egypt and visited the priests of Säis. Solon learned of the former existence of a great island located beyond the Strait of Gibraltar. This island, Atlantis, was larger than Libya and Asia and around 9500 B.C. was the home of a powerful empire. Its inhabitants invaded the Mediterranean basin and were locked in a war with Athens. In one horrible day and night, powerful earthquakes and torrential rains sank Atlantis beneath the sea, leaving a vast area of unnavigable mud.

The story of Atlantis continued in Plato's next dialogue, *Critias* (or *Kritias*), which he never completed. *Critias* provided a more detailed description of Atlantis and the Atlanteans, who Plato stated were descended from the sea god Poseidon (Neptune) and his son Atlas (not the Atlas who was condemned to hold up the earth). Atlan-

tis was a rich land with fine irrigated farmlands and vast, beautiful cities. Its inhabitants lived lives of justice and self-control befitting their divine ancestry, but as their divinity became diluted by breeding with mere humans, the Atlanteans became base and selfish. When Zeus, the king of the gods, observed the extent of this change, he decided to punish them—hence their destruction by earthquake and flood.

Plato was the first person to mention the existence of Atlantis. His dialogues form the ultimate source for all the subsequent and voluminous literature on Atlantis, although some authors claim to have psychic sources and contacts that supposedly predate Plato. Most serious scholars think Plato simply made up Atlantis as a fictional land designed to prove some of his points about the nature of humanity and the world. It is possible that Plato intended Atlantis to serve as an example of how the ideas presented in his greatest dialogue, *The Republic,* would have worked in an actual human society. Basically Plato's Atlantis is a fictional creation in the same manner that societies in futuristic science fiction novels are fictional. The descriptions of Atlantis found in *Timaeus* and *Critias* do not describe an actual place or literal events in the manner of historical documents. Certain events, such as the destruction of the Greek island of Thera in a huge volcanic explosion about 1500 B.C., may have inspired Plato's imagination.

Many people, however, believe that Plato's Atlantis did exist. Several religions and a number of archaeological theories are or have been based on its existence. Spanish historian **Francisco López de Gómara** in 1553 was the first of many to suggest Atlantis as a source for the Native American population. The Maya in particular were singled out as descendants of Atlantean colonists since Atlantis was supposedly the mother of all civilizations, especially the Mayan and **Egyptian.** While no serious twentieth-century scholar accepts such theories, they had tremendous impact in the past and continue to be an important component of pop and fringe archaeology.

Bibliography: de Camp, L. Sprague, *Lost Continents*, [1954], 1970; Pellegrino, Charles, *Unearthing Atlantis: An Archaeological Odyssey*, 1991.

Polynesian-American Contacts

Anthropologists and archaeologists generally agree that contacts occurred between Polynesia and the Americas during the pre-Columbian era. What they disagree about is how much contact occurred. Was it a two-way contact? Or, if it was one-way, which direction? Were Polynesians the descendants of American Indians or were some American Indians descended from the Polynesians?

Polynesia is a triangular region in the Pacific Ocean with New Zealand, the Hawaiian Islands, and **Easter Island** located at its three corners. The inhabitants are well known as a handsome people with dark, straight hair and much lighter skin than the Negrito peoples of Micronesia and Melanesia. All Polynesians speak a common language, although there are several local dialects that differ significantly from one another. Before European contact, their culture was technologically in the Stone Age. Most scholars, with the notable exception of **Thor Heyerdahl,** currently believe that the original Polynesians came from Southeast Asia and settled far earlier than had once been thought. Originally, scholars thought that the great settlement of Polynesia began about 500 and was completed about 1100. More recent archaeological study reveals that Polynesian Tonga was settled by 1140 B.C. and Samoa by 800 B.C. The geographical expansion of the Polynesians halted until A.D. 300, when they settled the Marquesa Islands and quickly moved on to Tahiti and the Society Islands. Occupation of Easter Island took place sometime between 300 and 500, the Hawaiian Islands by 600, and New Zealand by 1000.

Europeans began sailing the vast Pacific Ocean in the sixteenth century, but did not finish systematically exploring it until the

An oceangoing, Polynesian double canoe.

eighteenth-century voyages of Captain James Cook. These explorers found the Polynesians to be exotic, mysterious, and attractive, and they wondered about their origins. English missionary William Ellis worked in Polynesia from 1817–1825 and published a large study of his flock's culture, social institutions, history, and mythology in 1829. Basically he espoused **Hebrew** origins, but also noted their many cultural similarities with the indigenous peoples of Mexico and Peru. John Dunsmore Lang published a book on Polynesian origins in 1834, but not until its second edition of 1877 did he add the suggestion that the Polynesians also settled in the Americas. During the early decades of the twentieth century, English hyperdiffusionist Grafton Elliot Smith advocated the theory that **Egyptian** influence spread from Southeast Asia to Oceania, and from there to South America (see also **Diffusionism**). In 1947, American amateur archaeologist **Harold S. Gladwin** theorized in his book *Men out of Asia* that the **lost fleet of Alexander the Great** sailed east in 323 B.C. and eventually reached and civilized Central and South America. Along the way, members of the fleet populated Polynesia. Therefore, the Polynesians were descendants of this mixed company of Greeks, Persians, **Phoenicians,** and Egyptians. There is reason to believe that Gladwin concocted this theory as a joke. Meanwhile academic anthropologists such as Fritz Graebner and Erland Nordenskiöld cataloged many shared traits between Oceanian and South American cultures.

The basic assumption of all these theories, both the scholarly and the fantastic, is that the movement of people in the Pacific was predominantly from west to east. Thor Heyerdahl noted the same similarities, but he suggested the radical idea that contact took place from east to west and was largely one way. He quite rightly pointed out that sailing from west to east—from Polynesia to South America—is quite difficult because of the opposition from prevailing ocean currents and winds. Conversely, sailing from South America to Polynesia, an east-to-west journey, is relatively easy. The presence of the **sweet potato** in Polynesia provided another strong evidence for east-west contact from America. The sweet potato was definitely native to the Americas, but it was cultivated throughout Polynesia long before European contact in the sixteenth century. Furthermore, Heyerdahl cites linguistic similarities. The Peruvian or Quechua word for sweet potato is *cumar*. Among the Maoris of New Zealand it is *kumara*, for the Tahitians it is *umara*, and the Samoans call it *unala*. The Incas also told the Spanish conquistadors stories of islands to the west of Peru. Based on this evidence and other linguistic and cultural similarities, Heyerdahl suggested that Polynesia was populated by people from the Americas. He claims to have discovered broad similarities between Quechua, the language of the Incas, and Polynesian. One migration came from South America and coincides with the legendary westward flight of the sun god/king Kon Tiki, or **Viracocha**. Another migration originated among the Native Americans of the Pacific Northwest. These two groups merged to form the Polynesians. To help prove his theory, Heyerdahl successfully sailed the primitive balsa raft *Kon Tiki* from South America to Polynesia in 1947. Heyerdahl is not alone in supporting Native Americans as ancestors of the Polynesians. Mormons believe the same theory, although they ultimately base their thinking on theological evidence—the story of **Hagoth** in *The Book of Mormon.* More recent linguistic and archaeological evidence undermines Heyerdahl's thesis and reaffirms the traditional view that Polynesians originated in Southeast Asia.

Most anthropologists accept that sporadic contacts occurred between Polynesia and South America and that they went in both directions. The sweet potato had to reach Polynesia from America by human means because it could not have floated all that way in seawater. However it came, it arrived in the distant past because the Old World weevils in Polynesia have long been adapted to it. Polynesians were fantastically skillful sailors. Despite adverse winds and currents, they were fully capable of reaching the Americas. Accidental and purposeful voyages probably took place, although they normally would not have received a friendly welcome from Native Americans. These Polynesian visits would have provided very limited opportunities for cultural diffusion. Still, current anthropological thinking is that some of these Polynesian visitors to the Americas were able to return home, which is probably how the sweet potato reached Polynesia. In sum, pre-Columbian contacts between Polynesia and the Americas seem to have taken place but were rare and fairly insignificant in their cultural consequences.

Bibliography: Davies, Nigel, *Voyagers to the New World*, 1979; Heyerdahl, Thor, *American Indians in the Pacific*, 1952; Rivet, Paul, "Early Contacts between Polynesia and America," *Diogenes* 16 (1956): 78–92; Shutler, Richard, Jr., and Mary Elizabeth Shutler, *Oceanic Prehistory*, 1975.

Portuguese Policy of Secrecy

Also known as the Policy of Silence, in Portugal it is called *a política de sigilo* or *a política de mistério*. The name refers to a controversial historical thesis formulated in the first quarter of the twentieth century by various historians, primarily Portuguese, stating that Portugal made many voyages and discoveries in the Atlantic Ocean, including the discovery of the Americas sometime before 1492, but chose to keep those discoveries secret.

Before the nineteenth century, the historical record is frequently full of gaps and breaks. This condition certainly applies to the surviving records from the Age of Discovery. None of the original logs of Christopher Columbus's four voyages survives, although a partial transcript for the first voyage exists. John Cabot's voyages to North America in 1497 and Bartolomeu Dias's 1487 discovery of the Cape of Good Hope are practically without any contemporary documentation. Such losses of primary sources are tragic but all too common, and usually occur quite innocently as the result of accident or neglect. Some historians, however, question whether the gaps in Portuguese records are all that random. They suggest that some design or policy may lie behind the disappearance of some documents.

The thesis of a deliberate and systematic Portuguese government policy of secrecy concerning overseas exploration is a product of twentieth-century historians. Jaime Cortesão, a Portuguese historian, first formulated the thesis in 1924. He contended that surviving Portuguese chronicles about overseas explorations show definite signs of truncation and censorship, particularly Gomes Azurara's *Chronicle of Guinea*. Sixteenth-century Portuguese historian João de Barros's complaints about gaps and losses in the records are cited as further evidence of a policy of secrecy. Cortesão blames the censoring of the chronicles on a specific culprit—Ruy de Pina, secretary of King João II. Quite a lot of information was suppressed if one is inclined to believe Cortesão. When he first formulated his thesis, Cortesão claimed that Portugal discovered America prior to 1448 (see also **Biancho, Map of Andrea**). Later he added the contention that the discovery of an all-water route to India predated Vasco da Gama's famous voyage of 1497. Furthermore, he claimed that the fifteenth-century Portuguese secretly pioneered various developments in naval technology, such as the technique for calculating longitude while at sea, that were publicly credited to other nations at later dates. Such Portuguese explorers as **Diogo de Teive, Fernão Teles,** and **João Vaz Côrte-Real** all reached America before Columbus, and even they were not the first.

Jaime Cortesão was not alone in his support for the existence of a policy of secrecy. Of course, his brother Armando Cortesão, a prominent historian of cartography, supported it. But so did many other respected Portuguese historians such as Gago Coutinho. The thesis of a policy of secrecy attracted adherents among English-speaking historians such as Edgar Prestage and G. H. T. Kimble during the 1930s. In Portugal the thesis is a historical orthodoxy and a pillar of national pride. School textbooks at all levels teach it as fact. Lisbon's city government decorated its Avenida de Liberdade with a mosaic inscription that reads "Descoberta da America 1472 João Vaz Côrte-Real Descobridor da America."

Outside Portugal, historians generally reject Cortesão's thesis and its various claims of monumental but previously uncredited Portuguese achievements during the fifteenth century. G. A. Crone, a British historian of geography, rebutted Jaime Cortesão in 1937. Further devastating attacks on the policy of secrecy followed from prominent American historian Samuel Eliot Morison in 1940 and Brazilian T. O. Marcondes de Souza in 1944. Dissent exists even in the Portuguese historical community; respected historian Duarte Liete attacked Cortesão's theory as early as 1936. Despite all the controversy, the thesis of a Portuguese policy of secrecy still has enthusiastic supporters, and attracts equally determined opponents.

The basic complaint of skeptical historians concerning the policy of secrecy is the almost complete absence of solid evidence. Historians admit that monarchs and countries throughout history have attempted to protect their overseas commerce by maintaining secrecy about the how and where of

their sources. But ultimately these efforts failed. Supporters reply that the very lack of evidence is itself evidence of an extremely effective policy of secrecy. Their opponents, particularly Samuel Eliot Morison, find such an argument both circular and ridiculous. In his opinion, the only solid piece of evidence in favor of the policy of secrecy is the fact that in 1504 King Manuel forbade the making of maps and globes showing details of African geography below the Rio Manicongo. Morison also admits that João II had a secretive nature, but he feels that ultimately Cortesão's thesis requires the Portuguese to maintain their secrets for the sake of secrecy alone and often against their own best interests. He rightly argues that the Portuguese government's pursuit of a policy of secrecy needs to make sense and be of benefit to the national interest. If Portugal already knew about the Americas before 1492, why did João II relinquish virtually all that new land to Spain in the Treaty of Tordesillas? Another argument repeatedly brought to bear against the existence of such a policy is the well-documented and sustained participation in Portugal's overseas explorations of a substantial number of foreigners, of whom Alvise Cadamosto of Venice, **Ferdinand Van Olmen** of Flanders, **Martin Behaim** of Germany, and Christopher Columbus of Genoa are the best known. Historians identify the Pedro de Velasco of Spain who sailed with Diogo de Teive in 1452 as **Pedro Vasques de la Frontera** of Palos, who provided Columbus with so much moral support for his plan to sail west to Asia. Advocates of the secrecy policy claim that Portuguese ships quite thoroughly scouted out the American coast from Brazil to Newfoundland prior to 1492, but with so many foreigners involved, it would have been impossible to keep secret such important discoveries.

Details of Portugal's jealously guarded African trade leaked out with amazing rapidity.

Furthermore, little attempt was made to keep secret Bartolomeu Dias's discovery of the Cape of Good Hope in 1487, Vasco da Gama's voyage to India in 1497, and Gaspar Côrte-Real's voyage to Newfoundland in 1500. Why did the Portuguese let these important discoveries become public knowledge if they had such an effective policy of secrecy?

Outside Portugal, the thesis of the policy of secrecy and its accompanying suppression of information about various discoveries, most notably a pre-Columbian discovery of America, finds little support among historians. The evidence for its existence is too tenuous; the evidence against, too convincing. The thesis remains simply another fringe theory about pre-Columbian contact with the Americas, albeit with better scholarly support than most such. But it should also be remembered that much of that support derives from nationalistic wishful thinking on the part of many Portuguese historians.

Bibliography: Cortesão, Jaime, "The Pre-Columbian Discovery of America," *Geographical Journal* 89 (1937): 29–42; Crone, Gerald R., "The Alleged Pre-Columbian Discovery of America," *Geographical Journal* 89 (1937): 455–460; de Figueredo, Fidelino, "The Geographical Discoveries and Conquests of the Portuguese," *Hispanic American Historical Review* 6 (nos. 1–3, 1926): 47–70; Diffie, Bailey W., "Foreigners in Portugal and the 'Policy of Secrecy,'" *Terrae Incognitae* 1 (1969): 23–34; Morison, Samuel Eliot, *Portuguese Voyages to America in the Fifteenth Century,* 1940.

Powel, David
(1552–1598)

Sometimes spelled Powell, this Welsh historian and clergyman wrote *The Historie of Cambria* (1584), which incorporated **Humphrey Llwyd's** 1559 manuscript history of Wales including the story of **Prince Madoc's** discovery and colonization of unknown western lands in 1170 and 1171.

Born near Llangollen in Wales, Powel received a B.A. in 1573 from Oxford University and a B.D. and D.D. in 1583. During those years he served in various parishes and became the chaplain of Sir Henry Sidney, lord president of the Council in the Marches of Wales. In 1583 Sidney asked Powel to prepare for publication the manuscript of the deceased Humphrey Llwyd's English translation of Carado of Llancarfan's chronicle. In 1584 Powel published Llwyd's translation and historical notes under the title *The Historie of Cambria* and included extensive additions of his own, clearly distinguished by the use of a distinctive typeface. Powel's *Historie of Cambria* quickly became a major source for students of Madoc's voyages.

Bibliography: "Powel, David," in *Dictionary of National Biography*, 22 vols., 1908–1909; Williams, Gwyn A., *Madoc: The Making of a Myth*, 1979.

Preadamites

Some people postulated a separate race of humans who existed before the creation of Adam. They were sometimes known as Coadamites if they coexisted with Adam. Some early modern scholars used the theory of Preadamite humans to explain how the Americas became so densely populated in the relatively short period of time after Noah's flood.

Christopher Columbus's discovery of the Americas in 1492 created a dilemma that slowly dawned on the European worldview. How could the habitation of this unknown and apparently separate world with not only people but all sorts of plants and animals be reconciled with the universal destruction inflicted by Noah's flood? Some people responded by suggesting that **multiple crea-**

tions or polygenesis had occurred and that Noah's flood had not covered the entire earth. Therefore Native Americans were simply the descendants of Preadamites from a separate creation.

Swiss alchemist Philippus Aureolus Theophrastus, better known as Paracelsus (1493–1541), suggested the possibility of a second Adam for the New World. Orthodox Christians ignored the idea as unscriptural and heretical. Despite continued strong opposition, more detailed versions of the Preadamite theories reappeared in the middle of the seventeenth century. The reviver of the Preadamite theory was Isaac de La Peyrère (1594–1676), a French Huguenot. La Peyrère had written a study about Preadamites as early as 1643, but it was not until 1655 that he published two works on the subject: *Praeadamitae* (an English translation, *Men before Adam,* appeared in 1656) and *Systema theologicum ex prae-Adamitarum hypothesi* (an English translation, *A Theological System upon That Presupposition That Men Were before Adam,* appeared in 1655). Both works proved popular but controversial. The Parlement of Paris ordered the books burned, and La Peyrère was arrested at Antwerp and taken to Rome. After an audience with Pope Alexander VII, La Peyrère converted to Catholicism and published a retraction of his works in 1657. The retraction, however, does not appear to have been sincere.

La Peyrère argued for the existence of Preadamites on the basis of seeming contradictions and ambiguities in the Bible. He suggested that God made the Preadamites on the sixth day of Creation and then made Adam after the seventh day of Creation. In support of his theory, he pointed out that Adam, Eve, Cain, and Abel apparently had other humans for neighbors. According to La Peyrère, those neighbors were the Preadamites, not some unnamed children of Adam and his family. Finally La Peyrère limited Noah's flood to the descendants of Adam in Palestine. Therefore the Preadamites, including those in the Americas, escaped the deluge.

La Peyrère's ideas were widely known across Europe during the late seventeenth and early eighteenth centuries. They contributed to the development of the deistic ideology that was systematically critical of traditional Christianity. The belief in Preadamites provided an alternative for those who found it unbelievable that people, plants, and animals spread throughout the earth in the relatively short amount of time between Noah's flood and Columbus's voyage.

Bibliography: Huddleston, Lee Eldridge, *Origins of the American Indians: European Concepts,* 1492–1729, 1967; Maas, A. J., "Preadamites," in *The Catholic Encyclopedia,* 1913; McKee, David R., "Isaac de La Peyrère, a Precursor of Eighteenth-Century Critical Deists," *Publications of the Modern Language Association* 59 (June 1944): 456–485.

Quetzalcoatl

This Toltec and Aztec god/culture hero's name is variously translated as plumed serpent, feather serpent, precious serpent, or precious twin. He is commonly associated with the supposed **white god legends** of the Americas, which claim that various Old World peoples visited, bringing important civilizing knowledge with them.

Quetzalcoatl is a confusing god because the same name refers to two different personages, and those two personages are frequently combined into one composite person in some accounts. The first is the god Quetzalcoatl, one of four brother gods of creation along with Red Tezcatlipoca, Black Tezcatlipoca, and Huitzilopochtli. Next came Quetzalcoatl the culture hero, who was actually named Topiltzin Quetzalcoatl.

He was a priest-king of Tollan or Tula, the great city of the Toltecs of Mexico. Priests of the god Quetzalcoatl frequently combined his name with their own, and that appears to be what Topiltzin did. Topiltzin was a charismatic religious leader who opposed the common Mexican religious ceremony of human sacrifice. Although some scholars of the Toltec era consider Topiltzin a mythological figure, most feel he was a historical figure who lived toward the end of the Toltec empire (900–1100). Later Aztec legends frequently and confusingly seem to merge the culture hero Topiltzin/Quetzalcoatl with the old god Quetzalcoatl.

Topiltzin/Quetzalcoatl is the personage who was allegedly a white god. In its most developed form, the legend claims that the culture hero ruled over Tollan, bringing it a higher civilization and more humanitarian religious and ethical ideals. He was white-skinned, bearded, and possibly blonde. When his enemies forced him to leave Mexico, he promised to return in the year 1 Reed, which corresponded to 1519, ironically the year of Hernán Cortés's arrival on the coast of Mexico. According to one version of the legend, Topiltzin set himself on fire, rose into heaven, and reappeared as Venus, the morning star. In another version, he departed across the sea on a raft of serpents. Various writers and scholars identify Topiltzin with **Jesus Christ, St. Thomas, St. Brendan, Prince Madoc,** and other supposed pre-Columbian visitors. He has also been linked to supposed **Chinese** and **African** visitors to pre-Columbian America, which would actually make him a yellow or black god.

Some of the details of Topiltzin's legend have serious authenticity problems. Some scholars rightly ask: How much of it is genuinely pre-Columbian and how much is post-Columbian garbling and distortion from the chronicles and studies of sixteenth-century Spanish priests and historians? Eminent

Quetzalcoatl

historian and archaeologist Nigel Davies believes that the Spanish virtually invented the whiteness of Topiltzin and his promise to return. As Davies points out, native sources do not refer to him as white; they describe him with a black or black-and-yellow-striped face. He also points out that Topiltzin's beard is no proof of pre-Columbian visits from Europe or the Mediterranean world. Native Americans, while not as hairy as Europeans, can frequently grow beards. Moctezuma (or-Montezuma) II (r. 1503–1519) had a beard.

Quetzalcoatl.

Davies downplays the prophecy of Topiltzin's return, except symbolically as the planet Venus. He admits that Aztec Emperor Moctezuma II believed Cortés was the returned Topiltzin/Quetzalcoatl, but he

maintains that this idea was a unique conclusion reached by the nervous Moctezuma rather than a reflection of general Aztec religious beliefs. Davíd Carrasco, a historian of Mesoamerican religions, disagrees. In his opinion the prophecy of Topiltzin/Quetzalcoatl's return was a common belief among Aztecs. In fact, it hung over the shaky Aztec empire like an ideological sword of Damocles. Cortés's appearance caused the sword to fall, and with it fell the Aztecs. Both Davies and Carrasco think that Topiltzin/Quetzalcoatl is purely a figure of Mexican history and legend that later spread to the Mayan lands in the form of the gods **Kukulcan** and **Itzamná**.

Topiltzin/Quetzalcoatl was not a vague, legendary memory of visits by some Old World peoples. Certainly the chronology of Topiltzin at Tollan eliminates Jesus Christ, St. Thomas, or even St. Brendan as a possible model. He does not link up very well with the supposed chronology of African or Chinese visitors since he most likely lived in the late eleventh century, well after or well before visits by those groups. Even the Norse of **Vinland** and Prince Madoc do not make seriously acceptable candidates. Almost no professional archaeologist, anthropologist, or historian believes that Topiltzin/Quetzalcoatl was anything but a member of the Toltec civilization.

Bibliography: Carrasco, Davíd, *Quetzalcoatl and the Irony of Empire: Myths and Prophecies in the Aztec Tradition*, 1982; Carrasco, Davíd, *Religions of Mesoamerica: Cosmovision and Ceremonial Centers*, 1990; Davies, Nigel, *Voyagers to the New World*, 1979.

R

Ra Expeditions
(1969 and 1970)

Thor Heyerdahl made these voyages across the Atlantic Ocean in reproductions of ancient papyrus ships to prove that **Egyptian** and other ancient peoples were capable of reaching the Americas by using prevailing **ocean currents.**

Thor Heyerdahl has spent almost his entire anthropological career advocating the idea that oceans served as highways for the spread of early civilization rather than barriers to expansion. In his opinion, ancient peoples could easily have navigated across great stretches of ocean if they properly used the currents and winds. Therefore, he believes that many cultural exchanges could have taken place among the peoples of an-

tiquity, including those of the Old World and the Americas. Such ideas make Heyerdahl a supporter of **diffusionism,** although he maintains he is only a moderate diffusionist. In the case of the *Ra* expeditions, he attempted to demonstrate that the papyrus boats so frequently depicted on ancient Egyptian bas-reliefs were actually capable of transoceanic travel.

Theories advocating the existence of contacts between Egypt and Mesoamerica are common and have been around for a long time. One of the stumbling blocks to the credibility of those theories was the contention that ancient Egyptians were not a seafaring people and therefore lacked the means to cross the Atlantic safely. Heyerdahl's studies of old Egyptian vessels, however, caused him to reach the revolutionary conclusion that they were quite capable of oceanic voyaging. In 1954 archaeologists discovered the remains of the Cheops boat in a chamber at the base of the Pyramid of Cheops. It was a large boat, 140 feet in length, made of Lebanon cedar and designed along lines that would make it capable of sailing the high seas. But the Cheops boat was held together only by rope and glue; ocean waves would have quickly torn it to pieces. Heyerdahl concluded that the Cheops boat's function was merely ceremonial, but that its design was copied from papyrus boats fully capable of oceanic travel.

To prove his theory, Heyerdahl had tribal craftsmen from Lake Chad build him a papyrus vessel that copied, as much as possible, the designs of papyrus boats found on the bas-reliefs. No ancient papyrus vessels survive due to the perishable nature of their material. Papyrus boats are still in use on Lake Chad and a few other places in Africa, but seagoing papyrus boats have long since ceased to exist, having been replaced by more durable wooden ships. As a result, Heyerdahl and his craftsmen were copying a design without a clear understanding of all its functional aspects. That would prove to be a problem later.

Heyerdahl's plan was to sail his papyrus ship, named the *Ra*, from Safi, Morocco, to Barbados by taking advantage of the Canary and South Equatorial currents. Water and traditional foods were stored in the types of ceramic jars used by the ancient Egyptians so that everything about the voyage would be authentic. The *Ra* sailed on 17 May 1969 and was almost immediately plagued by problems with its equipment. The rudder oars broke on the first day out; on the second, a spar of the sail broke. All these problems were caused by the crew's inexperience. Having lost its steerage capabilities, the *Ra*'s journey was converted into a drift voyage. The *Ra* proved to be very seaworthy. The papyrus was very buoyant and did not become waterlogged as some predicted; in fact, it became stronger and more flexible when wet.

Unfortunately, one serious mistake had been made. Heyerdahl and the boat builders neglected to attach a tension rope to the *Ra*'s tail section as the old pictures indicated. Everyone assumed that the rope was there merely to preserve the curvature of the tail piece. In fact, its purpose was to prevent the rear section of the papyrus from buckling in heavy seas. Without that tension rope, the *Ra*'s stern section buckled, causing it to submerge. Slowly but surely the *Ra* was losing its back third. Although the front two-thirds remained quite buoyant, Heyerdahl decided to take no chances. He abandoned the *Ra* after traveling some 2,600 miles, with only 600 miles left to reach Barbados.

Despite the problems, Heyerdahl considered the *Ra*'s voyage a success. The very next year, he had another papyrus ship built and made a second ocean crossing. This time Bolivian Indians from Lake Titicaca built the papyrus boat, which was named the *Ra II*. Learning from their mistakes, the crew of the *Ra II* departed Safi on 17 May and crossed the Atlantic in 57 days without any

serious problems. For Heyerdahl, the *Ra* expeditions proved his theory that transoceanic contacts occurred in ancient times between Egypt and America. The majority of anthropologists and archaeologists continue to be skeptical about his conclusions. As archaeologist Brian M. Fagan recently put it, " . . . all it [the *Ra* expedition] proves is that a moderately seaworthy downwind vessel can navigate the tradewinds to the New World." Given the lack of supporting archaeological or historical evidence for Heyerdahl's theory of Egyptian visits to the Americas, Fagan's conclusion is correct.

Bibliography: Heyerdahl, Thor, *The Ra Expeditions*, 1971.

Rivet, Paul
(1867–1958)

This French anthropologist advocated the theory that the Americas were populated during prehistoric times by people from Australia and Melanesia who sailed across the Pacific Ocean, as well as by people coming across the **Bering Land Bridge**. He also believed that extensive contact occurred between the Native Americans and **Polynesians**.

Rivet studied medicine in France and obtained his degree in 1898. In 1901 he joined a scientific mission to Ecuador and decided to stay for an additional six years to study the Andean peoples. Rivet then became a lifelong student of anthropology and linguistics. After returning to France, he helped establish the Institut d'Ethnologie at the University of Paris in 1926 and the Musée de l'Homme in Paris.

Rivet strongly believed that significant interdependence existed, and always had, among the various societies and cultures of humanity. This belief made him a supporter of various **diffusionist** theories. A number of anthropologists noticed that some Native Americans showed Australoid physical characteristics rather than the expected Mongoloid traits. During his researches among the Andean peoples, Rivet also noticed the occurrence of such Australoid traits. To explain this apparent Australoid presence, he theorized that early Australian aborigines traveled from Australia to Antarctica and then to South America between 8000 and 4000 B.C. This initial migration was followed by later Melanesian and Polynesian migrations or visits.

Besides citing physical evidence for Australoid, Melanesian, and Polynesian presences, Rivet also amassed lists of various shared cultural traits. He compiled vocabularies of shared words, but this evidence did not convince other anthropologists since it is quite common for two completely unrelated languages to have many similar words. Rivet pointed out that certain plants such as the yam, calabash, **cotton**, coconut, and **sweet potato** were common to both the Americas and Oceania. In this case, many scholars agree with Rivet that contacts between Polynesia and the Americas occurred. The chronology and direction of such exchanges, however, remains undetermined and hotly debated (see also **Thor Heyerdahl**).

Rivet developed his theory of a prehistoric Australoid migration to the Americas during the early twentieth century. At that time, many scholars believed that humans had only arrived in the Americas around 4000–2000 B.C. Now they know that people came to America far earlier (see also **Bering Land Bridge/Strait Theory**). Such changes in the basic chronology have completely undermined Rivet's theory about an Australoid migration. As it was, the theory never received wide support; the proposed migration route across Antarctica seemed completely ridiculous, and the linguistic evidence was weak and generally unconvincing. Rivet's theory provides a tragic example of a respected scholar who developed a somewhat outlandish and improbable theory and continued to advocate it in the face of rejection by his colleagues.

Bibliography: Davies, Nigel, *Voyagers to the New World,* 1979; Rivet, Paul, "Early Contacts between Polynesia and America," *Diogenes* 16 (1956): 78–92; Ronze, Raymond, "Rivet, Paul," in *International Encyclopedia of the Social Sciences,* edited by David L. Sills, 1968.

Romans in Ancient America

This Italian people created the greatest and longest-lived empire of the ancient Mediterranean world. Although they dominated the western world from about 200 B.C. to about A.D. 500, the Romans have never been particularly popular as the subject of theories about pre-Columbian visitors to the Americas. The Romans are not commonly thought of as a seafaring people, although this impression is an unfair one. Seaborne commerce carried out on the Mediterranean Sea was one of the main things holding the Roman empire together. Other Roman merchants regularly reached India and may have known of China. Whether they reached the Americas is another question altogether.

The primary evidence for possible Roman visits to the Americas comes from **coin finds**. In 1533, miners in Panama supposedly found a Roman coin dating from the time of Caesar Augustus (27 B.C.–A.D. 14). Most sixteenth-century Spaniards, however, did not consider this discovery authentic, and modern scholarship shares their skepticism. In fact, research indicates that virtually all Roman coin finds in the Americas are the result of modern losses or deliberate hoaxes. Nevertheless, many **diffusionist** writers continue to use coin finds as evidence for Roman visits. **Cyrus Gordon** and Constance Irwin both cited a find of a large cache of Roman coins in Venezuela as evidence for Roman or Arabic voyages to the Americas.

After more than 20 years, this particular find remains undocumented and therefore increasingly unreliable as a piece of evidence.

Popular writer Frederick Pohl exemplifies the position that Roman visits to the Americas were accidental. Blown west by storms, they often shipwrecked on the coast of the Americas. It is his opinion that these visits mostly took place during the first century or later. He also feels that at least one ship managed to return home, bearing American pineapples. Supposed pictures of pineapples on Pompeiian wall paintings are presented as evidence for this contention. Unfortunately, like Gordon and Irwin, Pohl relies on discredited coin finds or the rather unconvincing pineapple evidence.

Other diffusionist writers view the Americas as a place of refuge for persecuted groups from the Roman world. In 1961 Charles M. Boland claimed that early Christians fleeing from Emperor Nero's persecutions in the year 64 went to America and settled in the vicinity of present-day Virginia and North Carolina. Supposed Roman bronze and iron artifacts, some bearing inscriptions, were found in 1943 on the farm of James V. Howe near Jeffress, Virginia. But archaeologists, classicists, and historians refuse to authenticate them as genuine, and the sites where the artifacts were found are considered Native American. To Boland, this reaction by the professionals smacks of a cover-up. Others simply consider it good debunking scholarship. Another similar late–Roman-era visit to the Americas is the so-called Roman-Jewish colony of Calalus that was supposedly established in Arizona about 700 by people fleeing from the Islamic conquest. The evidence for this settlement consists largely of the crosslike "Tucson Artifacts." Although **Barry Fell** and retired professor of history Cyclone Covey consider this evidence genuine, professional archaeologists and historians are equally convinced that it is a hoax, and a crude one at that.

The one intriguing Roman artifact found in the Americas is a bearded terra cotta head dated to approximately 220. As reported by Robert Heine-Geldern, Mexican professor José García Payon found it in a dig in the Toluca Valley in the region of Calixtlahuaca. Both the artifact and its pre-Columbian archaeological context appear to be authentic, so the question becomes, how did it get there? Heine-Geldern suggests that it may have been carried from the Roman world to India, Southeast Asia, or China. From one of these places, pre-Columbian visitors then carried it to Mexico. This interpretation essentially co-opted the Roman artifact as evidence substantiating Heine-Geldern's own theories of **Hindu** and **Chinese** contacts. He also accepts the possibility that the terra cotta head may have come directly across the Atlantic Ocean from the Roman world to Mexico, but does not discuss how and why. It seems fairly certain that Roman voyages to America were rare and one way, if they took place at all. Otherwise, some record would have survived in the literary heritage left by Rome.

Bibliography: Boland, Charles M., *They All Discovered America*, 1961; Heine-Geldern, Robert, "A Roman Find from Pre-Columbian Mexico," *Anthropological Journal of Canada* 5 (1967): 20–22; Pohl, Frederick J., "Did Ancient Romans Reach America?" *New Diffusionist* 3 (1973): 23–37; Williams, Stephen, *Fantastic Archaeology: The Wild Side of North American Prehistory*, 1991.

Rosicrucians

Rosicrucians is a collective name for a group of secret societies devoted to pursuing esoteric knowledge and ancient mysteries. The Rosicrucians believe that **Atlantis** and **Lemuria** existed in the distant past and were destroyed in great catastrophes. Before their destruction, the inhabitants of these two lost continents managed to spread civilizing colonies throughout the rest of the world, including the Americas.

Rosicrucianism arose out of Protestant Christianity during the early seventeenth century and was an active intellectual movement through the mid-eighteenth century. At that time, the lines between science and the occult were blurred, and Rosicrucians studied both as a unified whole. The movement became dormant for about a century but revived in the second half of the nineteenth century, firmly focused on the occult aspects of knowledge. By the early twentieth century there were several groups of Rosicrucians, of which the better known are the Ancient Mystical Order of the Rosae Crucis (AMORC), the Rosicrucian Society, and the Rosicrucian Fellowship.

Atlantis and Lemuria are the sources of human civilization according to the Rosicrucians. From those lost continents survivors spread throughout the earth bringing their culture and civilization. The terrible destruction of Atlantis and Lemuria, however, caused humanity to regress for a time, because only vestiges of their great civilization remained intact. Under H. Spencer Lewis, the founder of AMORC, belief in the existence and destruction of Atlantis became an official doctrine of Rosicrucianism. R. Swinburne Clymer, a leader of the Rosicrucian Foundation or Fraternity in Pennsylvania, attributed the destruction of Atlantis to the misuse of advanced scientific and magical knowledge by the Atlanteans. They attempted to use their knowledge to visit God but instead upset the balance of nature and caused Atlantis to sink under the ocean. Some of the survivors managed to establish a secret settlement on the Yucatán Peninsula, where they preserve the ancient wisdom of Atlantis to this very day.

The Rosicrucian Fellowship is a somewhat unique branch of Rosicrucianism that had its origin in **Theosophy.** Carl Louis van Graf, a German immigrant to the United States, under the pseudonym of Max Heindel, founded the Rosicrucian Fellowship in 1907. Heindel gathered together his teachings in a book titled *The Rosicrucian Cosmo-Conception,* first published in 1907. Heindel claimed that a Rosicrucian mystic converted him from Theosophy, but many of his ideas appear to have been gleaned from the teachings of Rudolph Steiner, the founder of **Anthrosophy.** According to Heindel, the Lemurians were a primitive people who were the ancestors of modern Negroes. Atlanteans were a more advanced race, although cunning, not reason, guided their decisions. Heindel identified the Jews as descendants of degenerate Atlanteans who still used cunning rather than reason. For him, the Aryans were humanity's next evolutionary step since they used reason. Obviously Heindel's version of Rosicrucian beliefs was heavily tainted by racist ideology, but that did not stop his organization from continuing to thrive after his death.

Rosicrucians, like Theosophists, claim to have acquired their knowledge of Atlantis and the ancient dispersal of humanity throughout the world by otherworldly communications with spirits or by other so-called occult means. No serious scholar gives any credence to their theories about pre-Columbian contacts between the Americas and Atlantis.

Bibliography: de Camp, L. Sprague, *Lost Continents,* [1954], 1970; Fogarty, Harry Wells, "Rosicrucians," in *Encyclopedia of Religion,* edited by Mircea Eliade, 10 vols., 1987; "Rosicrucianism," in *Encyclopedia of Occultism and Parapsychology,* edited by Leslie Shepard, 2 vols., 1978; Wauchope, Robert, *Lost Tribes and Sunken Continents,* 1962.

Sahagún, Father Bernardino de (1500–1590)

Missionary and historian, he wrote the great unpublished historical and ethnographic work *Historia general de las cosas de Nueva España* (General history of the things of New Spain) from 1547 until his death in 1590.

Born at Sahagún in Spain, he studied at the University of Salamanca and took the vows for entry into the Franciscan order in 1524. Coming to Mexico in 1529, he quickly learned the Native American language Nahuatl. Sahagún and his fellow Franciscans feared that the Spanish effort to Christianize the natives of Mexico was superficial and in danger of failing. To aid other missionaries, Sahagún began compiling *Historia general* as a sourcebook on native customs and beliefs, which he hoped would make it easier for other Spanish clerics to learn Nahuatl. In gathering his research materials, Sahagún interviewed native informants and trained native scholars as research assistants. Unfortunately, the sympathy shown for Native Americans by the Franciscans and Sahagún became increasingly incompatible with the general plan of the Roman Catholic Church during the years immediately after the Council of Trent (1545–1563). Whereas the Spanish Crown had called for preservation and study of the preconquest knowledge and artifacts of the Native Americans as recently as 1573, after 1576 royal orders called for those same materials to be locked up and forbade their further study. A somewhat bewildered Sahagún continued to fight for a sympathetic understanding of Native Americans until his death at the age of 90, despite suffering excommunication for his efforts. Sahagún died during an epidemic of respiratory disease in Mexico in 1590.

Sahagún was exclusively interested in the ideas the Native Americans had about their origins as represented by their myths and legends. There is no convincing evidence that he speculated about possible Old World origins. Edward King, **Viscount Kingsborough**, claimed that Spanish authorities ordered Sahagún to stop his attempts to prove the **Hebrew** origin of Native Americans, but supplied no evidence for this assertion. Scholars of the Church of Jesus Christ of the Latter Day Saints have attempted to establish a correspondence between the myths and legends preserved by Sahagún and the contents of *The Book of Mormon*. Non-Mormon scholars are unconvinced by such Mormon efforts to prove the historicity of *The Book of Mormon*, although they consider Sahagún an outstanding pioneer ethnographer.

Bibliography: Edmonson, Munro S., ed., *Sixteenth-Century Mexico: The Work of*

Sahagún, 1974; Huddleston, Lee Eldridge, *Origins of the American Indians: European Concepts, 1492–1729,* 1967; Sahagún, Bernardino de, *Florentine Codex: General History of the Things of New Spain,* 13 vols., 1982.

Sánchez, Alonso, of Huelva

This is the name given to the **Unknown Pilot of Columbus** by mestizo historian **Garcilaso de la Vega.**

In the beginning of his *Royal Commentaries of the Incas* (Bk. 1, ch. 3), Garcilaso de la Vega tells the story of the discovery of the New World. His narrative includes a very detailed version of the story of the Unknown Pilot, whom Garcilaso identifies as Alonso Sánchez. Sánchez lived in the coastal town of Huelva where he operated a small ship that carried goods in a triangular route from Spain to the Canary Islands to Madeira and back again to Spain. During a voyage in 1484, the ship encountered a great storm between the Canaries and Madeira that steadily drove it westward for 28 or 29 days. When the weather calmed, the survivors sighted an unknown island (which Garcilaso thought was probably Santo Domingo) and landed. After taking on fresh water and fuel and making some navigational measurements, the ship attempted to return to Spain. But the return voyage lasted so long that supplies ran out. By the time Sánchez and his companions reached Terceira in the Azores, only 5 of the original 17 crew members were still alive. The survivors were taken into the house of Christopher Columbus, who was at that time residing on Terceira. The physical damage inflicted by the long voyage, however, proved too great. One by one, the crewmen died despite careful ministrations by Columbus. Before they died, they left him the precious secret of their accidental but potentially world-shaking discovery of unknown lands in the western Atlantic.

For his evidence, Garcilaso cited stories told by his father, Sebastian Garcilaso de la Vega, who was a soldier, and his father's companions-in-arms. He also cited the far simpler version of the Unknown Pilot story told by the respected Spanish scholar **José de Acosta** in his *Natural and Moral History of the Indies* (Bk. 1, ch. 19). Garcilaso's elaboration of the Unknown Pilot story basically proves the staying power of an intriguing rumor rather than the truth of Alonso Sánchez's existence.

Bibliography: Garcilaso de la Vega, *Royal Commentaries of the Incas and General History of Peru,* 2 vols., 1966.

Sarmiento de Gamboa, Pedro (ca. 1532–1592)

This Spanish explorer and historian suggested that the natives of Peru were descendants of refugees from **Atlantis,** while those of Central America and Mexico were descendants of Greeks left behind by **Ulysses.**

Born at Alcalá, Spain, Sarmiento joined the Spanish army in 1550 and served in Europe for five years. In 1555 he traveled to Mexico and by 1557 had made his way to Peru. He immediately developed a strong fascination with the pre-Columbian history of the Andean region. From 1564–1567 he was imprisoned by the Inquisition for dabbling with the occult. After his release he sailed the Pacific Ocean from 1567–1569 in search of treasure islands that the Incas claimed lay to the west. This expedition, commanded by Alvaro de Mendaña de Nehra, reached a group of islands they named the Solomons after the hope that they were ancient **Ophir** and so contained King Solomon's fabled mines. After returning to Peru, viceroy Francisco de Toledo ordered Sarmiento to compile a history of the natives of Peru. Sent to Spain in 1572, it dealt with the years 565 to 1533 and was titled *Segundo parte de la historia general llamada índica* (translated into English as *History of the Incas*). The proposed first and third parts of that work would have dealt with geography and the history of the Spanish conquest, respectively, but they were never written. Even the completed manuscript of the second part remained unpublished until it turned up at the University of Göttingen in the nineteenth century. A German edition appeared in 1906.

Sarmiento believed that the natives of Peru were the descendants of survivors of the catastrophe that sank Atlantis in 1320 B.C. The prevalence of flood legends among the Peruvians was one of the evidences that convinced him that he was right. But Sarmiento also thought significant differences existed between the natives of Peru and Mexico that needed explaining. He suggested that the Greek hero Ulysses and his fleet had sailed to the Yucatán. Some of the Greeks in his expedition decided to remain behind when Ulysses's fleet returned home, and their descendants formed the population of Mexico and Central America. Interestingly enough, Sarmiento's Ulysses theory was revived in the twentieth century by **diffusionist** writer Henriette Mertz. After completing his history, Sarmiento went on to combat the piratical activities of Francis Drake off the coast of Peru in 1579. From 1580–1584 he explored the Strait of Magellan in hopes of fortifying it against future incursions like Drake's. He died in Manila in 1592.

Bibliography: Huddleston, Lee Eldridge, *Origins of the American Indians: European Concepts, 1492–1729,* 1967; Sarmiento de Gamboa, Pedro, *History of the Incas,* edited by Clements Markham, 1907; Wilgus, A. Curtis, *The Historiography of Latin America: A Guide to Historical Writing, 1500–1800,* 1975.

Scolvus, Voyage of Johannes (1472 or 1476)

Also known as Johannes Skolp or Jan of Kolno, this Polish or Danish explorer supposedly discovered America some 20 years prior to the first voyage of Christopher Columbus

by sailing past **Greenland** to Labrador and Newfoundland. Some people link him to the **voyage of Pining-Pothorst** and **João Vaz Côrte-Real,** in which he supposedly served as the pilot.

Almost nothing is known about Johannes Scolvus. The first mention of him appeared as a note on the globe that Gemma Frisius and Gerard Mercator designed in 1537. It stated that Scolvus was a Dane who made a voyage west of Greenland in 1476. Another reference by Spanish historian **Francisco López de Gómara** in his *La historia de las Indias y conquista de México* of 1552 asserted that Scolvus, a Norwegian, visited Labrador and possibly Newfoundland. An English document dated 1575 referred to John Scolvus, a pilot of Denmark, who in 1476 sailed the Arctic waters west of Greenland. Finally, in his *Descriptionis Ptolemaicae* (1597) Cornelis Wytfliet alluded to a "Johannes Sclolvus Polonus" exploring the Arctic waters in 1476 and visiting Labrador, which was also called **Estotiland.**

Both Poles and Danes claim Johannes Scolvus for their own. The Danes argue that Wytfliet's "Polonus" was actually a typographical error for "pilonus" (i.e., pilot). Poles are unimpressed by that argument, and Polish-Americans periodically agitate for a Jan of Kolno Day to match Columbus Day. It was the imaginative researches of Danish librarian Sofus Larsen in 1920 that first linked Johannes Scolvus as the pilot of the Pining-Pothorst and Côrte-Real voyage and moved its date up to 1472. To reduce the crowding on that expedition, some writers suggest that Scolvus and Hans Pothorst were the same person. One Portuguese scholar asserts that it was João Vaz Côrte-Real and Scolvus who were one and the same. Finally, Peruvian historian Luis Ulloa advanced the unique thesis that Christopher Columbus was the alias of Joan Baptiste Colom, a Catalan rebel. While Colom/Columbus visited Ireland and **Iceland** in the 1470s, he made a western voyage during

1477. The pronunciation of his Danish companions transformed his name from Colom to Scolom or Scolvus. Professional historians such as Samuel Eliot Morison concede that a Johannes Scolvus actually existed and most likely did explore the Arctic seas beyond Greenland in 1476, but without any significant historical consequences.

Bibliography: Larson, Laurence M., "Did John Scolvus Visit Labrador and Newfoundland in or about 1476?," *Scandinavian Studies* 7 (May 1922): 81–89; Larsen, Sofus, *The Discovery of America Twenty Years before Columbus*, [Danish, 1920], 1924; Morison, Samuel Eliot, *The European Discovery of America: The Northern Voyages,* 1971; Yarmolinsky, Avraham, *Early Polish Americana: A Bibliographical Study. With an Appendix: A Legendary Predecessor of Columbus*, 1937.

Scythians in Ancient America

The true Scythians were a nomadic people of Indo-European origin who lived in the area between the Carpathian Mountains and the Don River from about 1000 B.C. to A.D. 200. They were a warlike people and one of the first to develop the art of horsemanship.

During the Middle Ages, Europeans referred to any nomadic people living between the Black Sea and the Pacific Ocean as Scythians; they also used the term interchangeably with **Tartar** and **Siberian.** As a result, supporters of the early versions of the **Bering Land Bridge/Strait theory** would have considered the ancestors of the first Native Americans to be Scythians.

Bibliography: Huddleston, Lee Eldridge, *Origins of the American Indians: European Concepts, 1492–1729,* 1967; Rice, T. Talbot, *The Scythians,* 1958.

Sea Kings, Ancient

This theory, associated with geographer Charles H. Hapgood, suggests that an advanced civilization existed during the last ice age some 10,000 to 15,000 years ago. This civilization engaged in worldwide commerce that included the Americas.

Hapgood's theory is based primarily on a close study of the **Piri Re'is map** of 1513. Hapgood's ideas, published in 1966, are basically an elaboration of ideas first suggested by Arlington H. Mallery in 1956. Both men pointed out that the Piri Re'is map contains a number of accurate geographical details not yet known by Europeans in 1513. The map shows details of the Antarctic coast that had long been covered by ice. Other geographical anomalies include a supposedly accurate depiction of places not yet explored at that time, including the Andes, the island of Marajo at the mouth of the Amazon River, and details of the southern coast of South America. Furthermore, the map shows signs of certain catastrophic changes such as a large mid-Atlantic island where today there are only the tiny Rocks of Sts. Peter and Paul and a larger, more extensive group of Azores Islands. In the case of the Azores, Hapgood claims that the extra islands on the Piri Re'is map correspond to the location of now-submerged sea mounts. He explains these differences as the result of some ancient subsidence.

According to Hapgood, Piri Re'is had access to some very old maps containing this anomalous information. Piri Re'is himself claimed he had used source maps from the time of **Alexander the Great.** Since similar anomalous geographical knowledge appears on other medieval and early modern maps, Hapgood concludes that the source of this knowledge must be fragmentary survivals of the intellectual heritage of a very ancient and unknown civilization that existed during the ice age. He points out that much ancient knowledge was lost in the destruction of the library of Carthage and the three burnings of the vast library of Alexandria. In addition, Hapgood cites evidence of various ancient peoples having scientific knowledge far in advance of their supposed technical abilities, such as the navigational skills of the **Egyptians** and the mathematical precision of the Mayan calendar. These achievements are explained as survivals from that advanced but lost civilization.

The nature and location of Hapgood's ice age civilization cannot be determined from its meager remnants. Its navigational skills, however, were at least equal to those of eighteenth-century Europe, if not greater. Basing his argument on theories and speculations about the polar origins of various ancient peoples, particularly those of the protagonists of the **Hindu** Vedas, Hapgood locates the unknown advanced civilization on the unglaciated Antarctic continent of 15,000 years ago.

Hapgood's study of the Piri Re'is map and its supposed evidence for a lost ice age civilization makes for fascinating reading. Its cartographical and mathematical analyses seem quite complete and convincing if certain assumptions made by the author are accepted by the reader. That is, however, a problem. At times it seems that the Piri Re'is map is given credit for an accuracy that does not seem all that evident. The main difficulty is the lack of corroborating archaeological or historical evidence. No indisputable artifacts from this ice age civilization survive. Hapgood claims that the pyramid of Cuicuilco in Mexico is a survival from the ice age culture, but it is a claim that no professional archaeologist of the pre-Columbian Americas supports. Otherwise, the main centers of the unknown civilization remain inaccessible beneath hundreds of feet of Antarctic glaciers, if they exist at all. Hapgood's claim that any sophisticated mathematical and astronomical knowledge found among such peoples as the Egyptians and Mayas must ultimately derive from this lost civilization of the ice age smacks of excessive **diffusion-**

ism. It denies most ancient peoples any credit for creativity or intelligence; their best achievements are always attributable to some other civilization such as Hapgood's lost Antarctic civilization. Most archaeologists find that such claims are not borne out by the archaeological record, which clearly documents the slow but impressive acquisition of technical knowledge by the Egyptians and Maya.

Bibliography: Hapgood, Charles H., *Maps of the Ancient Sea Kings: Evidence of Advanced Civilization in the Ice Age*, [1966], rev. ed., 1979.

Seven Cities, Legend of

According to legend, early in the eighth century seven Portuguese bishops and their followers fled into the western Atlantic Ocean to escape Muslim invaders. They established seven rich cities on the island of **Antillia.** By the fifteenth century, Antillia and the Seven Cities appeared on maps, along with vague reports of various people sighting or landing on them. This legend inspired much of the early exploration of the Atlantic.

Muslims, led by Tariq, crossed the Strait of Gibraltar in 711 and invaded the Iberian Peninsula. They decisively defeated the army of the Christian king Roderick, and by the following year his Visigothic kingdom of Spain was destroyed. This Muslim invasion and conquest inspired the legend that the Archbishop of Oporto and six fellow bishops took ship with their Christian flocks and fled from the hated infidel invaders into the western Atlantic. They found the island of Antillia and took refuge. After burning their ships so that no one could return and reveal their location to the Muslims, they built seven cities and soon established a rich, even utopian, society. According to late–fifteenth-century cartographer **Martin Behaim,** their flight took place in 734, although Fernando, the son of Christopher Columbus, dated it more reasonably to 714.

Although the Seven Cities were supposedly founded in the eighth century, Europeans apparently remained unaware of them until the early fifteenth century. According to a notation Martin Behaim placed on his globe of 1492, a Spanish ship sighted the island of the Seven Cities in 1414. The oldest firsthand reference to the Seven Cities occurred on **Zuane Pizzigano's map** of 1424, which showed Antillia, including the Seven Cities, for the first time. Spanish historian Antonio de Herrera y Tordesillas (ca. 1549–1625) wrote that some Portuguese sailors reached Antillia in the time of Prince Henry the Navigator (1394–1460). They found a civilized people who spoke Portuguese. After their departure, they also discovered that the beach sand they had placed in their firebox was full of gold. Back in Portugal, Prince Henry ordered them to return to the island, but they refused. **Bartolomé de Las Casas** of Spain included the story in his *Historia de las Indias,* as did Portuguese historian Antonio Galvão (1503–1557), but he dated it to 1447. Some people consider these reports of the Seven Cities to be records of pre-Columbian visits to some location in the Americas.

The search for the Seven Cities inspired many Portuguese voyages of discovery during the fifteenth century, including **Diogo de Teive** in 1452, **Fernão Teles** in 1474–1476, and **Ferdinand Van Olmen** in 1487. All hoped to find the Seven Cities, but there is no record that they found anything at all, including any part of the Americas. By 1474 geographer **Paolo Toscanelli dal Pozzo** decided that the Seven Cities on Antillia would make a good rest stop for voyagers on their way to Asia. Meanwhile the fame and lure of the Seven Cities spread to England, where they inspired the **Bristol voyages** of

the 1480s. In his 1497 voyage for England during which he discovered Newfoundland, Genoese adventurer John Cabot returned home convinced that his discovery was a part of the island of the Seven Cities.

By 1500 the map of **Juan de la Cosa** located the Seven Cities on the North American mainland where Cabot had visited. Other cartographers, such as Gerard Mercator, continued to locate them on an Atlantic island as late as 1587. Some geographers placed the Seven Cities on the mainland of South America, although most people continued to think they were somewhere in North America. From that vague location they beckoned to conquistadors Hernando de Soto, who searched the southeastern region of the present-day United States from 1539–1543 but found only death, and Francisco Vásquez de Coronado, who vainly explored the southwestern region from 1540–1542.

Some people feel that the legend is evidence that the Portuguese discovered America before Columbus. In the absence of more convincing proof, their contention must remain just as legendary as the Seven Cities themselves.

Bibliography: Buker, George E., "The Seven Cities: The Role of a Myth in the Exploration of the Atlantic," *American Neptune* 30 (1970): 249–259; Clissold, Stephen, The Seven Cities of Cibola, 1962; Speck, Gordon, *Myths and New World Explorations,* 1979.

Siberians

Collective name for tribal peoples living in northern Asia from the Ural Mountains to the Pacific Ocean, their ancestors were related to the Paleo-Indians' ancestors, who first crossed from Asia to North America over the Bering Land Bridge between 20,000 and 15,000 years ago. See also **Bering Land Bridge/Strait Theory.**

Sinclair, Voyage of Prince Henry (1398)

Sinclair, or St. Clair, has been identified as the **Prince Zichmni** of the **Zeno Narrative** who supposedly sailed to **Estotiland** (Newfoundland or Nova Scotia) during the last decade of the fourteenth century.

Henry Sinclair (1345–1400) was the son of Sir William Sinclair from whom he inherited the barony of Roslin in Scotland. He obtained the disputed claim to the earldom of Orkney through his mother Isabel. These twin inheritances made Sinclair a noble of both the king of Scotland and the king of Norway since Orkney still owed obedience to Norway in the late fourteenth century. Despite growing fears about Scottish influence, the king of Norway confirmed Sinclair's title to the earldom in 1379. That recognition, however, did not assure him of the peaceful enjoyment of his possession since the Orkneys were very disordered at that time. Still, Sinclair gradually built the castles and ships needed to establish his control. By 1389 his efforts were so successful that his fleet was bigger than that of the king of Norway. As a result, the king ordered Sinclair to use his fleet to conquer the Shetland Islands.

Some proponents of the Sinclair/Prince Zichmni theory claim that Nicolò Zeno the elder entered the story at this point. In 1390 Sinclair supposedly rescued the shipwrecked Zeno while campaigning on the Shetlands. Finding Zeno well versed in the latest techniques of naval warfare, Sinclair took him into his service and made him his admiral. In turn Zeno found his service with Sinclair so lucrative and pleasant that he invited his brother Antonio to join him. Sinclair continued to serve the interests of Norway, although the Zeno Narrative seems to contradict what other sources say about his activities. He traveled to England in 1392 to lease some warships for Margareta, the queen of Norway, while the next year he

attempted to return **Iceland** to obedience to Norway. In 1394 Sinclair (Zichmni) supposedly sent Zeno on his ultimately fatal voyage to **Greenland**. When Nicolò died in 1395 from an illness contracted on that expedition, Sinclair promoted his brother Antonio to admiral.

It would have been shortly after Antonio's appointment in about 1396 that the **Fisherman of Frislanda** returned from Estotiland and told Sinclair about his adventures there. Impressed by the description of Estotiland's riches, Sinclair decided to send Antonio with a fleet to investigate. Enthusiasm ran high, and getting volunteers for the voyage was no problem. In fact, Sinclair decided to take personal command of the expedition, which probably would have sailed in 1397.

Sinclair's itinerary is unclear and confused. Apparently some Estotilanders, who had accompanied the recently deceased Fisherman of Frislanda, served as guides. Sailing west, on 1 July the fleet reached the islands of Ledovo and Ilofe, which are tentatively identified as Lille Dimon and Skyoe. After recommencing their journey, Sinclair's crew again sighted land. Although they located a good harbor, the local inhabitants proved hostile and prevented a landing. A parley took place in which Sinclair learned that the land was called **Icaria** and that it had been conquered in the past by Prince Icarus, son of the Scottish king Daedalus. The natives told Sinclair to leave them alone and not to meddle in their laws. Sinclair desperately needed to replenish his water supply, so he made a clandestine landing. He managed to get the water, but his ships barely got away before a hostile force arrived.

Sailing on to the west and southwest for another ten days, Sinclair discovered an excellent country with a fine harbor. A smoking mountain lay in the distance and this time no hostile natives appeared. The fleet landed and sent out 100 soldiers to explore. (This took place at the beginning of June, which is odd since the fleet reached the island of Ilofe on 1 July, supposedly only a few weeks before. Apparently the narrative skimmed over almost a year of travel.) After eight days the exploring party returned. They reported that the smoking mountain was burning inside, and that there was a spring of pitch near it. Later some natives made an appearance. They were small, timid, and quite primitive—"half wild, and living in caves."

Sinclair named the landing harbor Trin. Frederick Pohl, popular writer and student of Sinclair, considers the name a reference to the landing occurring on the ecclesiastical feast of Trinity, which in 1398 fell on 2 June. Although the new land was pleasant, some of Sinclair's crew demanded to leave because they wanted to get home before winter. Sinclair and others wished to continue exploring, so the fleet was divided between volunteers staying with the prince and a homeward-bound group under the reluctant command of Antonio Zeno. And there the Zeno Narrative ends because the rest of the manuscript was destroyed.

Despite the lack of surviving documentation, Frederick Pohl developed a theoretical reconstruction of events for the remainder of Sinclair's voyage. He claims that Sinclair's visit to North America is the source for the Glooscap legend of the Micmac Indians. Glooscap was a seafaring prince from across the eastern sea who settled among the Micmacs and engendered great respect. Such a description broadly matches Sinclair. After spending a winter in the Micmac homeland of Nova Scotia, Sinclair cruised south down the coast of New England. There he supposedly left the enigmatic drawing known as the Westford Military Effigy as a memorial for one of his deceased knights. He finally returned to the Orkneys in 1399, but the following year he died opposing an English invasion of his hard-won islands.

The above account is, of course, a very tentative combination of historical facts from the life of the real Prince Henry Sinclair, events concerning Prince Zichmni of the Zeno Narrative, and suppositions supplied by Sinclair's latest biographer, Frederick Pohl. Beyond the basic chronological framework of the Zeno Narrative, supporters of the veracity of Prince Henry Sinclair's voyage differ greatly over their identification of places. Sinclair's Frislanda is variously identified as the Orkneys, the Faeroes, the Shetlands, or Iceland. Icaria is commonly thought to be Kerry in Ireland, although some people think it is Newfoundland. The unnamed land with the smoking mountain is located either in Greenland or Nova Scotia. If Sinclair's Icaria was Kerry and the land of the smoking mountain was Greenland, then his expedition was not at all extraordinary and was not a pre-Columbian visit to North America. Certainly he failed to reach the civilized Estotiland described by the Fisherman of Frislanda. Finally, there is the question of the ultimate reliability of the highly suspect Zeno Narrative, which professional historians generally feel is a sixteenth-century hoax.

Bibliography: Morison, Samuel Eliot, *The European Discovery of America: The Northern Voyages*, 1971; Pohl, Frederick J., *Prince Henry Sinclair: His Expedition to the New World in 1398*, 1974; Pohl, Frederick J., "Prince 'Zichmni' of the Zeno Narrative," *Terrae Incognitae* 2 (1970): 75–86.

Skraelings

This is the Norse name used collectively for the various Native American groups they encountered in **Vinland, Markland,** and **Greenland.** It has also been suggested that the skraelings were descendants of a colony of **Irish Monks in America.**

The meaning and derivation of the word skraeling is uncertain, although possibly it is related to the modern Norwegian *skraela* for scream or the modern Icelandic *skraelna,* which means shrink. Skraeling is still used by modern Icelanders to refer to a rude person, while in modern Norway it means weakling. Most scholars of Norse voyages to North America think that skraeling was used to mean either "screamers" in reference to the Native Americans' war cries or "wretches," showing the contempt in which the Norse held the natives they encountered in America.

The skraelings are identified with one or more tribes living in the northeast section of North America during 1000–1500, the time of the Norse colonization of Greenland. Some popular writers like Charles M. Boland link the skraelings to the alleged colony of Irish monks in America known as **Great Ireland.** This identification is highly unlikely since there is no generally convincing evidence that Great Ireland ever existed. Furthermore, the Norse of Greenland and Iceland were quite familiar with Ireland and its monks. They had a special name for them: *papars.* If they had encountered any in Vinland, they would probably have called them *papars,* not skraelings.

Given the Norse descriptions of Vinland skraelings as being small and dark-complected with coarse hair, big eyes, and dark features, it is obvious that they encountered some type of American Indians. But since the suggested geographical locations for Vinland range from Newfoundland to Florida, that leaves a large selection of tribes. Those who place Vinland in New England or Nova Scotia think they were Micmacs. Those placing Vinland in Newfoundland think they were the extinct Beothuk tribe.

Skraelings as John White saw them in the sixteenth century.

Skraelings encountered in Markland or Labrador may have been Beothuks or an extinct group known as the Point Revenge Indians. It is more definite that the Norse met skraelings who were **Eskimos** or Paleo-Eskimos in Labrador, because Norse artifacts have been found in archaeological excavations of Dorset culture Eskimo sites. Skraelings in Greenland would have been Eskimos of the Thule culture. Archaeological digs and contemporary documents attest to this identification.

The Norse were not particularly good observers of the Native American cultures. All were lumped together as skraelings with no regard to the obvious differences between the Beothuks, Dorset Paleo-Eskimos, and Thule Eskimos. Descriptions of the skraelings of Vinland having skin boats complicate matters because Red Indians generally used birch canoes and Eskimos used skins for their kayaks and the larger umiaks. There is some evidence, however, that the Beothuks and Point Revenge Indians may also have used skin boats, which would eliminate the problem.

Norse relations with any of the skraelings do not appear to have been particularly good. In the **Vinland Sagas** attempts at trade invariably degenerated into warfare. Evidence shows that the Norse later did some trading with the Dorset Paleo-Eskimos in Labrador and the Thule Eskimos in Greenland for timber and ivory. Surviving Norse and Eskimo accounts also indicate that such trade was frequently punctuated by violence. The Norse failed to learn from the Thule Eskimos how to adapt to the worsening climate of Greenland, with the result that their colony slowly but inexorably died out. It has also been pointed out that it was the determined hostility of the skraelings of Vinland that persuaded the Norse not to attempt a permanent settlement there, delaying the European settlement of the Americas for 500 years.

Bibliography: Fitzhugh, William W., "Early Contacts North of Newfoundland before A.D. 1600: A Review," in *Cultures in Contact,* edited by William W. Fitzhugh, 1985; McGhee, Robert, "Contact between Native North Americans and the Medieval Norse: A Review of the Evidence," *American Antiquity* 49 (no. 1, 1984): 4–26; McGhee, Robert, "Norsemen and Eskimos in Arctic Canada," in *Vikings in the West,* edited by Eleanor Guralnick, 1982.

Smith, Joseph, Jr.
(1805–1844)

He was the founder of the Church of Jesus Christ of the Latter Day Saints and author/translator of *The Book of Mormon,* which presents a variation of the theory that **Hebrew** visitors to the New World were the ancestors of Native Americans.

Joseph Smith, Jr., was born at Sharon, Vermont, on 23 December 1805, the fourth child and third son of Joseph Smith and Lucy Mack. His father failed to establish a stable living in New England and moved to Palmyra, New York, in 1816. The area around Palmyra contained many Native American mounds, and speculations abounded regarding the origins and history of the **Mound Builders.** Superstitions were common among the residents of that region, and many people believed in and practiced magic. Other common Palmyran pastimes included counterfeiting, treasure hunting, and religious revivalism. Growing up in such an environment, the younger Joseph Smith developed a strong interest in the magical arts, treasure hunting, and the origins of the Mound Builders. At age 14 he claimed to have been visited by God the Father and Jesus, although this experience was not mentioned until 1834. Outwardly his early life revealed no extraordinary religious inclinations.

On 18 January 1827 Joseph Smith married Emma Hall of Harmony, Pennsylvania. She respected his intelligence and imagination, but disapproved of his fascination for treasure hunting and fortune-telling. Despite Emma's efforts, by the end of their first year of marriage it was widely rumored around Palmyra that Smith had found a fantastic treasure buried in the earth. That treasure was the golden plates upon which *The Book of Mormon* was based. According to Smith, on 21 September 1823 the angel Moroni visited him while he knelt at his bed praying for forgiveness. Moroni revealed the location of a book consisting of golden plates that contained the story of earlier inhabitants of America and God's revelations to them. Accompanying them were the urim and thummin, described as two stones, that Smith was to use to translate the plates. However, when Smith found the stone box containing these sacred objects, the angel Moroni would not allow him to touch them until he achieved greater knowledge and holiness. For the next four years Smith was permitted only to visit and look upon the gold book once a year. Finally, on 22 September 1827 Smith received permission to bring his holy treasures home.

The news of Smith's discovery aroused the curiosity of his neighbors and the greed of some. Several attempts were made to find and steal the plates. Martin Harris, a nearby farmer, contemplated aiding Smith in the translation and publication of the plates. Initially doubting their authenticity, Harris had Smith make a transcript of part of the plates, which were purportedly written in Reformed Egyptian. Harris took the transcript to New York City for verification by experts. He consulted Samuel Latham Mitchell, vice-president of Rutgers Medical College, and Charles Anthom, a classics professor at Columbia College. Mitchell, an early supporter of the **Bering Strait theory** of Native American origins, gave Harris no encouragement, but he directed him to Anthom. After viewing the transcript in February 1828, Anthom agreed that many of the figures were indeed characters from ancient scripts but did not commit himself as to whether they were part of an authentic ancient document. Eager to believe, Harris took this statement as a full confirmation. When Anthom learned that his name was being used to support the authenticity of Mormonism, he vigorously denied saying that the transcript was a copy of genuine ancient writing.

Twentieth-century painting of Joseph Smith, Jr.

The first phase of Joseph Smith's translation of *The Book of Mormon* took place from 12 April to 14 June 1828. Smith used the seer stones, or urim and thummin, as spectacles and dictated his translation to Martin Harris. The two men were separated by a curtain because Joseph Smith believed that only he could look at the gold plates and not die. A manuscript of 116 foolscap pages was written, but when a reluctant Smith gave Harris permission to take the manuscript home and show their work to his doubting wife Lucy, she stole it. Despite strenuous efforts by Harris, his wife refused to return the manuscript and it was never seen again.

Smith feared that the missing manuscript might be used to discredit his revelation by pointing up inconsistencies between the first translation and a second. Translation recommenced in early 1829 at the point where it had left off, with Smith dictating to his wife Emma or her brother Reuben Hale. In May 1829 Smith proclaimed that a divine visitation forbade retranslation of the first part. He also provided new plates that contained an account paralleling the missing material. On 7 April Oliver Cowdrey, a 22-year-old schoolteacher, took over the job of transcribing. By early July Smith and Cowdrey completed the task.

By 11 June 1829 Joseph Smith had filed for a copyright on *The Book of Mormon*. After some difficulty Egbert B. Grandin, publisher of the local newspaper the *Wayne Sentinel,* agreed to print the book. Martin Harris mortgaged his farm as security for the printing bills. Advertisements appeared in the 26 March 1830 issue of the newspaper, but sales were poor. Most people considered the book an affront to traditional Christianity.

The Book of Mormon claimed to be a history of the **Nephites** and **Lamanites,** two nations descended from Hebrews fleeing the destruction of Jerusalem and taking refuge in the New World about 600 B.C. Like the biblical Hebrews, the Nephites continually fell away from a proper faith in God. After his crucifixion and resurrection, Christ visited the New World inhabitants but brought about only a temporary reformation. Eventually the Lamanites destroyed the Nephites, ending Christianity in the New World about A.D. 400. *The Book of Mormon* also contained a briefer account of the **Jaredites,** who were even more ancient; they traveled to the New World at the time of the confusion of languages at the Tower of Babel.

The history in *The Book of Mormon* seemed more plausible at the time of its first appearance than it does today. Numerous theories on the origins of Native Americans and pre-Columbian visitors were quite prevalent then. Unfortunately for the adherents of these theories and *The Book of Mormon,* continuing archaeological research has only served to bolster the Bering Strait Theory (which was only just beginning to gain scholarly acceptance in Smith's day), while undermining the rest.

From its beginnings, Mormonism faced persecution. After an unsuccessful attempt in 1831 to settle in Kirtland, Ohio, Joseph Smith hoped to make northwest Missouri his headquarters. Violent opposition from Missourians during 1838–1839 forced the Mormons to move to Illinois. Initially welcomed, the Mormons built their town of Nauvoo. Rumors and increasing evidence that some Mormons practiced polygamy split the religious community and fueled the growing hostility and suspicions of the surrounding non-Mormon population. When Joseph Smith destroyed an opposition newspaper's press in Nauvoo, he finally aroused the fears of potential Mormon tyranny to fever pitch. Civil war threatened Illinois and compelled Smith to submit to arrest. He was jailed at Carthage, where a mob killed him on 27 June 1844. His church, along with its unique version of beliefs in pre-Columbian visitors to the New World, survived.

Bibliography: Brodie, Fawn M., *No Man Knows My History: The Life of Joseph Smith,* [1945], 2nd ed., 1971; Bushman, Richard L., *Joseph Smith and the Beginnings of Mormonism,* 1984.

Solon (fl. 594 B.C.)

This Athenian statesman and lawgiver is cited by **Plato** as the source for his information about the ancient lost continent of **Atlantis.**

It is well known that Solon traveled extensively in the world of the eastern Mediterranean Sea as a merchant. Therefore, when Plato's dialogue *Timaeus* mentioned that Solon visited Egypt, it supplied a plausible touch. According to Plato, Solon stopped off at the city of Säis and spent some time with the priests. They told him that the Greeks knew little or nothing about the history of the distant past. They proceeded to inform him of the glories of the Athens of 9,000 years earlier (ca. 9600 B.C.) and its war with the great island empire of Atlantis. The war was ended by great earthquakes and floods that annihilated the Athenian army and sank Atlantis under the waves of the ocean. Only unnavigable and muddy shallows were left where the once great continent had been. Oddly enough, Solon did not reappear as a source for the more detailed description of Atlantis supplied by Plato's next dialogue, *Critias*.

Most scholars do not consider Plato's Atlantis story or Solon's conversations with the **Egyptian** priests accounts of real events. None of Plato's dialogues was a literal recounting of real debates and conversations by Socrates, his students, or Plato's contemporaries; they were philosophical treatises dressed up as fictional exchanges among people who had actually existed. Solon also existed, but there is no other evidence to indicate that he brought back the Atlantis story from Egypt. No trace of the Atlantis story existed in Greek literature before the writing of Plato's *Timaeus*. Solon's story is almost certainly a fictional tale that Plato used as a didactic device. Nevertheless, it engendered widespread belief in **lost continent legends** along with their numerous connections to fringe theories about the origins of Native Americans and other pre-Columbian visitors to the Americas.

Bibliography: de Camp, L. Sprague, *Lost Continents*, [1954], 1970.

Songhay Traders in Fifteenth-Century Mexico

According to Ivan Van Sertima, an advocate of **African** contacts with pre-Columbian America, merchants from the Songhay empire traveled to the Caribbean basin and Mexico from 1462–1492 or earlier. His evidence is the supposed depiction of Negroid people from Africa in various Native American statuary and drawings. His identifications of these figures as Africans are highly problematic; a few scholars accept them, but most do not. Van Sertima also bases his argument on the alleged presence of **cotton** on the Cape Verde Islands by 1462. But it has not yet been satisfactorily proven that American cotton was growing on the Cape Verdes prior to 1492.

Other structural problems bedevil Van Sertima's theory. Prior to the reign of Sunni 'Alī the Great (1464–1492), the Songhay realm had either been under the suzerainty of the empire of Mali during the fourteenth century or suffered periodic depredations by the nomadic and warlike Tuareg tribes. Van Sertima is suggesting that some Songhay were traveling to Mexico for trade just as their empire was beginning its rise to power, which seems politically improbable. Even more troublesome is the fact that the Songhay homeland was located on the Great Bend of the Niger River in the vicinity of the cities of Gao and fabled Timbuktu. Even at their most successful, the Songhay armies never subdued the coastal regions of West Africa. It makes little sense that a landlocked people would be able to engage successfully in long-distance oceanic trade. Why would they even want to start? The Songhay already had the lucrative trans-Saharan trade in gold and slaves to keep them busy. Finally, Van Sertima has the Songhay trading with the Americas up until 1492. Why did they quit at that time? Why did the newly arriving Europeans never come across any of these Songhay merchants? Certainly no even moderately convincing archaeological or documentary evidence has been found to suggest that Songhay traders ever reached Mexico.

Bibliography: Oliver, Roland, *The Cambridge History of Africa*, vol. 3: *From c. 1050 to c. 1600*, 1977; Van Sertima, Ivan, *They Came before Columbus*, 1976.

Sumé

Also known as Tumé or Zumé, this so-called white god of the Tupinamba tribe of southeastern **Brazil** is thought by some **diffusionist** writers to be a regional variation of the legendary white god **Viracocha** of Peru.

Many theories regarding the supposed **white god legends** of the Native Americans and pre-Columbian contacts with the Old World have been suggested. In the case of Sumé, however, his name was claimed to be a corruption of Thomas, that is, **St. Thomas,** the so-called Apostle of the Americas. According to this explanation, the story of Sumé is a garbled memory of St. Thomas's missionary work among the Native Americans.

Sumerians in Ancient America

The Sumerians flourished in southern Mesopotamia from 3000–2000 B.C. until Semitic peoples invaded and overthrew them. Like the **Cretans** and **Hittites**, the Sumerians were a forgotten people until their history was restored by twentieth-century archaeologists. As knowledge of them increases, some **diffusionists** suggest they traveled to the Americas or that their culture traveled there through the process of diffusion.

An early advocate of Sumerian influences on the Americas was Lawrence A. Waddell who, in his *Makers of Civilization in Race and History* (1929), placed the Sumerians in the role of the source of all human civilization. Waddell's thesis mirrored contemporary Grafton Elliot Smith's better-known theory of Egypt as the original

source of all higher culture. The husband-and-wife archaeological team of A. Hyatt and Ruth Verrill believed that the Sumerians definitely established colonies in the Americas. Another diffusionist writer, Pierre Honoré, cites as evidence the technique of metalworking that produced granulated gold. It supposedly diffused from the Sumerians to the Chavin empire of South America rather than being independently invented. In his *The God-Kings and the Titans* (1973), James Bailey claimed that Sumerian traders reached the Americas. In 1958 Mormon writer Thomas S. Ferguson identified the **Jaredites** of *The Book of Mormon* as Sumerians. Subsequent Mormon scholarship, however, has moved away from Ferguson's identification. One problem for all writers advocating Sumerian visits to America is a lack of plausible evidence. Furthermore, the Sumerians do not seem to have had a seafaring technology of any great sophistication. Although **Thor Heyerdahl** has demonstrated that the simple technology of the Sumerians was capable of impressive voyages, it stretches credulity to suggest that they were making either one-way or two-way journeys to the Americas. So the Sumerians have never become one of the more popular candidates for being pre-Columbian visitors.

Bibliography: Bailey, James, *The God-Kings and the Titans: The New World Ascendancy in Ancient Times*, 1973; Honoré, Pierre, *In Quest of the White God*, 1964; Verrill, A. Hyatt, and Ruth Verrill, *America's Ancient Civilizations*, 1953.

Sweet Potato

There are two divergent claims regarding the sweet potato as evidence for pre-Columbian contact between the Americas and the Old World. One theory is that the sweet potato originated in Africa and was carried to the Americas. The other places the origin of the sweet potato in the Americas but claims that it was carried into Polynesia during the era before European contact.

The sweet potato (*Ipomoea batatas*) is considered by the vast majority of scholars to be a native of the Americas. A member of the morning glory family of plants, research indicates that it evolved in tropical Central America from a wild plant with the scientific name of *Ipomoea trifida*. The domesticated sweet potato differs from its wild relative in that it produces an edible swollen underground stem or tuber. In 1954 botanist Elmer Drew Merrill suggested a possible African origin for the sweet potato. Since that time, no evidence has been discovered that supports Merrill's position, and other scholars have either rejected or ignored it. Despite its lack of support from botanists, **diffusionist** writers occasionally use Merrill's theory of an African origin for the sweet potato to bolster their own ideas about **African voyages to pre-Columbian America.** However, botanical and archaeological evidence overwhelmingly puts the original home of the sweet potato in the Americas.

Except for a few Spanish landings in the sixteenth century, sustained European contact with Polynesia began in the eighteenth century with Jacob Roggeveen's discovery of **Easter Island** in 1722 and Captain James Cook's visits to the Hawaiian Islands in 1778 and New Zealand in 1769. When the Europeans arrived, the natives of these islands all cultivated the sweet potato. Obviously the plant came from the Americas, but how and when did it get to Polynesia? Some people suggest a natural transfer, in which a sweet potato seed or tuber floated from the Americas to the various Polynesian islands by accident. However, most experts feel that the sweet potato's seeds or tubers were not capable of floating such vast distances. Furthermore, prolonged exposure to salt water would also destroy the fertility of the seeds and tubers. Therefore their presence in Polynesia would seem to indicate **Polynesian-American contacts** during the pre-Columbian era. Supporters of Polynesian-American contacts also cite linguistic evidence. They claim that in the Lima region of Peru, the native Quechua word for sweet potato is *kumar* or *kumal.* The Polynesians know the sweet potato by variations of these Quechua words. It is called *uwala* in Hawaii, *kumara* in New Zealand and Easter Island, *umara* in Tahiti, and *unala* in Samoa. Unfortunately, this impressive linguistic evidence is inaccurate. *Kumar* or *kumal* is not the Quechua word for sweet potato; it is *apichu. Kumar* does not refer to sweet potato anywhere along the coastal region of Peru. So, the best linguistic evidence does not support the occurrence of Polynesian-American contacts.

Supporters of Polynesian-American contacts suggest two possible explanations for the sweet potato migration to Polynesia. One theory postulates that Polynesians in outrigger canoes made the epic voyage to the Americas. After they landed they possibly launched a raid, acquiring a few prisoners and some starts of the sweet potato before they beat a hasty retreat home. An alternate theory claims that Peruvians sailed to Polynesia on balsa rafts using the South Equatorial current (see also *Kon Tiki* **Expedition**). Either group could have spread the sweet potato throughout the myriad islands of Polynesia.

Donald D. Brand, a geographer from the University of Texas, has advanced a subtle theory claiming that the spread of the sweet potato occurred entirely during post-Columbian times. According to his scenario, Spanish settlers carried the sweet potato home to Spain. From there it reached Portugal in 1500. The Portuguese then carried it to their trading stations in India before 1505. Asian traders—Persians, Arabs, and **Hindus**—took the sweet potato into the Moluccas, or the Spice Islands. At that point the sweet potato entered a trading network connected to Melanesia. After spreading quickly across these islands, the sweet potato reached Polynesia before any Europeans set foot on those islands. Brand's theory is not the final word, of course. Many others still support the theories that either Polynesians or Peruvians somehow carried the sweet potato to Polynesia in pre-Columbian times.

Bibliography: Baker, Herbert G., *Plants and Civilization*, 2nd ed., 1970; Brand, Donald D., "The Sweet Potato: An Exercise in Methodology," in *Man across the Sea: Problems of Pre-Columbian Contacts*, edited by Carroll L. Riley, et al., 343–365, 1971; Yen, Douglas E., "Construction of the Hypothesis for Distribution of the Sweet Potato," in *Man across the Sea: Problems of Pre-Columbian Contacts*, edited by Carroll L. Riley, et al., 328–342, 1971.

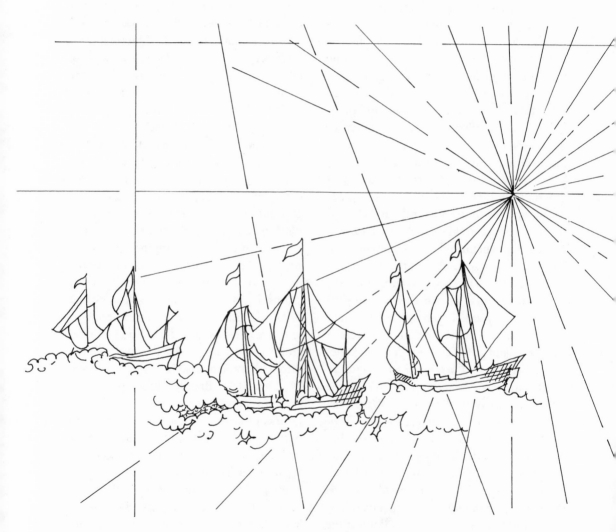

T

Tartars

Also spelled Tatars, this name refers collectively to the many nomadic tribes located in central and northern Asia between the Black and Caspian seas on one end and the Pacific Ocean on the other.

For centuries Europeans used the words Tartar and **Scythian** interchangeably. Tartar was also frequently used to mean the **Siberians.** According to some supporters of the **Bering Land Bridge/Strait Theory,** the Tartars and Native Americans or Red Indians were descended from the same peoples. Writers such as **Hugo Grotius** who opposed the Bering Land Bridge/Strait theory argued in turn that since the Tartars were a culture heavily dependent on the use of the horse, there could be no connection between them and the natives of pre-Columbian America,

who did not have horses. Such a belief was based on the assumption that Tartar culture was static and unchanging. Dutch scholar **Johan De Laet** refuted it as early as the 1640s, and showed that Tartars and Native Americans were almost certainly related.

Bibliography: Beazley, C. Raymond, *The Dawn of Modern Geography,* 3 vols., [1897–1906], 1949; Huddleston, Lee Eldridge, *Origins of the American Indians: European Concepts, 1492–1729,* 1967; Wright, Herbert F., "The Controversy of Hugo Grotius and Johan De Laet on the Origins of the American Aborigines," in *Some Less Known Works of Hugo Grotius,* edited by Herbert F. Wright, 1928.

Teive, Voyage of Diogo de (1452)

Besides discovering the islands of Corvo and Flores in the Azores group, Teive's expedition is alleged to have reached the Grand Banks of Newfoundland 40 years before the first voyage of Columbus.

Diogo de Teive came from Madeira. According to the accounts of **Bartolomé de Las Casas** and Ferdinand Columbus, in 1452 he departed from Faial in the Azores in the company of Pedro de Velasco of Palos (see also **Vasques de la Frontera, Pedro**). They sailed in a southwesterly direction in search of **Antillia,** the island of the **Seven Cities.** After traveling 150 leagues without finding anything, they headed back to the Azores and, by following a flight of land birds, discovered Flores. They proceeded northeast to the latitude of Cape Clear, Ireland. They found a calm stretch of sea, which they thought indicated land to the west. But it was already August and winter approached, so they decided to return home. Teive was later appointed the captain of Flores and Corvo.

Both Las Casas and Ferdinand Columbus, son of the great explorer, gleaned the story from Christopher Columbus's now-lost notebooks. Christopher Columbus learned of Teive's voyage from Pedro de Velasco of Palos, who encouraged him in his plans to sail west. None of these sources, however, claimed that Teive's expedition even sighted land, let alone landed.

In 1937 the modern Portuguese historian Jaime Cortesão put forward the claim that Teive discovered America in 1452. He contended that Teive really sailed northwest, not northeast, from Flores. As a result he sighted land, but the Portuguese government suppressed the full report because of its **"Policy of Secrecy,"** which was designed to guard jealously its discoveries. Cortesão's thesis is widely accepted in Portugal but nowhere else. Samuel Eliot Morison, the great American historian of Columbus, thoroughly refuted the Cortesão theory in several of his books, as have other reputable historians. Basically the prevailing direction of winds and currents in the North Atlantic makes it virtually impossible for Teive to have sailed to the northwest. Teive could not have come near the Grand Banks, let alone sighted North America.

Bibliography: Cortesão, Jaime, "The Pre-Columbian Discovery of America," *Geographical Journal* 89 (1937): 29–42; Crone, Gerald R., "The Alleged Pre-Columbian Discovery of America," *Geographical Journal* 89 (1937): 455–460; Morison, Samuel Eliot, *Portuguese Voyages to America in the Fifteenth Century*, 1940.

Teles, Voyage of Fernão (1474–1476)

According to some Portuguese historians, Portuguese seaman Fernão Teles discovered the island of Hispaniola in 1475 during his explorations of the western Atlantic. Later one of his pilots indiscreetly revealed that discovery to Christopher Columbus—and the rest is history.

Little is known about Fernão Teles and his western explorations. On 28 January 1474 King Afonso V granted Teles the right to search for and settle on any islands he might find, on the condition that they were not in the region of Guinea (i.e., West Africa). The king extended his grant on 10 November 1475 by including the right to settle the island of the **Seven Cities,** also known as **Antillia,** or any other inhabited island. This second grant led historian Brito Rebelo to speculate in his 1903 introduction to João de Lisboa's *Livro da Marinharia* that Teles had already discovered Hispaniola by 1475. In fact, there is no evidence that Teles had even sailed west by the time of the revision of his grant, or for that matter, that he sailed west after 1475. Of course, advocates of the theory that the Portuguese government practiced a **Policy of Secrecy** consider this lack of evidence a sure indication that Teles discovered something very important. Most historians believe that the voyage of Teles found nothing, if it took place at all.

Bibliography: Diffie, Bailey W., and George D. Winius, *Foundations of the Portuguese Empire, 1415–1580*, 1977; Morison, Samuel Eliot, *Portuguese Voyages to America in the Fifteenth Century*, 1940.

Ten Lost Tribes of Israel in Ancient America

From the sixteenth century to the present, many people have identified Native Americans as descendants of the Ten Lost Tribes of Israel.

The Assyrians carried the Ten Lost Tribes into captivity after the fall of Samaria in 722 B.C. In the Apocrypha of the Bible, 2 Esdras adds the story of how the Ten Lost Tribes fled from the Assyrians to the uninhabited land of Arzareth, to remain in hiding until the last days of the world. Although the Ten Lost Tribes and Arzareth have been placed all over Africa, Asia, and Europe, some writers suggest that Arzareth was the Americas and that the Ten Lost Tribes were the ancestors of Native Americans. See also **Hebrews in Ancient America.**

Terra Australis

Literally meaning southern land, it is the name for an unknown continent that people, from ancient Greeks through eighteenth-century Europeans, believed existed in the southern hemisphere.

The belief in Terra Australis originated in the Greeks' belief that the world consisted of four quarters: the oikoumene, the **antipodes,** the antoikoi, and the antichthones. Each quarter of the spherical earth supposedly contained an equal-sized landmass because the Greeks believed that an equal distribution of weight was necessary to keep the world in balance. The oikoumene, with its three continents of Africa, Asia, and Europe, was the world known to the Greeks. Each of the other quarters contained a similar landmass. The antipodes were the other northern quarter, the antoikoi were the southern quarter below the oikoumene, and the antichthones were the southern quarter below the antipodes. Two world-girdling oceans, the meridional and equatorial, separated the four quarters. It was commonly thought that the southern quarters were cut off from the northern quarters by the deadly heat of the equatorial region, which no one could cross and live. As a result, ancient and medieval maps simply showed a single large landmass circling the entire southern hemisphere. They also occasionally included an analogous unknown western continent, **Terra Occidentalis.** The geographical work *Liber Floridus,* written by the early–twelfth-century canon Lambert of St. Omer, is an excellent example of such a worldview.

During the classical and medieval eras, Terra Australis and the antipodes were frequently conflated. Some geographers, including Claudius Ptolemy, suggested that Terra Australis was not completely separated from the oikoumene by the equatorial ocean. Instead, Africa was simply a large peninsula connected to the great southern continent. The Indian Ocean was an inland sea, and therefore Africa could not be circumnavigated. Such a belief rendered Portuguese explorations down the African coast quite problematic. However, Europeans lost contact with Ptolemy's geographical concepts until the fifteenth century, so his ideas had little impact on the Portuguese program of African exploration. Basically the belief in the existence of unknown lands across the oceans served to spur further exploration and geographical speculation. The discovery of North America ended further speculation about Terra Occidentalis by showing that such a place actually existed. The search for Terra Australis continued off and on until the voyage of Captain James Cook in 1772. His explorations conclusively proved that the southern continent did not exist except for the frozen landmass of Antarctica.

Bibliography: Ramsey, Raymond H., *No Longer on the Map: Discovering Places That Never Were*, 1972; Wright, John Kirtland, *The Geographical Lore of the Time of the Crusades*, [1925], 1965.

Terra Occidentalis

Literally meaning western land, it is the name for an unknown continent the ancient Greeks and Romans believed to exist in the western hemisphere. The Greeks divided the spherical earth into four quarters: the oikoumene, the **antipodes,** the antoikoi, and the antichthones. Each quarter contained a landmass separated from the other three by the world-encircling equatorial and meridional oceans. The oikoumene quarter contained the known world, which consisted of Africa, Asia, and Europe. The opposite quarter of the northern hemisphere was the antipodes, also frequently called Terra Occidentalis. Many ancient and medieval world maps depict both Terra Occidentalis and its southern counterpart, **Terra Australis.** The geographical treatise *Liber Floridus,* written by Lambert of St. Omer in the early twelfth century, discusses both Terra Occidentalis and Terra Australis.

Both unknown continents served as inspirations for exploration, and Terra Occidentalis was the first to become known. When John Cabot sighted Newfoundland in 1497, he began a process by which the geographical concept of North America soon replaced the concept of Terra Occidentalis. It is important to remember that ancient and medieval speculations about unknown continents were just that—speculation. It was the symmetrical nature of the Greek worldview that demanded the creation of a western landmass, not the vague survival of stories concerning supposed pre-Columbian visitors to the Americas.

Bibliography: Wright, John Kirtland, *The Geographical Lore of the Time of the Crusades,* [1925], 1965.

Theopompus of Chios
(ca. 378 B.C.–?)

A Greek historian and younger contemporary of **Plato,** his writings mention the existence of a vast western continent inhabited by an advanced urban civilization.

Theopompus and his father Damasistratus were banished from Chios for their support of Sparta. **Alexander the Great** of Macedonia restored them to their homeland in hopes of displacing the pro-Persian rulers of the island. In his historical writings, Theopompus showed great psychological insights into various leaders' motives and actions. As a follower of Isocrates, he viewed history and politics as closely related. His two main works were *Hellenica* (a history of Greece continuing Thucydides's history of the Peloponnesian War) and *Philippica* (a history of Alexander's father Philip).

Theopompus's books survive only as fragments in the form of excerpts contained in the works of later writers. The Roman historian Aelian (ca. 170–235) quotes

Theopompus in his *Varia historia* concerning a visit King Midas received from Silenus, a follower of Dionysius and companion of the Satyrs. According to Silenus, Europe, Asia, and Africa were merely islands in the ocean, and one great continent lay beyond the waters of the ocean. Everything was bigger on this continent including the people, who were twice the size and lived twice as long as normal humans. These people lived in various cities, the two greatest being Eusebes, a place of piety and peace, and the warlike city of Machimus. Once, the people of Machimus made a voyage to Europe but they turned back after reaching the land of the legendary northern race of Hyperboreans. The Machimians learned that the ancient Greeks believed that Hyperboreans led the most blessed existence of all humans. Since they had found Hyperborean life so contemptible, the Machimians concluded it was not worth contacting the rest of humankind. Silenus's account mentions other wonders on the great continent, including mystical trees that bore fruit producing states of grief and pleasure.

Some students of pre-Columbian exploration take Theopompus's account as an indication of a vague knowledge of the island-hopping route across the North Atlantic later used by the **Vikings** (see also **Geographical Concepts: Norse**). Others argue that Theopompus's source may have been a satire written by the dramatist Thespis (fl. 535–533 B.C.) to criticize **Solon's** accounts of **Atlantis** and other western lands beyond the ocean.

Bibliography: Conner, W. R., *Theopompus and Fifth Century Athens*, 1965; Graves, Robert, *The Greek Myths*, 1958.

Theosophy

A pantheistic religion founded during 1875 in New York City by Madame Helena P. Blavatsky (1831–1891) and Colonel H. S.

Olcott, theosophy derives many of its teachings from the sacred books of Hinduism and Buddhism. Its adherents' beliefs consist of a curious mixture of magic and rationalism as well as the advocation of universal toleration. Theosophists also believe in the prehistoric existence of the lost continents of **Lemuria** and **Atlantis,** and a series of races that existed prior to the evolution of present-day humans. Some of these lost races helped to people and civilize the Americas millenniums before Columbus.

Madame Blavatsky presented her ideas on ancient history and lost continents in her three-volume work *The Secret Doctrine* (1888–1897). The factual basis for Blavatsky's book was nonexistent. She claimed to have received her information during trances in which she communicated with the mysterious Mahatmas of Tibet, who let her read from the ancient *Book of Dzyan*. The *Book of Dzyan* was composed in Atlantis in the lost language of Senzar. According to Blavatsky, the world would go through seven eras, each associated with a root race. Each of these main root races was further divided into seven subraces. The first root race had the form of astral jellyfish and were basically spiritual beings. The second had physical bodies and lived on the lost Arctic continent of Hyperborea. After Hyperborea sank below the sea, the Pacific continent of Lemuria arose and took its place. The Lemurians formed the third and rather strange root race of apelike hermaphrodites who reproduced by laying eggs, had four arms, and an eye in the back of their heads. Then disaster struck the Lemurians—they discovered sex and brought down upon themselves the wrath of the Theosophical gods. Lemuria suffered a rain of fire and sank into the Pacific Ocean. Meanwhile, Atlantis rose about 850,000 years ago to form the home of the fourth root race.

Atlanteans were quite human except that they were bigger, more intelligent, and generally better than humans of the present era. They invented airplanes and electricity, and spread their civilization to other parts of the world including Egypt and the Yucatán in Central America. Many of the Near Eastern pyramids, various Druid temples, and the Mesoamerican ruins are the remains of the Atlantean culture. But Atlantis too eventually suffered an apocalyptic catastrophe. Earthquakes destroyed that continent and it slipped under the sea about 11,000 years ago, just as **Plato** described it.

The humans of the present are the fifth root race of Theosophical doctrine, and there are sixth and seventh root races yet to come. New continents will also arise, such as Nulantis, which will appear out of the depths of the South Atlantic sometime in the future. Madame Blavatsky died in 1891, but Theosophy has survived her. New leaders, such as Annie Besant (1847–1933) and W. Scott Elliot, added considerable detail to Blavatsky's outline of the world's prehistory. They used some of the same basic sources such as "astral clairvoyance," that is, direct mental communication with those holy and very informative Mahatmas. Skeptical scholars find such sources rather difficult to check for accuracy. Meanwhile Theosophy and its related sect, **Anthrosophy**, still have a goodly number of followers who accept the basic teachings and doctrines of Madame Blavatsky including those concerning Lemuria, Atlantis, and pre-Columbian Atlantean colonies in the Americas.

Bibliography: de Camp, L. Sprague, *Lost Continents*, [1954], 1970; Williams, Stephen, *Fantastic Archaeology: The Wild Side of North American Prehistory*, 1991.

Thomas the Apostle in America, St.

The belief arose shortly after Christopher Columbus's first voyage to America that St. Thomas, along with St. Bartholomew, visited the natives of the Americas and brought them Christianity. St. Thomas was identified as the source for various Native American legends about **white gods** such as **Quetzalcoatl** in Mexico and Tonapa in the Andean lands.

For centuries Christian tradition credited St. Thomas and St. Bartholomew with evangelizing India during the early years of the Christian church. St. Thomas was said to be buried in India at Mylapore near Madras, a fact that was confirmed when the Portuguese located his tomb in 1522. Meanwhile, when Columbus encountered the outlying islands of the Americas, he and others initially mistook them for islands off the coast of Asia and therefore named them the Indies. Given this geographical confusion, Columbus's contemporaries began to compare him with St. Thomas and predicted the imminent discovery of evidence of St. Thomas's missionary work and his tomb.

It was not until 1519 that a clear distinction between the East Indies and the West Indies as widely separate geographical locations became common knowledge. By then, the connection between the Americas and the missionary activities of St. Thomas, and to a lesser extent of St. Bartholomew, had become fixed in the minds of many Europeans. They argued that the Bible claimed that Christianity had been carried to all parts of the world. Furthermore, some argued that the ancients had sufficient navigational skills to reach the Americas. Others argued that even if they did not, angels or some other miraculous force could have brought St. Thomas to the New World.

The first work to assert specifically that St. Thomas preached in the Americas was a German book titled *Tidings out of Brazil* that appeared in 1514, based on the account of a Portuguese or Italian trader. According to the book, the natives considered St. Thomas to be some sort of lesser god. Meanwhile, continued exploration by the Spanish brought them into contact with the more advanced civilizations of Central America. The expeditions of Francisco Córdoba in 1517 and Juan de Grijalva in 1518 observed what they thought was the use of the cross as a religious symbol by the Maya. Other travelers reported the same thing. More crosses were located in other parts of Mexico and later in Peru. Various figures from Native American religions and legends also seemed to resemble **Jesus Christ,** the Virgin Mary, and other Christian personages. Both **Diego Durán** and **Bernardino de Sahagún** identified the Aztec deity Quetzalcoatl/Topiltzin as St. Thomas. This identification confused Quetzalcoatl the god and Quetzalcoatl/Topiltzin, the hero of Tula. Quetzalcoatl/Topiltzin lived centuries after St. Thomas and therefore could not possibly have been him. At the same time, it was chronologically possible to link St. Thomas with the earlier Quetzalcoatl the god. Some writers argued that Thomas and Quetzalcoatl both meant twin. This interpretation means abandoning the usual Nahuatl (the ancient language of central Mexico) meaning for Quetzalcoatl of "feathered serpent" in favor of the alternative of "precious twin." Another Native American deity identified as St. Thomas was Tonapa (Thonapa) from Andean mythology. Tonapa was described as a bearded, blue-eyed man who wandered among the various groups of Andean peoples preaching love and performing miracles. **Sumé** (or Zumé), a benevolent god of the Tupinambas and other tribes of **Brazil,** was also identified as St. Thomas. Both Sumé and Tonapa were names that could be considered corruptions of Thomas. Many detailed stories of Sumé's (St. Thomas's) missionary work among the Brazilian Indians were collected by postconquest priests, although they appear for the most part to be spurious, latter-day additions. They attest, however, to the enduring nature of the belief that St. Thomas visited the Americas and brought Christianity there during the first century A.D. As the work of Roman Catholic historian Peter De Roo demonstrates, it remains an accepted, but unproven, belief into the twentieth century.

Bibliography: De Roo, Peter, *History of America before Columbus,* vol. 1, ch. 9: "The Apostle St. Thomas in America," 1900; Vigneras, Louis-André, "Saint Thomas, Apostle of America," *Hispanic American Historical Review* 57 (February 1977): 82–90.

Torquemada, Fray Juan de (1563–1624)

This Augustinian priest and historian is erroneously credited with supporting the theory that Native Americans were the descendants of the **Ten Lost Tribes.**

Torquemada was born in Spain but moved to Mexico during his boyhood. He became an Augustinian priest in 1583 and eventually rose to be provincial of the order. Like many of his contemporary Spanish clergy, he wrote a history of the conquest and conversion of the native Mexicans that included descriptions and narratives of preconquest customs and events. Completing his work in 1612, Torquemada published it under the title *Monarquia Indiana* in 1615 at Seville. It borrowed heavily from the earlier unpublished studies of **Bernardino de Sahagún,** Andrés de Olmos, and Toribio Motilinía. Torquemada particularly plagiarized Gerónimo de Mendieta's *Historia Eclesiástica Indiana,* often copying complete chapters except where he softened any criticisms of the conquistadors. Such a pro-European viewpoint allowed Torquemada's writings to be published and dominate Spanish thinking while better but more critical histories languished unpublished and unread until the nineteenth and twentieth centuries.

Torquemada is often erroneously credited with supporting the theory that the Ten Lost Tribes of Israel were the ancestors of

Native Americans. In fact, he rejected the theory. The supposed similarities between Native American and Jewish customs did not persuade him that such a connection existed. However, he mistakenly attributed **Bartolomé de Las Casas** with originating the Ten Lost Tribes theory; that distinction belonged to **Francisco López de Gómara.** If Torquemada supported any theory about Native American origins and pre-Columbian visitors, it was the **Tartar** theory that the first Native Americans came from Asia. He also contended that the ancient Greeks and **Romans** had no knowledge of the Americas, and cited for evidence their geographical worldview that the earth consisted of the three continents of Africa, Asia, and Europe. Later Mormon writers have frequently quoted Torquemada's history in support of the historical authenticity of *The Book of Mormon.*

Bibliography: Huddleston, Lee Eldridge, *Origins of the American Indians: European Concepts 1492–1729*, 1967; Wilgus, A. Curtis, *The Historiography of Latin America: A Guide to Historical Writing, 1500–1800*, 1975.

Toscanelli dal Pozzo, Paolo (1397–1482)

This Florentine physician, mathematician, astronomer, and geographer anticipated Christopher Columbus in 1474 by advocating sailing west across the Atlantic Ocean as the shortest and easiest way to reach Asia from Europe.

Toscanelli was a native of Florence who lived and died in that city. In 1424 he earned a doctorate from the University of Padua. Although he practiced medicine, his special love was the study of geography and astronomy as well as its then closely related discipline, astrology. His studies earned Toscanelli a reputation for expertise in astronomical measurement and a command of the geographical lore brought back from China by the Venetian traveler Marco Polo (1254–1324).

About 1474 Portuguese King Afonso V (1438–1481) sought Toscanelli's opinions on geography and the feasibility of sailing west across the Atlantic to Asia. Canon Fernão Martins, a royal councillor, contacted Toscanelli and the two men engaged in several discussions on the matter. Unfortunately, Christopher Columbus's copy of Toscanelli's letter to Martins dated 25 June 1474 is all that survives of their correspondence. In the letter, Toscanelli strongly advocated the western route across the Atlantic as shorter and easier than any potential sea route the Portuguese might find around Africa. A map illustrating his contentions accompanied Toscanelli's letter, but neither the original nor any copies survive. According to Toscanelli's calculations, only 8,000 miles of sea separated Lisbon and the Asian mainland. The actual distance on the open sea was even less because the Portuguese would begin their journey from the Canary Islands, which lay farther west than Lisbon. Furthermore, he pointed out that the islands of **Antillia** and Japan were nicely located to serve as convenient rest stops. There is no evidence that either Afonso V or his successor João II (1481–1495) was impressed by Toscanelli's plan. But Christopher Columbus was; he contacted the Florentine during or before 1481 as he was in the process of formulating his own arguments for attempting the sail to Asia using the western route.

Some scholars, notably Henry Vignaud in 1902, questioned the authenticity of the Toscanelli letter. However, most scholars now accept it as authentic. Afonso V's query and Toscanelli's letter show that by 1474 there was significant interest in the exploration of the western Atlantic. The letter intriguingly refers to "the island of Antillia, which is known to you [the Portuguese]," a phrase that some take to mean that the

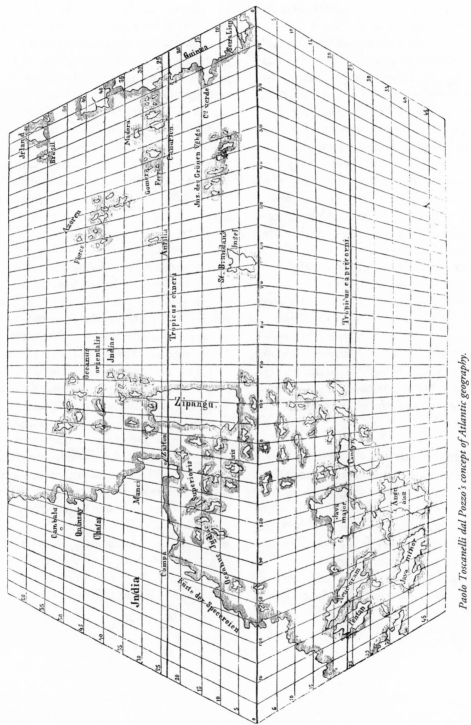

Paolo Toscanelli dal Pozzo's concept of Atlantic geography.

Portuguese had already reached Antillia (which would have been someplace in the Americas). But unless one accepts the arguments of the advocates of a **Portuguese Policy of Secrecy,** and with it the existence of secret voyages and discoveries, Portugal's kings showed relatively little interest in developing the western oceanic route to Asia. The most likely reason for their indifference is that they accepted larger estimates of the earth's circumference than those used by Toscanelli or Columbus, which would have made a western ocean voyage impossibly long, even with Antillia as a rest stop. Basically Toscanelli provides a good example of the geographical concepts and knowledge of an educated European during the late Middle Ages—concepts very similar to those held by Columbus and **Martin Behaim.**

Bibliography: Diffie, Bailey W., and George D. Winius, *Foundations of the Portuguese Empire, 1415–1580,* 1977; Dilke, D. A. W., "Toscanelli," in *The Christopher Columbus Encyclopedia,* edited by Silvio A. Bedini, 1992; Vignaud, Henry, *Toscanelli and Columbus: The Letter and Chart of Toscanelli,* [1902], 1971.

Trojans in Ancient America

The European discovery of the Americas and their inhabitants prompted much speculation over the possible origins of Native Americans. It was inevitable that the legendary Trojans would join the roll of progenitors of the American aborigines.

The leading advocate of the Trojan origin theory was English adventurer Thomas Morton (ca. 1590–1647), who wrote *New English Canaan; or New Canaan, Containing an Abstract of Three Books* in 1637. Morton claimed to discern Latin and Greek words in the languages of the native tribes of New England. That combination of languages caused him to suspect that the Trojans were the ancestors of Native Americans, since supposedly the Trojans would have used both Latin and Greek. In 1729 Spanish historian **Andrés González de Barcía Carballido y Zúñiga** added the Trojan origin theory to his revision of **Gregorio García's** 1607 work on Native American origins.

The undertaking of a long sea journey to America to start a new settlement was something the Trojans were perfectly capable of doing. After all, Aeneas and his Trojan refugees wandered the Mediterranean until eventually they stopped and founded Rome. So why not have a later Trojan leader, Brutus, lead other Trojans from war-torn Italy in search of a safer home, such as ancient New England? Morton's theory assumes that Troy and the Trojans existed just as Homer described them in the *Iliad* and as Virgil described them in the *Aeniad.* Troy did exist. Heinrich Schliemann's pioneering archaeological discoveries in the nineteenth century proved that. But it is also certain that these historic Trojans did not sail to North America. Morton's theory is pure speculation backed up by a few dubious linguistic parallels.

Bibliography: Huddleston, Lee Eldridge, *Origins of the American Indians: European Concepts, 1492–1729,* 1967; Morton, Thomas, *New English Canaan,* [1637], 1947.

U

Ulysses in Ancient America

Also known by the Greek version of his name, Odysseus, some writers claim that this legendary hero visited America either during his journey home after the fall of Troy, as described in Homer's *Odyssey*, or later in his life.

Ulysses was the king of Ithaca in Greece. When the Trojan War broke out, he joined the allied Greek army and participated in the siege. Renowned for his clever wiles, he proposed the strategy of building the Trojan horse. Because he offended the sea god Poseidon (or Neptune), it took Ulysses ten years to return home. Those ten years of adventures form the subject of the *Odyssey*. Later legends tell of how the restless Ulysses tired of life in Ithaca and returned to sea. Sailing west, he founded Lisbon, then sailed into the

Atlantic Ocean and was never heard from again. Geographers Strabo and Solinus repeated this legend, as did the great Italian poet Dante Aligheri of the Middle Ages. Spanish historian **Pedro Sarmiento de Gamboa** learned about it from their writings. Incorporating the legend into his *Historia de las Incas*, which he completed in 1572, Sarmiento speculated that after Ulysses sailed west into the Atlantic he reached the West Indies and eventually arrived at the Yucatán Peninsula and Campeche, where he brought civilization to the peoples of Mesoamerica.

During Sarmiento's time, people generally assumed that Ulysses was a historical personage rather than a mythological one. Even today it is assumed that the *Odyssey* at least reflected the Homeric age's concept of the geography of the Mediterranean world. In fact, some people still believe that Ulysses really lived and actually went on the Odyssey. In 1965 Henriette Mertz, a patent lawyer, wrote and privately published *The Wine Dark Sea: Homer's Heroic Epic of the North Atlantic*. Other writers have tried to trace Ulysses's journey around the Mediterranean Sea, but Mertz took him far beyond the Strait of Gibraltar and all the way across the Atlantic Ocean.

The *Odyssey* actually gives some credence to taking Ulysses into the Atlantic. In Book XI he and his crew sailed into the River Ocean, reached the land of the Cimmerians, and visited with their slain comrades in Hades. Mertz places all of Ulysses's adventures from the Laestrygonians onward into various locations around the North Atlantic. Circe's island is Madeira, Scylla and Charybdis are located in the Bay of Fundy, the River Ocean is the circular **ocean currents** of the North Atlantic, and Calypso's island is Santa Maria in the Azores. According to Mertz, Ulysses circled the North Atlantic twice, and on his second loop encountered a hurricane. Finally, on his second attempt, he was able to reenter the Mediterranean.

Mertz's reconstruction of Ulysses's itinerary during the *Odyssey* is interesting but not convincing. It is important to keep in mind that Ulysses was a fictional character. Furthermore, a journey of the magnitude that Mertz proposes seems just too incredible. Ulysses is just one of several travelers that Mertz attempts to place in the Americas. She also traced the routes that the **Chinese** and the tribe of Nephtali, one of the **Ten Lost Tribes**, took to reach the Americas. Lately Mertz appears to have joined forces with **Barry Fell** in an effort to locate supposed ancient inscriptions that prove the presence of more Old World visitors.

Bibliography: Mertz, Henriette, *The Wine Dark Sea: Homer's Heroic Epic of the North Atlantic*, 1965; Sarmiento de Gamboa, Pedro, *History of the Incas*, edited by Clements Markham, 1907.

Unknown Pilot of Columbus

Persistent stories have circulated from well before 1500 on into the twentieth century that a dying pilot from a storm-tossed trading vessel passed on sailing directions and a map to Christopher Columbus describing the accidental discovery of unknown, inhabited islands far across the Atlantic Ocean.

Many versions of this story have circulated, varying greatly in detail. Reduced to its basic, common elements, the story tells how a trading vessel in the Atlantic was blown off course to the west by a great storm that lasted many days. In the far western waters, the survivors landed on an unknown island inhabited by naked people. The sailors attempted to return to Europe, but since they did not know the best route for taking advantage of winds and currents, they remained at sea for a dreadfully long time. When their vessel eventually reached land, most of the crew had died from lack of food

and water, and the few survivors were beyond recovery. All but one, an unnamed pilot, died quickly. Christopher Columbus, who was a close friend of the last survivor, took him in and nursed him. Grateful for this hospitality, the dying man gave Columbus sailing directions and a chart to the location of the islands accidentally discovered during the ill-fated voyage. It was on the basis of this secret information that Columbus formulated his own "Enterprise of the Indies."

The details of the various stories differ significantly without affecting the core. Sometimes the ship is traveling from Spain or Portugal to England and/or Flanders. In other cases, the destination is Madeira, the Canaries, or Guinea. The dying crew returns variously to Graciosa or Terceira in the Azores, Madeira or Porto Santo, or the Canaries. The Unknown Pilot is called Andalusian, Basque, Galician, or Portuguese. **Garcilaso de la Vega** goes so far as to give the Unknown Pilot a name, **Alonso Sánchez**, and a specific hometown, **Huelva**.

Apparently rumors of the existence of the Unknown Pilot began to circulate with Columbus's first landing in the Americas. **Bartolomé de Las Casas** reported that the story was widely discussed when he arrived in Hispaniola in 1502. It first appeared in print in **Gonzalo Fernández de Oviedo's** *Historia general y natural de las Indias* in 1535, although he rejected it. Later, Las Casas included the story in his unpublished *Historia de las Indias* and took the ambiguous attitude that, while the story was probably not true, it was certainly possible. **Francisco López de Gómara** repeated the story in his *La historia de las Indias y conquista de México* (1552). A brief version appeared in **José de Acosta's** *Historia natural y moral de las Indias* (1590). The story's details were greatly expanded in *Primera parte de los comentarios reales de los Incas* (1609) by Garcilaso de la Vega, who very much believed that Alonso Sánchez was the

Unknown Pilot. Furthermore, knowledge of the Unknown Pilot story was not confined to the Spanish world. **Sir Thomas Herbert,** an Englishman, mentioned it in his *A Relation of Some Yeares Travaile . . .* in 1634 while advocating **Prince Madoc** as the first discoverer of America. The passage of time did not diminish the credibility of the Unknown Pilot story; it seemed almost to increase it.

However, the story has never gone unchallenged. Oviedo definitely dismissed its veracity, while Las Casas basically doubted it. Ferdinand, the youngest son of Christopher Columbus, was naturally the leading sixteenth-century debunker of stories that detracted from the glory of his father's achievement. To combat those stories, particularly Oviedo's own theories about the discovery of America by the Spanish king **Héspero** and the **Carthaginians,** Ferdinand wrote a biography of his father. Composed between 1535 and 1539, it was not published until 1571. Ferdinand skimmed lightly over the Unknown Pilot story by claiming that the pilot was Vicente Dias, a Portuguese seaman who had made several unsuccessful exploring voyages with Luca de Cassano into the western Atlantic around 1452.

Debate over the story continued over the intervening centuries, but gradually it lost credibility. The Spanish crown never attempted to use it during legal battles with Columbus's heirs over the cancellation of his lucrative concessions in the newly discovered lands. Although it would have worked in the crown's favor, it apparently was not given any credence. If the story had been true, it would also have meant that Columbus's geographical research and theories about the possibility of sailing west to reach Asia were a deception used to hide his secret, true destination. Finally in 1942, Samuel Eliot Morison, in his biography *Admiral of the Ocean Sea: A Life of Christopher Columbus,* pointed out that the winds and currents of the Atlantic would not allow a ship to be storm-blown in the manner of the Unknown Pilot story. In Morison's opinion, the true source of the story lay among the rumormongering, malcontented segment of Spain's first colonists in the New World who disliked Columbus. These arguments would seem to provide a final negative answer to the mystery of the Unknown Pilot.

But the debate flared up again in 1976 with the publication of Spanish historian Juan Manzano Manzano's *Colón y su secreto: El predescubrimiento,* which appeared in a second edition in 1982. In Manzano's opinion, one of the surest proofs that Columbus had secret information was his unshakable certainty that something lay to the west within reasonable sailing distance. Contrary to Morison, Manzano also claims that it was quite possible for a sailing ship to be blown to the West Indies by a storm while using the high seas route known as the *volta de Mina* from Guinea to Portugal. It was on just such a voyage that the supposed ship of the Unknown Pilot was fatefully and fatally blown west. Once Columbus gained possession of the secret, he used it at crucial junctures to persuade the doubting Ferdinand and Isabella to support him and to encourage the Pinzon brothers to keep sailing west for a little while longer. Manzano's argument is based on the assumption of the existence of an Unknown Pilot, and provides an extremely detailed interpretation of the events of Columbus's career. Still, certain serious problems remain. The traditional version of Columbus formulating his "Enterprise of the Indies" out of his own imagination and research continues to fit the known facts far better than any reliance on an Unknown Pilot as the true source of his inspiration.

Bibliography: Larner, John, "The Certainty of Columbus: Some Recent Studies," *History* 73 (no. 237, February 1988): 3–23; Morison, Samuel Eliot, *Admiral of the Ocean Sea: A Life of Christopher Columbus,* 1942.

Van Olmen, Voyage of Ferdinand (1487)

Other variations of his name are Ferdinand Van den Olm, Fernão d'Ulmo by the Portuguese, and Fernando de Olmos by the Spanish. This Flemish seaman, while in the service of Portugal, sailed west from the Azores in 1487 on a failed attempt to find western lands such as the island of the **Seven Cities.**

Van Olmen was one of many Flemings who settled on Portugal's various Atlantic islands. He did quite well in the Portuguese service and became a knight of the royal court. When he settled on Terceira in the Azores, he acquired the captaincy of part of that island. By early 1486, Van Olmen was engaged in negotiations with King João II of Portugal for a voyage of discovery into the

western Atlantic. João II confirmed their agreement by letters patent on 3 March giving Van Olmen the right to make such a voyage.

The single most important fact in the agreement was that Van Olmen, not the king, would pay for the expedition. Several years earlier Christopher Columbus had approached the Portuguese king with a similar plan, but when he asked for royal financing it was refused. João II was quite interested in the exploration of the western Atlantic, but only on the cheap. Van Olmen's destination was the legendary island of the Seven Cities, although no one knew if it was a single island, an island group, or a continent. In exchange for financing the voyage of discovery, Van Olmen would receive the rule of any lands he found and have full legal jurisdiction over them, whether inhabited or not. If the natives proved hostile, Van Olmen would also command any fleet sent to conquer them. His title to any discoveries would be hereditary, passing to either male or female heirs.

Apparently Van Olmen could not afford personally to finance the entire expedition, so he found a partner, João Afonso de Estreito of Funchal, Madeira. The two men reached an agreement on 12 June 1486, in which they would divide in half any lands they discovered. Estreito agreed to immediately supply Van Olmen with the sum of 6,000 reals. Van Olmen would pay for the crews and Estreito would pay for the expedition's two ships; each would command one ship. João II confirmed their contract by royal decree on 24 July. He added the clause that Van Olmen would hold overall command for the first 40 days, after which Estreito would command until the expedition returned to Portugal. On any lands they discovered, the two men would exercise joint authority.

The Van Olmen/Estreito expedition was scheduled to depart from Terceira in

March 1487. **Martin Behaim,** the famous German cartographer, was living on Faial in the Madeiras at that time and was supposedly allowed to take passage on the voyage. He apparently did not exercise that privilege, since there is no indication of Van Olmen's voyage on Behaim's globe of 1492. Some scholars speculate that Van Olmen himself never sailed, because no official documents survive mentioning the voyage's aftermath. The general scholarly consensus, however, is that Van Olmen's expedition sailed but failed to make a landfall. **Bartolomé de Las Casas** mentioned the expedition as a fact in his *Historia de las Indias,* although he never provided the further details that he promised his readers.

Ferdinand Van Olmen's expedition failed for two reasons. First, it started in March, which is a bad season for any relatively small sailing ship to attempt to cross the stormy North Atlantic. Second, it started from the Azores, which are located at a latitude in which the prevailing winds do not favor western voyages. Like many before and after him, Van Olmen took on virtually impossible sailing conditions and predictably failed.

Despite Van Olmen's failure, João II apparently retained an interest in western Atlantic voyages. When Columbus offered his services again in 1488, the king responded by inviting him to Portugal. Unfortunately for Columbus, Bartolomeu Dias returned from the Cape of Good Hope in December 1488, causing Portuguese interest in a western route to Asia to fade. The respected historian Charles Verlinden argued, along with other less respected writers, that the Portuguese made sightings of western lands and were well aware that something was out in the western Atlantic by the time of Van Olmen's voyage. Samuel Eliot Morison, an even more eminent historian, has argued strenuously for years against this idea of secret Portuguese discoveries in the western Atlantic. His opinion is that none of the Portuguese voyages managed to sight land, let alone make a landfall. Morison's argument has proven the more convincing to the great majority of scholars. In the absence of new and authentic evidence to the contrary, it should continue to represent the scholarly consensus.

Bibliography: Morison, Samuel Eliot, *Portuguese Voyages to America in the Fifteenth Century,* 1940; Verlinden, Charles, "A Precursor of Columbus: The Fleming Ferdinand Van Olmen (1487)," in *The Beginnings of Modern Colonization,* 1970.

Vasques de la Frontera, Pedro

Also known as Pedro de Velasco, this native of Palos accompanied **Diogo de Teive's** voyage of 1452.

The expedition sought but failed to find **Antillia** and unexpectedly discovered Flores and Corvo, the western islands of the Azores. Sailing farther to the northeast, the sailors became convinced that land lay nearby to the west because of the general calm of the sea. The approach of winter, however, forced them to return home to Faial in the Azores. Vasques later returned home to Palos, where he provided much moral support and encouragement to Christopher Columbus in his plan to reach Asia by sailing west. To his dying day, Vasques remained convinced that Teive just missed making a landfall. Unfortunately, he did not live to receive confirmation of his beliefs; he was murdered while Columbus was away on his first voyage.

Pedro Vasques de la Frontera exemplifies the fact that Columbus was certainly not alone in his efforts to explore the western Atlantic. Furthermore, Vasques's testimony proves that Teive never sighted land as modern Portuguese historian Jaime Cortesão alleges. If he had, Vasques would have informed Columbus. The presence of

Vasques, a Spaniard, on a Portuguese voyage of exploration shows why any **Portuguese Policy of Secrecy** regarding its oceanic explorations would have been ineffective even if it existed.

Bibliography: Cortesão, Jaime, "The Pre-Columbian Discovery of America," *Geographical Journal* 89 (1937): 29–42; Morison, Samuel Eliot, *Admiral of the Ocean Sea: A Life of Christopher Columbus*, 1942; Morison, Samuel Eliot, *Portuguese Voyages to America in the Fifteenth Century*, 1940.

Vikings in Paraguay

This theory contends that both the Irish and the Vikings (Norse) reached South America as well as North America between 950 and 1250.

The leading advocate of Viking visits to Paraguay and other parts of South America is Frenchman Jacques de Mahieu. He is the South American equivalent of **Barry Fell** and has found alleged ancient inscriptions, primarily runic, in many parts of South America. Some of Mahieu's Vikings supposedly even made it to **Easter Island.** The Viking presence is also used to account for the various **white god legends** and the so-called traces of Christianity among Native Americans. Mahieu believes that a Viking king

ruled over Paraguay before they fell from power. Afterward the Viking descendants regressed to become the white-skinned and blond-haired tribe known as the Guayakis.

Mahieu began writing on the subject of Vikings in Paraguay in 1971; through 1988 he produced 12 books on that and other closely related topics. His books have been published in French, German, and Spanish but not as yet in English. They also attracted, beginning in 1977, the harsh criticisms of Spanish-American scholar Juan Schobinger. Apparently Mahieu took this criticism very badly, and in 1981 threatened to sue Schobinger for libel. Schobinger refused to be intimidated, and stands by his criticisms.

Mahieu's writings are yet another example of the phenomenon of inscriptomania whose followers claim to have found large numbers of inscriptions from various ancient and medieval peoples of Europe and the Mediterranean all over the Americas. Mahieu's credibility is further diminished by claims that the **Trojans** also made it to the Americas and that the Knights Templar mined silver from the great ore deposits of Potosi, Bolivia, to finance the building of the great cathedrals of the twelfth and thirteenth centuries.

Bibliography: Sorenson, John L., and Martin H. Raish, *Pre-Columbian Contacts with the Americas across the Oceans: An Annotated Bibliography*, 2 vols., 1990.

Vinland

This pleasant land of woods, meadows, and rolling hills was temporarily settled shortly after the year 1000 by various medieval Norse explorers of North America including **Leif Ericsson** and **Thorfinn Karlsefni.**

Vinland's name and location have long been the subject of great controversy among scholars of Norse exploration in North America. The common translation for the word Vinland is wine land, which refers to the grapes the Norse supposedly found there. If this translation is correct, then the "vin" in Vinland is actually "vín," the word for wine. Some scholars suggest that the Norse word was simply "vin," meaning meadow or fertile. This philological interpretation is consistent with the **Vinland Sagas'** descriptions of Vinland containing rich grasslands. But it is inconsistent with the *Greenlanders' Saga's* detailed description of grapes, which is further corroborated by the description of Vinland and grapes contained in **Adam of Bremen's chronicle.** Furthermore, "vin" is an archaic Norse word that had long gone out of common use by the time of the Vinland voyages. Most scholars accept that Vinland literally means wine land, but do not necessarily believe that Leif Ericsson actually found grapes in Vinland. Some suggest that Leif named his new land Vinland for the same reason that **Eric the Red** named his **Greenland:** Such a ploy made it sound more inviting to potential settlers. Other scholars suggest that the Norse found some sort of berry plant that reminded them of grapes. Cowberries, squashberries, blueberries, and blackberries are among the suggested substitutes.

The problem of the grapes is directly related to the problem of the location of Vinland. Most scholars now accept Newfoundland as the location because of the discovery of the Norse site **L'Anse aux Meadows** in the early 1960s. Prior to that, various writers located Vinland anywhere from Newfoundland to Florida. New England, particularly the Cape Cod area, attracted many supporters since it was the northernmost place where wild grapes could grow in the manner described by the saga. Other writers point out that since the climate was warmer in the year 1000, grapes could have grown successfully much farther north than they do now. But there has been no consensus on where the northern limits of wild grapes might have been in the elev-

enth century. Helge Ingstad, the discoverer of L'Anse aux Meadows, feels it is possible that wild grapes might have grown as far north as Newfoundland.

Both the *Greenlanders' Saga* and *Eirik's Saga* describe Vinland as being two days' sail from **Markland.** Such a distance is consistent with Newfoundland being Vinland, if Markland is Labrador. The sagas describe Vinland as a rich land with rivers full of salmon, eliminating any locations south of the Hudson River. It also had such a mild climate and lush grasslands that no winter fodder was needed for the livestock. On the shortest day of the year, the sun rose over Vinland before 9:00 A.M. and set after 3:00 P.M. according to the *Greenlanders' Saga*. This description places Vinland somewhere between 40° and 50° north latitude, which is anywhere from New Jersey to the mouth of the St. Lawrence River. Furthermore, descriptions of Vinland may not all refer specifically to Leif Ericsson's camp called *Leifsbudir* (meaning Leif's booths or houses), which was probably located at L'Anse aux Meadows. *Leifsbudir* is also most likely the same place as Thorfinn Karlsefni's camp, which *Eirik's Saga* called Straumfjord. *Eirik's Saga* also mentions that Karlsefni tried to establish a second settlement called Hop, or Hope, farther to the south. Several scholars, including Magnus Magnusson and Hermann Pálsson, place Hop somewhere in New England. With only these rather general descriptions from the sagas, it is impossible to fix the true location of Vinland. That difficulty is not surprising since the sagas are not eyewitness accounts. Rather, they are written versions of oral narratives passed on for over two centuries before finally being written down. Information contained in the sagas needs to be used cautiously as it is a mixture of facts, conflations, errors, falsehoods, and fantasies.

Caution has not always dominated the debate over Vinland's location. For many

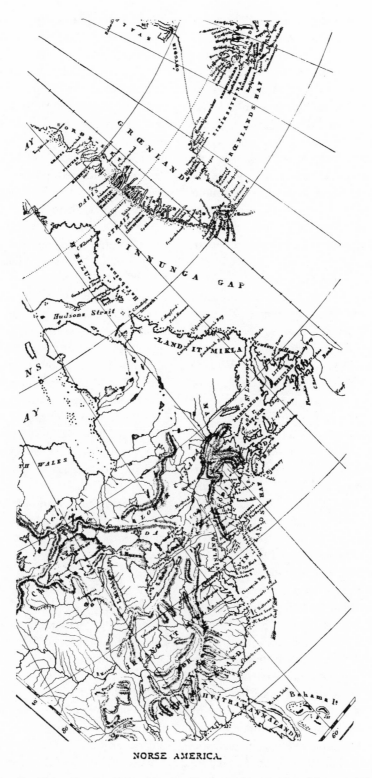

Nineteenth-century Danish map locating Hvítramannaland in the southeastern United States and Vinland in the middle Atlantic states.

centuries the Vinland Sagas and others received attention only from Scandinavian scholars. In 1705 Danish historian Torfaeus wrote the *Historia Vinlandiae antiquae,* placing Vinland in North America, but he made no attempt to determine an exact location. Benjamin Franklin learned about Vinland in 1750 from Swede Peter Kalm and considered the story authentic. Jeremy Belknap, an American clergyman and historian who was a harsh critic of tales about pre-Columbian explorations, cautiously declared in 1794 that the Vinland stories seemed credible. On the other hand, in an 1828 biography of Christopher Columbus, Washington Irving rejected the Vinland Sagas as reliable historical accounts. But American historian Henry Wheaton and Danish scholar Carl Rafn later persuaded him to change his mind.

Prior to 1830, scholars placed Vinland in Newfoundland or Labrador, if they made any attempt to locate it at all. That changed in 1831 when Henry Wheaton, the U.S. diplomatic minister in Denmark, published his *History of the Northmen,* which placed Vinland in New England. Wheaton's arguments convinced many of the antiquarians of New England. The great historian George Bancroft, however, remained quite skeptical of Wheaton's conclusions. Carl Christian Rafn (1795–1864) was a Danish scholar whose writings did even more than Wheaton's to revive interest in the story of medieval Norse visits to North America. His *Antiquitates Americanae* (1837) located *Leifsbudir* in Rhode Island, with the east coast of the United States from New Jersey to Maine being Vinland. As part of his evidence Rafn cited the Newport Tower in Rhode Island, a stone building thought by many to be a pre-Columbian structure. Later intensive research proved that the Newport Tower was actually built in the last half of the seventeenth century. Adherents of theories about Norse or other pre-Columbian

visitors ignore the Newport Tower's proven colonial origin and continue to cite it as evidence.

Thanks to Rafn's writings, many supporters of these theories appeared. Of course, Rafn was half right. The Norse voyages to America did take place, and well before the time of Columbus. But there is no credible evidence that Leif Ericsson's settlement was located in New England. Still, over the years others have accepted Rafn's location for Vinland, including **Benjamin Franklin De Costa** and Rasmus Anderson in the late nineteenth century, followed by Arlington H. Mallery, Hjalmar Holand, Charles M. Boland, Magnus Magnusson, and Frederick Pohl in the twentieth century. The finding of L'Anse aux Meadows and the close correspondence of that site to other topographical features mentioned in the Vinland Sagas has convincingly pulled the generally accepted location back to Newfoundland. Supporters of a New England location are now definitely on the fringes of scholarship. Oddly enough, the medieval Norse thought Vinland was an extension of Africa. They believed the Atlantic Ocean was virtually an inland sea and that Africa stretched west and then north toward Markland, **Helluland,** and Greenland to surround it. See also **Geographical Concepts: Norse.**

Bibliography: Jones, Gwyn, *The Norse Atlantic Saga,* 2nd ed., 1986; Magnusson, Magnus, and Hermann Pálsson, trans. and eds., *The Vinland Sagas: The Norse Discovery of America,* 1966.

Vinland Map

This controversial and possibly fraudulent mid–fifteenth-century map of the world is unique in showing **Greenland** as an island and also the region known as **Vinland**. It is cited as evidence that late-medieval Europeans had a significant awareness of earlier

Norse discoveries of lands in the western Atlantic Ocean.

Either the Vinland map is one of the most significant geographical manuscripts surviving from the later Middle Ages or it is the greatest of the many hoaxes related to the **Viking** presence in pre-Columbian America. When the Vinland map appeared in the 1950s, it was bound together with two medieval manuscripts. One manuscript was a section of Vincent of Beauvais's *Speculum historiale,* while the other was a previously unknown account of John de Plano Carpini's diplomatic mission to the Mongols in 1245–1247. Scholars title that manuscript the *Tartar Relation.* An examination of the paper used in the manuscripts indicates that it was manufactured about 1440, although the map itself may have been composed as early as 1425.

In its geographical concepts, the Vinland map is very similar to a world map made in 1436 by **Andrea Biancho** of Venice. Some skeptics suggest that the alleged forger of the Vinland map used the authentic Biancho map as a basis. It is the differences, however, that make the Vinland map significant. The Vinland map shows Greenland as an island, a piece of geographical knowledge that supposedly was not proven until long after the fifteenth century. More importantly, it shows the region of Vinland, which is labeled with a Latin caption reading "island of Vinland, discovered by Bjarni and Leif in company." Another long note right above Vinland states that Bjarni and **Leif Ericsson** while sailing together had discovered Vinland. It also provides the information that in 1117 **Bishop Eric Gnupsson** made an extended journey to Vinland. This apparent indication that Bjarni (**Herjolfsson?**) and Leif Ericsson sailed together to Vinland is not mentioned in either of the **Vinland Sagas**. The larger notation also provides evidence allowing the specific year of Bishop Eric Gnupsson's mission to be determined

as 1117. Besides showing Greenland as an island, the Vinland map's outline of that region's coastline is quite accurate by the standards of medieval cartography. By far the most significant and unique aspect of the Vinland map is its depiction of Vinland. No other medieval map shows the location of Vinland. If it is authentic, the Vinland map indicates that late-medieval Europeans had a greater awareness of the true geography of the western Atlantic Ocean than previously suspected.

The Vinland map is a document of mystery as well as controversy. It first appeared on the rare-book and manuscript market during the 1950s, but its true provenance remains a closely kept secret. The name and nationality of the person selling it have never been disclosed, allegedly because that person wished to avoid tax and customs difficulties. Experts at the British Museum declined to buy the manuscript when it was offered to them because of doubts about its authenticity. Laurence Witten, a rare-book dealer from New Haven, Connecticut, bought it in 1957. In 1959 a benefactor of Yale University bought the entire manuscript and gave it to that university in 1964.

In an effort to promote this apparently significant acquisition, R. A. Skelton, curator of maps at the British Museum, along with several librarians at Yale, brought out the massive volume titled *The Vinland Map and the Tartar Relation* in 1965. Considerable controversy followed its publication, culminating in the Vinland Map Conference held at the Smithsonian Institution in 1966. The gathering's results were edited by historian Wilcomb E. Washburn and published in 1971 as the *Proceedings of the Vinland Map Conference.* Basically, supporters and detractors of the Vinland map's authenticity found themselves in a scholarly standoff. Historical, geographical, and linguistic evidence did not conclusively support either side. Detractors argued that the accurate rendering of Greenland's coastline and its depiction as an island was an anachronism, proving the map was a fake. But a counter-argument pointed out that many speculative features appeared on authentic medieval maps; showing Greenland as an island could be simply speculation. Furthermore, the defenders of the map explained the accurate depiction of the coastline by arguing that it was a logical consequence of the centuries-long occupation of Greenland by the Norse. Those intrepid sailors knew that coastline very well.

As a result of the scholarly stalemate, officials at Yale University decided to authenticate the map by a scientific analysis of the physical evidence. In 1974 Walter C. McCrone, an analytical chemist, submitted a study of the chemical composition of the ink used to draw the Vinland map. He found that it contained a titanium-based substance called anatase that was not in use before 1920. This revelation resulted in the discrediting of the Vinland map, but its supporters were not ready to give up. Another team of chemists led by Thomas Cahill from the University of California–Davis performed further analyses of the inks of the Vinland map and other medieval manuscripts known to be genuine. They discovered that the post-1920 substance that McCrone called anatase was present in all the inks. Their revelation called McCrone's conclusions into question, although McCrone stood by the accuracy of his work and others joined in his defense. The authenticity of the Vinland map remains an open question, with scientists almost as stalemated as historians. In general, wary scholars treat the Vinland map with suspicion and will probably continue to do so until more conclusive evidence of its authenticity is brought forward.

Bibliography: Cahill, Thomas, et al., "The Vinland Map Revisited: New Composi-tional Evidence on Its Inks and Parchments," *Analytical Chemistry* 59 (1987): 829–833; McCrone, Walter C., *Chemical Analytical Study of the Vinland Map: Report to Yale University*, 1974; McCrone, Walter C., "The Vinland Map," *Analytical Chemistry* 60 (1988): 1009–1018; Skelton, R. A., et al., *The Vinland Map and the Tartar Relation*, 1965; Towe, Kenneth M., "The Vinland Map: Still a Forgery," *Accounts of Chemical Research* 23 (1990): 84–87; Washburn, Wilcomb E., ed., *Proceedings of the Vinland Map Conference*, 1971; Washburn, Wilcomb E., "The Vinland Map," in *The Christopher Columbus Encyclopedia*, edited by Silvio A. Bedini, 2 vols., 1992.

Vinland Sagas

This is the collective name for the two sagas dealing with Norse voyages to America: the *Greenlanders' Saga*, written around the 1190s, and *Eirik's Saga*, written about 1250–1260.

The Vinland Sagas are integral parts of the medieval literary genre of the Icelandic sagas. Two things about their nature as documents must be recognized in order to analyze them properly. First, 200 years or more separates the writing of these sagas from the events they describe, an observation that applies to most sagas. They are simply not eyewitness accounts. Second, compilers of sagas did not conceive of them as objective histories. While they contain some reasonably accurate descriptions of historical events, they also include various errors, inaccuracies, lies, and fantasies. Both points profoundly affect how the sagas can be used to reconstruct past events.

Saga writing began in **Iceland** during the early twelfth century as both a form of popular entertainment and an educational device. It reflected the Norse love for telling or listening to a good story, particularly during the long winter months. Thus sagas began as a form of oral poetry, although people soon began to write them down. After a while, Icelandic poets became so proficient at saga telling that there was a great demand for their employment throughout the royal and noble households of Europe. The Christian church in Iceland also contributed to the development of saga writing by its encouragement of the oral reading of edifying stories in public. Priests read about the lives of saints to their parishioners and encouraged the laypeople to do the same. A great demand for readable stories developed, while the subject matter became more secular and could be based on either historical or fictional events. The sagas also reflected Iceland's situation as a republic. Instead of concentrating on the activities of royalty, Icelandic sagas recorded the exploits of the first settlers and their descendants, events that began only about 250 years before the first written saga appeared.

Icelandic historian Ari Thorgilsson the Learned (1067/1068–1148) wrote the first saga, the *Islandingabók,* between about 1122 and 1125. He may have also written another important saga, the *Landnámabók,* possibly with the assistance of Kolskegg the Learned (d. before 1130). Both books are histories of the settlement of Iceland, and are important sources of information. The *Landnámabók* also contains the same account of **Eric the Red's** exploit that appears in the *Greenlanders' Saga* and *Eirik's Saga.* Many sagas followed these early works, providing a blend of history and fiction that reflected both the pagan and Christian values of the Icelanders.

The golden age of saga writing occurred between 1230 and 1280, the dates of the classic *Egil's Saga* and *Njal's Saga.* During this 50-year period sagas reached their most sophisticated level, with a more critical attitude toward the facts of the narrative, a wider historical perspective, and events explained in terms of cause and effect. These new developments help to explain the differences

between the *Greenlanders' Saga,* a preclassical composition of the 1190s, and *Eirik's Saga,* a classical saga from the 1250s. Compared with *Eirik's Saga,* the *Greenlanders' Saga* is a fairly crude although entertaining story. It does not present a tight narrative and can be coarse in its inclusion of pagan superstitions and violence such as **Freydis's** mass murders. *Eirik's Saga* is much more interested in telling a supposedly accurate history by the manner in which it presents its narrative. Many more details of description, names, and sailing directions are provided. The narrative is also more tightly integrated as it moves from **Leif Ericsson's** voyage to **Thorstein Ericsson's** failed voyage, and finally to **Thorfinn Karlsefni's** voyage. *Eirik's Saga* also reflects historical and geographical knowledge that the author of the *Greenlanders' Saga* did not have. A good example of this situation is the story of the uniped, or one-footed man. By the time of the composition of *Eirik's Saga,* the Norse believed that **Vinland** was part of Africa. Since Africa was the home of various monstrous races, including the unipeds, it only made sense that the Norse in Vinland should encounter some monstrous men. Most classical sagas contained a greater amount of such book learning than the early sagas.

The oldest surviving manuscript of the *Greenlanders' Saga* was found in a collection of sagas called the *Flateyjarbók,* which was compiled about 1390. *Eirik's Saga* survives in two distinct manuscripts. The older but more polished is a collection of sagas called *Hauksbók,* dating from about 1330, and also includes a version of the *Landnámabók.* The important Icelander Hauk Erlendsson put this collection together and subjected it to heavy editing and rewriting. The other surviving manuscript of *Eirik's Saga* appears in the *Skálholtsbók,* dating from about 1470. It is a rougher and longer version.

During the late nineteenth century, scholars tended to consider *Eirik's Saga* more historically accurate than the *Greenlanders' Saga.* As a result, Leif Ericsson received the credit for discovering Vinland, North America, instead of **Bjarni Herjolfsson.** Scholars now recognize that the *Greenlanders' Saga* is the significantly older and more accurate of the two. Furthermore, they attribute greater authenticity to the version of *Eirik's Saga* found in the *Skálholtsbók* than the more polished one in *Hauksbók,* even though the latter is older. Generally scholars agree that *Eirik's Saga,* despite its name, actually focuses on the activities and importance of Thorfinn Karlsefni, perhaps enhancing them more than the events merit. This is not surprising since *Eirik's Saga* was passed down through Thorfinn Karlsefni's descendants, including Hauk Erlendsson, the editor.

Obviously the Vinland Sagas are far from eyewitness accounts. They are a blend of history and fiction in which a core of truth can be readily discerned by the critical eye. Although in the past some scholars maintained that these sagas were totally fictional, the archaeological evidence of Norse settlement in America from **L'Anse aux Meadows** in Newfoundland both corroborates and vindicates their basic accuracy. Furthermore, a number of other sagas, such as the *Eyrbyggia Saga,* also contain mentions of western lands or Vinland. This knowledge of western lands in the Atlantic Ocean remained in common circulation among Icelanders and in other parts of the Scandinavian world into the Age of Discovery in the fifteenth and sixteenth centuries. Some scholars suggest that Columbus was influenced by these stories, but there is no definite evidence to support such a claim.

Bibliography: Jones, Gwyn, *The Norse Atlantic Saga,* 2nd ed., 1986; Magnusson, Magnus, and Hermann Pálsson, trans. and eds., *The Vinland Sagas: The Norse Discovery of America,* 1966.

Viracocha

Also known as Kon Tiki or Con Tiki, he was the supposed **white god** of the natives of Peru. The legend is cited by various **diffusionist** writers as evidence of visits to pre-Columbian Peru by various peoples of the Old World.

The name Viracocha means foam or fat of the sea, which was also a metaphor for the color white. According to some accounts of the beliefs of aboriginal Andean peoples, Viracocha was the supreme god and creator of the universe. He was associated with the sun but was more than a sun god. The worship of Viracocha included the sacrifice of children. Related to the god Viracocha was a story of the eighth king of the Incas who called himself Inca Viracocha, father of the great conqueror Inca Pachicuti. During his youth, Inca Viracocha briefly went into exile to escape his father's wrath. According to mestizo historian **Garcilaso de la Vega,** Inca Viracocha wore a beard.

It is widely reported that natives of the Andes believed Francisco Pizarro and his soldiers were the god Viracocha returning to bring the rule of justice. The white skin and beards of the Spanish supposedly reminded the Peruvian peoples of their god Viracocha and his promised return. Garcilaso de la Vega reported that Peruvian natives frequently called Europeans by the name "viracochas." But this reference may have been directed at their white skins and the color white being the ceremonial color associated with Viracocha rather than Viracocha's own skin color. Spanish historian Pedro de Cieza de León (ca. 1560–1591) also reported two native accounts of a second white god Viracocha who lived among the Andeans as a wandering preacher of love and kindness. This second Viracocha faced violent opposition because of his teachings but overcame it by miracles. Eventually he departed from Peru across the Pacific Ocean. Cieza stated that some people claimed these stories were native memories of visits by the apostles **St. Thomas** or St. Bartholomew, but he personally doubted it.

Nigel Davies, a modern prehistorian of the Americas, points out that the legends of Viracocha as reported by various diffusionist writers are not accurate versions of the original, authentic mythology. Most of the original native legends concerning Viracocha do not claim that he was white-skinned. Unlike in the case of the Mexican god **Quetzalcoatl**, it was never promised or prophesied that he would return and bring a restoration of a golden age. Furthermore, postconquest accounts of Viracocha seem to be filled with Spanish embellishments such as long white robes, benevolent missionary activities, and a flowing beard. Research shows that the Spanish elaborated on the existing Viracocha legends both to make Viracocha seem more like a visiting Spaniard and to have him predict his own (and, of course, their) triumphal return. All this was intended to enhance the prestige of the Spanish among the conquered Peruvians. Even the name *Kon Tiki* appears to be a Spanish invention, with the *Kon* having no apparent meaning. Etymologies claiming that *Kon Tiki* means "thunder vase" are spurious. Basically the modern versions of legends of Viracocha as a white god are an amalgamation of legends of the ancient god Viracocha, the narrative of the human ruler Inca Viracocha, and various Spanish additions. When the original legends concerning the god Viracocha are reconstructed, that deity no longer conforms to the basic characteristics of a legendary white god. He was not white-skinned, not bearded, not a benevolent ruler or preacher, and never promised to return. Viracocha the god cannot be used as evidence that white people from the Old World visited pre-Columbian Peru, whether they be **Alexander the Great's** sailors or the apostles St. Thomas and St. Bartholomew. Certainly the real god Viracocha bears no resemblance to the **Jesus Christ** of *The Book of Mormon,* contrary to the suggestion of Mormon writer Milton R. Hunter. It would appear that the legends of Viracocha were not nearly as convenient for the conquering Spanish to co-opt as were the legends of Quetzalcoatl and related Mesoamerican deities.

Bibliography: Davies, Nigel, *Voyagers to the New World,* 1979; Hagen, Victor Wolfgang von, ed., *The Incas of Pedro de Cieza de León,* 1959; Mercatante, Anthony S., *The Facts on File Encyclopedia of World Mythology and Legend,* 1988.

Vivaldi Expedition (1291)

This was the first European attempt to reach India by sea. Whether the two Genoese brothers who led the expedition sailed west across the Atlantic Ocean in anticipation of Christopher Columbus, or south to circumnavigate Africa in the manner of Vasco da Gama, is not known because the Vivaldis failed to return.

In 1291 the Mameluke Turks of Egypt captured the last Crusader outposts in Palestine, which prompted Pope Nicholas IV to order an embargo on trade with Egypt. As a result, European traders, particularly from the various Italian cities, sought ways to bypass or dislodge the powerful Mamelukes. One such response was the expedition of the Vivaldi brothers of Genoa.

A number of citizens of Genoa pooled their resources to outfit a substantial expedition to India. The fleet consisted of two galleys that were placed under the command of brothers Ugolino and Vadino Vivaldi and supposedly equipped with supplies for ten years. Two members of the new and vigorous Franciscan order also accompanied the galleys. Departing in May 1291, the fleet passed the Strait of Gibraltar and was last sighted at a place called Gozora. Some scholars identify Gozora as Cape Nun, and most agree that it was located somewhere between the Canary Islands and the beginnings of black Africa. The Vivaldi brothers may have been the first Europeans to rediscover the Canaries in the postclassical era.

Where the Vivaldis sailed after Gozora is uncertain. Their stated objective was to travel on the ocean to parts of India, a somewhat vague destination in light of European geographical concepts during the late thirteenth century. Most scholars feel that the Vivaldis intended to circumnavigate Africa, while a minority suggests they planned to sail west to Asia and therefore anticipated Columbus's first voyage by 200 years. Later fourteenth- and fifteenth-century reports of Vivaldi survivors and descendants in both West and East Africa tend to bolster the African-route hypothesis, although the reliability of these reports is questionable. Whichever route the Vivaldis took, their expedition marked the beginning of European expansion into the Atlantic Ocean and along the west coast of Africa that ultimately led to the voyages of Columbus and da Gama.

Bibliography: Fernández-Armesto, Felipe, *Before Columbus*, 1987; Rogers, Francis M., "The Vivaldi Expedition," *Seventy-Third Annual Report of the Dante Society* (1955): 31–45.

Vogado, Voyage of João (1462)

On 19 February 1462 King Afonso V of Portugal granted João Vogado the islands of Lovo and Capraria, which were supposedly located in the western Atlantic. Vogado failed to find the islands because they did not exist; Lovo and Capraria were the so-called False Azores. Still, the grant exemplifies Portugal's continuing interest in exploration of the western Atlantic in the years before Columbus's first voyage of 1492.

According to Portuguese historian Jaime Cortesão, voyages such as Vogado's actually reached America. But the **Portuguese government's Policy of Secrecy** led to the suppression of any news about successful voyages. The government wanted to guard Portugal's growing overseas interests from foreign interlopers. Cortesão's theory has little support outside Portugal. It is virtually certain that Vogado found nothing during the course of his voyage, if one even occurred.

Bibliography: Diffie, Bailey W., and George D. Winius, *Foundations of the Portuguese Empire 1415–1580*, 1977; Morison, Samuel Eliot, *Portuguese Voyages to America in the Fifteenth Century*, 1940.

Votan

Or Voton, this Mayan god or culture hero was said to have brought the basic components of civilization to the Tzentals, a Quiché or Highland Maya tribe. **Diffusionist** writer Constance Irwin identified Votan with supposed **Phoenician** visitors to pre-Columbian America. Votan supposedly taught the Tzentals to farm **maize** and **cotton,** invented writing and the calendar, created laws, and reformed religion. When his work was completed, he departed—to heaven, according to Mayan mythology, but in Irwin's version back to Phoenicia. See also **Viracocha.**

Bibliography: Irwin, Constance, *Fair Gods and Stone Faces*, 1963; Mercatante, Anthony S., *The Facts on File Encyclopedia of World Mythology and Legend*, 1988.

Waldeck, Count Jean Fréderic (1766?–1875)

Extremely long-lived artist of the Mayan ruins at Palenque and other sites, he advocated many theories attributing the origins of Native American civilizations to various Old World cultures including the Chaldeans, **Chinese, Egyptians, Hebrews,** and **Hindus.** But he also developed a hypothesis that civilization began in Central America and spread from there to the rest of the world.

Born in 1766, Waldeck was the son of a German noble of the Waldeck family, at least according to his own claims. After participating in an expedition to Africa during his teens, in 1785 he studied art under the neoclassicist Jacques Louis David. Numerous adventures followed, including partici-

pation in Napoleon's expedition to conquer Egypt in 1798–1799. In 1819 or 1821, he traveled to the ruins of the Mayan city of Cópan and sketched them. Unfortunately, the events of Waldeck's early life, as told by himself, seem to be fabrications.

After 1825 the facts of Waldeck's life can be verified independently. At that time he returned from Europe to Mexico to work as a hydraulic engineer for a silver mining company. The work did not agree with him, and he quit. He spent the next six years making a modest living by painting portraits and giving art lessons. He also began to collect pre-Columbian artifacts. The vice-president of Mexico provided him with support for a visit to the ruins at Palenque where he made 90 sketches. Those sketches included the supposed "elephant heads," which later turned out to be the head of a rain god. Over the years, **diffusionists** such as Grafton Elliot Smith have cited these supposed elephant heads as evidence for significant transoceanic contacts between the Americas and the eastern hemisphere. Waldeck became friends with another amateur archaeologist, Francis Corroy, who credited the **Phoenicians,** Egyptians, Greeks, **Arabs,** and Chinese as the sources of Mayan civilization. Later the two men would fall out and become bitter rivals.

Edward King, **Viscount Kingsborough,** the amateur scholar of Central American antiquities, began subsidizing Waldeck's work in 1834, allowing Waldeck to study the ruins at Uxmal. Political instability eventually caused Waldeck to leave Mexico in 1836, although not before local authorities confiscated many of his papers. Despite such troubles, in 1838 Waldeck published his *Voyage pittoresque et archéologique dans . . . Yucatan,* which was more of a popular account of southern Mexico than an archaeological monograph. Almost 20 years later the French government published the handsome but neglected volume *Recherches sur les* *ruines de Palenque,* which included 56 of his drawings.

Waldeck's weakest area as a scholar of the ancient Maya was his speculations on the origins of humans and civilization in the Americas. His initial feeling was that their origins were Asiatic or **Tartar,** a vague version of the **Bering Strait Theory.** At the same time, he claimed to see Egyptian, Chinese, and Hebrew influences in various Mayan sculptures. It was the Chaldeans, according to Waldeck, who founded Palenque, although they were later joined by a large influx of Hindus. During his later years, Waldeck reversed himself and claimed that civilization originated in Central America and spread throughout the rest of the world.

Jean Fréderic Waldeck.

After leaving Mexico in 1836, Waldeck spent the remaining 39 years of his long life as a familiar figure in the Parisian social scene. He enjoyed the company of women to the very end—so much that, according to one story, six weeks after reaching the age of 109 he died of a stroke while turning to eye a pretty girl. Waldeck's various archaeological theories were typical of the confused and fluid state of mid–nineteenth-century scholarship on the origins of Native Americans and the existence of pre-Columbian visitors.

Bibliography: Brunhouse, Robert L., *In Search of the Maya: The First Archaeologists,* 1973.

Welsh Indians, Legends of

The story of **Madoc's voyages** to America and his establishment of a colony led to persistent and widely believed travelers' tales of encounters with Welsh-speaking Indians from the sixteenth to the end of the nineteenth century in various parts of North America.

European visitors to the vast new world of the Americas speculated widely on the origins of the diverse tribes of Native Americans and linked them to different nations of the Old World. At the same time, the Elizabethan English were making special efforts to justify their encroachments on Spain's claim to the Americas by citing the legendary Madoc's pre-Columbian discovery and settlement of America. According to this story, the Welsh had settled in America, so it seemed quite reasonable that some of the Native Americans might be their descendants. Such a belief was further encouraged by the coincidental occurrence of words with similar sounds and meanings in both Welsh and various Native American languages.

Reports of Welsh Indians were rumored among both the English and Spanish who visited North America in the sixteenth century. The reliability of these stories is highly questionable, however, since the supposed witnesses seldom spoke Welsh themselves. **David Ingram** of Barking, Essex, reported encountering Indians using Welsh words in 1568. Along with 100 others, he had been marooned on the coast of the Gulf of Mexico by John Hawkins after the disastrous fight with the Spanish at San Juan d'Ulloa. Miraculously, Ingram and two others managed to travel cross-country for 12 months to what is now New Brunswick. A French ship picked them up and returned them to England. Sir Walter Raleigh also reported hearing Native Americans using greetings and other words that had the same meaning in Welsh during his visits to North America. Captain John Smith referred to Welsh Indians in his *General History of Virginia* in 1621, but he was merely copying speculations out of Welsh antiquarian **David Powel**'s *Historie of Cambria* (1584).

The first Welsh to claim an encounter with Welsh Indians was the Reverend Morgan Jones. While traveling in the Carolinas in 1666, some Tuscarora Indians called Doegs captured Jones and planned to execute him. When Jones inadvertently spoke Welsh, they became excited and spared him. Jones's experience contained all the basic elements of what would become the typical story of an encounter with Welsh Indians. A Welshman is captured by Indians and faces imminent execution, which is averted when the Indians discover that their captive speaks their language, Welsh. Another important element is that the Welsh Indians belong to an unidentified or unidentifiable group of Indians, making confirmation of their Welshness difficult or impossible. In Jones's case, no one ever located evidence of a Doeg band within the Tuscarora tribe. Still, Jones's story was widely repeated and republished with greater or lesser embroidering of the facts over the years.

Other stories of Welsh Indians followed. A shipwrecked Welsh sailor named Stedman reportedly encountered Welsh Indians along the southeast coast of North America sometime between 1660 and 1665. However, his story did not appear in print until 1777 in the Reverend N. Owens' *British Remains*. From then on, tales of Welsh Indians moved to the central Mississippi and upper Missouri river valleys. In 1721 Father Charlevoix worked as a missionary among the Iowa tribe, who informed him of a white tribe living to the west. Apparently such rumors were widespread and tended to identify white Indians as Welsh. As a result, a group of concerned Welsh wrote to the British Missionary Society of London on 1 March 1733 requesting money and advice on how to bring the gospel to the descendants of Madoc's colony now living deep in the interior of North America. Meanwhile, another French explorer, Sieur de La Vérendrye, reached the **Mandan** tribe. His personal observation was that the Mandans were indistinguishable from other tribes, but false rumors claimed that he had found them fair-skinned and speaking a language containing many words resembling Breton, which was closely related to Welsh.

The years 1750–1770 were the heyday of rumors about Welsh Indians. Most of the reports came from the Missouri-Mississippi or southeastern region of North America covering the present-day states of Virginia, the Carolinas, Florida, Kentucky, Tennessee, and Alabama. Major Robert Rogers (1731–1795), a famous Indian fighter, mentioned white Indians living west of the Mississippi River in his *Concise Account of North America* (1765). The famous frontiersman Daniel Boone (1734–1820) believed in Welsh Indians and claimed to have met blue-eyed Indians, whom he considered to be Welsh.

Accounts more detailed than Boone's accumulated from the mid-1750s onward. Benjamin Sutton claimed to have visited a light-complexioned, Welsh-speaking tribe on the upper Missouri in 1755. His story was flawed by the report that they had a Welsh Bible (the Bible was not translated into Welsh until 1588, well after Madoc's time). A geographically atypical story involved Francis Lewis, both a Welshman and a signer of the Declaration of Independence. In 1759 he was captured by Indians in upstate New York. As they prepared to burn him at the stake, Lewis spoke Welsh, which as usual caused the Indians to spare him since he was their kindred.

Sightings of Welsh Indians returned to the Missouri River area in 1764 when Welshman Maurice Griffith and some Shawnee Indians were captured and threatened with death by a tribe of white Indians. Griffith, of course, saved the day by speaking Welsh. About the same time, Captain Isaac Stewart was captured by Indians, but through good fortune, a traveling Spaniard ransomed him along with a Welshman named John David. Their party crossed the Mississippi River and proceeded up the Red River, where they encountered some Welsh-speaking Indians. For a change these Indians did not threaten anyone with death. But they did tell stories of how their ancestors had crossed the seas and landed at Florida. They also displayed some parchment rolls with writing on them. In still another story, sometime between 1770 and 1775 Captain Abraham Chaplain of Kentucky happened upon some Welsh Indians at Kaskaskia, Illinois. By 1791 William Owen could write with great certainty to the *Gentleman's Magazine* of London that Welsh Indians were far more civilized than other Native Americans. He even located them exactly at 38°N and 102°W (approximately the middle of the common border of Colorado and Kansas), but with settlements extending to 31°N and 97°W (about the site of Temple, Texas). Owen also specifically identified the Padouca tribe (or Comanche) as Welsh Indians.

All these stories created a virtual Welsh Indian fever among the members of London's Welsh community, an already highly nationalistic group. Events were further helped along when an American, William Bowles, arrived in London in 1791. He claimed to be a chief of the Creek tribe (falsely, it turned out) and also identified the Padoucas as Welsh Indians. Bowles's story prompted the Welsh of London to send an

expedition to locate these Welsh Indians. In 1792 they sent young John Evans to St. Louis, where he aroused the suspicions of nervous Spanish officials worried about the British laying claim to the Louisiana Territory or turning the Indians against them. In 1793 Evans joined frontier trader James Mackey on an expedition up the Missouri River. After several years of adventures, including a period of residence with the Mandan tribe, Evans returned to St. Louis. He sadly reported to his supporters in London that no Welsh Indians existed.

John Evans's report did not settle the question of Welsh Indians. Diehard Welsh nationalists believed that the Spanish bought off Evans and caused his true findings to be suppressed. This conspiracy theory still survives among supporters of the reality of the Madoc legend. Even when the famous Lewis-and-Clark expedition of 1804–1806 failed to find any evidence of Welsh Indians, some people still believed in their existence. A contemporary of Lewis and Clark and author of *Historical Sketches of Louisiana* (1812), Major Amos Stoddard maintained that Lewis and Clark had simply missed the Welsh Indians by following the wrong tributary of the Missouri. As a result, stories of Welsh Indians continued to be reported and believed throughout the nineteenth century. Frontier painter George Catlin lived some months among the Mandans during his travels through the American West during 1829–1838. He was convinced that they were descended from the Welsh. In 1865 Lieutenant Colonel Samuel Tappan identified the Navajo as Welsh on the basis of similarities of the two languages. Even at that time, however, enough was known about the Navajo language to discredit the theory in short order.

By the beginning of the twentieth century, belief in the existence of Welsh Indians was no longer respectable. In F. W. Hodge's two-volume *Handbook of Indians North of*

Mexico, published by the Bureau of American Ethnology of the Smithsonian Institution in 1910, the entry on "Welsh Indians" took a completely skeptical position on the question. But reports of contacts with Welsh Indians still occurred, and in 1947 the Kutenai tribe of British Columbia was identified as Welsh. Over the course of time, as historian Bernard De Voto calculated, 13 real tribes were identified as Welsh, along with 5 nonexistent named tribes and another 3 unnamed tribes. Besides the Mandans, the tribes of the Delaware, Cherokees, Comanche (Padoucas), Conestogas, Creeks, Hopis, Modocs, Navajo, Omans, Seneca, Shawnees, and Tuscarora all bore the honor of being considered the descendants of Madoc's settlers. Not to leave anyone out, various Indians in Mexico and Peru were also identified as Welsh, although those identifications did not have the staying power of the North American legends. Despite all the contrary evidence, the legend of Welsh Indians stubbornly remained a supposed historical truth in the popular consciousness. It even appeared as fact in some school textbooks for American history into the twentieth century.

Bibliography: De Voto, Bernard, *The Course of Empire*, 1952; Deacon, Richard, *Madoc and the Discovery of America*, 1966; Williams, Gwyn A., *Madoc: The Making of a Myth*, 1979.

White God Legends

This group of Native American myths purportedly describes memories of white gods, or pre-Columbian visitors from the Old World. Most of these legends relate to peoples from the ancient Mediterranean or Western European cultures, yet some adherents of pre-Columbian contacts between the Old World and the Americas claim that these legends actually refer to visitors from Africa or China (in which case the legends would be about yellow or black gods.)

The most common Native American white gods are **Quetzalcoatl, Kukulcan, Itzamná, Votan, Viracocha**, and **Sumé**. According to various nonacademic writers, such as Charles Boland and Pierre Honoré, all of these deities were bearded, white-skinned, established civilization and higher humanitarian values during the time they ruled over the various indigenous tribes and kingdoms in Mexico, Peru, and other parts of the Americas, and they departed from the Americas with a promise to return. It is claimed by many advocates of pre-Columbian contacts that these legends of white gods are almost universal among the aboriginal peoples of the Americas. The legends supposedly aided the Spanish conquest of the Aztecs, the Incas, the Maya, the Chibchas, and various other peoples, who mistakenly took the Spanish conquistadors to be their returning white gods. White god legends are also sometimes associated with legends of white people, living among or as Indians, who were the descendants of the white gods and were allegedly hidden away in remote areas of the Americas.

Among the pre-Columbian visitors to the Americas there are many candidates to serve as the inspiration for the white god legends. Almost any ancient or medieval people that allegedly visited the Americas is a possibility, but some groups or persons have been more popular than others. Two of the first candidates suggested as the source for the white god legends are the apostles **St. Thomas** and St. Bartholomew. Early Spanish settlers in Mexico saw definite parallels between Quetzalcoatl and St. Thomas, while those in Peru saw St. Bartholomew as the source for the Viracocha legends. St. Thomas, however, quickly supplanted St. Bartholomew in both places. Not everyone found this identification to be satisfactory. During the sixteenth century, the Spanish chronicler from Peru Pedro Cieza de León was particularly skeptical.

Another figure associated with pre-Columbian visits and white god legends is the Welsh **Prince Madoc.** His legend gained prominence in the late sixteenth century, and it has retained loyal adherents ever since. Some of them even claim that Madoc was the historic Quetzalcoatl.

During the first half of the nineteenth century, some Mormons believed that **Jesus Christ** visited and preached in the Americas after his death and resurrection. That made Jesus Christ quite literally a great white god and the logical inspiration for Quetzalcoatl, Viracocha, and the rest. In the same century, Scandinavian visitors were another group that became popular as possible progenitors of the white god legends.

In the twentieth century, the field of possible inspirers of the white god legends grows further. **St. Brendan the Navigator** has been suggested by some writers. Closely connected to the Brendan theory is that of Charles M. Boland. In *They All Discovered America* (1961), he claims that the missionary activities of wandering **Irish monks** from **Great Ireland** created the myth of Quetzalcoatl. Other writers have focused on anonymous groups of supposed pre-Columbian visitors rather than historical individuals as the inspirations for the white god legends. **Harold S. Gladwin,** in his iconoclastic and curmudgeonly *Men out of Asia* (1947), theorizes that members of the lost fleet of **Alexander the Great** sailed to the Americas and then spread out and civilized the indigenous peoples. In the process they created all sorts of white god legends. The French writer Pierre Honoré claims in his book *In Quest of the White God* (1963) that **Cretans** and **Phoenicians** visiting the Americas around 1200–600 B.C. were the white gods. Constance Irwin advances a similar theory in her *Fair Gods and Stone Faces* (1963), but while she focuses on the Phoenicians and Cretans, she adds the **Hittites** and the **Etruscans** as visitors to the Americas. In his *Before*

Columbus (1971), **Cyrus Gordon,** a specialist in the Semitic languages and civilizations of the Near East, agrees with Irwin's theory that many different Mediterranean peoples reached the pre-Columbian Americas and contributed to the white god legends. In *In Quest of the Great White Gods* (1992), Robert Marx also claims that various Mediterranean peoples, particularly the Phoenicians, visited the ancient Americas in the pre-Christian era and inspired the white god legends.

The problem with all of these twentieth-century theories is that they are not based on original and authentic Native American legends. Instead, they are based on legends that were embellished in post-Columbian times. Most of the so-called white gods were actual humans who filled the role of culture-hero. Like the Greek culture-hero Prometheus who brought civilizing fire to humanity, the Native American culture-heroes brought the benefits of agriculture, writing, the calendar, and true religion to the peoples of the Americas. Generally these gods are described as bearded, but that is no proof of their being white. Native Americans can grow beards, and these beards, such as the one worn by Aztec Emperor Moctezuma II, were observed by the Spanish. Many versions of the white god legends have been contaminated with post-Columbian additions by the Spanish. The whiteness of these white gods is not mentioned in the most authentic versions of the culture-hero legends. Quetzalcoatl is actually described as having a black or a black-and-yellow-striped face. It also appears that the white god's departure from and promise to return to the Americas are usually post-Columbian additions. The legend of Kon Tiki (Viracocha) is very incoherent and fragmentary, and the white god elements definitely appear to be post-Columbian additions, possibly done in imitation of the Quetzalcoatl legend. In the case of Quetzalcoatl, some historians, such as Nigel Davies, think that the belief that Hernán Cortés was the returned Quetzalcoatl was a delusion concocted by the nervous Moctezuma II. There was no general belief among the Aztecs that Quetzalcoatl would return. Davíd Carrasco, a historian of religion, disagrees. Instead, he claims that during its final years the Aztec empire lived in dread anticipation of Quetzalcoatl's return. In the case of the other Native American gods—Votan, Viracocha, and Sumé—however, scholars such as Nigel Davies consider the legend of the white gods a Spanish fraud.

Additional problems with linking white god legends to historic persons or peoples are chronological. Quetzalcoatl lived sometime during the years 900–1100 A.D., which eliminates most of the supposed ancient pre-Columbian visitors, including Jesus Christ, as candidates for inspiring his legend. Furthermore, the white god legends, like most tales of pre-Columbian visitors to the Americas, lack a convincing foundation in written and archaeological evidence. Close study of the Native American myths simply makes the white god legends seem less and less credible.

Bibliography: Carrasco, Davíd, *Quetzalcoatl and the Irony of Empire: Myth and Prophecies in the Aztec Tradition*, 1982; Davies, Nigel, *Voyagers to the New World*, 1979; Heyerdahl, Thor, "The Beard Gods Speak," in *The Quest for America*, edited by Geoffrey Ashe, 1971.

White Man's Land

This is the English translation of the Norse word **Hvítramannaland**, which refers to the legendary settlement of **Irish monks** in North America, also known as **Great Ireland**. This settlement existed prior to the **voyages of Bjarni Herjolfsson** in 986 and **Leif Ericsson** about 1001. According to historian Tryggvi Oleson, White Man's Land could also refer to the whole Arctic region, particularly **Greenland,** and not just the lands of the east coast of North America. These Arctic lands are also sometimes referred to as Albania or **Albania Superior.**

Oleson claims that the supposed references to Great Ireland are the result of a confusion between the Norse usage of White Man's Land for the western Arctic lands and the existence of a region in Ireland called Tir na-Fer Fin, which also means White Man's Land. Theories concerning the existence of Irish settlements in North America are simply false. See also **Irish Monks in America.**

Bibliography: Oleson, Tryggvi J., *Early Voyages and Northern Approaches,* 1964.

Wiener, Leo
(1862–1939)

He was an early advocate of **African voyages to pre-Columbian America,** particularly the **Mandingos** of West Africa during the fourteenth century.

Leo Wiener was born in White Russia where he received a strong education in foreign languages. In 1882 he arrived in the United States and from 1883–1895 served as a high school teacher and college instructor of foreign languages at various schools in the Midwest. Moving to Boston in 1895, he taught one year at Boston University. The following year he received an appointment as instructor of Slavic languages at Harvard University, the first such academic appointment in the United States, and in 1911 became department chairman. He retired in 1930 as a professor emeritus and is considered the pioneer of Slavic studies in the United States.

Wiener published many books including an English translation of Leo Tolstoy's complete works in 24 volumes and various studies of the history of Russian literature. But alongside this respected and prolific scholarly activity, Wiener also managed to write his massive work *Africa and the Discovery of America*, which argued that African traders had been in contact with the Americas since the twelfth century. Unable to find a commercial publisher for his work, he privately published the three-volume book between 1919 and 1922 with financial assistance from a rich benefactor, John B. Stetson. Wiener's work was not well received by other scholars. One of its controversial contentions was that tobacco had been brought from Africa to America, not the other way around as was commonly thought. However, Wiener's dating, chronology, and interpretation of archaeological evidence for tobacco smoking was erroneous. He also claimed to see African faces and hair styles in various statuettes from the southwestern United States. Anthropologists found his interpretations of such artistic evidence to be completely fallacious. Wiener's linguistic evidence for Mandingo contacts with pre-Columbian America was massive; however, its scholarly validity was slight. Other experts on African and Native American languages found it completely unconvincing. Wiener's work did not receive scholarly acceptance during his lifetime. Since his death in 1939, it has still not attracted much of a following outside of some African-American scholars who consider him a progenitor of the theories of African contacts with ancient America that they support.

Bibliography: Muffet, David J. M., "Leo Wiener: A Plea for Re-Examination," in *African Presence in Early America*, edited by Ivan Van Sertima, [1986], 2nd ed., 1992; Williams, Stephen, *Fantastic Archaeology: The Wild Side of North American Prehistory*, 1991.

Winsor, Justin
(1831–1897)

The scholarly interests of this librarian and historian focused on the discovery of America and its early explorations, including supposed pre-Columbian visitors.

Born into a family of Boston merchants, Winsor naturally attended Harvard College. He found its classical curriculum boring, so instead of studying the required subjects, he pursued historical and literary interests outside the curriculum. As a result, he earned such poor grades that he was suspended during his senior year. From 1854–1868 he failed in an attempt to establish a successful literary career. In 1868, Winsor finally found a congenial career when he became director of the Boston Public Library. He

Justin Winsor.

helped to found the American Library Association in 1876 and served as its first president from 1876–1885. After becoming the director of the Harvard College library in 1877, he was able to return to his beloved historical research.

In 1880 Winsor put together a prospectus for a cooperative history of the United

States titled *Narrative and Critical History of America*. It would be a combination of narrative and critical chapters surveying the existing writings on given topics. To help write the massive work, he recruited 39 contributors, although Winsor himself wrote about half of the work's eight large volumes. The *Narrative and Critical History* appeared between 1886 and 1889. Chronologically it covered from prehistory to 1850, although the colonial era received the most attention. Geographically Winsor included Latin America and British America, as well as the United States. Generally the *Narrative and Critical History* was well received although it also had definite weaknesses.

The first volume was titled *Aboriginal America*, although it was actually one of the last published, in 1889. It reflected nineteenth-century American society's great interest in the pre-Columbian history of the Americas as well as the myriad theories and hypotheses that attempted to explain that history. Winsor and his contributors took an evenhanded and open-minded approach. Although Winsor rejected the wilder theories about pre-Columbian visitors, he took a moderate approach to others. Unlike the great historian George Bancroft, Winsor believed that the Norse reached North America during the Middle Ages and that the **Vinland Sagas** were reliable historical documents. He also accepted the possibility of **Chinese** and **Japanese** visits as well as the plausibility of the story of Jan of Kolno (see also **Scolvus, Voyage of Johannes**). He rejected claims that the **Phoenicians, Carthaginians,** Greeks, **Zeno brothers,** and **João Vaz Côrte-Real** visited or colonized the Americas. Winsor's *Narrative and Critical History* provided a moderate, scholarly summary of the state of the late–nineteenth century's knowledge about pre-Columbian visits to the Americas that was unmarred by the sometimes uncritical enthusiasm of other writers such as **Benjamin Franklin De Costa.**

Bibliography: Simms, L. Moody, Jr., "Justin Winsor," in *Dictionary of Literary Biography*, vol. 47: *American Historians 1866–1912*, 1986; Winsor, Justin, ed., *Narrative and Critical History of America*, 8 vols., 1886–1889.

Zeno, Narrative of the Brothers
Nicolò and Antonio
(1390s)

According to accounts first published in 1558, these two Venetians traveled to **Greenland** and other unknown lands that may have been part of North America about 100 years before the first voyage of Columbus.

The Zeno family of Venice belonged to that city's political elite and even had a member who served as Doge. In 1558 Nicolò Zeno the younger published *Dei Commentarii . . . dello scoprimento de dell'Isole Frislanda, Eslanda, Engrouelanda, Estotilanda & Icaria da due fratelli Zeni, Nicolò e Antonio,* which besides providing descriptions of some of his ancestors' travels in Persia, also told of the northern voyages to unknown lands made by Nicolò Zeno the elder and his

brother Antonio. In about 1380 Nicolò the elder traveled north in search of adventure in England and France. A great storm wrecked his ship on the coast of a far northern island called Frislanda. The natives attempted to rob and kill the castaways, but they were saved by a local noble named **Zichmni,** the duke of Sorano (?) (see also **Sinclair, Voyage of Prince Henry**).

Zichmni quickly discovered that Nicolò was a far more experienced seaman than any of the men of Frislanda, so he recruited Zeno for his navy and made him a knight. Later Zichmni appointed him to command his entire navy in conquests of various northern islands and his wars with the king of Norway. Nicolò the elder wrote to his brother Antonio and invited him to bring more ships to Frislanda and share in the wealth and honors. Antonio accepted, and for the next four years served Zichmni under the command of his brother Nicolò.

Zichmni's wars continued and during the course of them, Nicolò visited Greenland. He stopped at the mysterious Dominican monastery of **St. Thomas,** which was heated by volcanic geysers and so could survive on Greenland's inhospitable eastern coast. During that visit, Nicolò also observed the natives' use of kayaks. The Arctic cold caused him to fall ill, and after returning to Frislanda he died. His brother Antonio inherited his offices and wealth. Antonio wanted to return to Venice, but Zichmni refused permission and instead compelled Antonio to serve as his admiral for ten more years.

Sometime after Nicolò's death, an old **Fisherman of Frislanda** returned from a 26-year absence. He claimed to have visited some unknown western lands called **Estotiland** and **Drogio**, which were inhabited by both civilized people of apparent European background and primitive savages. The Fisherman of Frislanda's story intrigued Zichmni, and he ordered Antonio Zeno to

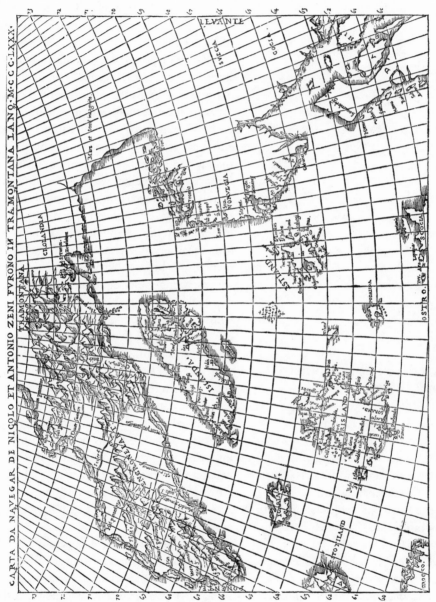

The Zeno map with its mixture of real and fictitious places.

lead an expedition to the west, using the old fisherman as a guide. Others shared Zichmni's interest and many volunteered for the voyage. Ultimately Zichmni resolved to take command personally. Three days before the expedition's departure, the old fisherman died. Several of his Estotilander companions remained, however, and Zichmni decided that they would be satisfactory replacements as guides.

Zichmni and his fleet sailed west. They landed on two small islands, then entered the high seas where they sailed through both stormy and fair weather for a number of days. Finally they sighted land and prepared to anchor in a fine harbor when a great force of natives arrived and barred them. A parley ensued in which Zichmni and Zeno learned that the island was called **Icaria.** The inhabitants called their kings Icari after their first king Icarus, the son of Daedalus, king of Scotland. Icarus had given the Icarians their laws, and they told Zichmni not to meddle. In the face of such hostility, Zichmni sneaked ashore farther along the coast and took on needed water. Signal fires soon brought howling hordes of natives to drive off the foreigners, and Zichmni resumed his search for Estotiland.

Continuing west and southwest for another ten days, at the beginning of June Zichmni's fleet reached an unknown land with an excellent harbor and a smoking mountain in the background. A hundred soldiers searched the area for inhabitants but found none. They observed the smoking mountain up close and saw that its interior burned, and that a spring of pitch bubbled nearby. Natives appeared, but they were timid, small of stature, and quite primitive. Zichmni found the surrounding countryside to be most pleasant, and decided to name the harbor Trin. Although he wanted to stay, many of his companions wanted to return to Frislanda before the arrival of winter. Zichmni called for volunteers to stay with him in the

new land, and the rest returned home under the command of Antonio Zeno, who also would have preferred to stay behind.

Zeno sailed eastward for 20 days, and then southeast for another 5 days. He came upon Neome Island, which was 3 days east of **Iceland.** Unfortunately, Antonio Zeno's letters describing the further adventures of Zichmni in the west did not survive to 1558. According to Nicolò the younger, Zichmni thoroughly explored the western lands and both coasts of Greenland before returning home. But the Estotiland of the Fisherman was never located.

The narrative of the Zeno brothers is full of problems despite the readiness of some writers to credit first the Fisherman of Frislanda and then Zichmni and Antonio Zeno with making pre-Columbian voyages to North America. Just what lands the Fisherman, Zichmni, and Zeno visited is difficult to determine from the vague descriptions in the surviving narrative. Some writers claim that Estotiland was Newfoundland or Labrador, while Drogio was Nova Scotia. Icaria also may have been Newfoundland, but others think it was Kerry in Ireland. Zichmni's unnamed land with the smoking mountain may have been either Nova Scotia or Greenland. Unfortunately, internal inconsistencies and a lack of corroborating evidence tend to undermine the credibility of the Zeno Narrative and any of the above identifications.

The surviving Zeno Narrative is supposedly only part of a larger original. Nicolò Zeno the younger claimed that as a boy he had played with the papers describing his ancestors' northern adventures and thoughtlessly destroyed some of them. When he matured, he realized their importance and had them published. His fellow Venetians responded with patriotic enthusiasm since his book purported to show that their countrymen reached America about a century before Christopher Columbus, who was a native of Genoa, their archrival. It was just what the proud but declining city needed to salve its bruised civic pride.

Some modern scholars also support the authenticity of the Zeno Narrative. R. H. Major's edition of the narrative for the Hakluyt Society in 1873 claimed that it was genuine. Arctic geologist William H. Hobbs also accepted it in 1951, as did the respected historian of geography E. G. R. Taylor in 1964. The consensus of modern historical scholarship, however, views the Zeno Narrative as a forgery and a hoax, a thesis that Frederick W. Lucas conclusively proved in 1898. C. Raymond Beazley in 1906, William H. Babcock in 1922, and Samuel Eliot Morison in 1971—all recognized authorities—supported Lucas's conclusions, but to no avail. The Zenos' claim to have discovered America before Columbus still occasionally attracts supporters.

Bibliography: Hobbs, William H., "The Fourteenth-Century Discovery of America by Antonio Zeno," *Scientific Monthly* 72 (January 1951): 24–31; Lucas, Frederick W., *The Annals of the Brothers Nicolò and Antonio Zeno*, 1898; Morison, Samuel Eliot, *The European Discovery of America: The Northern Voyages*, 1971.

Zichmni, Prince

This North Atlantic warlord appeared in the **Zeno Narrative** of 1558 with the title of Duke of Sorano. He is identified as **Prince Henry Sinclair**, the earl of Orkney (1345–1400). Around 1398, in the company of Antonio Zeno, Zichmni supposedly visited a land called **Icaria** and another unnamed land with a smoking mountain variously identified as Newfoundland, Nova Scotia, or **Greenland.**

Johann Reinhold Forster, a German scholar, first linked Zichmni with the historical figure Prince Henry Sinclair in 1786.

That identification has persisted well into the twentieth century among supporters of the veracity of the Zeno Narrative. Popular writer Frederick J. Pohl put forward several explanations for the seemingly unlikely reading of Zichmni for Sinclair in the documents. Basically he assumes the misreadings were caused by changes in European handwriting between the late fourteenth and mid-sixteenth centuries. Various letters written during the 1390s by the brothers Nicolò the elder and Antonio Zeno form the source of the published Zeno Narrative. Nicolò Zeno the younger transcribed these letters and published them in 1558. According to Pohl's theory, confusions over the writing of some words caused Nicolò to make certain errors of transcription. One explanation suggests that Sinclair was read as Zichmni and Roslin, the name for Sinclair's barony, was read as Sorano. Alternatively, d'Orkney (or Orkney), the earldom of Sinclair, may have been mistakenly read as Zichmni.

Frederick W. Lucas, an earlier historian of the problem, gave a more convincing explanation in 1898 by suggesting that Zichmni was actually a corruption of Wichmann, a Baltic pirate killed in 1401. If so, the Zenos went to work for a pirate, not a respectable nobleman, which could easily have been the case during the turbulent late fourteenth century in Europe. Assuming the truth of the Zeno Narrative, Zichmni was certainly a misreading of some other name. No person of that name appears in any other historical documents from that era.

Bibliography: Lucas, Frederick W., *The Annals of the Voyages of the Brothers Nicolò and Antonio Zeno in the North Atlantic*, 1898; Pohl, Frederick J., *Atlantic Crossings before Columbus*, 1961; Pohl, Frederick J., *Prince Henry Sinclair: His Expedition to the New World in 1398*, 1974.

Bibliography

The bibliography of pre-Columbian visitors to the Americas and the history of the theories about the origins of Native Americans is voluminous, as a casual inspection of the bibliographies listed below will indicate. It is the purpose of this bibliography to list the more important works on the subject as well as a comprehensive cross section of the many subtopics of Native American origins and pre-Columbian visitors. This bibliography lists many works not listed in the bibliographies of the individual entries of the encyclopedia.

I. Bibliographical Works

Bibliotheca Americana. Catalogue of the John Carter Brown Library in Brown University. 3 vols. Providence, RI: Brown University Library, 1919–1931.

Church, Elihu Dwight. *A Catalogue of Books Relating to the Discovery and Early History of North and South America.* 5 vols. 1907. Reprint. New York: P. Smith, 1951.

Dictionary of American Biography. 22 vols. New York: Charles Scribner's Sons, 1927–1958.

Dictionary of Literary Biography. Detroit: Gale Research, 1978–.

Dictionary of National Biography. [63 vols. 1885–1901], 22 vols. Oxford: Oxford University Press, 1908–1909.

Harrisse, Henry. *Bibliotheca Americana Vetustissima. A Description of Works Relating to America, Published between 1492 and 1551.* New York: G. P. Philes, 1866.

National Cyclopedia of American Biography. 63 vols. Clifton, NJ: J. T. White, 1892–1984.

Provost, Foster. *Columbus: An Annotated Guide to the Scholarship on His Life and Writings, 1750 to 1988.* Detroit: Omnigraphics, 1991.

Sorenson, John L., and Martin H. Raish. *Pre-Columbian Contact with the Americas across the Oceans: An Annotated Bibliography.* 2 vols. Provo, UT: Research Press, 1990.

Strayer, Joseph R. *Dictionary of the Middle Ages.* 12 vols. New York: Charles Scribner's Sons, 1982–1989.

Thomas, Jack Ray. *Biographical Dictionary of Latin American Historians and Historiography.* Westport, CT: Greenwood Press, 1984.

Wallace, B. J. "Transpacific Contacts: A Selected Annotated Bibliography." *Asian Perspectives* 11 (1968): 157–175.

Watson, Paul Barron. "Bibliography of the Pre-Columbian Discoveries of America." In *America Not Discovered by Columbus,* by Rasmus B. Anderson, 1930. (*See also* Anderson.) Bibliography was originally printed in *Library Journal* 6 (1882).

Bibliography

Winsor, Justin, ed. *Narrative and Critical History of America.* 8 vols. Boston: Houghton Mifflin, 1885–1889.

II. Primary and Secondary Works
General Works

Acosta, José de. *The Natural and Moral History of the Indies.* 2 vols. 1880. Reprint. New York: Burt Franklin, 1970.

Adair, James. *Adair's History of the American Indians,* edited by Samuel Cole Williams. New York: Promontory Press, [1775] 1973.

Adam of Bremen. *History of the Archbishops of Hamburg-Bremen.* Translated with an introduction and notes by Francis J. Tschan. New York: Columbia University Press, 1959.

Afetinan, A. *Life and Works of the Turkish Admiral: Piri Re'is.* Ankara, Turkey: Turk Tarin Kurumu Basimevi, 1954.

Akcura, Yusuf. *Piri Re'is Map.* Istanbul: Develet Bas Mevi, 1935.

Allen, Don Cameron. *The Legend of Noah: Renaissance Rationalism in Art, Science, and Letters.* Urbana, IL: University of Illinois Press, 1963.

Anderson, Rasmus Bjorn. *America Not Discovered by Columbus. A Historical Sketch of the Discovery of America by the Norsemen. . . .* 8th ed. 1874. Reprint. Madison, WI: Leif Erikson Memorial Association, 1930. Also contains Paul Barron Watson's bibliography. (*See also* Watson.)

———. *The Vatican Manuscripts Concerning the Church in America before the Time of Columbus.* New York: Norroena Society, 1906.

Armstrong, Zella. *Who Discovered America? The Amazing Story of Madoc.* Chattanooga, TN: Lookout Publishing Co., 1950.

Arocena, Luis A. "Father Joseph de Acosta (1540–1600)." In *Latin American Writers,* edited by Carlos A. Solé. 3 vols. 1989.

———. "Gonzalo Fernández de Oviedo y Valdés (1478–1557)." In *Latin American Writers,* edited by Carlos A. Solé. New York: Charles Scribner's Sons, 1989.

Ashe, Geoffrey. *Avalonian Quest.* London: Methuen, 1982.

———. *Land to the West: St. Brendan's Voyage to America.* New York: Viking Press, 1962.

———. *Mythology of the British Isles.* London: Methuen, 1990.

Ashe, Geoffrey, ed. *The Quest for America.* New York: Praeger, 1971.

Ayoob, Joseph Corey. *Ancient Inscriptions in the New World or Were the Phoenicians the First To Discover America?* 2nd ed. Aliquippa, PA: Privately published, 1964.

Babcock, William H. *Legendary Islands of the Atlantic: A Study in Medieval Geography.* New York: American Geographical Society, 1922.

———. "Atlantis and Antillia." *Geographical Review* 3 (1917): 392–395.

Bahn, Paul, and John Flenley. *Easter Island, Earth Island.* London: Thames & Hudson, 1992.

Bailey, James. *The God-Kings and the Titans: The New World Ascendency in Ancient Times.* New York: St. Martin's Press, 1973.

Baker, Herbert G. *Plants and Civilization.* 2nd ed. Belmont, CA: Wadsworth Publishing, 1970.

Batalha-Reis, J. "The Supposed Discovery of South America before 1448, and the Critical Methods of the Historians of Geographical Discovery." *Geographical Journal* 9 (February 1897): 185–210.

Beazley, C. Raymond. *The Dawn of Modern Geography.* 3 vols. 1897–1906. Reprint. New York: P. Smith, 1949.

Bedini, Silvio A., ed. *The Christopher Columbus Encyclopedia.* 2 vols. New York: Simon & Schuster, 1992.

Belfiglio, Valentino J. "Did Indian Texans Encounter the Ancient Romans?" *Italian Journal* 6 (1992): 51–55.

Blacket, W. S. *Researches into the Lost Histories of America; or The Zodiac Shown To Be an Old Terrestrial Map in Which the Atlantic Isle Is Delineated; So That Light Can Be Thrown upon the Obscure Histories of the Earthworks and Ruined Cities of America.* London: Trübner and Philadelphia: Lippincott, 1884.

Blanke, Gustav H. "Early Theories about the Nature and Origins of the Indians." *Amerikastudien* 25 (1980): 243–268.

Blegen, Theodore C. *The Kensington Rune Stone: New Light on an Old Riddle.* St. Paul, MN: Minnesota Historical Society, 1968.

Boland, Charles M. *They All Discovered America.* Garden City, NY: Doubleday, 1961.

Boudinot, Elias. *A Star in the West; or A Humble Attempt To Discover the Long Lost Ten Tribes of Israel.* 1816. Reprint. Freeport, NY: Books for Libraries Press, 1970.

Bradley, Michael. *The Black Discovery of America: Amazing Evidence of Daring Voyages by Ancient West African Mariners.* Toronto: Personal Library, 1981.

Brewster, Paul G. "The Melungeons: A Mystery People." *Ethnos* 29 (1964): 43–48.

Brodie, Fawn M. *No Man Knows My History: The Life of Joseph Smith.* 1945. 2nd ed., 1971.

Bruce, Erroll. *Challenge to Poseidon.* London: Hutchinson, 1956.

Brunhouse, Robert L. *In Search of the Maya: The First Archaeologists.* Albuquerque, NM: University of New Mexico Press, 1973.

Buker, George E. "The Seven Cities: The Role of a Myth in the Exploration of the Atlantic." *American Neptune* 30 (1970): 249–259.

Bunbury, E. H. *A History of Ancient Geography.* 2 vols. 1883. Reprint. New York: Dover, 1959.

Bushman, Richard L. *Joseph Smith and the Beginnings of Mormonism.* Urbana, IL: University of Illinois Press, 1984.

Cahill, Thomas, et al. "The Vinland Map Revisited: New Compositional Evidence on Its Inks and Parchments." *Analytical Chemistry* 59 (1987): 829–833.

Cameron, Ian. *Lodestone and Evening Star: The Epic Voyages of Discovery 1493 B.C.– 1896 A.D.* New York: Dutton, 1966.

Carrasco, Davíd. *Quetzalcoatl and the Irony of Empire: Myths and Prophecies in the Aztec*

Bibliography

Tradition. Chicago: University of Chicago Press, 1982.

———. *Religions of Mesoamerica: Cosmovision and Ceremonial Centers.* New York: Harper & Row, 1990.

Caso, Alfonso. "Relations between the Old and New World: A Note on Methodology." *Proceedings of the 35th International Congress of Americanists* (1962): 55–71.

Cassidy, Vincent H. "More Fortunate Islands—and Some That Were Lost." *Terrae Incognitae* 1 (1969): 35–40.

Catlin, George. *Letters and Notes on the Manners, Customs, and Conditions of the North American Indians.* 2 vols. 1844. Reprint. New York: Dover, 1973.

Ceram, C. W. *The First American: A Story of North American Archaeology.* New York: Harcourt Brace Jovanovich, 1971.

Chapman, Paul H. *The Man Who Led Columbus to America.* Atlanta, GA: Judson Press, 1973.

———. *The Norse Discovery of America.* Atlanta, GA: One Candle Press, 1981.

Chaunu, P. *European Expansion in the Later Middle Ages.* Amsterdam: North Holland Publishing Co., 1979.

Cheesman, Paul R., and Millie F. Cheesman. *Ancient American Indians: Their Origins, Civilizations, and Old World Connections.* Bountiful, UT: Horizon, 1991.

Childress, David Hatcher. *Lost Cities of Ancient Lemuria and the Pacific.* Stelle, IL: Adventures Unlimited Press, 1988.

Churchward, James. *The Lost Continent of Mu.* 1926. Reprint. Albuquerque, NM: BE Books, 1987.

Clissold, Stephen. *The Seven Cities of Cibola.* New York: Clarkson Potter, 1962.

Cobo, Bernabé. *History of the Inca Empire.* Austin, TX: University of Texas Press, 1979.

———. *Inca Religion and Customs.* Austin, TX: University of Texas Press, 1990.

Cole, J. R. "Anthropology beyond the Fringe." *Skeptical Inquirer* (Spring/Summer 1978): 62–71.

———. "Barry Fell, *America B.C.,* and a Cargo Cult in Archaeology." *Bulletin of the New York State Archaeological Association* 74 (1978): 1–10.

———. "Cult Archaeology." *Early Man* 2 (1980): 9–12.

———. "Cult Archaeology and Unscientific Method and Theory." *Advances in Archaeological Method and Theory* 3 (1980): 1–33.

———. "Inscription Mania, Hyper-Diffusionism, and the Public; Fallout from a 1977 Meeting." *Man in the Northeast* 17 (1979): 27–53.

Conner, W. R. *Theopompus and Fifth Century Athens.* Cambridge, MA: Harvard University Press, 1968.

Cortesão, Armando. *The Nautical Chart of 1424 and the Early Discovery and Cartographical Representation of America: A Study on the History of Early Navigation and Cartography.* Coimbra, Portugal: University of Coimbra, 1954.

Cortesão, Jaime. "The Pre-Columbian Discovery of America." *Geographical Journal* 89 (1937): 29–42.

Covey, Cyclone. *Calalus: A Roman Jewish Colony in America from the Time of Charlemagne through Alfred the Great.* New York: Vantage Press, 1975.

Crone, Gerald R. *The Discovery of America.* New York: Weybright & Talley, 1969.

———. "The Alleged Pre-Columbian Discovery of America." *Geographical Journal* 89 (1937): 455–460.

———. "Martin Behaim, Navigator and Cosmographer, Figment of Imagination or Historical Personage?" *Congresso Internacional de Historia dos Descobrimentos, Actas* 2 (1961): 117–133.

Crosby, Alfred W., Jr. *The Columbian Exchange: Biological and Cultural Consequences of 1492.* Westport, CT: Greenwood Press, 1972.

Cross, Frank M. "The Phoenician Inscription from Brazil, a Nineteenth Century Forgery." *Orientalia* 37 (1968): 437–460. (*See also* Gordon article.)

———. "Phoenicians in Brazil?" *Biblical Archaeology Review* 5 (January–February 1979): 36–43.

Crowley, Francis G. *Garcilaso de la Vega, el Inca, and His Sources in the "Comentarios reales de los Incas."* The Hague: Mouton, 1971.

Daly, D. "Mexican Messiah." *Popular Science* 39 (1891): 95–105. Identifies St. Brendan as Quetzalcoatl.

Daniel, Glyn Edmund. *Myth or Legend?* 1955. Reprint. New York: Capricorn Books, 1968. Book of essays about various legendary places.

———. Review of *America B.C.* by Barry Fell and *They Came before Columbus* by Ivan Van Sertima. *New York Times Book Review* (13 March 1977): 8, 12–13.

Davidson, Basil. "Africans before Columbus?" *West Africa* 27 (1969): 641.

Davies, Arthur. "Behaim, Martellus and Columbus." *Geographical Journal* 143 (1977): 451–459.

———. "Prince Madoc and the Discovery of America in 1477." *Geographical Journal* (1984): 363–372.

Davies, Nigel. *Voyagers to the New World.* New York: Morrow, 1979.

Davis, Richard A., Jr. *Oceanography: An Introduction to the Marine Environment.* 2nd ed. 1991.

de Camp, L. Sprague. *Lost Continents: The Atlantis Theme in History, Science, and Literature.* 1954. Reprint. New York: Dover, 1970.

De Costa, Benjamin Franklin. *Ancient Norombega, or the Voyages of Simon Ferdinando and John Walker to the Penobscot River, 1579–1580.* Albany, NY: Joel Munsell's Sons, 1890.

———. *Inventio Fortunata. Arctic Exploration with an Account of Nicholas of Lynn.* 1881.

———. *The Pre-Columbian Discovery of America by Northmen with Translations of*

Bibliography

the Icelandic Sagas. 1868. 3rd ed. Albany, NY: Joel Munsell's Sons, 1901.

de Figueredo, Fidelino. "The Geographical Discoveries and Conquests of the Portuguese." *Hispanic American Historical Review* 6 (nos. 1–3, 1926): 47–70.

De Roo, Peter. "The Apostle St. Thomas in America." In *History of America before Columbus.* Vol. 1. New York: Lippincott, 1900.

De Voto, Bernard. *The Course of Empire.* Boston: Houghton Mifflin, 1952.

Deacon, Richard. *Madoc and the Discovery of America.* New York: George Brazillier, 1966.

Desmond, Lawrence G., and Phyllis M. Messenger. *A Dream of Maya: Augustus and Alice Le Plongeon in Nineteenth-Century Yucatan.* Albuquerque, NM: University of New Mexico Press, 1988.

Diamond, Sigmund. "Norumbega: New England Xanadu." *American Neptune* 11 (April 1951): 95–107.

Diffie, Bailey W. "Foreigners in Portugal and the 'Policy of Secrecy.'" *Terrae Incognitae* 1 (1969): 23–34.

Diffie, Bailey W., and George D. Winius. *Foundations of the Portuguese Empire, 1415–1580.* Minneapolis: University of Minnesota Press, 1977.

Diller, Aubrey. "The Mysterious Artic Traveller of 1360, Nicholas of Lynn." *Isis* 30 (1939): 277–278.

Dincauze, D. "Monk's Caves and Short Memories." *Quarterly Review of Archaeology* 3 (no. 4, 1982): 1, 10–11.

Donnelly, Ignatius. *Atlantis: The Antediluvian World.* 1882. Reprint. New York: Dover, 1976.

Doran, Michael F. "Phoenician Contact with America? A Time Perspective." *Anthropological Journal of Canada* 12 (1974): 16–24.

Dunn, Joseph. "The Brendan Problem." *Catholic Historical Review* (January 1921).

Durán, Diego. *The Aztecs: The History of the Indies of New Spain,* translated by Doris Heyden and Fernando Horcasitas. New York: Orion Press, 1964.

———. *Book of the Gods and Rites and the Ancient Calendar,* translated by Fernando Horcasitas and Doris Heyden. Norman, OK: University of Oklahoma Press, 1971.

Durrett, Reuben T. *Traditions of the Earliest Visits of Foreigners to North America, the First Formed and First Inhabited of the Continents.* Filson Club Publications No. 23. Louisville, KY: The Filson Club, 1908.

Edmonson, Munro S., ed. *Sixteenth-Century Mexico: The Work of Sahagún.* Albuquerque, NM: University of New Mexico Press, 1974.

Eisner, Sigmund, ed. *The Kalendarium of Nicholas of Lynn.* Athens, GA: University of Georgia Press, 1980.

Ekholm, Gordon. "The Possible Chinese Origins of Teotihuacan Cylindrical Tripod Pottery and Certain Related Traits." *Proceedings of the 35th International Congress of Americanists* (1962): 39–45.

Elkin, A. P., and N. W. G. MacIntosh, eds. *Grafton Elliot Smith: The Man and His Work.* Sydney: Sydney University Press, 1974.

Elliott, J. H. *The Old World and the New, 1492–1650.* Cambridge, MA: Cambridge University Press, 1970.

Ellwood, T. *The Book of the Settlement of Iceland (Landnámabók).* Kendal, England: T. Wilson, 1898.

England, G. A. *Isles of Romance.* New York: Century Co., 1929.

Epstein, Jeremiah F. "Pre-Columbian Old World Coins in America: An Examination of the Evidence." *Current Anthropology* 21 (February 1980): 1–20.

Erasmus, Charles John. "Patolli, Pachisi, and the Limitation of Possibilities." *Southwestern Journal of Anthropology* 6 (1950): 369–387.

Fagan, Brian M. *Ancient North America: The Archaeology of a Continent.* New York: Thames & Hudson, 1991.

———. *The Great Journey: The Peopling of Ancient America.* London: Thames & Hudson, 1987.

Farmer, D. H., ed. *The Age of Bede.* New York: Penguin Books, 1965. Includes a translation of the *Navigatio.*

Feder, Kenneth L. *Frauds, Myths, and Mysteries: Science and Pseudoscience in Archaeology.* Mountainview, CA: Mayfield Press, 1990.

———. "American Disingenuous: Goodman's *American Genesis*—A New Chapter in Cult Archaeology." *The Skeptical Inquirer* 4 (no. 4, 1980): 36–48.

———. "Irrationality and Archaeology." *American Antiquity* 49 (no. 3, 1984): 525–541.

Feldman, M. *The Mystery Hill Story.* North Salem, NH: Mystery Hill, 1977.

Fell, Barry. *America B.C.: Ancient Settlers in the New World.* 1976. Rev. ed. New York: Simon & Schuster, 1989.

———. *Bronze Age America.* Boston: Little, Brown, 1982.

———. *Saga America.* New York: Times Books, 1980.

Ferguson, Thomas Stuart. *Cumorah— Where?* Independence, MO: Zion's Printing & Publishing Co., 1947.

———. *One Fold and One Shepherd.* 1958. Rev. ed. Salt Lake City, UT: Olympus Publishing Co., 1962.

Fernández-Armesto, Felipe. *Before Columbus.* Philadelphia: University of Pennsylvania Press, 1987.

———. *The Times Atlas of World Exploration.* New York: HarperCollins, 1991.

Figueredo, Fidelino de. "The Geographical Discoveries and Conquests of the Portuguese." *Hispanic American Historical Review* 6 (nos. 1–3, 1926): 47–70.

Fingerhut, Eugene R. *Who First Discovered America? A Critique of Pre-Columbian Voyages.* Claremont, CA: Regina Books, 1984.

Fisher, Raymond H. *Bering's Voyages: Whither and Why.* Seattle: University of Washington Press, 1977.

Fiske, John. *The Discovery of America.* 2 vols. Boston: Houghton Mifflin, 1902.

Fitzhugh, William W. "Early Contacts North of Newfoundland before A.D. 1600: A

Bibliography

Review." In *Cultures in Contact: The Impact of European Contacts on Native American Cultural Institutions A.D. 1000–1600,* edited by William W. Fitzhugh. Washington, DC: Smithsonian Institution Press, 1985.

Fogarty, Harry Wells. "Rosicrucians." In *Encyclopedia of Religion,* edited by Mircea Eliade. 10 vols. New York: Macmillan, 1987.

Fraser, Douglas. "Theoretical Issues in the Transpacific Diffusion Controversy." *Social Research* 32 (1965): 452–477.

French, Peter. *John Dee: The World of an Elizabethan Magus.* London: Rontledge and Kegan Paul, 1972.

Frost, F. "The Palos Verdes Chinese Anchor Mystery." *Archaeology* (January/February 1982): 23–27.

———. "Voyages of the Imagination," *Archaeology* 46 (March/April 1993): 44–51.

Gaddis, Vincent H. *American Indian Myths and Legends.* Radnor, PA: Chilton Books, 1977.

Gaffarel, Paul. *Histoire de la Decouverte de l'Amerique.* Vol. 1. Paris: A. Rousseau, 1892.

Galvano, A. *The Discoveries of the New World from Their First Original unto the Year of Our Lord 1555.* Hakluyt Society, 1862. Reprint. New York: Burt Franklin, 1962.

Gambier, James William. "The True Discovery of America." *Fortnightly Review* 61 (no. 325, 1894): 49–64.

Garcilaso de la Vega. *Royal Commentaries of the Incas and General History of Peru.* 2 vols. Austin, TX: University of Texas Press, 1966.

Gathorne-Hardy, G. M. *The Norse Discoverers of America.* Oxford: Clarendon Press, 1921.

Gladwin, Harold S. *Men out of Asia.* New York: McGraw-Hill, 1947.

Godbey, Allen H. *The Lost Tribes a Myth—Suggestions towards Rewriting Hebrew History.* 1930. Reprint. New York: KTAV Publishing, 1974.

Goddard, I., and W. Fitzhugh. "Barry Fell Reexamined." *Biblical Archaeologist* 41 (1978): 85–88.

———. "A Statement Concerning *America B.C.*" *Man in the Northeast* 17 (1979): 166–172.

Gómara, Francisco López de. *Historia general de las Indias.* 2 vols. 1552. Reprint. Barcelona: Obras Maestras, 1965.

Goodkind, Howard W. "Lord Kingsborough Lost His Fortune Trying To Prove the Maya Were Descendants of the Ten Lost Tribes." *Biblical Archaeology Review* 11 (September–October 1985): 54–65.

Goodman, Jeffrey. *American Genesis: The American Indian and the Origins of Modern Man.* New York: Summit Books, 1981.

Goodwin, William B. *The Remains of Greater Ireland in New England.* Boston: Meador, 1946.

Gordon, Cyrus. *Before Columbus: Links between the Old World and Ancient America.* New York: Crown, 1971.

———. *Riddles in History.* New York: Crown, 1974.

———. "The Canaanite Text from Brazil." *Orientalia* 37 (1968). (*See also* Cross article, which this one claims to refute.)

Graham, Ian. "Lord Kingsborough, Sir Thomas Phillipps, and Obadiah Rich: Some Bibliographical Notes." In *Social Process in Maya Prehistory,* edited by Norman Hammond, 45–55. London: Academic Press, 1977.

Graves, Robert. *The Greek Myths.* 2 vols. Baltimore: Penguin Books, 1955.

Greene, John C. *The Death of Adam: Evolution and Its Impact on Western Thought.* Ames, IA: Iowa State University, 1959.

Guralnick, E., ed. *Vikings in the West.* Chicago: Archaeological Institute of America, 1982.

Hagen, Victor Wolfgang von, ed. *The Incas of Pedro de Cieza de León.* Norman, OK: University of Oklahoma, 1959.

Hammond, N. G. L., and H. H. Scullard, eds. *The Oxford Classical Dictionary.* 2nd ed. Oxford: Oxford University Press, 1970.

Hanke, Lewis. *Bartolomé de Las Casas, Historian: An Essay in Spanish Historiography.* Gainesville, FL: University of Florida Press, 1952.

Hanson, P. M. *Jesus Christ among the Ancient Americans.* 1949. Reprint. Independence, MO: Herald Publishing House, 1945.

Hapgood, Charles H. *Maps of the Ancient Sea Kings: Evidence of Advanced Civilization in the Ice Age.* 1966. Rev. ed. Philadelphia: Chilton Books, 1979.

Harden, D. B. "The Phoenicians on the West Coast of Africa." *Antiquity* 22 (September 1948): 141–150.

Harley, J. B., and David Woodward. *The History of Cartography.* Vol. I: *Cartography in Prehistoric, Ancient, and Medieval Europe and the Mediterranean.* Chicago: University of Chicago Press, 1987.

Harris, Hendon. *The Asiatic Fathers of America.* Taitung, Taiwan: Privately printed, 1973.

Harris, Marvin. *The Rise of Anthropological Theory.* New York: Crowell, 1968.

Harrisse, Henry. *The Discovery of North America: A Critical, Documentary, and Historical Investigation.* 1892. Reprint. Amsterdam: N. Israel, 1961.

Harrold, F., and R. Eve, eds. *Cult Archaeology and Creationism: Understanding Pseudoscientific Beliefs about the Past.* Iowa City, IA: University of Iowa Press, 1987.

Haven, Samuel. *Archaeology of the United States.* 1856. Reprint. New York: AMS Press, 1973.

Heine-Geldern, Robert. "The Problem of Transpacific Influences in Mesoamerica." *Handbook of Middle American Indians.* Vol. 4. 1966.

———. "Representation of the Asiatic Tiger in the Art of Chavin Culture: A Proof of Early Contact between China and Peru." *Proceedings of the 33rd International Congress of Americanists* (1958): 321–326.

———. "A Roman Find from Pre-Columbian Mexico." *Anthropological Journal of Canada* 5 (1967): 20–22.

Bibliography

———. "Traces of Indian and Southeast Asiatic Hindu-Buddhist Influences in Mesoamerica." *Proceedings of the 35th International Congress of Americanists* (1962): 47–54.

Heine-Geldern, Robert, and Gordon Ekholm. "Significant Parallels in the Symbolic Arts of Southeast Asia and Middle America." *The Civilization of Ancient America,* edited by Sol Tax, 299–309. Chicago: University of Chicago Press, 1951.

Helweg-Larsen, Kjeld. *Columbus Never Came.* London: Jarrolds, 1963.

Herbert, Thomas. *A Relation of Some Yeares Travaile Begunne Anno 1626 into Afrique and the Greater Asia, Especially the Territories of the Persian Monarchie. . . .* London: William Stansby, 1634. Reprint. New York: De Capo, 1971.

Hess, Andrew C. "Piri Re'is and the Ottoman Response to the Voyages of Discovery." *Terrae Incognitae* 6 (1974): 19–38.

Heyerdahl, Thor. *Aku-Aku: The Secret of Easter Island.* Chicago: Rand McNally, 1958.

———. *American Indians in the Pacific: The Theory behind the Kon Tiki Expedition.* London: Allen and Unwin, 1952.

———. *Early Man and the Ocean: A Search for the Beginnings of Navigation and Seaborne Civilization.* Garden City, NY: Doubleday, 1979.

———. *Kon Tiki.* Chicago: Rand McNally, 1950. First English edition with many subsequent printings.

———. *The Ra Expeditions.* Translation of the 1970 edition. Garden City, NY: Doubleday, 1971.

Heywood, J. C. *Documenta selecta.* Vatican Press, 1893 (documents on Norse Christianity in America). Reprint. *Catholic Historical Review* (1917–1918): 210–227.

Hirth, Friedrich, and W. W. Rockhill, eds. *Chau Ju-kua: His Work on the Chinese and Arab Trade in the Twelfth and Thirteenth Centuries, Entitled Chu-fan-chi.* 1911. Reprint. New York: Paragon Book Reprint Corp., 1966.

Hobbs, William H. "The Fourteenth-Century Discovery of America by Antonio Zeno." *Scientific Monthly* 72 (January 1951): 24–31.

Hodgen, Margaret T. *Early Anthropology in the Sixteenth and Seventeenth Centuries.* Philadelphia: University of Pennsylvania Press, 1964.

Holand, Hjalmar R. *The Kensington Stone: A Study in Pre-Columbian American History.* Ephraim, WI: Privately printed, 1932.

———. *Explorations in America before Columbus.* New York: Twayne Publishers, 1956.

———. *Norse Discoveries and Explorations in America 982–1362.* 1940. Reprint. New York: Dover, 1968.

Hole, F. Review of *Saga America* in *Bulletin of the Archaeological Society of Connecticut* 44 (1981): 81–83.

Honoré, Pierre. *In Quest of the White God.* American edition. New York: G. P. Putnam's Sons, 1964.

Hopkins, D., ed. *The Bering Land Bridge.* Stanford, CA: Stanford University Press, 1967.

Hopkins, D., et al., eds. *The Paleoecology of Beringia.* New York: Academic Press, 1982.

Hovgaard, William. *The Voyages of the Norsemen to America.* New York: American-Scandinavian Foundation, 1914.

Huddleston, Lee Eldridge. *Origins of the American Indians: European Concepts, 1492–1729.* Austin, TX: University of Texas Press, 1967.

Hudson, Charles. "James Adair as Anthropologist." *Ethnohistory* 24 (Fall 1977): 311–328.

Huguemin, Charles A. "The Mystery of the Origins of the Melungeons." *NEARA Journal* 6 (1971): 47–52.

Hunter, Milton R. *Christ in Ancient America.* Salt Lake City, UT: Deseret Book Co., 1959.

Hunter, Milton R., and Thomas S. Ferguson. *Ancient America and the Book of Mormon.* Oakland, CA: Kolob, 1950.

Huyghe, Patrick. *Columbus Was Last.* New York: Hyperion Books, 1992.

Ingram, David. *The Relation of David Ingram.* 1589. Reprint. Ann Arbor, MI: University Microfilms, 1966.

Ingstad, Anne Stine, ed. *The Discovery of a Norse Settlement in America.* Oslo, Norway: Universitetsforlaget, 1977.

Ingstad, Anne Stine, and Helge Ingstad, eds. *The Norse Discovery of America.* 2 vols. Oslo and Oxford: Norwegian University Press and Oxford University Press, 1985.

Ingstad, Helge. *Westward to Vinland: The Discovery of Pre-Columbian House-Sites in North America.* New York: St. Martin's Press, 1969.

Irving, Washington. *Voyages and Discoveries of the Companions of Columbus,* edited by James W. Tuttleton. 1831. Reprint. Boston: Twayne, 1986.

Irwin, Constance. *Fair Gods and Stone Faces.* New York: St. Martin's Press, 1963.

Ives, R. "An Early Speculation Concerning the Asiatic Origin of the American Indians." *American Antiquity* 21 (1956): 420–421.

Jackson, Donald Dale. "Who the Heck Did 'Discover' the New World?" *Smithsonian* 22 (September 1992): 76–85.

Jacoby, Arnold. *Señor Kon Tiki.* New York: Rand McNally, 1967.

Jairazbhoy, Rafique Ali. *Ancient Egyptians and Chinese in America.* Totowa, NJ: Rowman and Littlefield, 1974.

Jeffreys, M. D. W. "Arabs Discover America before Columbus." *Muslim's Digest* (June 1953): 69.

———. "Maize and the Ambiguity in Columbus' Letter." *Anthropological Journal of Canada* 3 (no. 4, 1965): 2–11.

———. "Pre-Columbian Arabs in the Caribbean." *Muslim Digest* 5, I (August 1954): 26.

Johnston, Thomas Crawford. *Did the Phoenicians Discover America?* 1913. Reprint. Houston: St. Thomas Press, 1965.

Jones, Gwyn. *A History of the Vikings.* London and New York: Oxford University Press, 1968.

Bibliography

———. *The Norse Atlantic Saga.* 2nd ed. Oxford: Oxford University Press, 1986.

Jones, Tristan. "Madoc—A Persistent Legend." *Epigraphic Society Occasional Publications* 6 (no. 132, 1979).

Kaeppel, C. *Off the Beaten Track in the Classics.* Melbourne: Melbourne University Press, 1936.

Katz, David S. *Philo-Semitism and the Readmission of the Jews to England, 1603–1655.* Oxford: Oxford University Press, 1982.

Keen, Benjamin, ed. *The Life of the Admiral Christopher Columbus by His Son Ferdinand.* New Brunswick, NJ: Rutgers University Press, 1959.

Kimble, George H. T. *Geography in the Middle Ages.* 1938. Reprint. London: Methuen, 1968.

Kingsborough, Lord. *The Antiquities of Mexico.* 9 vols. London: Robert Havell and Conaghi, 1830–1848.

Kirchhoff, Paul. "The Adaptation of Foreign Religious Influences in Pre-Spanish Mexico." *Diogenes* 47 (1964): 13–28. With a reply by Alfonso Caso: 29–35.

———. "The Diffusion of a Great Religious System from India to Mexico." *Proceedings of the 35th International Congress of Americanists* (1964): 73–100.

Kjeldgaard, Linda Lane. "Did Columbus Discover the New World before 1492?" *Encuentro* (University of New Mexico/Latin American Institute) 2 (no. 1, 1986): 8.

Kline, Burton. "America Discovered Many Times before Columbus Came." *World's Work* (1925): 135–142.

Landa, Diego de. *Yucatan before and after the Conquest,* translated by William Gates. 1937. Reprint. New York: Dover, 1978.

Larner, John. "The Certainty of Columbus: Some Recent Studies." *History* 73 (no. 237, February 1988): 3–23.

Larsen, Sofus. *The Discovery of America Twenty Years before Columbus.* Danish, 1920. London: Hachette, 1924.

Larson, Laurence M. "Did John Scolvus Visit Labrador and Newfoundland in or about 1476?" *Scandinavian Studies* 7 (May 1922): 81–89.

Lawrence, Harold. "African Explorers in the New World." *The Crisis* (June–July 1962): 321–322.

LeHuenen, Joseph. "The Role of Basque, Breton, and Norman Cod Fishermen in the Discovery of North America from the XVIth to the end of the XVIIIth Century." *Arctic* 37 (December 1984): 520–527.

Leland, Charles G. *Fusang or the Discovery of America by Chinese Buddhist Priests in the Fifth Century.* 1875. Reprint. London: Curzon Press, 1973.

Lewis, David. *We, the Navigators.* Honolulu: University Press of Hawaii, 1979.

Li, Hui-Lin. "Mu-lan-p'i: A Case for Pre-Columbian Transatlantic Travel by Arab Ships." *Harvard Journal of Asiatic Studies* 23 (1961): 114–126.

Little, George A. *Brendan the Navigator.* Dublin: M. H. Gill and Son, Ltd., 1945.

Little Turtle. "The Fell Trilogy: Synopses & Commentary." *NEARA Journal* 19 (1985): 79–95.

Lucas, Frederick W. *The Annals of the Voyages of the Brothers Nicolò and Antonio Zeno in the North Atlantic.* London: H. Stevens Sons & Stiles, 1898.

Maas, A. J. "Preadamites." In *The Catholic Encyclopedia.* 17 vols. New York: Catholic Encyclopedia Press, 1907–1922.

McCarthy, Charles Hallan. *Columbus and His Predecessors: A Story in the Beginnings of American History.* Philadelphia: J. J. McVey, 1912.

McCrone, Walter C. *Chemical Analytical Study of the Vinland Map: Report to Yale University.* 1974.

———. "Authenticity of Medieval Document Tested by Small Particle Analysis." *Analytical Chemistry* 48 (no. 8, 1976): 676A–679A.

———. "The Vinland Map." *Analytical Chemistry* 60 (1988): 1009–1018.

McDermott, Robert A. "Anthrosophy." In *Encyclopedia of Religion,* edited by Mircea Eliade. 10 vols. New York: Macmillan, 1987.

McGhee, Robert. "Contact between Native North Americans and the Medieval Norse: A Review of the Evidence." *American Antiquity* 49 (no. 1, 1984): 4–26.

McGovern, Thomas H. "The Economics of Extinction in Norse Greenland." In *Climate and History: Studies in Past Climates and Their Impact on Man,* edited by T. M. L. Wigley, et al., 404–433. Cambridge: Cambridge University Press, 1981.

———. "The Vinland Adventure: A North Atlantic Perspective." *North American Archaeologist* 2 (no. 4, 1980–1981): 285–308.

McGrath, Patrick. "Bristol and America 1480–1631." In *The Westward Enterprise: English Activities in Ireland, the Atlantic, and America 1480–1650,* edited by K. R. Andrews, et al. Detroit: Wayne State University Press, 1979.

McKee, David R. "Isaac de La Peyrère, a Precursor of Eighteenth-Century Critical Deists." *Publications of the Modern Language Association* 59 (June 1944): 456–485.

McKusick, Marshall B. *The Davenport Conspiracy.* Iowa City, IA: Office of the State Archaeologist, University of Iowa, 1970.

———. *The Davenport Conspiracy Revisited.* Ames, IA: Iowa State University Press, 1991.

———. "Canaanites in America: A New Scripture in Stone?" *Biblical Archaeologist* 42 (Summer 1979): 137–140.

———. "Contemporary American Folklore about Antiquity." *Bulletin of the Philadelphia Anthropological Society,* 1976.

———. "A Cryptogram in the Phoenician Inscription from Brazil." *Biblical Archaeology Review* 5 (July–August 1979): 50–54.

———. "The North American Periphery of Antique Vermont." *Antiquity* 53 (1979): 121–123.

———. "Some Historical Implications of the Norse Penny from Maine." *Norwegian Numismatic Journal* 3 (1979): 20–23.

McKusick, Marshall B., and Erik Wahlgren. "The Norse Penny Mystery." *Archaeology of Eastern North America* 8 (1980): 1–10.

———. "Vikings in America—Fact and Fiction." *Early Man* 2 (1980): 7–11.

Bibliography

Madsen, Brigham D., ed. *Studies of the Book of Mormon*. Urbana, IL: University of Illinois Press, 1985.

Magnusson, Magnus, and Hermann Pálsson, trans. and eds. *The Vinland Sagas: The Norse Discovery of America*. New York: New York University Press, 1966.

Mahan, Joseph B. *The Secret: America in World History before Columbus*. Columbus, GA: Mahan, 1983.

Major, R. H. *The Voyages of the Venetian Brothers Nicolò and Antonio Zeno*. London: Hakluyt Society, 1873.

Mangelsdorf, Paul C. *Corn: Its Origin, Evolution, and Improvement*. Cambridge, MA: Harvard University Press, 1974.

Marble, Samuel B. *Before Columbus*. South Brunswick, NJ: A. S. Barnes, 1980.

Marcus, G. J. *The Conquest of the North Atlantic*. American edition. New York: Oxford University Press, 1981.

Markham, Sir Clements. *Toscanelli and Columbus: A Letter from . . . and a Reply from Mr. Henry Vignaud*. London: Sands & Co., 1903.

Marx, Robert F. *In Quest of the Great White Gods: Contact between the Old and New World from the Dawn of History*. New York: Crown, 1992.

Mason, Gregory. *Columbus Came Late*. New York: Century Co., 1931.

Meggers, Betty J. "Did Japanese Fishermen Really Reach Ecuador 5,000 Years Ago?" *Early Man* 2 (1980): 15–19.

———. "The Transpacific Origin of Mesoamerican Civilization: A Preliminary Review of the Evidence and Its Theoretical Implications." *American Anthropologist* 77 (1975): 1–27.

———. "Yes If by Land, No If by Sea: The Double Standard of Interpreting Cultural Similarities." *American Anthropologist* 78 (1976): 637–669.

Meggers, Betty J., and Clifford Evans. "A Trans-Pacific Contact in 3000 B.C." *Scientific American* 214 (1966): 28–35.

Meltzer, D. J. "Why Don't We Know When the First People Came to North America?" *American Antiquity* 54 (no. 3, 1989): 471–490.

Mercatante, Anthony S. *The Facts on File Encyclopedia of World Mythology and Legend*. New York: Facts on File, 1988.

Mernitz, Susan Curtis, "Palmyra Revisited: A Look at the Early Nineteenth Century and the Book of Mormon." *John Whitmer Historical Association Journal* 2 (1982): 30–37.

Mertz, Henriette. *Pale Ink: Two Ancient Records of Chinese Exploration in America*. Privately published, 1953. 2nd rev. ed. Chicago: Swallow Press, 1972. Also in paperback under the title *Gods from the Far East: How the Chinese Discovered America*. New York: Ballantine Books, 1972.

———. *The Wine Dark Sea: Homer's Heroic Epic of the North Atlantic*. Chicago: Privately printed, 1965.

Meyer, Roy W. *The Village Indians of the Upper Missouri: The Mandans, Hidatsas, and Arikaras*. Lincoln, NE: University of Nebraska Press, 1977.

Mielche, Hakon. *After You, Columbus.* London: W. Hodge and Co., 1950.

Moltke, Erik. "The Ghost of the Kensington Stone." *Scandinavian Studies* 25 (1953): 1–14.

Montesinos, Fernando. *Memorias antiguas historiales y políticas del Perú.* London: Hakluyt Society, 1920.

Morison, Samuel Eliot. *Admiral of the Ocean Sea: A Life of Christopher Columbus.* 2 vols. Boston: Little, Brown, 1942.

———. *The European Discovery of America: The Northern Voyages, A.D. 500–1600.* New York: Oxford University Press, 1971.

———. *The European Discovery of America: The Southern Voyages, 1492–1616.* New York: Oxford University Press, 1974.

———. *Portuguese Voyages to America in the Fifteenth Century.* Cambridge, MA: Harvard University Press, 1940.

Morton, Thomas. *New English Canaan; or New Canaan, Containing an Abstract of Three Books.* 1637. Reprint. New York: Burt Franklin, 1967.

Moscati, S. *The World of the Phoenicians.* New York: Praeger, 1968.

Musmanno, Michael Angelo. *Columbus Was First.* New York: Fountainhead Publishers, 1966.

Nansen, Fridtjof. *In Northern Mists.* 2 vols. 1911. Reprint. Westport, CT: Greenwood Press, 1970.

Nebenzahl, Kenneth. *Rand McNally Atlas of Columbus and the Great Discoveries.* Chicago: Rand McNally, 1990.

Needham, Joseph. *Science and Civilization in China.* 6 vols. Cambridge: Cambridge University Press, 1954–1988, 1988–.

Neilsen, Richard. "The Kensington Runestone." *Epigraphic Society Occasional Publications* 15–17 (1986–1988).

Neudorfer, G. *Vermont Stone Chambers: An Inquiry into Their Past.* Montpelier, VT: Vermont Historical Society, 1980.

Newman, Marshall T. "The Blond Mandan: A Critical Review of an Old Problem." *Southwestern Journal of Anthropology* 6 (1950): 255–272.

Newton, Arthur Percival. *Travel and Travellers of the Middle Ages.* 1926. Reprint. London: Routledge and Kegan Paul, 1949.

Niane, D. T., ed. *Africa from the Twelfth to the Sixteenth Century.* Berkeley, CA: University of California, 1984.

Nibley, Hugh. *An Approach to the Book of Mormon.* 1957. 3rd ed. Salt Lake City, UT: Deseret Book Co., 1989.

———. *Collected Works of Hugh Nibley.* Vol. 5: *Lehi in the Desert, The World of the Jaredites,* and *There Were Jaredites.* Salt Lake City, UT: Deseret Book Co., 1988. Reprints of articles from the 1940s and 1950s.

———. *The Prophetic Book of Mormon.* 1967. Reprint. Salt Lake City, UT: Deseret Book Co., 1989.

———. *Since Cumorah: The Book of Mormon in the Modern World.* Salt Lake City, UT: Deseret Book Co., 1967.

Nowell, Charles E. "The Toscanelli Letters and Columbus." *Hispanic American Historical Review* 17 (1942): 346–348.

Bibliography

Nunn, George E. *The Mappemonde of Juan de La Cosa: A Critical Investigation of Its Date.* Jenkintown, PA: George H. Beans Library, 1934.

O'Dea, Thomas F. *The Mormons.* 1957. Rev. ed. Chicago: University of Chicago Press, 1964.

O'Gorman, Edmundo. *The Invention of America: An Inquiry into the Historical Nature of the New World and the Meaning of Its History.* Bloomington, IN: Indiana University Press, 1961.

Oldham, H. Yule. "A Pre-Columbian Discovery of America." *Royal Geographical Society Journal* (1895): 221–233.

Oleson, Tryggvi J. *Early Voyages and Northern Approaches, 1000–1632.* Toronto: McClelland and Stewart, 1964.

Oliver, Roland. *The Cambridge History of Africa.* Vol. 3: *From c. 1050 to c. 1600.* Cambridge: Cambridge University Press, 1977.

Oviedo, Gonzalo Fernández de. *Natural History of the West Indies,* translated and edited by Sterling A. Stoudemire. Chapel Hill, NC: University of North Carolina Press, 1959.

Parker, John. *Antilia and America.* Minneapolis: James F. Bell, 1955.

Parry, J. H. *The Age of Reconnaissance: Discovery, Exploration and Settlement 1450 to 1650.* 1963. Reprint. Cleveland: World Publishing Co., 1981.

———. *Manco Capac, the First Inca of Peru, Being a Critical Inquiry into the Pretensions Concerning the Discovery of America by Prince Madawg ap Owen Gwynedd; with Reflections upon the Final Discovery of That Continent by Christopher Columbus.* Pwlhelli, Wales: W. Llewelyn Ellis, 1908.

Pellegrino, Charles. *Unearthing Atlantis: An Archaeological Odyssey.* New York: Random House, 1991.

Penrose, Boies. *Travel and Discovery in the Renaissance, 1420–1620.* 1952. Reprint. Cambridge, MA: Harvard University Press, 1963.

Petersen, Mark E. *Those Gold Plates!* Salt Lake City, UT: Bookcraft, 1979.

Pfefferkorn, Ignaz. *Sonora: A Description of the Province,* edited by Theodore E. Treutlein. Albuquerque, NM: University of New Mexico Press, 1949.

Phelan, John L. "The *Apologetic History* of Fray Bartolomé de Las Casas." *Hispanic American Historical Review* 49 (1969): 94–99.

Phillips, J. R. S. *The Medieval Expansion of Europe.* Oxford: Oxford University Press, 1988.

Pohl, Frederick J. *Atlantic Crossings before Columbus.* New York: Norton, 1961.

———. *The New Columbus.* Rochester, NY: Security Dupont Press, 1986.

———. *Prince Henry Sinclair: His Expedition to the New World in 1398.* London: Davis-Poynter, 1974.

———. "Did Ancient Romans Reach America?" *New Diffusionist* 3 (1973): 23–37.

———. "Prince 'Zichmni' of the Zeno Narrative." *Terrae Incognitae* 2 (1970): 75–86.

Pollitzer, William S. "Ancestral Traits, Parent Populations, and Hybrids." *American Journal of Physical Anthropology* 30 (1969): 415–420.

Posnansky, Arthur. *Tihuanacu: The Cradle of American Man.* 3 vols. New York: J. J. Augustin, 1945. Discusses Phoenicians in the New World.

Pupo-Walker, Enrique. "El Inca Garcilaso de la Vega (1539–1616)." In *Latin American Writers.* 3 vols. Charles Scribner's Sons, 1989.

Putnam, C. E. "The Davenport Tablets." *Science* 7 (no. 157, 1886): 119–120.

Quinn, David Beers. *England and the Discovery of America, 1481–1620.* New York: Alfred A. Knopf, 1974.

————. *North America from the Earliest Discovery to First Settlements: The Norse Voyages to 1612.* New York: Harper & Row, 1977.

————. *North American Discovery, circa 1000–1612.* Columbia, SC: University of South Carolina Press, 1971.

————. "The Argument for the English Discovery of America between 1480 and 1494." *Geographical Journal* 127 (1961): 277–285.

————. "John Day and Columbus." *Geographical Journal* 133 (June 1967): 205–209.

Ralling, Christopher. *The Kon Tiki Man: Thor Heyerdahl.* London: BBC Books, 1990.

Ramsay, Raymond H. *No Longer on the Map: Discovering Places That Never Were.* New York: Viking Press, 1972.

Rands, Robert L. "The Water Lily in Maya Art: A Complex of Alleged Asiatic Origin." *Smithsonian Institution, Bureau of American Ethnology Bulletin* 151 (1953): 75–153.

Ranking, John. *Historical Researches on the Conquest of Peru, Mexico, Bogata, Natchez, and Talomeco, in the Thirteenth Century, by the Mongols, Accompanied by Elephants.* London: Longman, 1827.

Ravenstein, Ernest G. *Martin Behaim—His Life and His Globe.* London: G. Philip and Son, Ltd., 1908.

Reman, Edward. *Norse Discoveries and Explorations of America.* 1949. Reprint. Berkeley, CA: University of California Press, 1976.

Renfrew, Colin. *Before Civilization: The Radiocarbon Revolution and Prehistoric Europe.* London: Penguin Books, 1973.

Rice, T. Talbot. *The Scythians.* New York: Praeger, 1958.

Riley, Carroll L., et al., eds. *Man across the Sea: Problems of Pre-Columbian Contacts.* Austin, TX: University of Texas Press, 1971.

Rivet, Paul. "Early Contacts between Polynesia and America." *Diogenes* 16 (1956): 78–92.

Rogers, Francis M. "The Vivaldi Expedition." *Seventy-Third Annual Report of the Dante Society* (1955): 31–45.

Ronze, Raymond. "Rivet, Paul." In *International Encyclopedia of the Social Sciences,* edited by David L. Sills. 17 vols. New York: Macmillan, 1968.

Rosenstein, N. "How Wide the Biblical World? A Challenge for Recognition and

Bibliography

Preservation." *Biblical Archaeologist* 41 (Summer 1978): 84–85.

"Rosicrucianism." In *Encyclopedia of Occultism and Parapsychology,* edited by Leslie Shepard. 2 vols. Detroit: Gale Research, 1978.

Ross, A., and P. Reynolds. "Ancient Vermont." *Antiquity* 52 (1978): 100–107.

Rowe, John Howland. "Diffusionism and Archaeology." *American Antiquity* 31 (January 1966): 334–337.

Ruddock, Alwyn A. "Columbus and Iceland: A New Light on an Old Problem." *Geographical Journal* 136 (June 1970): 177–189.

———. "John Day of Bristol and the English Voyages across the Atlantic before 1497." *Geographical Journal* 132 (June 1966): 225–233.

Russell, Jeffrey Burton. *Inventing the Flat Earth: Columbus and Modern Historians.* New York: Praeger, 1991.

Sahagún, Bernardino de. *Florentine Codex: General History of the Things of New Spain.* 13 vols. Salt Lake City, UT: University of Utah Press, 1982.

Sanchez, Joseph P. "The Juan de La Cosa Map—1500." *Encuentro* 2 (no. 4, 1987): 3.

Sanders, Ronald. *Lost Tribes and Promised Lands: The Origins of American Racism.* New York: Little, Brown, 1978.

Sanderson, Ivan T. *Follow the Whale.* Boston: Little, Brown, 1956.

Sarmiento de Gamboa, Pedro. *History of the Incas,* edited by Clements Markham. Cambridge: Hakluyt Society, 1907.

Sarton, George. "The Mysterious Arctic Traveller of 1360: Nicholas of Lynn?" *Isis* 29 (1938): 98–99.

Sauer, Carl O. *Northern Mists.* Berkeley, CA: University of California Press, 1968.

Schach, Paul, trans. *Eyrbyggia Saga.* 1959. Reprint. Lincoln, NE: University of Nebraska, 1977.

Schoolcraft, Henry R. *Historical and Statistical Information Regarding the History, Condition, and Prospects of the Indian Tribes of the United States.* Pt. 4. Philadelphia: Lippincott, 1854.

———. "Archaeological Evidences That the Continent Had Been Visited by People Having Letters Prior to Columbus." In *Indian Tribes of the United States,* 106–108. Washington, DC: Bureau of Indian Affairs, 1851.

Schwartz, Stuart B. *The Iberian Mediterranean and Atlantic Traditions in the Formation of Columbus as a Colonizer.* Minneapolis: University of Minnesota, 1986.

Schwerin, Karl. "Winds across the Atlantic: Possible African Origins for Some Pre-Columbian New World Cultigens." In *Mesoamerican Studies.* No. 6. Carbondale, IL: University Museum, Southern Illinois University, 1970.

Scisco, Louis Don. "Pre-Columbian Discovery by Basques." *Proceedings and Transactions of the Royal Society of Canada* (3rd Series) 18 (1924): 51–61.

Selmer, C., ed. *Navigatio S. Brendani Abbatis.* Notre Dame, IN: University of Notre Dame Press, 1959.

Severin, Timothy. *The Brendan Voyage.* London: Hutchinson, 1978.

Shao, Paul. *Asiatic Influences in Pre-Columbian American Art.* Ames, IA: Iowa State University, 1976.

———. *The Origin of Ancient American Cultures.* Ames, IA: Iowa State University, 1983.

Shipps, Jan. *Mormonism: The Story of a New Religious Tradition.* Urbana, IL: University of Illinois Press, 1985.

Shutler, R., and M. Shutler. *Oceanic Prehistory.* Menlo Park, CA: Cummings, 1975.

Silverberg, Robert. *Mound Builders of Ancient America: The Archaeology of a Myth.* Greenwich, CT: New York Graphic Society, 1968.

Simpson, Lesley Byrd, ed. *Cortés: The Life of the Conqueror by His Secretary Francisco López de Gómara.* Berkeley, CA: University of California Press, 1964.

Sinclair, Andrew. *The Sword and the Grail: Of the Grail and the Templars and a True Discovery of America.* New York: Crown, 1992.

Skelton, R. A., et al. *The Vinland Map and the Tartar Relation.* New Haven, CT: Yale University Press, 1965.

Smith, Ethan. *View of the Hebrews; or the Tribes of Israel in America.* 1823. Reprint. New York: Arno Press, 1977.

Snow, D. "Martians and Vikings, Madoc and Runes." *American Heritage* 32 (no. 6, 1981): 102–108.

Sorenson, John L. *An Ancient American Setting for the Book of Mormon.* Salt Lake City, UT: Deseret Book Co., 1985.

Sorenson, John L., and Martin H. Raish. *Pre-Columbian Contacts with the Americas across the Oceans: An Annotated Bibliography.* 2 vols. Provo, UT: Research Press, 1990.

Spaulding, Solomon. *The "Manuscript Found." Manuscript Story, by Rev. Solomon Spaulding.* Liverpool: Millennial Star, 1911. (There are many editions of this book.)

Speck, Gordon. *Myths and New World Explorations.* Fairfield, WA: Ye Galleon Press, 1979.

Stephens, S. G. "Some Problems of Interpreting Transoceanic Dispersal of the New World Cottons." In *Man across the Sea: Problems of Pre-Columbian Contacts,* edited by Carroll L. Riley, et al. 1971.

Stewart, Ethel G. *The Dene and Na-Dene Indian Migration 1233 A.D. (Escape from Genghiz Khan to America).* Columbus, GA: ISAC Press, 1991.

Stiebing, W. *Ancient Astronauts, Cosmic Collisions, and Other Popular Theories about Man's Past.* Buffalo, NY: Prometheus, 1984.

Taylor, E. G. R. "The Fisherman's Story, 1354." *Geographical Magazine* 37 (1964): 709–712.

———. "A Fourteenth-Century Riddle—and Its Solution." *Geographical Review* 54 (1964): 573–576.

———. "A Letter Dated 1577 from Mercator to John Dee." *Imago Mundi* (1956): 56–69.

———. "A Pre-Columbian Discovery of America." *Geographical Journal* 67 (January 1926): 282–283.

Tena, T. Luca de. "The Influence of Literature on Cartography and the Vinland Map." *Geographical Journal* 132 (December 1966): 515–518.

Thomas, Cyrus. *Report on the Mound Explorations of the Bureau of Ethnology.* 1894. Reprint. Washington, DC: Smithsonian Institution Press, 1985.

Thompson, Gunner. *Nu-Sun—Asian American Voyages, 500 B.C.* Fresco, CA: Pioneer Press, 1989.

———. *American Discovery—The Real Story.* Seattle, WA: Argonauts O.T.M.I., 1992.

Thorndike, J. J., ed. *Mysteries of the Past.* New York: American Heritage Press, 1977.

Tompkins, Peter. *Mysteries of the Mexican Pyramids.* New York: Harper & Row, 1976.

Towe, Kenneth M. "The Vinland Map: Still a Forgery" *Accounts of Chemical Research* 23 (1990): 84–87.

Tozer, H. F. *A History of Ancient Geography.* 1897. Reprint. New York: Biblo and Tanner, 1964.

Trento, Salvatore Michael. *The Search for Lost America: Mysteries of the Stone Ruins in the United States.* New York: Penguin, 1978.

Trigger, Bruce G. *A History of Archaeological Thought.* Cambridge: Cambridge University Press, 1990.

Unwin, Raynor. *The Defeat of John Hawkins.* New York: Macmillan, 1960.

Van Sertima, Ivan. *They Came before Columbus.* New York: Random House, 1976.

Van Sertima, Ivan, ed. *African Presence in Early America.* 1986. 2nd ed. New Brunswick, NJ: Transactions Publishers, 1992.

Varner, John Grier. *El Inca: The Life and Times of Garcilaso de la Vega.* Austin, TX: University of Texas Press, 1968.

Verlinden, Charles. "A Precursor of Columbus: The Fleming Ferdinand Van Olmen (1487)." In *The Beginnings of Modern Colonization: Eleven Essays with an Introduction,* by Charles Verlinden. Ithaca, NY: Cornell University Press, 1970.

Verrill, A. Hyatt, and Ruth Verrill. *America's Ancient Civilizations.* New York: Putnam, 1953.

Vignaud, Henry. *The Columbian Tradition on the Discovery of America and the Part Played Therein by the Astronomer Toscanelli.* Oxford: Clarendon Press, 1920.

———. *Toscanelli and Columbus: The Letter and Chart of Toscanelli.* 1902. Reprint. Freeport, NY: Books for Libraries Press, 1971.

Vigneras, Louis-André. "The Cape Breton Landfall: 1494 or 1497." *Canadian Historical Review* 38 (1957): 219–229.

———. "Saint Thomas, Apostle of America." *Hispanic American Historical Review* 57 (February 1977): 82–90.

Vining, Edward Payson. *An Inglorious Columbus: Or, Evidence That Hwui Shan and a Party of Buddhist Monks from Afghanistan Discovered America in the Fifth Century A.D.* New York: Appleton, 1885.

Viola, Herman J., and Carolyn Margolis, eds. *Seeds of Change: A Quincentennial Commemoration.* Washington, DC: Smithsonian Institution, 1991.

Vogel, Dan. *Indian Origins and the Book of Mormon: Religious Solutions from Columbus to Joseph Smith.* [n.p.]: Signature Press, 1986.

Waddell, Lawrence A. *The Makers of Civilization in Race and History.* London: Luzac, 1929.

Wagner, Henry Raup. "Francisco López de Gómara and His Works." *Proceedings of the American Antiquarian Society* (October 1948): 263–282.

Wagner, Henry Raup, and Helen Rand Parish. *The Life and Writings of Bartolomé de Las Casas.* Albuquerque, NM: University of New Mexico Press, 1967.

Wahlgren, Erik. *The Kensington Stone: A Mystery Solved.* Madison, WI: University of Wisconsin Press, 1958.

Wallace, Brigitta Linderoth. "L'Anse aux Meadows Gateway to Vinland," *Acta Archaeologica* 61 (1990): 166–197.

———. "The Vikings in North America: Myth and Reality." In *Social Approaches to Viking Studies,* edited by Ross Samson. Glasgow: Cruithne Press, 1991.

Warmington, B. H. *Carthage.* Rev. ed. New York: Praeger, 1969.

Warren, Bruce W., and Thomas S. Ferguson. *The Messiah in Ancient America.* Provo, UT: Book of Mormon Research Foundation, 1987.

Washburn, Wilcomb E. "James Adair's 'Noble Savages.'" In *The Colonial Legacy,* edited

by Lawrence H. Leder. Vol. 3. New York: Harper & Row, 1973.

Washburn, Wilcomb E., ed. *Proceedings of the Vinland Map Conference.* Chicago: University of Chicago Press, 1971.

Waters, E. G. R. *The Anglo-Norman Voyage of St. Brendan.* Oxford: Clarendon Press, 1928.

Wauchope, Robert. *Lost Tribes and Sunken Continents: Myth and Method in the Study of American Indians.* Chicago: University of Chicago Press, 1962.

Weiner, George. "America's Jewish Braves." *Mankind* 4 (October 1974): 56–64.

Weise, Arthur James. *Discoveries of America to 1525.* New York: G. P. Putnam's Sons, 1884.

West, F. H. *The Archaeology of Beringia.* New York: Columbia University Press, 1981.

Westropp, Thomas Johnson. "Brasil and the Legendary Islands of the North Atlantic: Their History and Fable. A Contribution to the 'Atlantis' Problem." In *Proceedings of the Royal Irish Academy* 30 (Sec. C, 1912): 223–260.

Whittall, James P., Jr., ed. *Mythmakers: Epigraphic Illusion in America.* Long Hill, Rowley, MA: Early Sites Research Society, 1990.

Wiener, Leo. *Africa and the Discovery of America.* 3 vols. Philadelphia: Innes and Sons, 1919–1922.

Wilgus, A. Curtis. *The Historiography of Latin America: A Guide to Historical Writ-*

ing, 1500–1800. Metuchen, NJ: Scarecrow Press, 1975.

Willey, Gordon R., and Jeremy A. Sabloff. *A History of American Archaeology.* San Francisco: Freeman, 1980.

Williams, David. *John Evans and the Legend of Madoc 1770–1799.* Cardiff: University of Wales Press, 1963.

Williams, Gwyn A. *Madoc: Making of a Myth.* London: Methuen, 1979.

Williams, Stephen. *Fantastic Archaeology: The Wild Side of North American Prehistory.* Philadelphia: University of Pennsylvania Press, 1991.

Williamson, J. A., ed. *The Cabot Voyages and Bristol Discovery under Henry VII.* Cambridge: Cambridge University Press, 1962.

Wilmsen, E. "An Outline of Early Man Studies in the United States of America." *American Antiquity* 31 (1965): 172–192.

Winter, Heinrich. "New Light on the Behaim Problem." *Congresso Internacional de Historia dos Descobrimentos, Actas* 2 (1961): 399–410.

Wirth, Diane E. *A Challenge to the Critics: Scholarly Evidences of the Book of Mormon.* Bountiful, UT: Horizon Publishers, 1986.

Wright, Herbert F. "The Controversy of Hugo Grotius with Johan De Laet on the Origins of the American Aborigines." In *Some Less Known Works of Hugo Grotius,* edited by Herbert F. Wright. Leiden, the Netherlands: Brill, 1928.

Wright, John Kirtland. *The Geographical Lore of the Time of the Crusades: A Study in the History of Medieval Science and Tradition in Western Europe.* 1925. Reprint. New York: Dover, 1965.

Wuthenau, Alexander von. *The Art of Terracotta Pottery in Pre-Columbian Central and South America.* New York: Crown, 1969.

———. *Unexpected Faces in Ancient America: The Historical Testimony of the Pre-Columbian Artist.* New York: Crown, 1975.

Yarmolinsky, Avraham. *Early Polish Americana: A Bibliographical Study. With an Appendix: A Legendary Predecessor of Columbus.* New York: New York Public Library, 1937.

Young, Peter A. "Voyages from Fantasyland," *Archaeology* 46 (March/April 1993): 2.

Illustration Credits

Page 8
From *In Quest of the Great White Gods* by Robert and Jenifer Marx. © 1992 by Robert and Jenifer Marx. Reprinted by permission of Crown Publishers, Inc.

Page 10
Drawing by Campbell Grant. *Men out of Asia.* Harold Sterling Gladwin. New York: McGraw-Hill, 1947.

Page 13
Narrative and Critical History of America, Vol. I: *Aboriginal America.* Justin Winsor, ed. Boston: Houghton, Mifflin, 1889.

Page 19
Narrative and Critical History of America, Vol.I: *Aboriginal America.* Justin Winsor, ed. Boston: Houghton, Mifflin, 1889.

Page 26
Narrative and Critical History of America, Vol. II: *Spanish Exploration and Settlements in America from the Fifteenth Century to the Seventeenth Century.* Justin Winsor, ed. Boston: Houghton, Mifflin, 1886.

Page 28
Detail of 1729 map. By Permission Map Collection, British Library, London.

Page 38
Narrative and Critical History of America, Vol. I: *Aboriginal America.* Justin Winsor, ed. Boston: Houghton, Mifflin, 1889.

Page 39
St. Brendan's Seefahrt, fol 168v. Universitätsbibliothek Heidelberg.

Pages 58–59
Museo Naval, Madrid.

Page 63
St. Brendan's Seefahrt, fol 179v. Universitätsbibliothek Heidelberg.

Page 70
From the collections of the Library of Congress.

Page 80
"Leiv Eirikson Discovering America" by Christian Krohg, 1893. Nasjonalgalleriet, Oslo.

Page 83
By Permission British Library, London.

Page 93
Narrative and Critical History of America. Vol. I: *Aboriginal America.* Justin Winsor, ed. Boston: Houghton, Mifflin, 1889.

Page 100
Copy of a Skaholt map from 1670. Det Kongelige Bibliotek, Copenhagen.

Page 101
Drawing by Campbell Grant. *In Men out of Asia.* Harold Sterling Gladwin. New York: McGraw-Hill, 1947.

Illustration Credits

Page 103
Photo by Birgitta L. Wallace.

Page 117
By Permission Department of Prints & Drawings, British Library, London.

Page 120
From *In Quest of the Great White Gods* by Robert and Jenifer Marx. © 1992 by Robert and Jenifer Marx. Reprinted by permission of Crown Publishers, Inc.

Page 145
Photo by Birgitta L. Wallace

Page 154
Environment Canada Parks Service.

Page 156
From the collections of the Library of Congress.

Page 167
"Mih-Tutta-Hang-Kusch, Mandan Village." After Karl Bodmer. Joslyn Art Museum, Omaha.

Page 176
Negative 335020. Photo Logan. Courtesy Department of Library Services, American Museum of Natural History, New York.

Page 208
Engraving by Sydney Parkinson. By Permission Manuscripts Department, British Library, London.

Page 216
Quetzalcoatl based on the *Codex Borbonicus.*

Page 231
By Permission British Library, London.

Page 233
National Portrait Gallery, Washington, D.C.

Page 247
Narrative and Critical History of America, Vol. II: *Spanish Exploration and Settlements in America from the Fifteenth to the Seventeenth Century.* Justin Winsor, ed. Boston: Houghton, Mifflin, 1886.

Page 257
Narrative and Critical History of America, Vol. I: *Aboriginal America.* Justin Winsor, ed. Boston: Houghton, Mifflin, 1889.

Page 266
Narrative and Critical History of America, Vol I: *Aboriginal America.* Justin Winsor, ed. Boston: Houghton, Mifflin, 1889.

Page 272
Narrative and Critical History of America, Vol. I: *Aboriginal America.* Justin Winsor, ed. Boston: Houghton, Mifflin, 1889.

Page 276
Narrative and Critical History of America, Vol. I: *Aboriginal America.* Justin Winsor, ed. Boston: Houghton, Mifflin, 1889.

Index

Index

Index

Index

Index

Index

Index

Index

Index

DATE DUE

GAYLORD			PRINTED IN U.S.A.

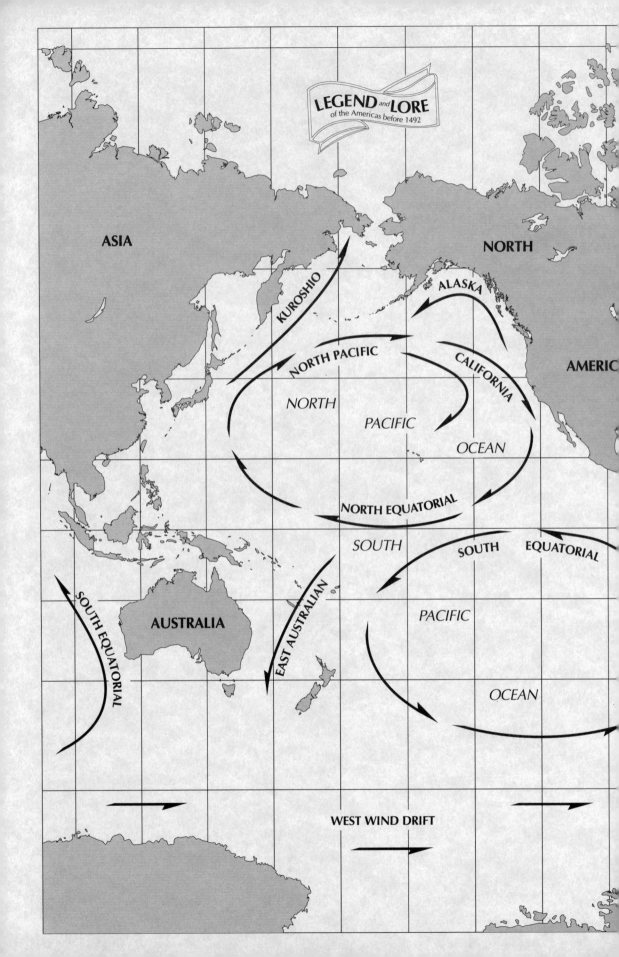